MY MCCABE HISTORY AND THE GREATER WORLD

EBE MCCABE

MY MCCABE HISTORY AND THE GREATER WORLD

iUniverse books may be ordered through booksellers or by contacting:

iUniverse
1663 Liberty Drive
Bloomington, IN 47403
www.iuniverse.com
844-349-9409

Because of the dynamic nature of the Internet, any web addresses or links contained in this book may have changed since publication and may no longer be valid. The views expressed in this work are solely those of the author and do not necessarily reflect the views of the publisher, and the publisher hereby disclaims any responsibility for them.

Any people depicted in stock imagery provided by Getty Images are models, and such images are being used for illustrative purposes only. Certain stock imagery © Getty Images.

ISBN: 978-1-6632-2770-6 (sc)
ISBN: 978-1-6632-2769-0 (e)

Library of Congress Control Number: 2021916576

Print information available on the last page.

iUniverse rev. date: 10/01/2021

[Ed. Note. The Viking-style helmet in the front cover graphic is based on the great diversity of medieval battle helmets, on Gallowglass adoption of Viking warfare gear and tactics, on the distinctive nature of the McCabe Gallowglass battle helmet indicated by the Cába name origin being most likely based on their warrior profession and distinctive headgear, and on the additional protection provided by face and neck covering chain mail (with the chain mail mesh being open enough to enable communications like giving/hearing orders and uttering cacophonous battle cries to strike fear in the opposition).]

Contents

Purpose and Dedication

To Supplement and Expand Upon
My and Mankind's Ancestry and World

For

McCabes,

Our Genetic and Ethnic Kin,

Ancestry Buffs,

And my own Edification.

Acknowledgements

My writing is indebted to the host of contributors to my education and to my knowledge of my family history.[1] Especially notable in regard to this book are:

Mrs. Eliot Ann (Yehle) Evans McCabe (deceased), whose superior interpersonal skills, unflagging encouragement, and positivity still improve my writing.

Vernon McCabe, my 5th Cousin, who provided the foundation for my family history work by researching and documenting the Revolutionary War service of our ancestor Private John McCabe (1727-1800), and cataloging over 11,000 of his descendants.[2]

Marjorie Adams, whose research into the McCabe family history provided a long-sought extension of the history of the Delmarva McCabes .

Andrew MacLeod, Genealogy Coordinator for his Clan and an invaluable source of related information and perspective.

Brian McCabe, Secretary of Ireland's McCabe Clan Society and Compiler and Editor of its newsletter. His perceptive comments led to my developing a more correct perspective on our surname—including but far from limited to providing details about the McCabe Castle that led me to search out the proliferation of fortified Tower Houses in Ireland.

The iUniverse staff who, during the pandemic panic that has disrupted personal and professional lives world-wide, have maintained their professionalism and positivity during the publication of this work. Especially notable among these are Publishing Services Associate Reed Samuel and the Cover Production Staff Management.

Preface

This family history update expanded when imbalanced, out-of-context depictions of Ireland's Gallowglass became apparent. That led to trying to put my ancestry and the world in a more realistic perspective—by condensed depictions of War, Slavery, cultures, and asides.

Scientific validity being a goal, Evolution was credited. Several Christian faiths (including Methodism and Roman Catholicism) consider it credible too. But we're humans (Genus Homo), not Chimpanzees or Bonobos (Genus Pan), not Gorillas (Genus Gorilla), not Orangutans (Genus Pongo), and not monkeys. [Many millions of years ago, humans, great apes, and monkeys began evolving separately from a common primate lineage.]

Hopefully, this work is improved by my inherited, learned, and self-developed views, which are largely based on:

- Age 0-4. Being born in Philadelphia, during the *Great Depression*, into a Protestant family with an Irish-English father from rural Lower Delaware and a Polish mother raised in a rural Canadian Catholic family. (My father lost his job as a surveyor during the depression and supported his family by becoming a milkman.)
- Age 4-10. Living in New York City (Astoria), where my father was employed as a fruit inspector. I was eight years old when Pearl Harbor was attacked.
- Age 10-17. Living in rural Frankford, Delaware, my father's home town. He worked in the Post Office, then in the Wartime Office of Price Administration (OPA), then as a bookkeeper, and then as a State Highway Inspector. We admired the WWII leadership of President Roosevelt and Prime Minister Churchill, and honored the Gold Star families who lost sons in the war. I worked summer jobs beginning at age 12.
- Age 18-24. Studied at the University of Delaware for a year. Worked the next at the Dupont Nylon Factory. Then attended and graduated from the U.S. Naval Academy.
- Age 24-37. Served on a WWII era destroyer, then two diesel-electric submarines, and then two Fleet Ballistic Missile submarines (the second as Executive Officer). Had several WWII veteran submariners as shipmates. Spent my last active-duty year on the staff of the Atlantic Submarine Force Commander.
- Serving in and eventually becoming a Captain (O6) in the U.S. Navy Reserve (USNR).
- ~Two years as a nuclear controls engineering section manager for a commercial nuclear power plant manufacturer's subsidiary.

- ~22 years performing and supervising safety inspections of commercial nuclear power plants for the Atomic Energy and Nuclear Regulatory Commissions.
- Striving to think independently, and to heed my father's injunction about the need to satisfy the face that stares back at me from the mirror.

Another hope is that my many multi-generational references, parenthetically enclosing many editorial comments, and being long retired has made this work more reflective of human nature than akin to E.L. Doctorow's assertion that what most people see as history is the present—a myth generated anew by each generation.[3]

1

Private John S. McCabe
(1727-1800)[4]

1.1 Chronology

06/20/1632	King Charles I granted Maryland (including present Pennsylvania and Delaware) to Cecil Calvert, the 2nd Lord Baltimore.[5]
03/04/1681	King Charles II granted Pennsylvania (Delaware was then the lower three counties of Pennsylvania.) to William Penn. Pennsylvania's boundaries were disputed by Maryland, with Maryland claiming (and continuing to administer) most of present Sussex County, Delaware.
05/13/1727	John S. McCabe (1727 John) was born in New Jersey.
1750-1751 [6]	The Transpeninsular Line Survey by John Watson & William Parsons of Pennsylvania and John Emory & Thomas Jones of Maryland[7] lowered the Maryland-claimed Southern boundary of Delaware to a line running East-West from Fenwick Island,[8] South of Sandy Branch.
Before 2/27/1752:[9]	1727 John wed Mary Hudson of Sandy Branch, which was in the area of Delaware that Maryland claimed and administered.
09/22/1753	Mary (Hudson) McCabe gave birth to Obediah McCabe.
March 1754	John Machainde petitioned the Annapolis, Maryland Hall of Records for a warrant for 5 acres of partly cultivated land in Sandy Branch, Worcester County, Maryland.

05/02/1754	Rounds Survey noted a survey based on a previous warrant for 170 acres called John's Delight to John Mackaide
07/02/1756	Mary (Hudson) McCabe gave birth to Matthew McCabe.
09/17/1756	Resurvey renamed the 170-acre property John's Luck, indicated a size of 120 acres since 50 acres had been taken away by a previous survey, and stated that the parcel was based on a special warrant to Benjamin Handy (who turned the warrant over to 1727 John) for 5 acres of vacant, partially cultivated land. Handy stated that John Mackaid had not paid caution money for the 165 acres over the 5 acres, or for the improvements on the land.
08/12/1759	Mary (Hudson) McCabe gave birth to John McCabe, Jr.
01/28/1761	Mary (Hudson) McCabe gave birth to Arthur McCabe.
04/02/1767	Mary (Hudson) McCabe gave birth to Alexa (Ercha?) McCabe.
01/11/1769	King George III approved the Mason-Dixon survey boundaries affirming the Transpeninsular Line,[10] ending the Delaware boundary dispute.
03/02/1772	1727 John bought 50 acres (Mumford's Choice) from William Mumford
Dec., 1776	1727 John enlisted in the Continental Army's Delaware Regiment.
12/25/1776	General Washington, leaving 2400 of his soldiers on the Pennsylvania side of the icy Delaware River, crossed over late in the day, and routed the Hessian forces at Trenton the next morning.[11] (Unconfirmed Information passed down to John McCabe's son Arthur's descendants states that John McCabe crossed with General Washington.[12])
09/03/1783	The Revolutionary War Peace Treaty was signed in Paris.
03/11/1784	1727 John was paid for his Revolutionary War military service from 08/01/1780-01/01/1782, and from 01/01/1783-11/03/1783.
Feb. 1785	George Mitchell of Kent County, Maryland was charged with keeping a Tippling House.
Aug. 1786	George Mitchell, 1727 John, Newt Hickman, John Buckwork, Levi Lynch, and Richard Hudson appeared before the Court. George was convicted.
05/09/1787	The Sussex County Sheriff ordered a levy for John McCabe's debt of £40 9d and damages of £3 5s 6d to George Mitchell.

05/09/1792	Mumford's Choice was seized for non-payment of the debt. It was sold at auction to George Mitchell.
06/09/1797	Mary (Hudson) McCabe died at about age 70.
11/13/1797	A bond of conveyance of Mumford's Choice from George Mitchell to 1727 John's son Arthur McCabe was recorded.
1/20/1800	72-year-old 1727 John died. {His memorial headstone is in Red Men's Cemetery in Selbyville (formerly Sandy Branch), Sussex County, Delaware, where about 106 McCabes are buried.[13]}
04/29/1806	The sale of Mumford's choice to Arthur McCabe was completed. (George Mitchell had died earlier.)
03/31/1834	Arthur McCabe requested, for himself and his brothers Obediah and John Jr., as their father's only heirs, 100 acres of bounty land for their father's War service. Supporting testimony asserted that John McCabe had enlisted for the term of the war and served until its end in the Delaware Regiment under Col. David Hall.

1.2 The Delaware Line

The Delaware Line (one infantry regiment), authorized on December 9, 1775, was recruited for a one-year enlistment early in 1776. Its first Colonel was John Haslett. Having a former British captain as adjutant contributed to the regiment being well trained. The regiment gained fame in the unsuccessful battles for New York City, after which General Washington retreated to Pennsylvania and crossed the Delaware River to route the Hessians at Trenton. In 1777, under Col. David Hall, the Line re-enlisted for the duration of the war. It served in the Maryland Division until a 1778 assignment to a Virginia Division, and rejoined the Maryland Division in 1779. In the Spring of 1780, it was shattered at the Battle of Camden and then had only enough men to form two companies. Those stayed in action through General Nathan Greene's campaign, which harried Cornwallis' British forces out of the South. Two more companies were recruited, joined General Washington's forces in the siege of Yorktown, and then relieved the two veteran companies in Greene's campaign. The Line was furloughed early in 1783 and was formally disbanded on November 15, 1783.[14, 15, 16]

1.3 Locale

Colonial Sussex County was less populated than neighboring Kent County because of *there being great quantities of poor land in Sussex County.*[17] And the farm I spent my teens on five miles North of Selbyville had a shallow topsoil layer over a hard layer of "irony" soil that took a pickaxe to penetrate. Also, Josiah Campbell (1810-1890) stated that the sandy soil of his family's Sandy Branch area farm produced less income than beehive honey and wax—and his family worked hard at harvesting cedar trees buried under decaying vegetation in the Cedar (Burnt) swamp.[18]

A "Hundred" was originally considered big enough for 100 farms.[19] Hundreds were tax reporting and voting districts until the 1960s. They are now used as real estate title descriptions.[20] {Sussex County's economy improved after Wilmer and Cecile Steele of Ocean View (in Baltimore Hundred) began the broiler industry in 1923—when Cecile ordered 50 chicks, received 500, and they raised them for meat instead of for eggs.[21]}

The tract John McCabe claimed in 1754 bordered on the Sandy Branch waterway extending Northwest from Collins Branch, which extended Northwest from the Bishopville Prong of the St. Martins River. Until the mid-19th Century, the area was a forested wilderness. An old trail that also served as a stagecoach route went through Snow Hill and Berlin in Maryland to Sandy Branch, and passed on to Frankford, Dagsboro, Millsboro and Lewes (pronounced Lewis) in Delaware. In 1842, Sampson Selby opened a general store in the area. He bought his stock in Philadelphia, was asked where to deliver it, and reputedly said *It will have to go by Indian River vessel then to—just put Selbyville.* [22, 23]

A Google map of Selbyville[24] shows Sandy Branch extending Northwest, past the point where Polly Branch branches off to the Northeast, then curving to the West and then Southwest between Hosier Street and Park Street in Selbyville and ending just Northwest of the intersection of Hosier Street and School Road.

Scrolling to Frankford (4.3 miles North along Pepper Road) shows Vines Creek, which extends to the Northeast in a still uninterrupted pathway to Indian River Bay. When I was a boy in Frankford, my brother and I played in Vines Creek, which was about 40 unpaved yards down Pepper Road from my grandfather's house on the corner between Vine Street and Main Street. It was only about a foot deep. When my father, who was born in 1900 in that house, called it the Vine's Street Canal, I said it was just a creek. He explained that it had much bigger when he was a boy, and had been the way goods were brought to Frankford. (Before the railroad arrived in the 1870s, canals were the primary means of transporting goods because they were superior to horse-drawn wagons and hand-maintained dirt roads/ trails. And Colonial settlers were very familiar with canals because they were widely used for the same purpose in Europe.)

Scrolling Southeast from Sandy Branch shows the St. Martins River's exit into Isle of Wight Bay. The Assawoman Canal from Indian River Bay provided a waterway to Assawoman Bay and to Isle of Wight Bay in 1890. How much of its length was previously traversable by water isn't evident.

A waterway may have existed between Frankford and Selbyville in 1842—Vines Creek extends Southwest from Frankford and many branches come close to it, including Polly Branch. No interconnection between Vines Creek and Polly Branch is now evident.

The waterway from Sandy Branch to the St. Martins River also isn't continuous now— for a short distance near Bishopville. And if an inland water route traversable by Indian River Vessels interconnected Indian River Bay with Selbyville in 1842, it no longer exists.

The Ocean City, Maryland Inlet did not exist until 1933. So the water route to present day Selbyville from Philadelphia in 1842 may have been the about 100 mile longer one running

South past the Indian River Inlet and Assateague and Chincoteague, Virginia—then inland into Chincoteague Bay and North through Sinepuxent Bay to Isle of Wight Bay—and then up St. Martins River. (Ocean-going ship cargos would have had to be reloaded into shallow draft vessels upon or before reaching St. Martin's River.)

1.4   Finances

Low or no pay made seven years of Revolutionary War service a financial drain. (Privates reportedly got a monthly pay of $6, sergeants $8, and Captains $20. And they had to provide their own weapons, gear, and uniforms.[25]) That and damp, unsanitary living conditions and near starvation made the Continental Army's size vary between 5,000 and 20,000—due to desertions, mutinies, and enlistment expirations.[26] But Private John McCabe reportedly served continuously as a foot soldier from age 49 to 56. His ankle wound at the siege of South Carolina in 1781[27] didn't alter that. And it wasn't until six months after the Peace Treaty was signed that he was paid for military service from 7/1/1780-1/1/1782 and from 1/1/1783-11/3/1783. (He may not have been paid for much of his other service because the Revolutionary War Colonial Government was very strapped financially.) So, as is still the case for Army Privates, during the Revolutionary War even paid ones were too poor to support a family.

Converting Colonial pounds (£) to today's dollars is highly inexact, but John McCabe's unpaid £43.5 postwar debt was roughly the value, in England, of eight cows.[28] A cow costs about $1500 today[29] and values in the Colonies and in England could vary by a third. So John McCabe's £43.5 debt would be about $12,000 ± $4000 in 2018. Today's >$30,000 median salary indicates that that wasn't insurmountable. But 1727John might may have suffered from one or more of the following possible effects of wartime service:

- His debts may have been more than his ~$204 "mustering out" pay.
- The effect of seven years of war's privations on his mind and aging body.
- A distractive association with George Mitchell.
- Differences with his wife about his war service.

Its aftermath notwithstanding, Private John McCabe's Revolutionary War service was quintessentially that of the Colonial Scotch-Irish and in full accord with the pledge in the final sentence of the *Declaration of Independence: And for the support of this Declaration, with a firm reliance on the protection of divine Providence, we mutually pledge to each other our Lives, our Fortunes, and our sacred Honor.*

1.5   Gaelic Ancestors

The Gaelic Celts settled in Ireland and expanded into Scotland and the Isle of Man. The Brythonic Celts occupied Brittany (Northwest France) and "Brittain." Except for Wales and Cornwall, the Brythonic Celts were driven out of Brittain by Gaelic and Anglo-Saxon invasions.[30] {Some Brythonic Celts had responded to the earlier Roman invasion by going North of the walls the Romans built (e.g., Hadrian's Wall), and attacking the Romans, who didn't pursue them into the rugged Scottish terrain which, like Wales and Cornwall, adds a geographic barrier to the cultural one.}

The Gaelic Celts, despite their ethnic commonalities, did develop significant ethnic/societal individualities. For example, before 1868, Scotland's Primogeniture Laws awarded estates as follows:[31]

- Immoveable property (e.g., real estate, buildings) went to the eldest son.
- Moveable property (goods, gear, money and debts) was divided into thirds, the widow's part, the bairns' (children's) part, and the deid's part (which went to whomever or whatever the deceased specified).

Estate owners often were land-rich but in debt, so second and later sons who did not marry the eldest daughter of a property owner with no sons had to establish themselves from scratch. And second and subsequent sons no doubt swelled the ranks of the clergy, adventurers, fortune-seekers, the politically disfavored, and hired warriors (Gallowglass) in Ireland. (Some of those may have changed their names to further free themselves from yesteryear or become more "Irish.")

Ireland's ancient Brehon Laws and traditions were different. They provided that lands were inherited equally among the sons of the deceased (partible inheritance).[32] That gave the offspring of the wealthy less financial motivation to undertake the warrior trade. But Ireland was not a wealthy nation, and the Christian mandate to *go forth and multiply* often produced successive subdivisions of property to the point where inherited land became an insufficient income source. That fostered the taking up of arms to increase a family's or clan's or country's holdings. But Christianity ruled out measures like the practice, in the Himalayan Mountains, of a form of polyandry that keeps a family's property intact by having one wife being shared by all of a family's brothers.[33]

The Irish, like other Celts, warred against their country's invaders and against each other. In addition to the records of Invasions of Ireland by the Vikings, the British, the Normans, etc., prehistory (myth/legend) tells of invasions by Partholonians, Nemedians, the Fir Bolg, the Tuatha de Danann, and Milesians.[34] Despite embellishment with fanciful tales (e.g., magic), myth and legend credibly depict warfare as inherent to Ireland's prehistory. And the reputed raids of High King Niall of the nine hostages[35] show that the Irish, like other nationalities, warred to extend their realm.

1.6 John's Ancestral Ethnicity

As is later addressed, the MacCabes who were in Ireland as Gallowglass in the 14th Century and afterwards were involved in supporting Catholic Ireland's resistance to England and Irish Clans' wars against each other. And religious early Gallowglass were Catholic because the Protestant Reformation didn't begin until the 16th Century.

John McCabe's Gallowglass ancestors lost their lands to the British. And the ancestral/

ethnic linkage of the Gallowglass to Scotland gave them much in common with those Ulster-Scots disaffected with the British Crown, with loyalty to it, and with the Anglican religion. But John McCabe's ancestors had been far more Irish than Scotch for centuries when his father reputedly emigrated to America.

Religious faith is strong among warriors. And Catholicism was and is Ireland's and Northern Ireland's largest religion. But John McCabe would have found it difficult, if not impossible, to practice Catholicism in the then rabidly Protestant English Colonies. Also, John McCabe married Mary Hudson, who carried an ancient Anglo-Saxon English name. Henry Hudson (1580-1611) discovered the "Northwest Passage" and Hudson's Bay in Canada[36] and had New York's Hudson River named after him. And strong loyalty to the Crown was shown by Michael Hudson (1605-1648), a Chaplain to England's King Charles I (1600-1649). Michael was killed defending Woodcroft Castle against the Parliamentarians in the war that resulted in Charles' death too.[37]

That the Anglican (Episcopal) Church of England may have been important to Mary Hudson is suggested by the about five-mile distance from her childhood home in Sandy Branch to the Chapel of Ease in All Hallows Parish, the predecessor of Worcester Parish on the site of historic St. Martin's Episcopal Church[38] in Showell, Maryland. (St Peter's Episcopal Church in Lewes, Delaware began serving its community in 1680.[39] But It was some 29 miles away—further than the about 22 miles to the Episcopal Church in Milton, Delaware, which was founded in 1728. And St. Georges Chapel, the next Episcopal church in Sussex County, wasn't established until 1794.[40])

Reputedly, the Colonial Scotch-Irish were Presbyterians, like the Ulster-Scots, who came to Ireland centuries after the Gallowglass did. And not only was Catholicism anathema to England's Anglicanism (Episcopalianism), Presbyterianism was too.

John's and Mary's marriage is consistent with his acceptance (or endorsement) of the Episcopalian (Anglican) denomination when they wed—because America's Methodist-Episcopal Church (where my family historically worshipped) was established in the mid-18th Century by Anglican Priest John Wesley (1703-1791).[41]

Mary Hudson and John McCabe had biblical forenames. So did their first three children: Obediah (Servant of God), Matthew, and John Jr. But then came Arthur, whose Celtic name may have come from the ancient Welsh term Arto-uiros (bear-like man) but is best known from the legend of King Arthur.[42] The baby of the family was Alexha, a feminine diminutive of the Greek name Alexander.[43] So religion wasn't the basis for the names of John McCabe's children. (Their ancestry, as is later shown, was a major factor.)

1.7 John's Sons' Ethos

That the Patriot Armed Forces were about 13% of the populace and male means that roughly 26% of the Colonies' eligible males were under arms. The ineligibility of the young and the inability of the elderly and/or disabled to serve indicates a more than 74% probability that a Colonial man did not join the army or militia. That correlates to a less than 30% probability that four randomly selected eligible males were all noncombatants. But applying such a guesstimate to John McCabe's four sons seems less realistic than considering why none of them shared their father's dedication to Independence enough to follow him into the Continental Army, despite all four being old enough to serve.

John's sons may have been incapable of killing or physically unfit for war. Or John may have counseled against their going to war. Or Mary Ann (Hudson) McCabe may have inculcated gentleness in them. She may even have been a Tory whose influence kept her sons out of the war. (The hand that rocks the cradle....) But it also may be, especially if Mary's upbringing were harsh (as was far from uncommon), she endorsed her husband's Scotch-Irish views rather than the Tory association implied by her quintessentially English maiden name. (That's all unconfirmed speculation.)

1.8 John's Parents

Marjorie Adams, a 7th generation descendant of John McCabe, identified John's parents as Edward McCabe (1700 – >1758) and Lydia (Winter) McCabe. (7/1709 – c.1758).[44]

Marjorie's references include the Holland Society of New York,[45] the U.S. Dutch Reformed Church,[46] the Miller File,[47] the 1758 Will of an Edward McCabe,[48] and the New York Genealogical and Biological Record.[49] Edward's parents are unidentified. His birthplace is (uncertainly) identified as Dublin, Ireland.[50] Lydia was born in Ulster, New York, New York Colony, and probably died in the New Jersey Colony.[51] So the prior, unconfirmed identification of John McCabe's parents {i.e., James McCabe and Katherine Mary Sheridan being the parents of a John McCabe born 13 May 1727 in "Worchester" (Worcester) County, MD[52]} is now contraindicated.

Edward's and Lydia's youngest son, Edward McCabe (c.1790 – >1800), is not now known to have had children or to have married.[53] (But he may have done both.)

Matthew McCabe, aka McKeeby, McCaby, (c.1729 – >1802)[54] was Edward's and Lydia's middle son. He was born in the Colony of New York and died in Dutchess, New York. His wife was Mary (Conklin) McCabe. He and his sons Benjamin and Matthew (Junior) are listed on the 1802 tax list for Philips, Dutchess, New York. Matthew (Junior) was Matthew McCabe (c.1750 – c.1810),[55] aka McCaby, McCavy, McKeeby. He was born in Fishkill, Dutchess, Colony of New York, and died in Montague, Sussex, New Jersey. All of Matthew Junior's and his wife Jannetje Tappan's 10 children took either McKeeby or McCaby as their surname. And their four sons had no known offspring.

Edward's and Lydia's oldest son was John McCabe (c.1727 – c.1800).[56] He is identified on Wikitree as the progenitor of the McCabes of the Selbyville, Delaware area, with the reference for that progenitorship[57] identifying the following namesakes:

- Obediah McCabe (1753-1794), John McCabe and Mary (Hudson) McCabe's firstborn. {Lydia Winter's father was Obadias (Obadia) "Obadiah" Winter.[58]}
- Matthew McCabe (1756 – 1811), John and Mary (Hudson) McCabe's 2nd son. {Edward and Lydia's 2nd son was Matthew McCabe (c.1729 – >1802)}
- Lydia Winter McCabe (1794-1878) was a granddaughter of John and Mary (Hudson) McCabe (their 4th son Arthur McCabe's 5th child).

[That children and grandchildren of John and Mary (Hudson) McCabe were deliberately given forenames of their recent ancestral families is very likely while such names choices being coincidental is so unlikely that that's an unreasonable speculation.]

Confirmation of the kinship of John McCabe to Lydia Winter McCabe's husband through Y-DNA analysis of the father's patrilineal descendants is desirable. But even without that, the information available as of this writing credibly identifies Edward McCabe (1700 – >1758) and Lydia (Winter) McCabe. (7/1709 – c.1758) as the parents of Revolutionary War Private John McCabe (1727-1800).

1.9 John's Maternal Lineage

Lydia McCabe's father, Obedias Winter (d. >1739) was born and died in New York. In 1739 he was living in Port Richmond, Staten Island (a neighborhood on the North Shore of Staten Island.[59]) His parents are unknown.[60] He married Susannah Magdalena DePue (c.1669 – >1723), aka Palmerton, DePuy, DePuis), a daughter of Nicholas (Depuy) Dupuis and Cateryntje (de Vos) Depuis.[61]

The ancient surname Depue was first found in Languedoc, France, where they held lands and estates. Name variants include: Dupuis, Dupuits, Dupuit Dupuy, du Puy, Dupuy, Du Peu, dePeu, DuPeux, LePeu, Dupè, Pouey, Poueigh, Pouy, Dupouy, Poy, Puig, Delpuy, Pouet, LePuy, LePuis, DePuis, DePuy, Le Pouey, DuPouy, LePeux, Dupée, etc.[62]

Nicholas (Depuy) Dupuis (c.1625 – 1690) was born in Arras, Pas-de-Calais, Nord-Pas-de-Calais, Frankrijk, and died in New York, New York. He married Cateryntje (de Vos) Depuis (c.1634 – 1705) in 1656 in Leiden, Netherlands. Nicholas Dupuis was the son of Nicholas du Puy II and Chevalier—whose birth surname and parents are unknown.[63]

Catryntje (Catharina) "Catalyna, Cathalijna" (De Vos) Dupuis. aka Renaer, Reynardt, Duvois, Depuy was born in Leiden, Zuid Holland, Nederland and died in Staten Island, New York. Her mother is unknown. Her father was Moses Duvois De Vos Renard, whose parents are unknown.[64] (Vos is Dutch for fox; renard is French for fox.)

Nicholas Du Puy II (c. 1594 – 1625) was born in France and died 6/25/1625 at the Battle of Sarragosse (the French spelling of Zaragosa, Spain, an unconfirmed 1625 battle locale). He married Chevalier (b.1610). His parents were Nicholas Du Puy I and Claudine "Claudia" Sanguin.[65] Chevalier's maiden name and parents are unknown.[66]

Nicholas Du Puy I (b. 1576), aka Depuy, Dupuy, the French-born son of Claude DuPuy and Guigonne de Joven,[67] married French-born Claudine Sanguin (b.1576). She was born in France to Jacques Sanguin (b.~1550)[68] and Barbe de Thou (b. ~1150),[69] The parents of Jacques Sanguin[70] and of Barbe de Thou[71] are unknown.

Claude DuPuy (b. 1540), aka Depuy, the son of Francois Du Puy and of Jeanne Pelissier,[72] married Guigonne de Joven, whose parents are unknown.[73]

Francois Du Puy, aka Depuy (1515-1571), who married Jean Peilissier, was the son of Honorat Dupuy and Peronette de Claveyson.[74] Jean Pelissier's parents are unknown.[75]

Honorat Dupuy (d. c.1588), the son of Jacques Dupuy and of Francise Astraud,[76] wed Peronnette de Claveyson (b. c.1490), the daughter of Louis de Claveyson and an unknown mother.[77] Louis de Claveyson's parents are unknown.[78]

Jacques Dupuy (1475 - >1505),[79] the son of Eynier Dupuy and Catherine de Bellecombe,[80] married Francise Astraud (b.1476), whose parents are unknown.[81]

Eynier "Aimer" Dupuy (b. 1444), the son of Giles du Puy II and Florence (Hauteville) Puy,[82] married Catherine de Bellecombe (b. c.1450), whose parents are unknown.[83]

[There is an unresolved discrepancy between the 1444 birth of Eynier Dupuy and the 1420 death of his reputed father Giles (Puy) du Puy II.]

Giles (Puy) du Puy II (1365 – 1420), aka Signeur de Pereins Autres Villes, the son of Giles Gillet (Puy) du Puy and Alix (Bellecombe) du Puy,[84] wed Florence (Hauteville) Puy (b. c. 1420). Her father was Florimond (Hauteville) de Hauteville, her mother is unknown.[85] Florimond (Hauteville) de Hauteville's parents are unknown.[86]

Giles Gillet (Puy) du Puy (c.1328 – 1390), aka Chevalier, Signeur de Pereins, married Alix (Bellecombe) du Puy (b. c.1335). He was the son of Alleman (Dupuy) DuPuy V and Ainarde (Roland) du Puy.[87] Alix (Bellecombe) du Puy's parents are unknown.[88]

Alleman (Dupuy) DuPuy V (c.1305 – <1362), who was born and died in Pereins (Peyrins), Dauphne (Drome), France, married Ainarde (Roland) Du Puy (c.1310 – >1362). He was the son of Alleman Dupuy and Eleanor (Alleman) Dupuy, and the 5th oldest son of his name to be *Seigneur de Pereins, Rochefort, Apifer, et Ansenix*,[89] Ainarde (Roland) Du Puy's father was Gillet de Roland. Her mother is unknown.[90] Gillet de Roland (1285 – c.1339), parents unknown, was born and died in Dauphne (Drome), France.[91]

Alleman DuPuy (b. c. 1265), the son of Alleman DuPuy and Beatrix Artaud, married Eleanor (Alleman) Dupuy (b. c.1276),.[92] Eleanor's father was Jean Alleman (b. c.1265 to unknown parents.[93] Eleanor's mother is unknown.[94]

Alleman Dupuy (c.1235 – >1304), who married Beatrix Artaud (b. c.1235), was the son of Alleman Dupuy and Alix (unknown) DuPuy.[95] Beatrix Artaud's parents are unknown.[96]

Alleman Dupuy (b. c.1200), who married Alix (unknown) DuPuy, was the son of Hugues Dupuy and Floride de Moran.[97] The parents of Alix (unknown) DuPuy are unknown.[98]

Hugues Dupuy (b. c.1145), who married Floride de Moiran (b. c.1175), was the son of Allemande Dupuy and Veronique Ademar.[99] Floride de Moiran was the daughter of Berlion de Moiran and an unknown mother.[100] The parents of Berlion de Moiran (b. c.1150) are unknown.[101]

Allemande Dupuy (1077 – c.1150), who married Veronique Ademar, was the son of Hugues DuPuy and Deurand de Poiseu,[102] Veronique Ademar's father was Gerard Adhemar. Her mother is unknown.[103] Gerard Adhemar's parents are unknown.[104]

Hugues (Hugo the Crusader) Dupuy (c. 1055 – >1096), the son of Raphael de Podio and an unknown mother, wed Deurand de Posieu (b. c.1070 of unknown parents[105]). Hugo was the first Seignor de Perens, d'Apifer and de Rocheport en Dauphine. He joined the First Crusade, led by Bishop Adhemar of Le Puy (Adhémar de Monteil), in 1096.[106, 107]

Raphael de Podio (<990 – >1033[108]) was born in Rome, Italy and died in Le Puy, Dauphine, France.[109] (de Podio is another variant of du Puy[110])

2
Colonial Times

2.1 Initial Colonization

The Spanish and French established settlements in the New World in the 1500s. In 1609 the English Navigator Henry Hudson claimed the land that became New Netherlands for the Dutch[111] (after sailing past the English settlement of Jamestown, Virginia). The Dutch land claim extended from the Delmarva Peninsula to Cape Cod,[112] and the Dutch made the first settlement in Delaware in 1631. That it was wiped out by the Amerinds didn't prevent the establishment of a Swedish Colony and Trading Post in 1638 at Fort Christina (Wilmington). Then the Dutch built a fort near New Castle in 1651, forced out the Swedes, and retook Delaware.

The Dutch, who vastly outnumbered the English in America, were governed from Manhattan (New Amsterdam). But four English warships with several hundred soldiers came to New Amsterdam's Harbor in 1664 and demanded its surrender. The Dutch community opposed fighting them and Governor Peter Stuyvesant signed over the Colony to the English. They did not evict the Dutch, but Holland's North American venture was over—and the Dutch shifted their focus to Surinam in South America.[113, 114] The English then became the great majority of European immigrants to the present United States of America.[115]

2.2 Delmarva

Mary Land (Terra Mariae) was conceived by George Calvert (the first Lord Baltimore, and a Catholic) as a colony where Catholics and Protestants could live harmoniously.[116] He died before Maryland was granted to him, and Charles I granted it to his son Cecilius.[117]

The first Maryland settlers were a selected group of Catholics and Protestants who arrived in 1634 on St. Clement's Island (in the Potomac River), where Catholics took their first Mass in Britain's American colonies. But many strongly anti-Catholic Puritans came to Maryland, and long-lasting religious conflict ensued.[118]

Captain Richard Ingle (1609-1653), who carried goods to and from England, sided with the Puritans and England's Parliament during England's Civil War between the Catholic Royalists and the Protestant Parliamentarians. Ingle escaped when his ship was seized by Maryland's Catholic Governor Leonard Calvert (Cecillius' younger brother). Then, claiming the permission of Protestant England and a Letter of Marque to cruise the "Shesapeake," he returned In February 1645 in the ship *Reformation*, took St. Mary City (Colonial Maryland's Capitol) and imprisoned its leaders. Governor Calvert fled to Virginia but returned with an armed force in 1646 and quashed the rebellion. Most of Ingle's men were granted amnesty but Captain Ingle reputedly was hanged for piracy in 1653.[119]

Protestants overthrew Maryland's Catholic government in 1654. And anti-Catholicism grew over the years. In 1704 an *Act to Prevent the Growth of Popery within this Province* forbade any *Popish Bishop, Priest, or Jesuite* from proselytizing and from baptizing any person other than those with *Popish Parents*. Another 1704 statute limited Catholic Mass to private homes. Other laws prohibited Catholics from practicing law and from teaching children. And in 1718 the requirement that voters swear to anti-Catholic declarations denied the vote to Catholics. Also, to discourage Irish immigration, severe taxes were imposed on hiring Irish *Papist* servants. In effect, Roman Catholicism was banned in Maryland (except in or near Baltimore?) until the 1750s.[120]

In 1681, King Charles II granted part of Maryland to William Penn.[121] He named it Pennsylvania. Its lower three counties, which now, from North to South, are New Castle, Kent, and Sussex, were formerly New Amstel, St. Jones, and Deale.[122]

Maryland claimed Delaware South of Lewes (38°46'28" N Latitude). (That's a bit more than 48% of the landmass of Delaware.) But the 1751 Transpeninsular Line Survey, made by two Pennsylvania surveyors and two Maryland surveyors, put Delaware's southern boundary 16-17 miles South of Lewes, at Fenwick Island (~38°27' N Latitude), where the Transpeninsular Line's Eastern marker was placed on 4/26/1751.[123] But it wasn't until November 1760 that Frederick Calvert, the 6th Lord Baltimore, approved that survey, paving the way for Its results to be accepted and its Middle Marker placed.[124] The 1768-1774 Mason-Dixon survey later affirmed that Transpeninsular Line and established Delaware's western boundary.[125]

William Penn espoused religious freedom. But English law effectively denied public office to Catholics.[126] And Sussex County's first Catholic Church was St. Agnes-by-the-Sea, built in Rehoboth Beach in 1905.[127] (Protestantism is still predominant in the county. In the 1940s, when a Catholic family moved into Millsboro, about six miles North of my parents' residence, a neighbor wryly commented that *the papists aire a'comin*. And in 2010 Sussex County had 197,145 inhabitants,[128] four cities and 21 towns,[129] over 100 unincorporated communities,[130] but just seven Catholic Churches.[131])

Except for those brought by Lord Calvert and those who soon followed, sensible Catholics didn't settle in Colonial Delmarva. And the boundary dispute that began when Penn and Calvert met in 1683 in New Castle wasn't resolved until 1/11/1769, when George III approved the Calvert-Penn petition that the Mason-Dixon Survey be accepted.[132] [So lower Sussex County residents weren't sure until then that they didn't live in Maryland.]

2.3 Tories and Patriots

The Continental Army, Navy, Marines, and Militia represented about 13% of the about 2.8 million people in the Colonies—more than double the 6% typical of warring nations.[133] But Delaware's majority and mostly Anglican Court Party favored reconciliation and was strongest in Kent and Sussex Counties. The largely Ulster-Scot (Scotch-Irish?) Country Party, centered in New Castle County, advocated independence.[134]

According to Richard Purcell of Catholic University, during the American Revolution over half the people of Delaware's Kent and Sussex Counties were of the *Established Church of England* (I.e., Anglicans), *and many of them were pronounced Tories*. Purcell used W.A. Powell's 1928 *History of* Delaware (and inexact arithmetic) to show the Anglican Anglo-Saxon and Presbyterian character of the people: in 1743, of 1020 men in Kent County, there were Anglicans (484), Quakers (56), Presbyterians (397), and the religiously unaffiliated (20). That there was virtually no Catholic presence in Delaware then also is evident in the record of the holding of Catholic services in New Castle by missionaries as "early" as 1804, with a brick church begun there in 1807.[135]

Political disturbances in Sussex County kept anyone from being elected there in 1777. When Whigs were finally chosen in March 1778, the Friends of American Independence considered that a miracle. And the 1780 Black Camp rebellion showed that Toryism was still strong. As Harold Bell Hancock put it:

> With the removal of the British from Philadelphia in the spring of 1778, ... activities of Sussex Counties Tory's diminished except for the 1780 Black Camp Rebellion in which insurrectionists, mainly from Sussex Counties Cedar Creek and Slaughter Neck, who had headquarters in this swamp about six miles north of Georgetown where 'leaders' Bartholomew Barnum and William Dutton had near 400 men under arms formed into militia units. These people, it was said, were ignorant, opposing all laws, favored the Kings Law and the payment of tax, and thought that the South of Chesapeake Bay had laid down arms and taken Kings Law and thought Sussex should do the same. A Continental Militia from upper Delaware dispersed these insurrectionists, some were placed in the Continental Army, some were to be "hung by the neck until most dead, then cut their bowels out and be burnt before your face, then the head be severed and the body quartered". By good fortune, this sentence, common for treason, was never carried out and all were pardoned in 1780 Session of the General Assembly on November 4th.

Colonial Toryism[136] undoubtedly diminished when the Revolution succeeded. But England's trade sanctions on the U.S., opposition to U.S. expansion, and impressment of British-born American sailors into the Royal Navy brought about the *Second War of Independence* (The War of 1812).[137] After Andrew Jackson finished that war off at New Orleans, Tories in the United States must have been deep in the closet.

The U.S. and UK have long since mended their differences. [And intermarriage between the English, Irish, Scotch, and Welsh in the New World has resulted in virtually all U.S. citizens with European Colonial ancestors having both Tory and Patriot ancestry—by a combination of their patrilineal and matrilineal lineages.]

2.4 Sussex County, Delaware's First Town

Early Lewes, Delaware is an example of what our ancestors brought to and encountered in the New World. (It's also illustrative of the character of the Amerinds and Colonists.)

The initial European settlement of Lewes was under the auspices of the Dutch West India Company (DWIC). Samuel Godyn and Samuel Bommaert, DWIC patroons (landowners with lordship-like manorial rights), sent the 18-gun ship *Walvis*, commanded by Captain Pieter Heyes, there from Texel, Holland. Godyn and Bommaert and Heyes were in a "Land Pool" that also included Kilian van Rensalaer (a Founder of DWIC, one of its first patroons and the only successful one), Captain David Pietersz. de Vries, a navigator from Hoorn, Holland (the first choice to command the expedition), and four others. [138]

Walvis could carry at least 162 people (the number aboard when she broke up on Indonesia's Selayar reef on 1/7/1663[139]). When she set sail for Godyn (Delaware) Bay in December 1630, she carried ~30 immigrants, cattle, food, and whaling implements (DeVries had been told that whales were abundant) and was accompanied by a yacht.

Heyes sailed up the West shore of Delaware Bay, found a navigable stream just above present Cape Henlopen in April 1631, and named it the *Hoornkill*. (It seems to have been known as Lewes Creek before it became the Lewes-Rehoboth Canal. And Lewes still has a *Hoornkill Avenue*.[140]) Gillis Hossett, the expedition's Commissary, led the settlers in laying out a manor and building Fort Oplandt. The Colonists put up a pillar with a tin plate with a tracing of the Coat of Arms of the Netherlands' United Provinces, and named their settlement *Zwaanendael* (Swan Valley). Then, after crossing the Delaware to buy a 12 square-mile bayside tract running Northwest from Cape May from the Amerinds, Heyes left Hossett in charge and set sail for Holland in September.

Early in 1632, New Amsterdam Governor Peter Minuet returned to Holland from Manhattan. He carried news of a massacre at *Zwaanendael*. Captain de Vries, who was preparing to sail from Texel to bring more settlers to Zwaanendael, sailed anyhow. On December 6, he found the stockade burned, human bones and heads, cattle remains, and no survivors. The Amerinds reportedly told him (a cock and bull story?) that an Indian Chief had taken the tin from the pillar to make pipes, causing settler indignation.

To make amends, the Siconese brought that chief's head to the settlers, whom they claimed to revere almost as much as the Indian God Manitou. They were rebuked for the killing. But the chief's friends, under the guise of visiting a sick settler, slaughtered the whole (revered?) colony, putting 25 arrows into a chained mastiff in the process. De Vries reputedly considered the massacre the result of misbehavior by the White Settlers. And when whaling proved inadequate to sustain *Zwaanendael*, he removed its new settlers and returned, via Manhattan, to Holland.[141, 142] (His ship's cannons may have influenced the Amerind's behavior and led to the conclusion that they were peaceful.)

Exactly how *Zwaanendael* and *Hoornkill* became *Hoerekill-Whorekill* is uncertain, but the massacred settlers were raised in a society that placed great emphasis on female pre-marital virginity. Its women were chattels expected to provide their husbands sex upon demand and to be monogamous. But men were free to *sow their wild oats*. And non-whites were considered inferiors who could be mistreated without fear of punishment.

Militant evangelism eventually converted many Amerinds to White mores. But the earlier Amerinds had equal sexual rights. Their adult sexual relationships were mostly exclusive and heterosexual, but polygamy and pre-marital and extra-marital sex were allowed. "Marriage" was mostly entered into without ceremony. Divorce could be effected simply by moving out, and involved no penalty, stigma, or property settlement. Children were expected to experiment with heterosexual and homosexual behavior, were tribal members with their own rights, and were part of a family with many fathers, mothers, and siblings. When a French Jesuit Priest said that the Amerind men did not know which children were theirs, a male Montagnais (of Quebec) responded: *You French people love only your own children but we love all the members of our tribe*. The Amerinds also knew that we all have both male and female traits, and saw "Two-Spirit" humans as created by Manitou—with spiritual and shamanistic value. Two-Spirit behavior probably began among the Eastern Seaboard Tribes substantially before European settlement.[143, 144]

[Asserting that there had been no misbehavior by the settlers attributes remarkable restraint to young men newly away from their sexually restrictive culture—with sexually active women available. Some settlers may not only have exploited the availability of the Amerind women, they may have tried to enforce a sexual exclusiveness inconsistent with the women's right to sexual polyandry. The Amerinds could have seen that as depriving them of the sexual availability of desirable partners. (Sexual permissiveness does not eliminate male or female competition for sexual advantage.) So a perception of lessened availability of sexual partners could have fostered Amerind retaliation.]

[Another potential contributing factor was the White Man's profiteering from Amerind vulnerability to alcohol. Their prior lack of exposure to intoxicants that strong may have set the stage for a drunken orgy of Amerind violence. The statement that the massacre involved shooting 25 arrows into a chained mastiff is consistent with drunkenness—sober warriors being unlikely to have wasted their limited arrow supply on a restrained mastiff, at least after enough arrows had been fired to assure that the animal could no longer be a threat. Finding cattle bones also is consistent with an orgiastic slaughter—it suggests wastage of a source of meat by attackers who could ill afford to waste protein.]

[Another factor was Walvis' crew and cannons. Heyes' return to Holland gave the Amerinds the military advantage. Moreover, the settler left in charge was a supplier (commissary) and builder, not a warrior. And destroying *Zwaanendael* before more settlers and armed ships arrived was a great opportunity. Other factors may have contributed or even been primary, but it also seems likely that the Amerinds simply recognized *Zwaanendael's* numeric and combat inferiority and mounted a well-planned attack—and then orgiastically killed everything in sight (as happened when Jericho fell?).]

2.5 The Scotch-Irish

In 1728, Anglican Reverend William Beckett of Lewes (then still the only town in Sussex County) wrote:

> *the first settlers of the county were mostly English, with a few Dutch families, but of late years great numbers of Irish (who call themselves Scotch Irish) have transported themselves and their families from the North of Ireland unto the Province of Pennsylvania, where many families settled in County Sussex— and are Presbyterians by profession.*

Both of the county's Anglican Rectors were sympathetic to the Tories, who were for rule by England.[145] {Beckett's statement that Sussex County's Irish immigrants came from the North of Ireland isn't borne out by the surnames of my 15 high school classmates and acquaintances. Of their eight Irish names,[146] one (Quillen) is from County Antrim in Ulster, Ireland's Northern Province. The others trace to Leinster (the Eastern Province) Connacht (the Western Province), and Munster (the Southern Province)}.

Hebridean/Highland Scots voluntarily emigrated to Ireland as crack infantry and bodyguards as early as the 11th Century.[147] Their Northwest (Highland) culture began separating from the Lowlands during the 5th Century Anglo-Saxon invasion and extension of the Kingdom of Bernicia into Southern Scotland. Many Lowlanders are considered to be descended from those Anglo-Saxons or from the Vikings (who began raiding and settling late in the 8th Century). That resulted in Highlanders considering Lowlanders not true Scots but Germanic. {The Highland Line running Southwest from Stonehaven on the East to Campbelltown on Kintyre (corresponding to the Highland Geologic Fault) became the putative line of demarcation between the Highlands and Lowlands}.[148]

Lowlanders have spoken Saxon English for over a millennium, and the Lowlands became the "cradle" of Scotland when its people (e.g., William Wallace) led the way to temporary Scottish independence. Also, Capitalism took hold in the Lowlands early in the 18th Century, while the Highlands held on to feudalism and tribal communal cultures until the early 19th. Lowlanders have been described as quiet moral, and hardworking—and Highlanders as carefree, exuberant, and unreliable. (That may be overstatement.) Typically, neither Highlanders nor Lowlanders consider themselves English[149] or the same as each other. As a Glaswegian (Lowlander) stated: *You have to understand Scots to know how this pans out…. Scots don't like other Scots. Scots from further away aren't quite as bad as the ones down the road, but if you try and do down any of the disparate roaming tribes…gods help you.* Another Scot commented: *The lowlands has a similar culture to the North of England. Apart from things like kilts at weddings, burns nights there's not much difference between the lowlands and England. Being proud Scots though runs through us all.*[150] (Burns' Night is on January 25, Robert Burns' birthday.)

In 1605, impoverished Lowland and Border Scots began emigrating to Ireland's North, primarily Ulster, during England's "Plantation" of conquered Irish territory. They had to swear loyalty to the English Crown, and became known as *Ulster-Scots* in the Isles. America's Ulster-Scots Society considers all descendants of the Scots who came to Ireland from the

1400s onwards to be Ulster-Scot descendants.[151] But the only "Plantation" of Ireland before Ulster was by Anglican Queen Elizabeth I, who unsuccessfully sent English and Welsh to Munster in 1586. Most survivors returned to England.[152] {Some American Scotch-Irish (e.g., Revolutionary War Private John McCabe) had Hebrides/Highland ethnic roots.}

In the 1688-1691 Williamite War, Ireland's Gallowglass supported the Catholic Jacobite and England's and Scotland's King (England's James II, Scotland's James VII). Protestant William of Orange won that war and the conquerors took the losers' lands.

Presbyterianism came to Scotland with John Knox (1513-1572).[153] Presbyterian and Anglican differences were like the Protestant and Catholics ones. But the Ulster-Scots supported the Williamites and Anglican King William III allowed them to practice Presbyterianism. That changed when he died in 1702—because his successor, Anglican Queen Anne, despised both Catholics and Dissenters (non-Anglican Protestants).[154] Repressive penal laws were enacted, ostensibly to unify England, Ireland, and Scotland. For example, Catholics were excluded from most public offices in 1607. Enforcement of the Penal Laws apparently varied based on local magistrates' attitudes. But the Penal Laws were made harsher starting in 1695, and in 1737 Presbyterians were banned from public office. Other restrictions included: [155]

On Catholics and on Dissenters

A ban on Irish or English Parliament membership (from 1652-1662 & 1691-1829).
Voting disenfranchisement (from 1728-1793).
A ban on foreign education (until 1782) or entry to Trinity College Dublin (until 1793).
Exclusion from the legal profession (until 1793) and the judiciary (until 1829).

On Catholics

No holding of firearms or service in the armed forces (until 1793).
No intermarriage with Protestants (until 1778).
If an eldest son and heir converted to Protestantism, he became the sole tenant of estate and the other children's inheritance was limited to one-third of the estate.
A prohibition on leasing land that lasted more than 31 years (until 1778).
No custody of orphans without a £500 donation to Dublin's Blue Coat Hospital.
No inheritance of Protestant land.
No owning of a horse valued at over £5 (i.e., with military value).
Lay priests could register to preach under the 1704 Registration Act, but seminary priests and Bishops couldn't preach until 1778.
If allowed, new churches were to be built of wood, not stone, and away from main roads.
No school teaching or learning instruction upon pain of a £20 fine and three months imprisonment (until 1782).

<u>On Protestants</u>

Presbyterian marriages were not legally recognized by the State. Converting to Catholicism meant forfeiting all property and legacy to the Monarch, remaining imprisoned at the Monarch's pleasure, and forfeiting the Monarch's protection (thereby prohibiting any action against any injury, however atrocious).

2.6 Scotch-Irish Discontent

Author Raymond Campbell Patterson, a Glaswegian (Lowlander), studied the "Scots-Irish" and documented the following.[156]

In 1704, Queen Anne's Anglican-dominated government passed an act requiring all office holders to take communion in the Anglican Church, eliminating much of the civil administration in Ireland. It was even seriously suggested that Presbyterian ministers could be charged in Anglican Church Courts with fornicating with their own wives. The Toleration Act of 1719 removed the worst features of that legislation, but the discrimination it fostered against Presbyterians lasted until the mid-19th Century. Among its critics was Daniel Defoe (the author of Robinson Crusoe), who stated:

> It seems somewhat hard, and savours of the most scandalous ingratitude, that the very people who drank deepest of the popish fury, and were the most vigorous to show their zeal and their courage in opposing tyranny and popery, and on the foot of forwardness and valour the Church of Ireland recovered herself from her low condition, should now be requited with so injurious a treatment as to be linked with the very Papists they fought against...There will certainly be no encouragement to the Dissenters to join with their brethren the next time the Papists shall please to take arms and attempt their throats. Not but they may be fools enough as they always were to stand in the gap.

Another source of Irish rage was the expiration of most immigration-fostering farm leases by 1710, with renewals being unaffordable. Anglican Archbishop of Dublin William King rated that rack-renting as the primary force behind emigration to the Americas by stating:

> Some would insinuate that this in some measure is due to the uneasiness dissenters have in the matter of religion, but this is plainly a mistake; for dissenters were never more easy as to that matter than they had been since the Revolution [of 1688] and are at present; and yet never thought of leaving the kingdom, till oppressed by the excessive rents and other temporal hardships: nor do any dissenters leave us, but proportionally of all sorts, except Papists. The truth is this: after the Revolution, most of the kingdom was waste, and abandoned of people destroyed in the war: the landlords therefore were glad to get tenants at any rate, and let their lands at very easy rents; they invited abundance of people to come over here, especially from Scotland, and they

lived here very happily ever since; but now their leases are expired, and they are obliged not only to give what they paid before the Revolution, but in most places double and in many places treble, so that it is impossible for people to live or subsist on their farms.

Whatever their reason for immigrating, the Scotch-Irish made a major contribution to the Revolutionary War. British Army Hessian Captain Johann Henricks said: *Call it not an American rebellion, it is nothing more than an Irish-Scotch Presbyterian Rebellion.* Paterson also wrote that General Washington stated that, if the cause was lost, he would take a last stand among the Scots-Irish of his native Virginia. (A General might make statements to encourage his forces and not affirm them later, and that one isn't supported by Washington's writings.) Paterson's eulogizing of the Scots-Irish also included:

With the outbreak of the Revolution in 1775 the Scots-Irish, in interesting contrast to many of their Scottish cousins, were among the most determined adherents of the rebel cause. Their frontier skills were particularly useful in destroying Burgoyne's army in the Saratoga campaign...It was their toughness, virility and sense of divine mission that was to help give shape to a new nation, supplying it with such diverse heroes as Davy Crocket and Andrew Jackson. They were indeed God's frontiersmen, the real historical embodiment of the lost tribe of Israel.

2.7 Colonial Religion

Religious freedom was a factor in the colonization of America. But most residents came primarily to better themselves, some of them believing the equivalent of streets are paved with gold lunacy. And Colonial churches by and large denied religious freedom to and persecuted other denominations. Also, those churches were not separate from the State. And their behavior is a trenchant example of basic human nature.

Quakers today are peaceful. But the Quakers of the Colonies of the 1600s were self-righteous, shouting in church, yelling in the streets pot- and pan-bangers who sometimes stripped off their clothes. The Puritans responded by whipping them, branding them, cutting off their ears, boring holes through their tongues, and hanging them. "Christian" Reverend John Norton, a leading Boston minister, cried: *I would carry fire in one hand and faggots in the other, to burn all the Quakers in the world.*[157]

Those Quakers began arriving in the Colonies in 1656. The General Court in Massachusetts repeatedly banned them, and the punishments they meted out were far from limited to whipping and branding. In 1660, for example, Massachusetts executed four Quakers who refused to renounce their faith.[158]

Such treatment didn't stop the Quakers. In 1682, three young English Quaker women in Dover, New Hampshire, preached against professional ministers, restrictions on individual conscience, and church-ruled customs. A petition for relief from their spreading of wicked errors was presented to Crown Magistrate Waldron. He ordered:

> *To the constables of Dover, Hampton, Salisbury, Newbury, Rowley, Ipswich, Wenham, Linn, Boston, Roxbury, Dedham, and until these vagabond Quakers are carried out of this jurisdiction, you, and every one of you are required in the name of the King's Majesty's name, to take these vagabond Quakers, Ann Coleman, Mary Tompkins, and Alice Ambrose, and make them fast to the cart's tail, and driving the cart through your several towns, to whip their naked backs, not exceeding ten stripes apiece on each of them, in each town; and so to convey them from constable to constable, till they are out of this jurisdiction.*

That meant whippings in at least eleven towns and traveling over 80 miles in bitterly cold weather. By George Bishop's recounting:

> *Deputy Waldron caused these women to be stripped naked from the middle upwards, and tied to a cart, and after awhile cruelly whipped them, whilst the priest stood and looked and laughed at it.*

According to Sewall's History of the Quakers:

> *The women thus being whipped at Dover, were carried to Hampton and there delivered to the constable...The constable the next morning would have whipped them before day, but they refused, saying they were not ashamed of their sufferings. Then he would have whipped them with their clothes on, when he had tied them to the cart. But they said, 'set us free, or do according to thine order. He then spoke to a woman to take off their clothes. But she said she would not for all the world. Why, said he, then I'll do it myself. So he stripped them, and then stood trembling whip in hand, and so he did the execution. Then he carried them to Salisbury through the dirt and the snow half the leg deep; and here they were whipped again. Indeed their bodies were so torn, that if Providence had not watched over them, they might have been in danger of their lives.*

A better side of human nature was shown In Salisbury, where Sergeant Major Robert Pike stopped the persecution of those Quaker women. Dr. Walter Barefoot, who was with him, dressed their wounds and brought them back to the Piscataqua, setting them up on the Maine side of the river at the home of Major Nicholas Shapleigh of Kittery.[159]

The Colonial mindset of New England also was revealed in witchcraft hysteria. The source of the belief in witchcraft was evident in English Puritan Joseph Glanvilel's 1668 book, *Against Modern Saddicism*. In it, Glanville claimed to be able to prove the existence of witches and ghosts, and that men who doubted the reality of spirits not only denied demons but also almighty God.[160]

The carryover of that in Colonial New England showed when Boston North Church Puritan

Reverend Cotton Mather became convinced that Irish Catholic washerwoman Goodwife (Goody) Glover was a witch. That resulted in her being tried for witchcraft (casting spells on Boston mason John Goodwin's children). During the trial, Mather called Glover *a scandalous old Irishwoman, very poor, a Roman Catholic and obstinate in idolatry.* He also said that *the court could have no answers from her, but in the Irish, which was her native language.* Robert Calef, a Boston merchant who knew Goody, said: *Goody Glover was a despised, crazy, poor, old woman, an Irish Catholic who was tried for afflicting the Goodwin children. Her behavior at her trial was like that of one distracted. They did her cruel. The proof against her was wholly deficient. The jury brought her guilty. She was hung. She died a Catholic.*[161]

Goody Glover was hanged in Boston on 11/16/1688. And Mather's 1689 Book *Memorable Providences Relating to Witchcrafts and Possessions* described how witchcraft had afflicted the children of Boston mason John Goodwin—whose oldest child had stolen linen from washerwoman Goody Glover, a disagreeable old woman whose husband described her as a witch.[162]

About 78% of the witchcraft accusations and convictions were of women. Puritan belief and New England's culture held that women were inherently sinful and more susceptible to damnation than men. Puritans, especially women Puritans, actively tried to thwart the Devil's attempts to take their souls. And Puritans believed that men and women were equal in God's eyes but not in the Devil's, and that women's souls were unprotected in their weak and vulnerable bodies.

Colonial women were more likely to admit to witchcraft than Colonial men. According to Historian Elizabeth Ross, some probably believed that they had given in to the Devil while others may have believed to have done so temporarily. An associated factor was the repentant being forgiven and the convicted deniers being executed.

Nonconformist women, especially those not married or mothers, were more likely to be accused of witchcraft. Over 200 people were accused of witchcraft during the 1692-3 Salem Witch Trials, with 30 found guilty and 19 (15 women, 4 men) executed. Another man was pressed to death for refusing to plead, and at least 5 more accused died in jail. That Witch Hunt has been used to caution against the dangers of isolationism, extremism, false accusations, and lapses in due process. And, according to Historian George Lincoln Burr, *...Salem witchcraft was the rock on which theocracy shattered.*[163]

On 3/27/1692, Massachusetts Governor Phips appointed a seven-judge *Court of Oyer and Terminener* to conduct the Salem Witch Trials. Lieutenant Governor Willian Stoughton was the Chief Judge (and prosecutor). The Witch Trial judges believed in the Devil and in his making secret contracts with people (witches) to do his evil. Under that framework, witches could leave their bodies in spectral form and assault their victims.[164]

The judges accepted Spectral Evidence—an accusing witness' testimony that the accused's spirit or spectral shape appeared to the witness in a dream while the accused's body was at another location. (Only the accusing witness could see the specter.) On 8/1/1692, the Rev. Increase Mather (Cotton Mather's father and the President/Rector of Harvard College) led a group of Boston ministers in a meeting during which the group reversed its position and held that spectral evidence is acceptable.[165]

An example of the nature of the Salem Witch Trials is the case of Abigale (Dane) Faulkner (1652-1730).[166] There is no record of her being accused of any criminality or misconduct before her neighbors accused her of witchcraft. On 10/12/1675, the day before her 23rd birthday, Abigail married Lieutenant Francis Faulkner—joining two prominent and wealthy Andover families. Francis' father bequeathed most of his wealth to Francis that year, and Francis inherited almost all of the rest when his father died 12 years later. Soon after that, Francis' convulsions, confusion, and memory loss resulted in Abigail being granted control of his estate until their sons came of age. But until her witchcraft tribulations, Francis and Abigail led the life of the prominent well-to-do.

Abigail's father, Rev. Francis Dane, Andover's minister for over 40 years, had sued, a decade before his daughter was accused of and tried for witchcraft, Andover's residents for a salary increase, and won. He also had opposed the proposed separation of Andover into two districts. The fanatical nature of the witchcraft proceedings disturbed him, and he openly expressed doubts about the accusations against his daughter. He was initially alone in in that—and was deserted by his own deacons, who considered him an old and failing man too far behind the times to appreciate modern science. And he too was accused of witchcraft in 1692. He was never charged, but his support of his daughter risked his reputation and life and those of all the women in his family.

On 8/10/1692, Elizabeth Johnson, the daughter and namesake of Abigail's sister, confessed that she had consorted with the Devil, meeting with him at a gathering of *about six score*. (She had been arrested for witchcraft earlier that August.)

On 8/11/1691, Abigail, the mother of seven children and pregnant with her eighth, was arrested for witchcraft for afflicting her neighbors' children. She was taken to Salem and interrogated. Most of her accusers were young women (e.g., Ann Putnam, Jr. and Mary Warren). Another was William Baker, Sr., who stated that he had: been afflicted by the Devil for three years; signed the Devil's book; and been promised that Satan would *pay all his debts* and let him live in luxury. Baker named *George Burroughs* as the ringleader, and Abigail and her sister Elizabeth as his *enticers to this great abomination*.

Abigail's accusers fell to the floor in hysterics when she entered the trial room. And when she squeezed or twisted the handkerchief she was holding, they had grievous *fitts*. Magistrates asked Abigail to look at the girls' distress and demanded to know why she harmed them. She said she was sorry the girls were afflicted and that it was the Devil [who] does it in my shape. The magistrates asked why, if she was innocent, she shed no tears over the girls' suffering. Abigail insisted that God would not have her confess what she was not guilty of.

Once during the interrogation, Mary Warren fell into *fitts* and was pulled under the table. She seemed unable to come out but was freed after receiving *a touch of said Faulkner*.

On 8/19/1692, George Burroughs was hanged.

On 8/29/1692, Abigail's 11-year-old niece Abigail and 14-year-old nephew Stephen and their mother, Elizabeth Johnson Sr. were arrested and charged with witchcraft.

On 8/30/1692, Abigail was reexamined in prison. She still insisted that she had never consorted with the Devil or signed his book.

Abigail also stated that, when her niece was taken up for witchcraft, neighbors had crowded around the Johnson home, laughing, taunting Abigail, and saying that her sister also would soon be arrested for witchcraft. She had been angry at what folks said and, her spirit being roused, had looked with an evil eye on ye afflicted persons and wished them ill. Abigail suggested that the Devil had used that to frame her for witchcraft.

On 8/31/1692, Abigail's sister Elizabeth and nephew Stephen testified that: at a gathering, they were baptized by the Devil, who promised them *happiness and joy*; and at the Devil's behest, they had afflicted Martha Sprague and several people in Andover. But they refused to implicate anyone else in their activities.

On 9/6/1692, Deliverance Dane, Abigail's sister-in-law, was examined and confessed to witchcraft. She later recanted, insisting that she had *wronged the truth* by confessing.

On 9/16/1692, Abigail's 9-year-old daughter and namesake was arrested for witchcraft.

On 9/17/1692, Abigail's 12-year-old daughter Dorothy was arrested for witchcraft. She and Abigail Jr. soon confessed, and condemned their mother as a witch.

On 9/18/1692, Ann Putnam, Jr. testified that Abigail had afflicted her on 8/9/1692—and that she had witnessed Abigail or her specter tormenting two other young women. Abigail was convicted. Her sentence read:

> *The Jury find Abigail Faulkner, wife of Francis Faulkner of Andover, guilty of ye felony of witchcraft, committed on ye body of Martha Sprague, also on ye body of Sarah Phelps. Sentence of death passed on Abigail Faulkner.*

Abigail's execution was postponed because she was pregnant.

On 10/3/1692, Rev. Increase Mather denounced the use of Spectral Evidence.

On 10/6/1692, Stephen and Abigail Johnson were released, and Abigail's daughters Abigail Jr. and Dorothy were released to the care of Abigail's brother Nathanial Dane and John Osgood, Sr. Each release cost £500.

In January 1693, Abigail's niece, Elizabeth Johnson, Jr. was found guilty of witchcraft and sentenced to death. Her death warrant was signed by (zealot) Lieutenant Governor Stoughton. Governor Phips spared her the gallows.

On 10/18/1692, 25 citizens, including Abigail's father, condemned the Salem Witch Trials in a letter to Governor Phips and the General Court

In December 1692, Abigail petitioned Governor Phips for clemency, claiming that her husband's illness had gotten worse and there was no one to watch their children. He pardoned and released her. And her sister-in-law, Deliverance Dane, was released when her case was dismissed.

In January 1693, Abigail's sister, Elizabeth Johnson, Sr. was acquitted and released. And Abigail's father wrote to fellow ministers that, knowing the people of Andover and being its senior minister, *I believe many innocent persons have been accused and imprisoned.* He also denounced the use of spectral evidence.

On 3/20/1693, Abigail gave birth to a son. She named him Ammi Ruhamah, a Hebrew phrase meaning *my people have obtained mercy.*

In 1703, Abigail began and continued petitioning the Court for exoneration.

On 10/17/1711, the Massachusetts General Court reversed the convictions and cleared the names (mostly posthumously) of Abigail, George Burroughs, Giles Corey and 18 others.[167]

3

The American Revolution

This abbreviation of the Revolution[168, 169] is intended to provide a more realistic view.

3.1 Prelude in the Ohio River Valley

As the Colonial population increased, survivors of indentured service and the desire to advance produced a huge thirst for land. In the early 1750s, France and England were vying for land and power in the Ohio River Valley, which comprises parts of today's Ohio, Indiana, Kentucky, Pennsylvania, and West Virginia. Amerind nations vying for this land allied with France, or with England, or remained neutral.[170]

3.2 George Washington's First Combat

12/17/53: Robert Dinwiddie, Virginia's Royal Governor, sent Colonial LtCol. George Washington to Fort LeBeouf in the Ohio Territory (in Northwest Pennsylvania, 15 miles from Lake Erie) to deliver a letter telling the French to leave. Washington knew the area from surveying for his older brothers. His party included the Mingo Chief Tanacharison.

Fort Le Boef's commander, Jacque Legardeur de Saint Pierre, told 21-year-old Washington that the letter should have been sent to Saint-Pierre's Commanding Officer in Canada. Washington returned to Virginia and told Governor Dinwiddie that the French refused to leave. Dinwiddie ordered him to raise a regiment to hold the Forks of the Ohio (today's Pittsburgh), and issued a Captain's commission to William Trent and sent him to build a fort at the Forks.

2/1754: Trent's company, assisted by Tanacharison and the Mingos, began constructing a storehouse and stockade at the Forks.

3/1754: Dinwiddie sent Washington back to the Ohio River Valley—with the following orders (which Historian Fred Anderson called *an invitation to start a war*):

Act on the [defensive] but in case any attempts are made to obstruct the works or interrupt our [settlements] by any persons whatsoever. You are to restrain all such Offenders, & in case of resistance to make prisoners of or kill & destroy them.

4/16/1754: An ~500-man force of Canadians, French, and Amerinds led by Claude-Pierre Pécaudy de Contrecoeur arrived at the Forks—with orders not to attack unless provoked.

4/17/1754: Trent's 36-man force agreed to leave. The French tore down their work and began building Fort Duquesne.

5/23/1754: Contrecoeur sent Ensign Joseph Coulon de Villiers de Jumonville and 35 men to see if Washington had entered French territory—with a summons ordering Washington's troops to leave.

When Washington reached Winchester, Pennsylvania, Trent and Tanacharison arrived with news of Jumonville's advance. Tanacharison promised warriors to help the British. Washington decided to build Fort Necessity 37 miles Southeast of the Forks.

5/27/1754: Washington sent Captain Hog and 75 men out to pursue French troops who had threatened Hog's house and property, and then told some young Mingos that the French had come to kill Tanacharison, prompting them to also set out after the French. That evening, after receiving Tanicharison's message that he had found the French encampment, Washington and 40 soldiers went toward Tanacharison.

5/28/1754: At *Jumonville Glen*, Tanacharison and Washington attacked, killing 10-12, wounding 2, and capturing 21. Jumonville was one of the dead. Just how he died is uncertain but there were several reports that Tanicharison had crushed his head with a tomahawk and washed his own hands in the brains.[171] (So George Washington's first combat was a reputedly gory victory.) A Mingo warrior claimed that Washington fired the first shot, but that's still in dispute. Dartmouth College History Professor Colin Gordon Calloway's view is that Tanicharison manipulated Washington into attacking.

The French claimed that Jumonville and his men had diplomatic, not military orders— and that Washington led an unprovoked attack against them in peacetime. Washington maintained that the attack was a justified defense against French aggression.

And that's how Robert Dinwiddie, George Washington, and Tanicharison started the French and Indian War. It led to the Seven Years War (1756-63) between France and England. Their allies, and their African and Asian colonies, also were involved. [172]

3.3 George Washington's Only Surrender

6/3/1754: Washington (with half the Virginia regiment) completed Fort Necessity.

6/9/1754: The rest of the Virginia Regiment arrived at Fort Necessity. Its Colonel, Joshua Fry, had fallen from his horse enroute, died of a broken neck, and was buried in Cumberland, Maryland. A noted mapmaker and a William and Mary college professor, Fry commanded the Virginia Regiment and was Commander-in-Chief of the Colonial forces.[173] Washington took command of the regiment. 100 British Regulars arrived a few days later and camped outside the fort. Their leader was Major Mackay, whose Royal Commission made his rank higher than Washington's Colonial one.

6/16/1754: Washington led 300 Virginians to widen the road to Fort Duquesne, reputedly defended by 500 French troops. Tanicharison's Mingos declined to help.

6/28/1754: Louis Coulon de Villers, Jumonville's older brother, left Fort Duquesne with 600 Frenchmen and 100 Amerinds. Washington retreated to Fort Necessity, abandoning most of his supplies to facilitate keeping ahead of the French.

7/1/1754: The Virginians reached Fort Necessity. Its provision hut had been depleted.

7/2/1754: Rain turned Fort Necessity's trenches into streams. The woods being within musket range, Washington ordered trees cut down and made into breastworks.

7/3/1754: Using Washington's road, Villiers reached Jumonville Glen, found several scalped bodies, had them buried, and neared Fort Necessity by 11 am. The Virginians were digging a trench. Their pickets fired and fell back. The French and Amerinds advanced, miscalculated the fort's location, and redeployed into the woods. Washington ordered his entire force to attack across the open field. Villiers ordered his force, led by Amerinds, to charge. Washington ordered his men to hold and fire a volley. Mackay's troops did, and inflicted a few casualties. But the Virginians fled to the fort, and Washington ordered the then greatly outnumbered British regulars to retreat to it. The French spread out, kept up a heavy fire, and felt little effect from the aimed too high return fire. Heavy afternoon rain made the defenders (but not their attackers?) unable to fire because their gunpowder was wet. (The maxim *Put your trust in God; but mind to keep your powder dry* is attributed to English General Oliver Cromwell's address to English troops about to cross a river during their 1649-53 conquest of Ireland.[174])

Villiers, because British reinforcements might arrive, sent an officer under a flag of truce to negotiate. Washington did not allow him near the fort, but sent his translator (Van Braam) and another man to Villiers. As negotiations began, Virginians broke into the fort's liquor supply and got drunk. Villiers' said that Washington could surrender and return to Virginia, and risked being stormed by the Amerinds and being scalped if they didn't. Washington agreed but couldn't read the French surrender document. {Van Braam might not have translated its statement that Jumonville was "assassinated" (and/or the condition that no British fortifications be built in the Ohio River Valley for a year?)}. Both Washington and MacKay signed. That was Washington's only military surrender.

7/4/1154: Washington, to avoid a potential bloodbath, didn't try to stop the looting of his force's baggage as they marched away, drums beating and flags flying.

7/17/1754: Expecting a rebuke, Washington reported the combat to Governor Dinwiddie. The Governor and the House of Burgesses attributed the defeat to poor supply and the refusal of aid by the other Colonies, and gave him a vote of thanks. [175]

3.4 Braddock's Failure

August 1754: The news reached England where, months later, the decision was made to send an expedition led by Major General Edward Braddock to remove the French the next year. When Louis XV learned that, he sent a large body of French troops to Canada. They arrived too late to fight Braddock but aided in a later string of French victories.

5/29/1755: Braddock set out from Fort Cumberland in Maryland to attack Fort Duquesne, ~110 miles away through the densely wooded Allegheny Mountains. Benjamin Franklin helped to procure his wagons and supplies. His waggoneers included Daniel Morgan (a future Revolutionary War hero) and Danial Boone. British Lieutenant Colonel (and future General) Thomas Gage was among his 2100-man force. George Washington was an aide-de-camp. The only Amerind support was eight Mingo scouts.

Braddock decided to build a road for resupply of Fort Duquesne after he captured it. That and a shortage of healthy draft animals slowed his progress. Contracoeur, the French Commander, had about 250 French regular and Canadian troops in Fort Duquesne, and about 650 Amerind allies outside. His fort could not withstand English cannons, and he decided to ambush Braddock at the Monongahela River [176]

6/8/1755: England's Vice Admiral Edward Boscawen, with 11 ships dispatched to thwart the arrival of the forces sent by Louis XV, was patrolling along the Southern shore of Newfoundland. Three of his warships, *HMS Dunkirk* (60 guns), *HMS Defiant* (58 guns), and *HMS Torbay* (74 guns) were sighted by the French warships *Dauphin Royal* (60 guns), *Alcide* (64 guns), and *Lys* (22 guns). Those French vessels had become separated by fog from the French fleet (which eluded the British). Toussant Hocquart, captaining *Alcide*, called out to *Dunkirk*'s Captain Richard Howe *Are we at war or at peace?* He was told *At peace, at peace*. Then, after a brief discussion, the British opened fire. *Alcide* fought bravely for five hours but was badly damaged. She and *Lys* surrendered. *Dauphin Royal* escaped in the fog. Britain had 32 casualties. The French had 130 casualties and 2000 captured (mostly troops). Ten thousand scalping knives intended for the Amerinds and Canada's Acadians (French descendants) were found on the captured ships.[177]

7/8/1755: Braddock sent his chief scout, Lieutenant Fraser, and Washington to meet with the Amerinds who had requested a conference. The Amerinds asked the British to halt their advance so they could negotiate a peaceful French withdrawal from Fort Duquesne. Washington and Fraser recommended doing that. Braddock decided against it.

7/9/1755: Washington's warning of flaws in Braddock's plan was ignored. Braddock's advance force, Lieutenant Colonel Thomas Gage, 300 grenadiers and Colonials, and two cannons, crossed the Monongahela unopposed about 10 miles South of Fort Duquesne. They moved ahead and encountered the oncoming French. The first British volley killed the French Field Commander. The French and Amerinds fired at both sides of the column from the woods beside the road, and their advancing regulars pushed the British back. Gage fell back and collided with Braddock's main body. Braddock was shot. British resistance was collapsing. Washington (who was subsequently dubbed *Hero of the Monongahela*) imposed some order and formed a rear guard that aided the retreat. According to his letter to his mother:

> *We marched to that place, without any considerable loss, having only now and then a straggler picked up by the French and scouting Indians. When we came there, we were attacked by a party of French and Indians, whose number, I am persuaded, did not exceed three hundred men, while ours consisted of about*

one thousand three hundred well-armed troops, chiefly regular soldiers, who were struck with such a panic that they behaved with more cowardice than is possible to conceive. The officers behaved gallantly, in order to encourage their men, for which they suffered greatly, there being near sixty killed and wounded, a large proportion of the number we had.

Braddock died during the retreat. The survivors reached their reserve and rear supply units, which were led by Colonel Dunbar. They outnumbered the opposition but were demoralized and not combat capable. Dunbar ordered the supplies and cannons destroyed, burned about 150 wagons, and withdrew. The French and Amerinds looted and scalped, and did not pursue.[178]

[Braddock's tactics have been much debated. A disciplined withdrawal and regrouping might have enabled him to use his numeric advantage—or to return to fight another day. But the French were practicing Amerind-style warfare instead of the European practice of having opposing forces frontally confront each other. And the disarray that that produced among the British was compounded by dependence on the mortally wounded Braddock. Perhaps no British general of the era would have been innovative enough, or would have had forces sufficiently disciplined and trained, to deploy to a better position than the sorely disadvantaged one of a column under attack on both flanks.]

[Disciplined forces, advantageously positioned, can overwhelm superior numbers. For example, multiple sources, citing Roman Historians Tacitus and Cassius, state that Celtic Queen Boudica's Britons' 60 AD vengeful attacks destroyed ancient Colchester, St. Albans, and London (Rome's three largest cities in Britain), massacred everyone in them, and cut the Roman 9th Legion to pieces. Another defeat supposedly would have forced Rome to leave Britain. The Roman Governor, General Gaius Suetonius Paulinus, with 10,000 men, fled to a location protected by woods and gorges on three sides. Boudica's Britons, vastly superior numerically, brought their families to watch their victory from carts among the wagons of the supply train in their rear. They made a frontal attack on the Roman's narrow fourth side. The Romans threw their javelins and advanced in a triangular wedge—behind long shields around which their swords were thrust. Panicked but prevented by their supply train from fleeing, the Britons and their families and their baggage animals were all slaughtered. And Rome ruled Britain for 350 more years.[179]]

3.5 Taking Fort Duquesne

<u>1758:</u> Britain sent a military expedition under Brigadier General John Forbes to take Fort Duquesne. Then Full Colonel George Washington and a Virginia contingent made up one-fourth of Forbes' ~6000-man force. Forbes, stricken by dysentery, was unable to keep up and entrusted his lead force to his second-in-command, Lieutenant Colonel Henry Bouquet. Most of the summer was spent on Forbes' Road and supply depots.[180]

<u>9/11/1758:</u> Major James Grant of the 77th Regiment of (Highland Scot) Foot Soldiers was sent with 800 men to scout Fort Duquesne.

<u>9/13/1758:</u> Grant arrived two miles from the fort, and sent 50 men to reconnoiter. They saw no defenders outside, burned a storehouse, and returned.

<u>9/14/1758:</u> Bouquet believed that the fort was held by 500 French and 300 Amerinds. Grant believed there were only 200 defenders. He sent Captain MacDonald and a company of the 77th to decoy them out by approaching at daylight, drums beating and bagpipes playing. He also set a 400-man force to ambush them. Several hundred more, under Virginia Major Andrew Lewis, lay in ambush near Grant's baggage train. When the drums and bagpipes sounded, the Amerinds swiftly deployed to the banks of the Monongahela and Allegheny. From there they surrounded the Highlanders, who were in ranks in close order, and attacked from higher ground. Lewis' attempt to aid was repulsed. Grant and Lewis were captured. Their 800-man "scouting" force suffered 342 casualties, 242 of whom were from the 77th. The Franco-Amerind force suffered 8 dead and 8 wounded.[181] But most of Grant's men made it back (from what is now Grant's Hill and Grant Street in Pittsburgh) to Bouquet.

<u>10/12/1758:</u> French Captain Charles Philippe Aubrey, with 440 French troops and Canadian militia, attacked the under construction British Fort Ligonier, ~42 miles Southeast of Fort Duquesne. Bouquet was away at another post. The fort, with over 2000 British and Colonial troops, was commanded by Pennsylvania Militia Colonel James Burd. Upon hearing gunfire from about 1.5 miles away—where his men were guarding the expedition's grazing animals—Burd sent the Maryland Battalion of about 200 and the 1st Pennsylvania Battalion toward it. They, along with the guards for the animals and supplies, were driven back to the fort. Artillery drove the attackers back. About 9 pm, one of the fort's redoubts was attacked, but the fort held. The Franco-Amerind force killed or took about 200 horses and withdrew.

The Amerinds reputedly stated that Forbes' men were learning the art of war, the firing from the trees had made them retreat, and they could have subdued the redcoats but not the Great-Knifes (Virginians). Reported French losses were 2 dead and 7 wounded, with 100 scalps and 7 prisoners taken. The British reported 12 dead, 18 wounded, and 31 missing. Bouquet wrote Forbes that *[this] enterprise, which should have cost the enemy dearly, shows a great deal of comtempt for us, and the behavior of our troops in the woods justifies their idea only too well.* The British continued building Fort Ligonier.[182]

<u>10/26/1758:</u> Thirteen Amerind Nations and the Governors of Pennsylvania and Maryland ceremonially celebrated ending the week of negotiations that produced the Treaty of Easton (Pennsylvania). It specified:

- No Amerind fighting on the side of the French in the current war.
- Recognition of Amerind rights to their Ohio River Valley hunting grounds.
- Return to the Iroquois of large blocks of land ceded to Pennsylvania.
- No post-war Colonial settlements West of the Allegheny Mountains.
- No Iroquois intervention in Pennsylvania or Lenape-Delaware negotiations.
- Lenape ceding of all claims to New Jersey (for 1000 Spanish dollars).[183]

<u>11/2/1758:</u> Forbes reached Fort Ligonier. An advance on Fort Duquesne began.

<u>11/24/1758:</u> Because their 600-man force could not hold off the about 10:1 manpower advantage of the British and Americans, the French set fire to Fort Duquesne and escaped in the night. Many of the captured Highlanders' heads were impaled on sharp stakes atop the

fort's walls, with their kilts displayed below.[184] Forbes briefly visited the ruins. He was then taken by litter to Philadelphia and soon died.[185]

3.6 Pontiac's Rebellion

5/1//1763: The Amerind Ottawa Chief Pontiac rebelled against British arrogance, fort building, and Colonial settlement on Amerind land.[186] His Ottowas, the Wyandots, the Potawatomis, and the Ojibwas began an unsuccessful siege of Fort Detroit. Pontiac's Amerind allies, the Delaware, Seneca, and Shawnee, destroyed many British outposts, putting the borders of Pennsylvania, Maryland, and Virginia in a state of terror.

7/31/1763: About 250 British soldiers attacked Pontiac's Parent's Creek camp and were defeated. Their 50 casualties included 20 dead, including their Commander. The Creek, which reputedly ran red with blood, became known as Bloody Run.[187] Pontiac's Rebellion continued until December when, after failing to gain support from tribes farther West and South, he signed a peace treaty and was pardoned by the English.

The frontier warfare was characterized by atrocities. Prisoners were killed and civilians were targeted. The British attempted to inflict smallpox on the Amerinds by giving them blankets used by smallpox victims at Fort Pitt. (Whether that had a substantial impact is controversial.) That preceded the request by British General Jeffrey Amherst, 1st Baron Amherst, the British Commander-in Chief, that such an attempt be tried. Amherst had previously written to the Commander of Fort Detroit that captured Amerinds should *immediately be put to death, their extirpation being the only security for our future safety.*

The coalition of Amerind tribes involved in Pontiac's Rebellion provided about 3500 warriors. Over 200 of them were killed. The British had about 3000 soldiers. About 450 of them died, as did about 450 civilians. And about 4000 civilians were displaced.[188]

3.7 The Appalachian Proclamation

10/7/1763: To limit Colonial autonomy, appease Amerinds, and halt attacks by Amerinds and Colonists on each other, King George III issued the Appalachian Proclamation. It forbade Colonial expansion West of the Appalachian Divide. (The Appalachian Divide separates the Atlantic Seaboard watershed from the Gulf of Mexico watershed. It nearly spans the U.S. from South of Lake Ontario through the Florida Peninsula, and encompasses the Appalachian Mountains to the North and the Southern Piedmont Plateau and lowland ridges in the Atlantic Coastal Plain to the South.[189]) Only licensed agents were authorized to go West of the Divide or deal with the Amerinds. Private citizens and Colonial governments couldn't buy land from or make agreements with the Amerinds. Colonists, even those already granted their land, were ordered to return from West of the Divide. But enforcement of the Proclamation was weak and land-hungry Colonists, including George Washington, ignored it. Its consistency with the Treaty of Easton notwithstanding, the Proclamation produced the first strong aversion to the Crown common to all 13 Colonies. (It also established three new colonies—Quebec,

West Florida and East Florida—extended Georgia's southern border, and granted land to soldiers who had fought in the Seven Years War.)[190]

3.8 The Stamp and Townshend Acts

3/22/1765: Over protestations that the Colonies could only be legitimately taxed by Colonial Legislatures, Britain imposed the Stamp Act. It taxed wills, deeds, pamphlets, newspapers, playing cards, and dice. The rationale was that the French and Indian (and Seven Years) War had put England deeply in debt, the Colonies had benefitted from it, and they should pay some of the costs. (The Colonists' prior tax burden was about 5% of that of England's citizenry.) Among the Act's provisions was trial without juries in Vice-Admiralty Courts for offenders (because of Colonial juries not convicting smugglers). Patrick Henry, a vocal opponent, submitted a series of resolutions adopted by Virginia's legislature—denying England's right to tax the Colonies and calling for resistance to the Act. Those resolutions were widely reprinted throughout the Colonies.[191]

Early Summer, 1765: Shopkeepers and artisans formed the *Loyal Nine,* a forerunner of the *Sons of Liberty.* Its Leaders included the printer Benjamin Eddes and John Gill of the Boston Gazette. Their stream of Anti-Stamp Act advocacy presaged the organization of ~2000 men under Ebenezer McIntosh, a South Boston shoemaker.[192]

8/1765: The paramilitary *Sons of Liberty* was founded by Samuel Adams of Boston to advance the "English" right to a representative government and judiciary, and to combat taxation. It spread to Massachusetts, Rhode Island, New Hampshire, New York, New Jersey. Maryland, and Virginia. Their motto, *No Taxation Without Representation,* became a Colonial rallying cry. John Hancock and Paul Revere were members. [Some head taxes in U.S. communities are taxation without representation.]

Samuel Adams was John Adams' 2nd cousin, a Harvard graduate, a political theorist who believed in the anti-authoritarian philosophy of John Locke, and a newspaper publisher. He was proud of his Puritan heritage, a reputed Boston Tea Party planner, a delegate to the Constitutional Convention (ill health forced him out in 1781), and he helped draft the Articles of Confederation. After John Hancock died, Samuel Adams became Governor of Massachusetts from 1794 until ill health forced him to retire in 1797.[193]

8/14/1765: An effigy of wealthy merchant and Loyalist Andrew Oliver was hanged from an elm tree in front of Deacon Eliot's house—a few weeks after Boston learned that Oliver would be the Massachusetts Stamp Act Commissioner. After dusk, a mob paraded the effigy through the streets, destroyed the brick building that Oliver had recently built on the waterfront, beheaded the effigy in front of his home, threw stones through his windows, demolished his carriage house, and drank his wine cellar's contents.

8/15/1765: Oliver, who had not asked to be a Stamp Act Commissioner and was appointed to be one without his knowledge, resigned that position.

8/26/1765: A mob attacked one of the finest mansions in Boston, the home of Oliver's brother-in-law—Lieutenant Governor Thomas Hutchinson. They stripped it of its doors, furniture, paintings, silverware, and the slate on its roof.

Riots also broke out in seaports from Portsmouth, New Hampshire to Savannah,

Georgia, causing Crown officials to resign. The *Sons of Liberty* formed local Committees of Correspondence to keep abreast of Colonial Protests.

October 1765: In New York, the Stamp Act Congress (delegates from nine Colonies) composed a *Declaration of Rights and Grievances* stating that only Colonial Assemblies had the authority to tax the Colonists. Boycotts of British imports in seaports (e.g., Boston, New York, and Philadelphia) caused British merchants to lobby for Stamp Act Repeal.

11/1/1765: The Stamp Act was to be effective this date. That didn't happen because of mass resignations of its officials and because the Colonists ignored it.

3/18/1766: Parliament repealed the Stamp Act and passed the Declaratory Act stating that England had the power to impose laws binding on the Colonies.

May 1766: News of Stamp Act repeal reached Boston. The *Sons of Liberty* gathered at the elm tree from which Oliver's effigy was hanged to commemorate that and label the elm the *Liberty Tree*—a gathering repeated every August 14 until 1775, when Boston was under siege. And when Andrew Oliver died in 1774, four years after becoming Lieutenant Governor, a *Sons of Liberty* delegation gave three cheers at the graveside as his coffin was lowered into the ground. The British chopped the elm into firewood before evacuating Boston, and a final commemoration was held at its stump in 1776.[194, 195]

11/20/1767: Parliament enacted The Townshend Acts imposing duties on glass, lead, paint, paper, and tea imported to the colonies. The expected £40,000 revenue was to pay the salaries of Colonial Governors and Judges and ensure their loyalty to the Crown. A pamphlet titled *Letters from a Farmer in Pennsylvania* with essays by Pennsylvania Legislator John Dickenson, and another titled the *Massachusetts Circular Letter*, written by Samuel Adams and James Otis, put the Colonists behind a boycott of British goods.

January 1768: Encouraged by the *Sons of Liberty*, 24 towns in Massachusetts, Connecticut, and Rhode Island agreed to a one-year boycott of British goods, except for necessities like fishing hooks and wire.

April 1768: New York established a stronger boycott than Massachusetts had.

12/31/1768: A total of 2000 redcoats were occupying Boston.[196]

3.9 The Sloop Liberty and Smuggling

5/9/1768: John Hancock's sloop *Liberty* anchored in Boston Harbor. Customs officials (tidesmen) inspected the ship the next morning and found 25 pipes (casks) of Madeira wine, one-quarter of her capacity. Two tidesmen who had stayed on *Liberty* overnight swore that nothing was unloaded. A month later, with the 50-gun *HMS Romney* in port, one of the tidesmen claimed to have been forcibly held on the *Liberty* while it had been illegally unloaded. (Prior to the Townshend Acts, it had been common for tidesmen to ask what cargo was subject to customs duty, for part of the cargo to be declared, for the rest to be unloaded duty free, and for the tidesmen to receive a sample of the cargo.)

6/10/1768: Sailors and marines coming to seize the *Liberty* were mistaken for a press gang. Bostonians, already angered by *Romney's* Captain's prior forcible conscription of Colonists, beat two tidesmen senseless and broke other tidesmen's windows and destroyed their property. The tidesmen fled to British ships in the harbor.

6/22/1768: A lawsuit was filed against *Liberty*. It resulted in her confiscation in August. She was refitted, armed, named *HMS Liberty*, and used to enforce trade regulations.

10/1768: Hancock and five others were charged with unloading 100 pipes of wine from *Liberty* without paying the duties. Conviction meant a £9,000 fine, triple the wine's value. John Adams defended Hancock in the highly publicized trial—in a Vice-Admiralty Court. There was no jury and defense cross-examination of witnesses was not always allowed. After almost five months, the charges against Hancock were dropped without explanation.

The flamboyant, very wealthy, extravagant, luxury-loving John Hancock graduated from Harvard at the age of 17. A former Loyalist, he was a political protégé of the Puritanical Samuel Adams, and beloved of Colonists. His smuggling was described by Harvard's Winthrop Research Professor of History Stephan Thernstrom (b. 1934):

> *Owing mainly to the lack of enforcement of the Navigation Acts and of the impossible Molasses Act, smuggling was no longer looked upon as reprehensible. Everyone, even leading merchants like John Hancock, smuggled regularly. Owing to the lightness of his character, excessive vanity and his love of popularity, unballasted by either moral depth or intellectual ability, John Hancock's motives for joining the patriot party are difficult to appraise correctly or even perhaps fairly. But there was no question of patriotism in much of his smuggling. That was for profit.*

The preceding perspective on Hancock and *Liberty* was extracted from partially consistent sources.[197, 198, 199]

7/19/1769: *HMS Liberty*, under Captain William Reid, seized two Connecticut ships and towed them to Newport. Captain Joseph Packwood of New London, Connecticut and a Rhode Island mob (mostly *Sons of Liberty*) boarded *HMS Liberty*, and scuttled and then burned her—an overt defiance of Britain.[200] (A Naval Ship is its nation's territory.)

3.10 The Boston "Massacre"

1770: Colonists skirmished with the over 2000 British soldiers in Boston. Stores selling British goods were vandalized. Their merchants and customers were intimidated.

2/22/1770: Patriots attacked a Tory store. Customs Officer Ebenezer Richardson fired from a window in his nearby home to try to break up the rock-pelting mob. He killed 11-year-old Christopher Seider. A fight between Colonists and soldiers a few days later set the stage for further bloodshed. (Richardson was convicted of murder but got a royal pardon and a new customs job on the grounds that he had acted in self-defense.[201])

3/5/1770: British Private Hugh White was guarding the Custom House on King Street. Colonists insulted him and threatened violence. He struck one with his bayonet, and was pelted with snowballs, ice, and stones. Boston's fire bells began ringing. A mass of male Colonists came out. Private White fell and called for help. Captain Thomas Preston and several soldiers took up a position in front of the Custom House. Reportedly, some Colonists pleaded that the soldiers not shoot while others dared them to. The soldiers were being struck with clubs and sticks. Someone fired, someone cried *Fire!* and other soldiers shot too. Six Colonists were wounded. Five others were killed: Crispus Attucks, a stevedore (of African and Natick, Massachusetts Amerind descent); Samuel Gray, a rope maker; James Caldwell, a 17-year-old sailor; Samuel Maverick; and Patrick Carr.

Samuel Maverick was a 17-year-old apprentice carpenter or dentist (whose grandfather Samuel Maverick had immigrated to Massachusetts in 1623, three years after the Mayflower landed). Young Samuel had supped at the home of a friend's father, ran out when the bells rang, and worked his way to the front of the mob harassing the soldiers. Some were screaming *Kill Them!* When the soldiers raised their muskets, Samuel shouted *Fire away, you damned lobsterbacks!* A musket ball went through his belly. He died the next morning. Boston's Maverick Square commemorates him. Private Matthew Kilroy was charged with his murder.[202] (There's no evident link between that Kilroy and the *Kilroy was here* WWII phrase.[203])

Patrick Carr, a 30-year-old Irish Catholic immigrant who worked in a leather business, came outside when the bells rang, and was shot through the abdomen while crossing King Street. He suffered painfully—and died nine days later. Dr. Jeffries tended him and testified at the trial that Carr had said that the soldiers had been greatly abused, fired in self-defense, would have been hurt if they hadn't, and that none of the soldiers he had seen quell mobs in Ireland had borne half as much before firing. Carr also said that he had malice toward no one. Founding Father Samuel Adams reportedly "denounced" this dying man.[204] [As well as militant anti-British activism, that denunciation (whoever made it) may well have involved Colonial (Puritanical?) opposition to Catholicism.]

Captain Preston and his soldiers were promptly jailed. Patriot leaders (e.g., John Hancock and Samuel Adams) incited Bostonians. The British troops were removed to Castle William in the harbor—as Hancock "demanded." Paul Revere etched an engraving depicting the soldiers as vicious, murdering instigators and the Colonists as gentlemen. The trials were held seven months later. John Adams, a defense attorney, convinced the judge to seat a jury of non-Bostonians. Eyewitnesses presented contradictory evidence on whether Preston had ordered his men to fire. One, Richard Palmes, testified:

> *After the Gun went off I heard the word 'fire!' The Captain and I stood in front about half between the breech and muzzle of the Guns. I don't know who gave the word to fire.*

Adams argued reasonable doubt and Preston was found *Not Guilty.* His soldiers pled self-defense. All were found *Not Guilty* of murder. But two, Hugh Montgomery and Matthew Kilroy, were convicted of manslaughter and branded on the thumbs—as first offenders per English law.[205] Captain Preston opined:

> *None of them was a hero. The victims were troublemakers who got more than they deserved. The soldiers were professionals...who shouldn't have panicked. The whole thing shouldn't have happened.* [206]

A statement by Robert Kennedy (JFK's brother) about mob violence follows:[207]

What has violence ever accomplished? What has it ever created? No martyr's cause has ever been stilled by an assassin's bullet. No wrongs have ever been righted by riots and civil disorders. A sniper is only a coward, not a hero; and an uncontrolled or uncontrollable mob is only the voice of madness, not the voice of the people.

[Insofar as the inciters of the Boston "Massacre" claimed to represent the common people, incited their intense passions, exploited their reactions in order to gain power, and threatened or broke established rules of conduct, they were demagogues.[208]]

April 1770: The Townshend Acts were repealed, except the 3 pence tax per pound of tea. (Parliament kept it to show it could tax the Colonies without their approval.)[209]

3.11 The Gaspee Incident

2/17/1772: HMS *Gaspee,* commanded by Lieutenant William Dudingston, a Scot, stopped the sloop *Fortune* in Narragansett Bay and seized 12 hogsheads of undeclared rum. To prevent the rum from being reclaimed by Colonists, Dudingston sent *Fortune* to Boston. That violated the 1663 Rhode Island Royal Charter, which required that arrests in Rhode Island be tried there. Dudingston then began stopping merchants on shore and searching their wares. Rhode Island Governor Joseph Wanton wrote to him demanding that he "produce me your commission and instructions, if any you have, which was your duty to have done when you first came within the jurisdiction of this Colony." Dudingston refused to leave his ship or to acknowledge Wanton's authority.

6/9/1772: While chasing the packet ship *Hannah*, HMS *Gaspee* ran aground on a small peninsula, now named Gaspee Point, in the Providence River at Warwick, Rhode Island. Dudingston decided to wait for high tide, hoping it would set *Gaspee* afloat. John Brown (a Brown University founder) led a band of Providence Colonists (mostly *Sons of Liberty*), who rowed out and boarded *Gaspee* at dawn on June 10. Dudingston was shot and wounded, and *Gaspee* was burned to the waterline. To determine who had enough evidence against them to warrant extradition to England for trial for treason, a Royal Commission of Inquiry was established. Its members were the chiefs of the Supreme Courts of Massachusetts, New York, and New Jersey, the Judge of the Vice-Admiralty of Boston, and Rhode Island's Governor Wanton. They stated they were unable to deal with the case. And Governor Wanton, based on conflicting assertions about the culprits' whereabouts, decided not to take them to trial. But the prospect of Colonists being tried in England alarmed all 13 Colonies. And a Reverend John Allen sermon at Boston's Second Baptist Church warned about greedy monarchs, corrupt judges, and conspiracies in the London government. It was printed seven times in four colonial cities, and Colonial newspaper editorials intensified the discontent.[210] (Dudingston, though lamed by his wounds, became an Admiral in His Majesty's Navy, and left a considerable estate.[211])

3.12 The Boston Tea Party

<u>5/1/1773:</u> A new Tea Act gave the near-bankrupt British East India Company a monopoly on tea exported to the colonies—enabling it to sell the tea through its agents, with the three pence tax intact, at a price less than smuggled Dutch tea. That allied conservative Colonial merchants with radicals led by Samuel Adams and his *Sons of Liberty.*[212]

<u>12/16/1773:</u> A Colonial town meeting was held at Boston's Old South Church. After another attempt to persuade Governor Hutchinson to send the three tea ships in the harbor back to England failed, moderator John Hancock told the crowd of ~5000 *Let every man do what is right in his own eyes.* Hancock approved of but didn't take part in the Tea Party that followed.[213] And shortly after Samuel Adams announced that *This meeting can do nothing further to save the country,* people started leaving to prepare for action. Some donned Amerind costumes to hinder retaliation. Over a three-hour period that evening, they dumped all three ships' tea, 342 chests, into the harbor. The East India Company put the cost at £9,659, ~$1,700,000 today.[214]

John Adams, who was not in Boston that night, was shocked when he found out what the *Sons of Liberty* had done. But he endorsed it in a diary entry stating *There is a Dignity, a Majesty, a Sublimity, in this the last Effort of the Patriots, that I greatly admire. I can't but consider it as an Epocha in History.* He also noted that dumping the tea was an *Attack upon Property,* and asked *What measures will the ministry take in consequence of this? Will they punish us? How? By quartering troops upon us? —by annulling our Charter? By laying on more duties? By restraining our Trade?*[215]

The dumping of the tea was controversial. George Washington wrote to George William Fairfax that *the Ministry may rely on it that Americand will never be tax'd without their own consent that the cause of Boston the despotick measures in respect to it I mean now and ever will be considerd as the cause of America (not that we approve their cond[uc]t in destroyg the tea).* Benjamin Franklin argued for restitution. New York merchant Robert Murray, along with three other merchants, went to England's Prime Minister Lord North and offered to pay for the losses. He rejected their offer.[216]

[The Tea Party was facilitated by the British troops having been removed from Boston. And the discipline that prevented harming the tea ships' crews or damaging the ships was a major difference from the Boston "Massacre" mob's behavior.]

3.13 Coercive Acts

<u>3/31/1774.</u> The Boston Port Act closed Boston Harbour until restitution was made to the Crown and the East India Company.[217]

<u>5/20/1774:</u> The Massachusetts' Government Act annulled Massachusetts' Charter, put the Colony under military administration, and made it a Royal Colony in which the Judges and local officials were appointed by the Crown.[218]

<u>5/20/1774:</u> The Administration of Justice Act allowed British Officials charged with capital offenses to be tried in England or in another Colony.[219]

5/20/1774: The Quebec Act prescribed French Civil Law and allowed Roman Catholicism between the Mississippi and Ohio Rivers by giving that territory and fur trade to Quebec Province. That waved the red flag of "popery" in the Protestant Colonies.[220]

6/2/774: The Quartering Act expanded the 1765 requirement that Colonists provide barracks for British Troops by giving military commanders the authority to billet soldiers in empty houses, barns, and other outbuildings if Colonial Officials didn't provide adequate housing within 24 hours of it being requested.[221]

Those five *Coercive Acts*, known in the Colonies as the *Intolerable Acts*, isolated Massachusetts. Blockaded Boston faced starvation. Samuel Adams asked for and got food and supplies from the other Colonies. Committees of Correspondence raised anti-British feeling. A Boston resolution called for Massachusetts to boycott British goods and stop commerce with England.

3.14 The 1st Continental Congress

9/5/1774: The 1st Continental Congress met in Philadelphia for a 51-day long development of the response to the *Intolerable Acts*. Georgia did not attend. Some delegates wanted to pressure the Crown to rescind the *Acts*. Others wanted to craft a statement of Colonial Rights and Liberties. The outcome was:[222]

- A petition to the King for redress of grievances and repeal of the *Intolerable Acts*.
- Each Colony was urged to set up and train its own militia.
- A boycott of British goods starting 12/1/1774. (English imports dropped 97%.)
- Exports to Britain were to cease on 9/10/1775 if the *Intolerable* Acts were not repealed.

3.15 War Begins in Massachusetts

4/18/1775: Paul Revere and William Dawes rode to warn of a British attack on Concord. (Listen my children, and you will hear, Of the midnight ride of Paul Revere...[223])

4/19/1775: The Revolutionary War began at dawn, when ~700 British troops found 77 Colonial militia on Lexington's town green. A British major yelled *Throw down your arms! Ye villains, ye rebels*. A shot rang out. British volleys followed. Eight militiamen died, nine were wounded. One Redcoat was injured. The British went on to their primary objective, Colonial arms at Concord. Most had been removed. What they found they burned. Minutemen outside Concord, fearing that the town would burn too, went to Concord's North Bridge. British soldiers on it fired and fell back when the Militiamen returned fire (*the shot heard round the* world[224]). In the about four hours that the British spent searching Concord, nearly 2000 minutemen arrived, and more were coming. During the 18-mile British return to Boston, their column was fired upon by up to 3500 militiamen—from behind trees, walls, houses, and sheds. British soldiers abandoned weapons, clothing, and equipment to get away faster. The harassment continued after a reinforcing brigade of Redcoats met the column at Lexington. Newly arrived minutemen from Salem and Marblehead didn't try to cut off the British, who escaped to the safety of naval support at Charlestown Neck. There were roughly 250 British and 90 Colonial casualties, and the Colonists gained confidence in their ability to stand up to England's military.[225]

[These Minutemen vastly outnumbered an enemy fleeing in a column, out in the open and discarding their weapons. Their courage and (Amerind-like) tactics drove a unit of the best military in the world from the field in disarray, but their inexperience enabled their bloodied foe to get to get to a location protected by British Naval power—whereupon the attackers sensibly avoided attacking into cannon fire.]

Patriots had begun seizing British arms from royal storehouses, provincial magazines, and supply ships months before the Battles of Lexington and Concord. Still, when the war began, captured weapons and Colonial arms production wasn't sufficient and the American soldiers mostly supplied their own weapons. France began supplying arms and ammunition in 1776, and the hundreds of thousands of arms supplied by France and Spain were essential to the American victory in the War.[226]

4/19/1775: Colonial Militia began a siege of Boston by blocking land access.[227]

4/21/1775: Israel Putnam, a farmer, and a Colonel in and a hero of the French and Indian War, heard about Lexington and Concord. He literally left his plow in the field, arrived in Cambridge after an eight-hour, 100-mile ride, offered his services, and was made a Major General in the Army of Observation, the predecessor of the Continental Army. Putnam became a primary planner of and participant in the *Battle of Bunker Hill*.[228]

3.16 The 2nd Continental Congress

5/10/1775: The 2nd Continental Congress became the Colonies' Central Government. It raised armies, directed strategy, and appointed diplomats (and generals).[229] (Colonels and below were appointed by the Colonies.)[230]

6/15/1775: Congress unanimously elected George Washington Commander-in-Chief of the yet-to-be-created Continental Army at a $500 a month salary.

6/16/1775: The newly elected General and Supreme Commander of the Colonial Military said that he would enter upon that momentous duty, but sincerely believed that he did not think himself equal it. He also stated:

> As to pay, sir, I beg leave to assure the Congress, that, as no pecuniary consideration could have tempted me to have accepted this arduous employment, at the expence of my domestic ease and happiness, I do not wish to make any profit from it. I will keep an exact Account of my expences. Those, I doubt not, they will discharge, and that is all I desire.[231]

Had Washington been paid that $500/month salary, he would have received $48,000 for his generalship. His "highly creative" expense account was, by comparison, for $449,261.51. In addition to his out-of-pocket costs, there was a 6% interest charge for the first two years costs, and a surcharge for depreciation. At the war's end, his account was promptly settled. When he again offered to serve unpaid when he was elected President, the Congress denied that and begged him to accept an annual salary of $25,000, which he did. His wartime expense account amounts were reportedly flawlessly written in beautiful script with the reasons barely legible and more vague the greater the amount—and included items like >$800 for a saddle and tack, and $6000 for liquor for himself and his officers over a 7-month period.[232, 233] And during his second term as president, his expense account was 2% of the federal budget.[234] A reviewer dubbed him the father of expense account living as well as of his country. [But Washington's war "expenses" of $56,157.69 per year and his presidential expenses were invaluable.]

3.17 Bunker Hill

6/16/1775: The Colonial militia besieging Boston learned that the British planned to send troops to occupy the hills surrounding it—to assure control of the harbor. Militia led by Colonel William Prescott were ordered to fortify Bunker Hill. They hurriedly put their major redoubt on nearby Breed's Hill, which was closer to Boston and overlooked it better.[235]

6/17/1775: The British attacked Breed's Hill, where Colonel Prescott's statement *Don't fire until you see the whites of their eyes!* appears to have been made, and not just by him, in response to Major General Israel Putnam's injunction that

> *Powder is scarce and must not be wasted. Do not fire until you see the whites of their eyes. Then Aim low. Aim at their waistbands, aim at the handsome coats, pick off the officers.*[236]

There was disarray in the rear of the attacking and defending forces. The British brought the wrong caliber of cannon ammunition. And they made frontal attacks across a hayfield hiding uneven ground—against defenders protected by a rail fence that absorbed British volleys and allowed the Patriots to take a steadier aim by resting their muskets on it. Some Patriots disobeyed orders. (Several officers were court-martialed and cashiered.) There also was significant Patriot desertion, and some reinforcements didn't get to the battle because they didn't try to make an opposed crossing of the Charles River. Also, their ammunition was in short supply and few had bayonets.

The attacking forces were commanded by Maj. Gen. William Howe, with Maj. Gen. Henry Clinton in charge of the reserves. The senior American officer was Maj. Gen. Israel Putnam, on Bunker Hill. Col. Prescott led the defenders on Breed's Hill.

The British attacked in line abreast and were repulsed with heavy casualties. So was their next assault, again in line abreast, across the first assault's dead and wounded (some moaning). The third assault was made in a column reinforced by 400 soldiers from Boston and with 200 re-formed walking wounded. The rebels ran out of ammunition and the bayonet-equipped redcoats used hand-to-hand combat to turn the tide. The rail fence defenders' controlled withdrawal prevented British encirclement of Breed's Hill, and the Patriots made an orderly retreat over Bunker Hill. Britain's Maj. Gen. John Burgoyne described the retreat as *no flight, it was even covered with bravery and military skill.* And the withdrawing rebels took most of their wounded with them.

The British casualties (226 dead, 828 wounded), with a disproportionately high numbers of officers among them, was their greatest single battle loss in the War. The Americans' ~450 casualties included ~140 dead and 30 captured (20 of whom died as POWs). Most American casualties occurred while retreating. According to General Clinton's diary:

> *A few more such victories would have shortly put an end to British dominion in America.*

Bunker Hill increased Colonial support for independence, especially in the South. King George III received General Gage's report on the battle, declared the colonies to be in a state of open and avowed rebellion—and refused to receive the Continental Congress' Olive Branch Petition, the last substantive try to end the conflict peacefully. Gage was fired as Commander-in-Chief three days after his Bunker Hill report was received.[237]

3.18 Invasion of Canada

5/9/1775: Skenesboro, New York, the first permanent settlement on Lake Champlain, was taken by American forces. British Army Captain Philip Skene's trading schooner *Katherine* and several bateaux (flat-bottomed, double-ended boats, the largest of which were capable of carrying up to 10 tons of cargo) were seized.[238]

5/10/1775: Col. Benedict Arnold, Col. Ethan Allen and his ~100 Green Mountain Boys (Vermont Militia), and ~60 other Colonials crossed Lake Champlain to Northeast New York and captured Fort Ticonderoga—catching its small garrison asleep. The fort became a staging ground for invading Canada and its cannons were used at Boston.[239]

5/18/1775: After rowing all night, Arnold and ~35 men, in the now armed *Katherine*, renamed *Liberty*, and several bateaux, raided Fort Saint-Jean on the Richelieu River North of Lake Champlain. (The Richelieu runs North from Lake Champlain and empties into the St. Lawrence.) Supplies and the 70-ton sloop *HMS Royal George* were seized. Warned by their captives that British forces were enroute, Arnold's men loaded captured supplies and cannons on the *George*, renamed *Enterprise*, sank the boats they couldn't take along, and withdrew. They met Allen and his bateaux 15 miles into Lake Champlain, fed Allen's men (who had rowed 100 miles without food), and headed South. Allen continued on to Fort Saint-Jean, believing he could seize and hold it.

5/19/1775: At Fort Saint-Jean, Allen was warned by a sympathetic Montreal merchant, who had raced ahead of the British force, that the British were coming. Allen withdrew as the British were arriving, and returned to Fort Ticonderoga two days later.[240]

6/19/1775: Philip Schuyler, a French and Indian War Major, New York Assemblyman and Continental Congress delegate, was commissioned a Major General.[241]

6/271775: Congress reversed its decision to abandon New York territory, including Ticonderoga. They also authorized Maj. Gen. Schuyler to investigate the Quebec situation and, if it seemed appropriate, to invade. Their basis was:

- A New York and New England outcry against the abandonment.
- Arnold and Allen's separate reports that Ticonderoga needed to be held to prevent British splitting of the Colonies, and suggesting that a 1200-1500 man force could drive the British out of Quebec Province.
- Quebec Province's Governor, General Guy Carleton, was having Fort Saint-Jean fortified and trying to get the Iroquois in Northern New York to enter into the conflict.

Benedict Arnold went to Boston to meet with George Washington, and convinced him to send a supporting force, under Arnold's command, to support the Quebec invasion.

Schuyler's plan was to cross Lake Champlain and attack Montreal and then Quebec City, with a force from New York, Connecticut, New Hampshire, and Vermont (the Green Mountain Boys). His caution was enhanced by reports that Carleton was fortifying positions outside Montreal and some Amerinds were supporting the British.

8/25/1775: With Schuyler away at a conference with the Amerinds, his subordinate, Brigadier General Richard Montgomery (an Irish immigrant, a British French and Indian War veteran, and a former New York Provincial Congressman), was informed that ships under construction at Fort Saint-Jean were nearing completion. Without orders, he invaded with 1200 troops that had mustered at Fort Ticonderoga.

9/4/1775: Montgomery arrived at Île aux Noix, South of Fort Saint-Jean in the Richelieu River. Schuyler had caught up with him enroute.

9/5/1775: After a skirmish with mostly Amerinds at Fort Saint-Jean, the attackers returned to Île aux Noix. Schuyler was ailing and turned over his command to Montgomery. The Fort had not supported the skirmish, and their Amerinds withdrew from the conflict. Other Amerind support of the British was prevented by Oneidas who intercepted a Mohawk war party moving toward the Fort and convinced them to go home.

9/17/1775: With his force augmented by another 800-1000 men, Montgomery began besieging Fort Saint-Jean—cutting off communications with Montreal and capturing supplies that were intended for the Fort. The next week, Ethan Allen overstepped his instructions to raise local militia, tried to take Montreal, and was captured. (He was a British prisoner until being exchanged in 1778.[242]) Local militia support for the British increased. Desertions made that effect short-lived.

10/30/1775: General Carleton's attempt to relieve Fort Saint-Jean failed.

11/3/1775: Fort Saint-Jean surrendered.[243]

11/13/1775: Montreal fell without significant fighting. Carleton, suffering from desertions after the fall of Fort Saint-Jean, decided that Montreal was indefensible. He narrowly escaped capture and made his way to Quebec City with his fleet.

Montgomery sent messages to the inhabitants of Quebec City stating that Congress wanted Quebec to join the fight against England. And he held discussions with American Sympathizers about holding a provincial convention to elect delegates to the Continental Congress. He then left 200 troops in Montreal under the command of Brigadier General David Wooster and departed for Quebec City in captured boats, adding 200 men from the newly created 1st Canadian Regiment to his 300 along the way.

11/19/1775: After encountering a boat carrying a surrender demand and the allegation that downstream batteries would destroy the fleet if it didn't, the British fleet surrendered. Carleton sneaked off his ship and made his way to Quebec City in disguise.

12/2/1775: At the Plains of Abraham near Quebec City, Montgomery and his 500 men met with Benedict Arnold and the 600 nearly starving men he had left from the 1100 he had started with. Carleton refused their surrender offer, as he had Arnold's earlier one

12/31/1775: Montgomery and Arnold attacked Quebec City, separately and during a snowstorm. Both attacks were repulsed. Montgomery was killed. After several more tries, his force retreated. Arnold's left leg was shattered while he was leading the advance force. Daniel Morgan took command, but the British reorganized and repulsed the attack before Arnold's main force arrived. Over 400 attackers were killed, wounded, or captured (including Morgan). British casualties were minor. Carleton decided to remain in the fortified city and await reinforcements that would arrive after the Spring thaw. Arnold maintained an ineffectual siege until he was ordered to Montreal in March 1776. Major General David Wooster replaced him in April 1776. (Arnold was promoted to Brigadier General for his role in reaching Quebec.[244])

At Montreal, Wooster arrested Loyalists and threatened to arrest and punish anyone opposed to the American cause. He disarmed several communities and tried to force local militia members to renounce their Crown Commissions, arresting and imprisoning those who refused. American supplies were paid for in paper money instead of coin and the city's inhabitants became highly disillusioned with the Americans.

3/20/1776: Wooster left Montreal to take charge at Quebec City. By the end of the month, reinforcements arriving during the winter had swelled the attacking force to 3000 men, about one-quarter of them disabled, mostly by smallpox.

4/19/1776: Arnold arrived at Montreal and took command.

4/29/1776: A five-man delegation sent by the Continental Congress arrived at Montreal to assess the Quebec situation and sway the populace to their cause. Benjamin Franklin was a member. They brought no hard currency, could not alleviate the accumulating debt incurred to support the invasion, and were unsuccessful.

5/11/1776: Franklin and Delegate Catholic Priest John Carroll left Montreal when news arrived about Carleton's sortie from Quebec City with reinforcements from the newly arrived British Fleet—and about the panicked retreat of the besiegers of Quebec. Father Carroll had been unable to influence the Catholic clergy to support the American War Effort. Fleury Mespit, the printer on the delegation, had set up his press but was unable to do any printing before events overtook the delegation's efforts.

5/21/1776: Maj. Gen Frank Thomas, now commanding the remainder of the Quebec City attackers, met with the Congressional delegation at Sorel, Canada.

5/27/1776: The other two Congressional delegates, Samuel Chase and John Carroll, after analyzing the military situation to the South and East of Montreal and writing their report to Congress, left Montreal and headed South.

6/2/1776: Thomas died of smallpox. He was replaced by Brigadier General Thompson.

6/14/1776: Carleton sailed his army upriver (South) to Sorel and found that the Americans had abandoned it earlier in the day and were retreating Southward, this time in a more orderly fashion. He ordered General Burgoyne and 4000 troops to pursue the retreating force and continued to sail upriver toward Montreal.

6/15/1776: Upon receiving word of the sighting of the masts of Carleton's fleet, Arnold and his command abandoned the Montreal area.

6/17/1776: Carleton reached Montreal. Arnold caught up with the main invading army near Fort Saint-Jean. They retreated South, reportedly just before Burgoyne's vanguard arrived, and arrived at Crown Point early in July. Isaac Senter, a doctor who had been with the invaders for most of the now ended invasion, described it as *a heterogeneal concatenation of the most peculiar and unparalleled rebuffs and sufferings that are perhaps to be found in the annals of any nation.*

In early July, Adjutant General (Chief Administrative Officer) Horatio Gates was given command of the Continental Army's Northern forces, left an ~300-man force at Crown Point, moved the bulk of the army to Ticonderoga, tasked Arnold with building up the American fleet at Crown Point, and began improving Ticonderoga's defenses. Reinforcements made his force an estimated 10,000 strong by the end of summer.

10/11/1776: Benedict Arnold had used his sea trader (and smuggler) expertise to get a host of shipwrights and carpenters to cobble together 15 schooners, sloops and gunboats. Carleton's fleet met them on Lake Champlain, between Valcour Island and the Western shore. The 25 British vessels virtually destroyed Arnold's 15 in a two-day battle. Arnold retreated to Crown Point, and then withdrew to Ticonderoga.

10/17/1776: Carleton occupied Crown Point. Some of his troops approached Ticonderoga in an unsuccessful attempt to draw Gates' army out.[245] But Arnold's "fleet" had given the British pause and they withdrew to Winter Quarters in Quebec—a strategic victory credited by many historians as having saved the Revolution.[246]

3.19 War Comes to Virginia

March 1775: Rebellious Whigs, who controlled Virginia's Provincial Assembly, began recruiting troops. Virginia's Royal Governor, John Murray, 4th Earl of Dunmore, had British marines take gunpowder from Williamsburg's storehouse to a Royal Navy ship.[247]

June 1775: Safety concerns prompted Lord Dunmore to take his family from Williamsburg and go aboard a Royal Navy ship. A small British fleet assembled at Norfolk.[248]

11/30/75: Lord Dunmore wrote that he soon would be able to *reduce this colony to a proper sense of their duty.*[249]

12/9/1775: South of Norfolk, Colonial Colonel Woodford's force, reinforced to 700 men by militia from surrounding counties and North Carolina, was entrenched on the South side of Great Bridge. Lord Dunmore's forces had fortified the North side and tried to dislodge Woodford. They were decisively repulsed, and withdrew to the British fleet at Norfolk—along with most of Norfolk's remaining Tories. Woodford's force grew further when Colonel Robert Howe and North Carolina regulars arrived the next day.[250]

12/14/1775: Virginia's Whig forces had grown to ~1200. Colonel Howe, who was senior, denied supply deliveries to the overcrowded British ships, and insisted on parity in prisoner exchanges, The Whig forces moved into Norfolk. Realizing the vulnerability to isolation by British Fleet maneuvers, Colonels Howe and Woodward recommended to the Virginia Assembly that Norfolk be abandoned and rendered useless to the British.[251]

12/21/1775: *HMS Liverpool* and a stores ship arrived at Norfolk. Lord Dunmore stationed *Dunmore, Liverpool, Otter,* and *Kingfisher* along the waterfront, prompting mass departures from Norfolk.[252]

12/24/1775: *HMS Liverpool*'s Captain Bellew messaged Norfolk stating that he preferred purchasing supplies to taking them by force. Colonel Howe rejected that overture.[253]

12/30/1775: Captain Bellew demanded that the Whigs cease parading and changing the guard on the Norfolk waterfront, and said that it would not be imprudent for women and children to leave Norfolk. Colonel Howe told Bellew that *I am too much an Officer…to recede from any point which I conceive to be my duty.*[254]

3.20 The 1776 Transition

January 1776: King George III's October 1775 message to Parliament reached the Colonies. In it the King railed against the Colonies and ordered the enlargement of the Royal Army and Navy. That strengthened the Colonial Radicals and caused many Conservatives to abandon hope of reconciliation with Britain. And Thomas Paine, a recent immigrant from Britain, published the pamphlet *Common Sense.* It labelled Independence a *Natural Right* and the only possible Colonial course. Over 150,000 copies sold in the next few weeks.[255] [That's equivalent to ~18 million copies today.] That and King George's message to Parliament marked the turning the focus of the Revolution from gaining the rights of British citizens toward achieving independence from England. [And the Revolutionary War was no longer essentially one precipitated by New England and joined into by Virginia.]

1/1/1776: In Norfolk, between 3 and 4 pm, an over 100-gun British cannonade began and lasted well into the evening. Landing parties set fire to buildings used by Whig snipers. Most of the waterfront was set ablaze. The landing parties were resisted, but little was done to stop the fires, which continued spreading after the cannonade.

1/2/1776: Col. Howe reported that *the whole town will I doubt not be consum'd in a day or two.* The British had destroyed 19 Norfolk buildings (modern value £410,000). Lord Dunmore had done £270,000 in damage earlier. The Whigs destroyed 863 buildings (£16,000,000). But Howe did not report the Whig's role and it was generally assumed that most of the damage was done by the British. The Virginia Convention approved the recommendation that Norfolk be destroyed, and its other 416 buildings were destroyed by February 6. The extent of the Whig destruction was not acknowledged until 1777.[256]

1/5/1776: Congress had, two weeks earlier, appointed Brigadier General and Commander of Rhode Island's military Esek Hopkins as the Commander-in-Chief of the Continental Navy (eight merchant ships reconfigured as men-of-war).[257] They now ordered him to *proceed to Chesapeake Bay, gain intelligence and, if the enemy there is not greatly superior, to take or destroy all its naval force that you find. If you are successful, then immediately proceed South and make yourself master of such enemy forces as are in North and South Carolina. If bad winds, storms, or other unforeseen accident or disaster disenable you from doing so, follow such courses as your best judgement shall suggest as best useful to the American cause and to distress the Enemy by all means in your power.*

2/17/1776: Commodore Hopkins [sensibly] decided not to risk destroying the infant

Continental Navy. Knowing that British Nassau would be poorly guarded and his friends there would help, he set sail for Providence in the Bahamas. (John Paul Jones was a Lieutenant under Hopkins then.)[258]

March 1776: General Charles Lee took command of the Continental Army's Southern Department. He mobilized to evict Virginia Governor Lord Dunmore from his camp near Portsmouth. Lord Dunmore left Virginia for good in August.[259]

3/3/1776: In "a bold stroke, worthy of an older and better trained service," marines and sailors from Commodore Esek Hopkins' Continental Navy made the U.S. Navy's first amphibious landing, raided Nassau, and captured stores of badly needed munitions.[260]

4/6/1776: Hopkins severely damaged *HMS Glasgow* but didn't capture her.

4/8/1776: Hopkins' "fleet" returned to New London with two British merchantmen and a six-gun schooner as prizes.

Continental Congress President John Hancock wrote Hopkins:

> *I beg leave to congratulate you on the success of your Expedition. Your account of the spirit and bravery shown by the men affords them [Congress] the greatest satisfaction..."*

Hopkins's successful raid caused the British Navy to divert ships to non-belligerent areas. But Southern Congressmen were upset about the orders he didn't carry out. That added to Congress' political, social, economic, religious, and philosophical differences.

Thousands of Letters of Marque were issued to privateers. They took the British ships they conquered as renumeration and could pay crews nearly twice what the Continental Navy could. And the additional men-of-war Congress built couldn't be manned.[261]

Mid-June 1776: Congress appointed a committee to prepare a Declaration of why the Colonies were seceding. Its 33-year-old John Adams (MA), 70-year-old Benjamin Franklin (PA), 55-year-old Roger Sherman (CT), and 58-year-old Robert B. Livingston (NY) convinced the eloquent 33-year-old Thomas Jefferson (VA) to draft it.

7/4/1776: Congress adopted the *Declaration of Independence*—after the Committee and the Congress had modified one-fifth of what Jefferson had written (86 changes). They did not alter its most famous passage:

> *We hold these truths to be self-evident; that all men are created equal; that they are endowed by their Creator with certain inalienable rights; that among these are life, liberty and the pursuit of happiness; that to secure these rights, governments are instituted among men, deriving their just powers from the consent of the governed.*

That *American Dream* was the world's first statement by a national government that it is the peoples' right to choose their own government.[262]

[That dream greatly facilitated the success of the American Revolution and of the U.S. In practice, *all men* meant *White Men of means* then. But the as practiced *American Dream* has blossomed far beyond that initial state.]

Jefferson's condemnation of Slavery in the *Declaration* was deleted without explanation.

But the political reality was that the South's Economy depended on Slavery and New England profited from the Slave trade.[263] [Otto von Bismarck, the brilliant German who autocratically dominated European politics from 1871-90, two peaceful decades, labeled politics *the Art of the Possible*. (He also said that *Laws are like sausages, it is better not to see them being made*, and *There is a Providence that protects idiots, drunkards, children and the United States of America*.)[264]]

8/12/1776: Commodore Esek Hopkins, though defended by John Paul Jones and Congressmen John Adams (MA), Samuel Adams (MA), Benjamin Franklin (PA), Richard Henry Lee (VA) and Robert Treat Paine (MA), was censured by Congress. John Hancock (MA), the non-voting president of the Congress, wrote a resolution to have a schooner remade into a man of war and named the Hopkins. No records show that to have been done. And short staffing and superior British seapower kept Hopkins' force mostly blockaded in Narraganset Bay while he remained Commander-in-Chief.[265]

12/25/1776: Washington crossed the icy Delaware River late that Christmas Day (leaving several hundred of his men on the Pennsylvania side).

12/26/1776: Washington's early attack routed the Hessian mercenaries at Trenton.

3.21 Mid-Atlantic State and Connecticut Battles

1/3/1777: Washington returned to Trenton to lure the British South, made a daring night march, and captured Princeton, New Jersey. That and the Trenton victory regained control of much of New Jersey and boosted Patriot morale.[266]

February 1777: Upon learning that he had been passed over for promotion to Major General, Benedict Arnold offered to resign. Washington rejected the offer and wrote to members of the Continental Congress that *two or three other very good officers might be lost if they persisted in making politically motivated promotions*.[267]

4/22/1777: Former New York Royal Governor Tryon, a temporary Major General in command of 1800-1900 British troops, sailed from New York on an expedition against the Danbury, Connecticut Continental Army Depot.

4/26/1777: At Danbury, Tryon's force destroyed 4000-5000 barrels of pork, beef, and flour; 2000 bushels of grain, 1600 tents, and other supplies.

4/27/1777: At ~1 am, Tryon was alerted to the presence of American responders in nearby Bethel, roused his force, and ordered Patriot houses burned. (Tory houses had identifying marks on their chimneys.) Over 20 buildings were burned. To avoid the ~700 Patriots led by Major General David Wooster and Brigadier General Benedict Arnold, Tryon marched South toward Ridgefield. Wooster and ~200 men harassed the British. The 67-year-old Wooster was mortally wounded in his second assault on the column. His assault enabled Arnold and Connecticut Militia Brigadier General Gold Selleck Silliman and the remaining troops to set up crude defenses in Ridgefield. Tryon, with a 3:1 numeric advantage in troops, breached the barricade in an ~15-minute attack that chased the defenders out of town. Arnold's horse was hit by 9 musket balls during the retreat, and fell with Arnold entangled in his trappings. A British soldier charged, calling for him to surrender. Arnold said *Not Yet*, shot and killed the soldier, and escaped with his troops.

4/28/1777: In the morning, after camping just South of Ridgefield, the British set fire to 6 houses and the Episcopal Church (a Patriot supply depot and field hospital), and departed to re-embark in 12 transports at Campo Point at the mouth of the Saugatuck River. Silliman led 500 reinforced Colonials in harassing attacks on the fleeing column. Benedict Arnold and 500 men and a small company of artillery took a strong position on Campo Hill. The fast-moving British, aided by fresh marines from the ships, gained the high ground, blunted the opposition with a bayonet charge, shot another horse out from under Arnold, re-embarked, and sailed for New York.

This tactical success for the British cost them a reported 26 dead, 117 wounded, and 29 missing. The Americans had a reported 20 dead and 40-80 wounded. No more ship-based sallies against inland Colonial strongholds and no more inland operations in Connecticut were attempted by the British during the war.[268]

7/5/1777: British General John Burgoyne, who had come from Canada with 7400 men in an effort to split the Colonies, put artillery atop Sugar Loaf Mountain, overlooking Fort Ticonderoga. (The Americans had thought that the steep incline would prevent that.) General St. Clair began a night withdrawal. Burgoyne captured the Americans' supplies, but their rear guard (led by Colonel Long) escaped in a running battle in which they badly mauled the British 9th Foot. St Clair bivouacked at Fort Hubbardton. The British devastated his rear guard, the 11th Massachusetts, and killed its Commander, Colonel Ebenezer Francis. But the Americans fought well and their main body escaped.[269]

9/11/1777: Covered by dense fog, British Generals Sir William Howe and Charles Cornwallis split their 18,000 troops. With Howe leading a frontal attack and Cornwallis one from the right flank, they surprised Washington and his 11,000 troops at Brandywine Creek near Chadds Ford in Delaware County, Pennsylvania. In danger of being surrounded, Washington retreated to Germantown (then outside Philadelphia), losing most of his cannons and suffering 1000 casualties to 600 British ones.

9/26/1777: Howe outmaneuvered Washington, entered Philadelphia, and put 9000 troops in Germantown. [270]

10/3/1777: Washington made a poorly coordinated four-pronged attack on Germantown. General John Sullivan's prong got ahead and received "friendly fire" from General Nathanial Greene's prong. A punishing British counterattack drove the Americans off, with 1000 American casualties to the British 500. A vocal military and Congressional minority began suggesting that General Horatio Gates, who was besting the British in Central New York, replace Washington as Commander-in-Chief.

Washington retreated to and wintered at Valley Forge, Pennsylvania. During that infamously brutal winter, with Prussian General Von Steuben's skillful assistance, the retrained Continental Army became a much improved fighting force.[271]

10/17/1777: Burgoyne was surrounded at Saratoga in upstate New York by Patriot forces that had swelled to about 15,000 from the about 9000 that had opposed him on September 19 and the about 12,000 he faced on October 7. He surrendered. During the Saratoga Campaign, the Americans suffered 90 dead and 240 wounded. The British losses were 440 dead, 695 wounded, and 6222 captured.[272]

3.22 Naval Activity and French Aid

<u>1/2/1778:</u> Commodore Esek Hopkins's Nassau raid, the "escape" of *HMS Glasgow*, and unsubstantiated allegations by a group of Hopkins' officers had been used by politically charged Congressmen to impugn his character and ability. Congress terminated his commission despite an impassioned defense by John Adams.

The allegations against Hopkins included ones by whistle-blowers Richard Marvin and Samuel Shaw that he had tortured British prisoners of war. Hopkins also reportedly played a part in Marvin and Shaw being arrested for having made those allegations. And his libel suit against Marvin and Shaw resulted in a Congressional resolution stating:

> *That it is the duty of all persons in the service of the United States, all well as all other inhabitants thereof to give the earliest information to Congress or any other proper authority of any misconduct, frauds or other misdemeanours committed by any persons in the service of these states, which may come to their knowledge.*

The tactics used in Hopkins' raid on Nassau also were used effectively by John Paul Jones. But the Nassau raid was on an area where the British felt more threatened than in the American Colonies—because of trade concerns and the pivotal role of the West Indies in naval conflicts with France. That deflected British interests and military assets away from the war in America. England's concern over losing the West Indies nearly caused it to abandon the war in 1778—and even may have cost her the war. So Hopkins' Nassau Raid also was a great strategic victory.[273]

[It is not obvious that either Hopkins or the Continental Congress were aware of the strategic aspects of his raid on Nassau.]

<u>2/6/1778</u>: Treaties negotiated by Benjamin Franklin with France were signed. They were:

- The Franco-American Treaty of Amity and Commerce. It recognized U.S. independence and established commercial relations with France.
- The 1778 Treaty of Alliance. Enabled by the victory at Saratoga, it gave the U.S. the support of France's Army, Navy, and Treasury, and an American-French combined force militarily superior to England's. France promised not to increase its possessions in America. And the U.S. guaranteed, *from the present time and forever, against all other powers…the present Possessions of the Crown of France in America.*[274]

<u>4/24/1778:</u> John Paul Jones had the first U.S. victory over a Royal Navy warship in British Waters. Jones, in the 18-gun *Ranger*, killed 5 crew members (including Captain Burdon) of the 14-gun Sloop *HMS Drake* in a one-hour battle in the North Channel near Carrickfergus, Northern Ireland. He then took *Drake* to Brest, France and sold her.[275]

<u>9/23/1779:</u> With *Poor Richard's* Almanac author Benjamin Franklin's invaluable support, France had given the supremely audacious John Paul Jones seven ships. The largest was an old and creaky 42-gun, 998 tonne vessel that Jones named *Bonhomme Richard* and captained. While sailing *Bonhomme Richard, Alliance, Pallas, Vengeace, and Cerf* down the

East coast of England (off Yorkshire), Jones encountered Britain's 41-ship Baltic merchant fleet. Its escort was the 44-gun, 879 tonne *HMS Serapis* and the hired, 22-gun, 500 tonne *Countess of Scarborough*. They battled Jones for four hours, enabling the escape of the merchantmen. *Serapis'* copper-clad hull gave her a maneuverability advantage, and she felled half of *Bonhomme Richard's* crew and disabled all but three of her cannons. Jones nonetheless maneuvered alongside *Serapis* and put grappling hooks over. And in response to *Serapis'* Captain Pearson's asking if he had struck his colors, Jones gave the famous reply ***I have not yet begun to fight!*** One of Jones' topmen crawled onto *Serapis* and dropped a grenade into her munitions, and the explosion disabled all but four of *Serapis's* cannons. She struck her colors. The *Countess of Scarborough* also surrendered. Jones transferred his crew to *Serapis*, cast the battered *Bonhomme Richard* adrift (she sank the next day), and returned to France a hero.[276]

3.23 Dark Days and Treachery

5/12/1780: After a 6-week British land and sea siege, American Maj. Gen. Benjamin Lincoln surrendered Charleston to British General Clinton. The British had 78 dead and 89 wounded. The Patriots had 89 dead, 138 wounded, and 5266 captured, along with 311 artillery pieces, 9178 artillery rounds, 5916 muskets, 33,000 rounds of ammunition, 49 ships, 120 boats, 376 barrels of flour, and large amounts of rum, rice, and indigo.[277]

8/16/1780: At Camden, South Carolina, 1500 British regulars and 600 militia commanded by Lt. Gen. Charles, Lord Cornwallis routed Maj. Gen. Horatio Gates' Patriot force of 1500 regulars and 2500 militia (~1000 of whom were disabled by dysentery). The British suffered 68 dead, 245 wounded, and 11 missing; the Patriots had 900 killed or wounded, and 1000 captured. Gates was replaced by Maj. Gen. Nathanial Greene.[278]

9/23/1780: British Major John Andre was arrested with papers showing that Norwich, Connecticut-born Major General Benedict Arnold had agreed to surrender his command, the strategically located West Point, New York fort to the British.[279] Arnold, chagrined at not getting the accolades and precedence over other Continental Army Generals that he demanded (his battlefield achievements were superior), had been providing the British information on American dispositions and troop movements. He fled to the British upon hearing of Andre's arrest. They made him a Brigadier General and he led successful British attacks on Richmond, Virginia and New London, Connecticut, burning much of New London to the ground and slaughtering the surrendering opposition after the Battle of Groton Heights. Arnold received his promised £360 annual income but, because the West Point surrender was averted, was paid only £6,000 of his £20,000 sellout price.

Historian W.D. Wetherell stated that the shortest explanation for Arnold's treason was marrying the wrong person, and that Arnold is::

> (a)*mong the hardest human beings to understand in American history. Did he become a traitor because of all the injustice he suffered, real and imagined, at the hands of the Continental Congress and his jealous fellow generals? Because of the constant agony of two battlefield wounds in an already*

gout-ridden leg? From psychological wounds received in his Connecticut childhood when his alcoholic father squandered the family's fortunes? Or was it a kind of extreme midlife crisis, swerving from radical political beliefs to reactionary ones, a change accelerated by his marriage to the very young, very pretty, very Tory Peggy Shippen?

Arnold's profiteering, mercurial temperament, and turn-coating made him despised in England and in America. His name became a synonym for traitor, and his battlefield heroics received no acclaim.[280]

[Benedict Arnold had a very rare combination of inspirational courage and military skill. In that regard, he stands out much as did John Paul Jones, Horatio Lord Nelson, and George S. Patton. But his battlefield heroics and successes greatly increased the anathema that his traitorship produced. His name is still a synonym for traitor.]

3.24 King's Mountain: the Tide Turns

10/7/1780: 900 American Patriots battled 1100 American Loyalists at King's Mountain (in the Charlotte, North Carolina metropolitan area). The Patriots were split into eight 100-200 independently operating groups, each led by a different Colonel. There was one British Regular with the Loyalists, Major Patrick Ferguson, their Commander.

The Patriots crept up King's Mountain, firing from cover. Surprised but combative, the Loyalists charged with fixed bayonets. Their attackers, who had no bayonets, scattered, reformed, and re-attacked. Ferguson rallied his men but was shot. His horse dragged him behind Patriot lines. A rebel officer demanded his surrender. Ferguson shot him dead and was immediately killed by a fusillade. (His corpse had 7 bullet holes.) The Loyalists surrendered. They suffered 290 dead, 167 wounded, and 668 captured. Patriot losses were 28 dead and 62 wounded.

Cornwallis postponed invading North Carolina and withdrew further into South Carolina

Thomas Jefferson called King's Mountain *The turn of the tide of Success.*

Theodore Roosevelt wrote of it: *This brilliant victory marked the turning point of the American Revolution.*

President Herbert Hoover, speaking there, said:

This is a place of inspiring memories. Here less than a thousand men, inspired by the urge of freedom, defeated a superior force entrenched in this strategic position. This small band of Patriots turned back a dangerous invasion well designed to separate and dismember the united Colonies. It was a little army and a little battle, but it was of mighty portent. History has done scant justice to its significance, which rightly should place it beside Lexington, Bunker Hill, Trenton, and Yorktown. [281]

10/14/1780: George Washington placed Major General Nathanael Greene in charge of the Southern Continental Army (1482 men, 949 of whom were Regulars). Greene considered his "army" too weak to face the British head on, unconventionally split his force, and put the brilliant, experienced Brigadier General Daniel Morgan in command of a wing sent to the West of the Catawba River to raise local morale and garner supplies.

3.25 Cowpens

Cornwallis was planning to resume his postponed invasion of North Carolina. To counter Morgan's threat to his left flank, he sent 26-year-old LtCol Banastre Tarleton (who had had several spectacular victories over the Americans) to the West to protect the American Loyalist Fort 96. Tarleton marched hard to get there, didn't find Morgan, learned Morgan's location and marched hard to confront him. To avoid being caught between Tarleton and Cornwallis, Morgan retreated to Hanna's Cowpens (in Northern South Carolina, about 60 miles West-Southwest of Charlotte, North Carolina). He decided to stand and fight there rather than risk being caught trying to cross the floodwater-swollen Broad River. Having the river at his back also prevented his Patriot militia from breaking and fleeing, which had been a problem in previous battles.

1/17/1781: At 3 AM, after marching overnight (and under orders to be aggressive), Tarleton approached Cowpens. He had 1158 men (531 of them were Loyalists recruited in the Colonies) made up of 552 Regulars, 300 Cavalry, 281 militia, and 24 artillerymen. And he had two grasshopper cannons that fired 3 lb. cannonballs.

Morgan had about 1900 men: 1255-1280 militia infantry, 300 Continental infantry, 150 State infantry, 82 Continental dragoons (light Cavalry), and 55 State dragoons. About 855 of them were South Carolinians, 442 were Virginians, 300 were North Carolinians, 180 were of the Maryland Line, 60 were of the Delaware Line, and 60 were Georgians. He placed his force between the Broad and Pacolet Rivers, safeguarding his flanks and eliminating the possibility that his troops would flee. His center was a low hill. Its flanks were exposed but protected by a ravine on the right flank and a creek on the left. Anticipating that Tarleton would attack head on, he established three lines of defense. The first was 150 sharpshooters from North Carolina and Georgia, the second 300 militia, and the third (on the hill) about 550 battle-hardened troops made up of Brooklyn veterans, the famed Maryland and Delaware Lines, and Georgia and Virginia militiamen. ((Historian John Buchanan wrote that Morgan may have been *the only general in the American Revolution, on either side, to produce a significant original tactical thought*.)

Tarleton—despite five days of hard marching, running out of food, and allowing his men only four hours sleep in the last 48—was confident of victory against a force that couldn't retreat. Just before sunrise, his vanguard emerged from the woods and he ordered his dragoons to attack. The first line of Patriot skirmishers shot 15 of them and the rest retreated. Tarleton, without pausing to study the defenses or give the rest of his force time to get out of the woods, ordered an infantry charge and deployed his main body and cannons. The first defense line kept firing and withdrew into the second line. As the British attacked it, the second line fired two volleys, especially targeting officers. The confused attackers, with 40% of their casualties being officers, reorganized and continued to advance. The second defense line withdrew around the American left flank. Mistaking that for a full-blown retreat, the British charged into the disciplined third line, with the 71st Highlanders ordered to flank the American right. The Virginians there were ordered to face them but misunderstood and initially withdrew. Believing that they were on the run, the British broke ranks and charged chaotically. The Virginians wheeled and halted the charge by firing into the attackers from no more than 30 yards. A Patriot bayonet charge was carried out by the Continentals in the center. Tarleton's force began surrendering and fleeing. Their cannons were seized. Cavalry from the American left and the reformed first and second line hit the British right flank and rear and, along with the Virginians on the American right, enveloped the British left flank. Doubly enveloped, hungry, exhausted, and utterly demoralized, nearly half the attacking infantrymen, wounded or not, fell to the ground. Tarleton ordered his only whole unit, the British Legion Cavalry, to charge. But they fled. Unable to retrieve his cannons with the 40 dragoons he had left, Tarleton fled with them.

At Cowpens, the Americans had 25 killed and 124 wounded. The British had 86% casualties: 110 killed, 229 wounded, and 629 captured—in a brigade constituting the cream of Cornwallis' army. The battle gave the Patriots a big boost by *spiriting up the people* in all the Southern States.

Cornwallis abandoned his campaign in South Carolina, stripped his army of excess baggage, and pursued Nathaniel Greene into North Carolina.[282]

2/15/1781: Nathanial Greene crossed the Dan River into Virginia, two hours before Cornwallis arrived. The British couldn't cross because Greene had taken all the boats. Cornwallis went South to Hillsborough, North Carolina to let his army recuperate from the exhaustive marching, freezing weather, and near starvation of the chase—and to recruit Loyalists. Greene's men recuperated, resupplied, and also gained reinforcements during their seven-day stay in Virginia.

2/18/1781: Col. Henry (Light-Horse-Harry) Lee (Robert E. Lee's father) with his cavalry and Col. Andrew Pickens with Maryland infantry crossed the Dan to monitor British activity. They set up a hidden camp between Hillsboro and the Haw River. The next morning, Lee's scouts reported that Tarleton was moving. He camped near the Haw before moving on.

2/24/1781: Lee and Pickens interrogated two captured British staff officers, learning that Tarleton was a few miles ahead. As the day waned, they encountered two of the 300-400 men that Loyalist Dr. John Pyle had recruited when Cornwallis asked for volunteers. Lee's cavalry wore short green jackets and plumed helmets and were mistaken for Tarleton's dragoons. Learning that Pyle's troops were nearby, Lee had Pickens flank them, and trotted into Pyle's camp in full salute. He exchanged civilities with Col. Pyle and was shaking his hand when Pickens attacked.

The militia at Lee's rear told their Captain Eggleston, a new arrival unfamiliar with Tory markings, that the red cloth strips on Pyle's men's hats were Loyalist badges. Eggleston asked one what side he was on, was told *King George*, and whacked the man on the head with his sabre. Lee's and Pickens' men then attacked in force. Pyle's men broke and ran. Many believed the attack to be a mistake and insisted that they were on King George's side. In 10 minutes, 93 Loyalists were dead. The rest fled, taking some of their wounded. Cornwallis reported that most of Pyle's men were *inhumanly butchered, when begging for quarters, without making the least resistance.* Lee's memoirs noted that those who wished to run away were allowed to do so, not chased down and butchered. [Both of those statements may be exaggerated.] The incident, known as Pyle's massacre, strongly inhibited British recruitment. Lee and Pickens stopped pursuing Tarleton when he came too close to Cornwallis' main force for an attack to be feasible.

3.26 The End Begins

<u>3/15/1781:</u> Cornwallis, a day after learning that Greene, with 4000-5000 men, was encamped at the Guilford Courthouse (in what is now Greensboro, North Carolina), arrived there about noon to attack with 2100 men.

The Americans were arrayed in three lines of defense—too far apart for mutual support. North Carolina militia formed the first line, behind a fence extending on both sides of the road. A six-pound cannon was deployed on each side of the road. Backwoods riflemen were on the first line's flanks. The second line was Virginia militia, with two more six-pound cannons in the center. Delaware infantry and the 1st and 2nd Maryland regiments were in the third and strongest line, 400 yards further on.

Initial contact was about 4 miles from the courthouse— between Tarleton's dragoons and Light Horse Harry Lee's Cavalry. Lee withdrew when infantry reinforced the British.

After a short cannonade on the first line, Cornwallis ordered his men forward. At about 150 yards from the fence, the Americans fired a volley. The British responded in kind and charged forward. About 50 yards from the fence, they were halted by the precision of the North Carolinians' musket fire, which was enhanced by shooting with their weapons resting on the fence. The Patriots had been ordered to fire two or three volleys but fled back through the woods before the third, some perhaps before the second. And the first two lines of defense inflicted considerable damage on the British before retreating

The British attacked the Continental infantry at the courthouse, captured two six-pounders, and pursued the defenders into the woods. They were repulsed by LtCol. William Washington's light cavalry and the 1st Maryland regiment. Cornwallis ordered two newly arrived three-pounders to fire at the light cavalry and British alike, killing many British soldiers. The Americans left the field, and the British didn't pursue very far.

Cornwallis' tactical victory in this 90-minute battle cost him an irreplaceable ~25% of his force. Greene came away with a strategic victory. He reported 79 killed, 185 wounded, and 1048 missing. Historians Lawrence Babits and Joshua Howard concluded that the casualties were probably 15-20% higher. They also noted that most of the unwounded missing were North Carolina militia who went straight home after the battle.

Cornwallis reported his casualties as 3 officers and 88 men of other ranks killed and 24 officers and 384 men of other ranks wounded. That toll resulted in his withdrawal to the coast at Wilmington, North Carolina to refit and recruit. British Whig Party Leader and war critic Charles James Fox restated Pyrrhus' famous 29 BC words by saying *Another such victory would ruin the British Army*. Cornwallis also overstated the American force strength by describing it as being over 7000 men, and stated that 200-300 of them were left dead on the field. He also lavished praise on his force (and thereby himself) by stating:

The conduct and actions of the officers and soldiers that composed this little army will do more justice to their merit than I can by words. Their persevering intrepidity in action, their invincible patience in the hardships and fatigues of a march of above 600 miles, in which they have forded several large rivers and numberless creeks, many of which would be reckoned large rivers in any other country in the world, without tents or covering against the climate, and often without provisions, will sufficiently manifest their ardent zeal for the honour and interests of their Sovereign and their country.

From Wilmington, Cornwallis raided farms and plantations, took hundreds of horses for his dragoons, and mounted 700 infantrymen. He also freed thousands of Slaves, many joining him, and planned to march into Virginia to hold the Southern States firmly.

Greene's command of the Southern arm of the Continental Army was described by him as *We fight, get beat, rise, and fight again.*[283]

3/16/1781: The 23-year-old Maj. Gen. Marquis de Lafayette, in charge of 1200 troops and supported by a small French Fleet, was enroute from Yorktown, Virginia with the objective of capturing now British Brig. Gen. Benedict Arnold, who was in Virginia to raid military supply bases, gather Loyalist support, and weaken Virginia's aid to Nathanial Greene in the Carolinas. Near the mouth of the Chesapeake Bay, the British won a naval battle with the French, who returned to Rhode Island. Arnold was reinforced by 2000 troops commanded by Maj. Gen. William Phillips, who commanded the British troops in Virginia. Lafayette's troops were still at Annapolis, Maryland, and he practiced Washington's tactic of limited engagement while preserving his forces.

4/25/1781: Phillips took Petersburg, Virginia and set his sights on Richmond. But Lafayette's troops were there and Phillips returned to Petersburg.

5/13/1781: Phillips died from fever, and Arnold commanded the King's army in Virginia.

5/20/1781: Cornwallis and 1500 men arrived in Petersburg from the Carolinas. He took command, was reinforced to 7000 troops by New Yorkers, and raided as far West as Charlotte. Lafayette, reinforced to 4000 men by Pennsylvania Continental Line troops under Brig. Gen. "Mad" Anthony Wayne and Virginia militia under Maj. Gen. Baron Friedrich von Steuben, began shadowing Cornwallis.

6/26/1781: After turning toward the coast and a skirmish at Spencer's Tavern West of Williamsburg, Cornwallis made plans to cross the James River at Jamestown. He also planned to, as ordered by Clinton, proceed to Portsmouth to establish a naval base there.

7/6/1781: Lafayette saw a chance to attack Cornwallis' rear guard for the river crossing. But Cornwallis deceptively sent across only his baggage and a small cavalry group, and had disinformation leaked that only a small part of his army remained at Jamestown. Lafayette sent Wayne and his 800 men to reconnoiter. Mad Anthony, trying to assess Cornwallis' strength, stopped at Green Spring Plantation, a couple of miles from Jamestown. Lafayette joined him, and they received more disinformation stating that most of Cornwallis' force had crossed the river. Wayne proceeded toward Jamestown, encountering British pickets. Lafayette moved alongside the river, got a better view, and saw that Wayne was going to encounter most of Cornwallis' force. By the time he got back to Wayne, Cornwallis had engaged Wayne. Lafayette called up reinforcements that arrived as the British were flanking Wayne. Mad

Anthony, seeing his plight, charged. That temporarily halted the British, whereupon Wayne made a disorderly withdrawal to Green Spring. Cornwallis had ~75 casualties, Lafayette ~140 (~28 killed, ~99 wounded, ~12 missing). That night, Lafayette moved his vastly outnumbered force further away.

Cornwallis moved on to Portsmouth and loaded his army onto transports. Lafayette surmised that they were headed for New York. But the British Fleet and Cornwallis' army arrived at Yorktown early in August and began fortifying it. The surprised Lafayette wrote to the French Minister to the U.S., stating: *If the French army could all of a sudden arrive in Virginia and be supported by a squadron, we would do some very good things.*[284]

3.27 Yorktown

7/6/1781: The French and American armies met at White Plains, New York. The French Commander, Lieutenant General Jean-Baptiste Donatien de Vimeur, comte de Rochambeau, also was Commander-in-Chief of the French Expeditionary Force sent to assist America. {French Lieutenant général des armées navales (Vice Admiral) François Joseph Paul, Comte de Grasse, Marquis of Grasse-Tilly de Grasse, commanded the French Naval Force.} Rochambeau, who had nearly 40 years of military experience, told Washington he had come to serve, not command.

Washington had earlier proposed attacking New York City, England's principal base. Rochambeau preferred attacking Virginia, and privately so informed de Grasse, whose support was essential to either action. Washington was still focused on New York (Manhattan). His staff and Rochambeau disagreed.

8/14/1781: Washington received a letter from de Grasse stating that he was enroute (from Haiti) to Virginia with 28 warships and 3200 soldiers, could only stay until October 14, and encouraging a joint operation. Washington prepared to march to Virginia, sent fake dispatches (which reached Clinton) stating that New York would be attacked, and left some troops behind to prevent Clinton from deducing his intentions.[285]

8/21/1781: Lafayette wrote to Washington, who was already enroute, stating:

> In the present State of affairs, My dear General, I Hope You will come Yourself to Virginia, and that if the french Army Moves this way, I will Have at last the Satisfaction of Beholding You Myself at the Head of the Combined Armies... When a french fleet takes possession of the Bay and Rivers, and we form a land force Superior to His, that Army must Soon or late Be forced to Surrender as we may get what Reinforcements we please.[286]

8/27/1781: Comte de Barras, who Rochambeau had contacted, sailed from Newport for the Chesapeake—with 8 ships of the line. 4 frigates, and 18 transports carrying siege guns and equipment.

8/30/1781: De Grasse disembarked 3200 troops at Chesapeake Bay. His presence trapped two British frigates in the Bay, denying New York information on his fleet.

9/5/1781: About 9:320 AM, frigates of British RAdm Sir Thomas Graves, with 19 ships of the line, and frigates of French RAdm de Grasse, sighted each other. Graves headed toward the Bay and de Grasse, whose ships were anchored.

At 11:30 AM, 24 of de Grasse's ships of the line cut their anchor lines and sailed out of the Bay on the noon tide—forming a line in order of speed. Their shore parties were left behind and understaffing prevented some ships from firing all their guns. About 2 PM, Graves (apparently sailing Southwest with the wind on his starboard quarter) altered course to avoid Middle Ground Shoal and close on de Grasse's line, wearing ships (bringing their sterns through the wind) to do so. That reversed his line of battle and put his most aggressive squadron leader, 1st Viscount RAdm Samuel Hood, last.

By 3:45 PM, the first four ships of de Grasse's East-heading line were so far ahead of the rest that it could have been cut off. Graves continued closing on an East-Southeast heading. The wind was from the North-Northeast, putting the British to windward. That enabled the French to fire full broadsides while the British had to keep their lower gunports closed to keep the sea out. The French also had more ships and more, and bigger, guns.

Graves hoisted two signals: *Line Ahead*, close in line and then come parallel (enabling broadsides); and *Close Action*, turn toward and come parallel when close. Hood saw the *Line Ahead* signal as taking precedence, closed slowly, and got only a few shots off.

About 4 PM, the British line turned to attack the French, subjecting their van to broadsides and limiting their response to bow guns. The French van's 4 ships, though engaged by 7-8 British ships, suffered less than the British van.

After two hours, sunset ended the battle. The British suffered 336 casualties (90 dead, 246 wounded), and had 5 ships badly damaged (scuttling one 6 days later). There were 220 French casualties, with two ships notably damaged.

9/6/1781: Ongoing ship repairs decided Graves against re-attacking then.

9/9/1781: After their fleets kept each other in sight for several days while de Grasse was luring Graves away from the Chesapeake, French scouts sighted de Barras' ships. De Grasse broke off that night and headed back to the Chesapeake.

9/10/1781: Comte De Barras entered the Chesapeake unharmed.

9/12/1781: De Grasse arrived back at the Chesapeake

9/13/1781: Graves and his subordinates, RAdm Hood and RAdm Drake, conferenced. They decided against further attacking *due to the truly lamentable state we have brought ourselves*. Graves then turned back toward New York, where he prepared a larger force. It sailed two days after the Siege of Yorktown ended.

De Grasse's victory, though less than decisive, secured the Chesapeake and enabled the complete encirclement and cutting off of Cornwallis at Yorktown.

King George III wrote:

> *after the knowledge of the defeat of our fleet...I nearly think the empire ruined.*[287]

9/14/1781: Washington met up with Lafayette in Williamsburg. (Rochambeau had loaned him half of his gold Spanish coins in Philadelphia to meet the American soldiers' demand for a month's pay in coin rather than in worthless Continental paper.)

9/26/1781: Transports brought artillery, siege tools, and French infantry and shock troops from the North of Chesapeake Bay. Washington now had an army of close to 19,000 (7800 Frenchmen, 3100 militia, and 8000 Continentals)—versus Cornwallis' 8000.

9/28/1781: Washington surrounded Yorktown. Cornwallis' defenses included a chain of redoubts and batteries linked by earthworks—and batteries covering the York River narrows. Washington concluded that Yorktown could be bombarded into submission.

9/29/1781: After a night in the open, and some foraging, Washington moved the army closer to Yorktown—receiving cannon and rifle fire but suffering few casualties.

Cornwallis, who had a letter from Clinton promising a 5000-man relief force within a week, pulled back from his outer defenses, except for the Fusiliers Redoubt on the West side of town. The attackers manned the abandoned fortifications, and began to set up artillery batteries. Both sides worked on improving their defenses.

9/30/1781: A two-hour French assault on the Fusiliers Redoubt was repulsed.

10/1/1781: British deserters revealed that, to conserve food, the defenders had slaughtered hundreds of horses and left them on the beach. The attackers cut down thousands of trees to provide wood for earthworks, and prepared to construct the 1st Parallel—a (Rochambeau proposed) 2000 yard long, 10' wide, 4' deep trench with earthworks on the Yorktown side, located 1000 yards from the town.

10/2/1781: Attacker casualties were suffered during the placement of siege artillery. And the British opened up a storm of fire to cover their cavalry-escorted foragers that night.

10/3/1781: A Banastre Tarleton-led British foraging party lost 50 men while retreating.

10/6/1781: Masked by stormy weather and a heavily overcast sky that obscured the full moon, the 1st Parallel was dug from the head of Yorktown to the York River. Washington started the digging. When a support trench was dug North of the French half, information supplied by a French deserter enabled the Fusiliers Redoubt to fire on the diggers.

10/9/1781: At 3 PM, with all their siege guns in place, the French began a barrage, driving HMS Guadalupe across the York River, where she was scuttled. At 5 PM, Washington fired the first gun of the American barrage. He ordered that the guns be fired all night. The British guns on the left were soon silenced. Some shells damaged British ships in the harbor. The British took shelter in their trenches. Many deserted.

10/10/1781: Cornwallis sank over a dozen of his ships in the harbor. French fire ignited HMS Charon. That set 2-3 other ships afire too. Clinton's message that the British Fleet would leave New York on 10/12 was received. Cornwallis stated that he could not hold out for long.

10/11/1781: After nightfall, the Americans dug the Washington-ordered 2nd Parallel—400 yards closer to Yorktown than the 1st. Redoubts 9 and 10 were in the way, so the 2nd Parallel could not be extended to the river. The British did not detect the digging and fired at the old line all night. By morning, the attackers were in position on the new line.

10/14/1781: With the trenches within 50 yards of Redoubts 9 and 10, Washington ordered all guns within range to fire at them all day—to weaken them for an attack during the coming moonless night. To better assure surprise, he ordered the attackers to fix bayonets and to not load their muskets before reaching the redoubts.

The redoubts were fortified by abatis (rows of tree trunks and/or sturdy branches, aligned to provide a barrier against attack and with sharpened ends pointed outward to impale attackers). Each Redoubt also had a surrounding muddy ditch about 25 yards away. Redoubt 9, a quarter-mile inland, had 120 defenders, and was attacked by 400 French soldiers led by the Count of Deux-Ponts. Redoubt 10, near the river, had 70 defenders, and was attacked by 400 infantrymen led by LtCol. Alexander Hamilton.

At 6:30 PM, a French diversionary attack was made on the Fusiliers' Redoubt. And movements consistent with an assault on the town were made along the lines to mislead the defenders. At 7 PM, simultaneous assaults were made on Redoubts 9 and 10.

When Hamilton's force began chopping the Redoubt 10 abatis, a British sentry challenged and then fired at them. They charged with fixed bayonets, hacked through the abatis, crossed the ditch, and stood on the shoulders of their mates to get onto the Redoubt. One shouted *Rush on boys, the Fort's ours!* They took the Redoubt, capturing most of its garrison and Major Campbell, its Commander, at a cost of 8 dead and 25 wounded.

The French assault on Redoubt 9 was halted by the abatis, which the artillery fire hadn't damaged. When they hacked at them, a Hessian sentry came out, asked who was there, and he and the Hessians on the parapet opened fire. The French returned fire and charged. The Germans then charged them as they climbed over the parapet, but a French volley drove the Germans back. The Hessians took defensive positions behind barrels, and surrendered when the French prepared a bayonet charge.

Putting artillery onto the Redoubts enabled bombarding Yorktown from three directions. The Americans and French competed to see who could most damage the defenses.

10/15/1781: Cornwallis turned all his guns on the attackers' nearest position and sent Col. Robert Abercromby and 350 men to storm out and spike (hammer an iron plug into the touchhole of) enemy cannons. They caught the artillerymen asleep, and charged with Abercromby's shout: *Push on my brave boys, and skin the bastards!* The six guns they spiked before being repulsed by the French were repaired overnight.

10/16/1781: More siege guns were added. The bombardment intensified. Cornwallis tried to evacuate across the York River to Gloucester Point, hoping to break out and march to New York. One wave of boats did get across, but a squall halted the evacuation. Cornwallis and his officers conferenced and agreed that their situation was hopeless.

10/17/1781: An officer waving a white handkerchief came out. The barrage stopped.

10/18/1781: Surrender negotiations began between LtCol. Thomas Dundas and Major Alexander Ross (for the British), LtCol. Laurens (for the Americans) and the Marquis de Noailles (for the French, for whom Washington ordered equal participation). At 2 PM, the victorious army entered the British positions.

10/19/1781: The British request for traditional honors, which they had not given to the Americans defeated at Charleston, was refused by Washington. They marched out with flags furled and muskets shouldered, to a *British or German march* instead of, with flags flying and fixed bayonets, to an American or French tune honoring the victors.

Brig. Gen. Charles O'Hara represented the reputedly ill Cornwallis at the Surrender. He offered his sword to Rochambeau, who shook his head and pointed to Washington, who also refused and had Maj. Gen. Benjamin Lincoln (who had surrendered at Charleston) take the surrender. Lincoln briefly held the sword and returned it.

The British marched out in new uniforms, some weeping, some drunkenly. Until O'Hara stopped it, some threw their muskets down between the French and Americans, as if to smash them instead of laying them down.

Cornwallis estimated that half his men had been unable to fight because of malaria. But its month-long incubation period resulted in very few French soldiers being incapacitated, and it didn't affect many Americans because most were resistant.

Britain suffered 156 dead, 326 wounded, 70 missing, and surrendered 6000 soldiers, 214 artillery pieces, thousands of muskets, 24 transport ships, and horses and wagons. The French had 60 dead and 194 wounded. The U.S. had 28 dead and 107 wounded.

The Articles of Capitulation were signed by Washington for the U.S, Rochambeau for the French Army, the Comte de Barras for the French Navy, Cornwallis for the British Army, and Captain Thomas Symonds for the Royal Navy. British officers were paroled and allowed to return home. British troops were taken prisoner and promised good treatment.

That evening, the American and French officers entertained the British officers at dinner with civility. Some French officers were said to have offered their sympathy to the British. The coolness of the British under the circumstances was remarked upon.

10/24/1781: Graves' fleet arrived to rescue Cornwallis. Learning of the surrender and seeing that the French fleet outnumbered his by nine ships, Graves returned to New York.

Philadelphia celebrated for several days when Congress was informed of the victory. British Prime Minister Lord North's reputed reaction was: *Oh God, it's all over.*

Washington moved his army to New Windsor, New York. No additional significant campaign or battle occurred. In March 1782, Parliament agreed to cease hostilities. The war formally ended with the Treaty of Paris on 9/3/1783.[288]

4
Slavery and Dominance

4.1 Basic Aspects

An awareness of the roles of Dominance and of Slavery is necessary to understand one's own and mankind's history.

Exercising power over others is common human behavior. That encompasses good (moral), evil, and in-between aspects, including war, criminality, altruism, leadership, salesmanship, law enforcement, punishment, con-artistry, Slavery, etc.

Slaves live miserably because of the Master's corruption and absolute power. Lord Acton described that as: *Power tends to corrupt. Absolute power corrupts absolutely.* And Slavery was the lot of most Blacks in the U.S. until the Emancipation Proclamation became effective on 1/1/1863. But there still are over 20 million Slaves in Africa, Asia, and the Middle East.[289] Moreover, child and sexual Slavery still exists in the U.S.

4.2 Slavery's Beginnings

Human anatomy has changed little in 120,000 years.[290] And Evolutionary Psychology holds that we inhabit a modern world with the ingrained mentality of Stone Age (~3.4 million year ago) hunter-gatherers.[291] Human Slavery very probably began in archaic humans or in our antecessor species—long before anatomically modern humans (AMHs) developed. [Other than among humans, only a few ant species practice Slavery.] Some more recent aspects of Slavery's known history[292] follow:

> **6800 B.C.** The first city-state emerged in Mesopotamia. Land ownership and the technology of the day brought war—with enemies being captured and enslaved.
> **2575 B.C.** Temple art showed Egypt's capture of Slaves in battle.
> **550 B.C.** The city-state of Athens used as many as 30,000 Slaves in its silver mines.
> **120 A.D.** Rome captured thousands of Slaves, and may have been over half-Slave.

500. Anglo-Saxons invaded England and enslaved the Britons.

1000. Destitute agricultural workers and their families placed themselves in a form of debt bondage to landowners.

1380. Europe's Slave trade thrived in the labor shortage after the Black Plague, The Slaves came from all over Europe, the Middle East, and North Africa.

1444. Portuguese sea traders brought a large cargo of Slaves from West Africa to Europe, beginning the Atlantic Slave Trade.

1526. Spanish explorers brought the first African Slaves to what is now the United States. They staged the first known Slave revolt in the Americas.

1550. Slaves were depicted as conspicuous consumption objects in Renaissance art.

1641. Massachusetts became the first British colony to legalize Slavery.

4.3 American Slavery

Amerinds sometimes enslaved conquered Amerinds instead of killing them. Some of those Slaves were allowed to assimilate into or be adopted by their conquerors' tribes, and some became roughly equivalent to indentured servants. The Amerinds' Slaves were in some cases considered ethnically inferior. But it was not Amerind practice to buy or sell them until, after contact with Europeans, some Amerinds adopted the chattel property aspect of Slavery.[293]

Colonists enslaved Amerinds before and after Black Slaves were imported. According to Brown University Associate History Professor Lindford D. Fisher, from 1492 to 1880, some 2-5.5 million Amerinds were enslaved in addition to 12.5 million Africans.[294] Enslaving Amerinds was a failure because many escaped and hid among neighboring tribes—or were stricken by the White Man's diseases. The recourse was Black Slavery.

When the *White Lion*, an English privateer, arrived at present Hampton, Virginia in August 1619 with "20 and odd" African captives "bought for victuals." Governor Sir George Yeardley and merchant Abraham Piersey bought most of them. and kept them in Jamestown. The early Black Slaves were valued for their farming skills and labor. They associated with other laborers, and many ran away together.[295]

England, France, Holland, Spain, Portugal, and Denmark brought Black Slaves to the Americas. The Massachusetts Slave trade began after a Slave voyage sailed from Boston in 1644. Rhode Island joined in about 1700. Colonial Slave ships carried sugar and molasses from Caribbean plantations to New England, where it was distilled into rum. The rum was taken to Africa and traded for Slaves, who were taken to the Caribbean and traded for sugar and molasses. By the 1750s, over 20 ships a year were sailing from New England (mostly from Newport) and the two-thirds of Rhode Island's fleet making Slave voyages made up over 60% of the Colonial Transatlantic Slave Trade.

Most Black Slaves ended up on sugar plantations in the Caribbean and South America. But ~500,000 of them ended up on the North American mainland. By 1755, the high cost and lack of Colonial labor resulted in there being over 13,000 Black Slaves in New England. In Connecticut, Massachusetts, and Rhode Island, it is likely that, by the mid-18th Century, there were as many as one Black for every four White families. And many prominent New England merchants made vast fortunes from the slave trade.[296]

An extreme example of the hardships faced by enslaved Blacks enroute to the Americas was the abortive 15-month voyage of the Slave ship *Sally*. Her Captain was Esek Hopkins, a member of a prominent Rhode Island family (his brother became Rhode Island's Governor in 1755). Esek had been a privateer during the French and Indian War, and became Commander-in-Chief of the United States' Revolutionary War Navy. When he arrived in the West Indies on *Sally*, 109 of his 196-Slave cargo had died and the rest were in such poor condition that they sold for very little.[297]

Slavery was most advantageous to those who, like plantation owners, could work Slaves profitably and breed replacements. [There were few, if any, such estates in Southern Delaware, where poor soil made hardscrabble farming common.]

[That well-treated people work better had to have disposed some Slave owners against cruelty. But the myth of natural (God-given) White superiority and cruelty continued to scourge *the American Dream* long after Slavery was abolished.]

Rhode Island and Connecticut prohibited the overseas Slave trade in 1774, without banning inter-Colony Slave trading. Vermont banned Slavery 1n 1777—and moved to provide full voting rights for Blacks while still allowing the existing Slavery to continue. (Vermonters did not want to remain a Crown Colony, but were not eager to join the United States.) [298] The Colonial Abolition Movement had begun much earlier—with the *1688 Germantown Quaker Petition Against Slavery*. Georgia, the last of the original 13 Colonies, initially prohibited Slavery. Pennsylvania passed *An Act for the Gradual Abolition of Slavery* in 1780. But most early Anti-Slavery laws prohibited the Transatlantic Slave Trade, not Slavery itself.[299]

Inferiority-alleging denigration of Blacks was still part of the culture of lower Delaware when I grew up. [My Polish-descended mother nonetheless expressly forbade it.] Until 1954, Delaware had the *Separate but Equal* schools for Blacks instituted when Slavery was abolished. The schools weren't equal, and neither was Black opportunity. And the White culture also suffered from conformity to: *Bad men need nothing more to compass their ends, than that good men should look on and do nothing.*[300] [Two-thirds of a century has passed since I lived in Delmarva. But old ways die hard and I would be unsurprised to hear instances of the N-word used epithetically there by some Whites.]

4.4 Thomas Jefferson's Ambivalence

The conflict between Slavery and Freedom is very apparent in the life of Thomas Jefferson (4/13/1743-7/4/1826). He entered William and Mary College at age 16, graduated in two years, and became a lawyer, diplomat, statesman, architect, philosopher, plantation owner, Founding Father, our 2nd Vice-President, our 3rd President, and the founder of the University of Virginia. At the age of 21, he took over full control of his inherited 5000-acre estate. When he was 29, he married his 3rd cousin, Martha (Wayles) Skelton, a 23-year-old widow who had borne two children who didn't survive. Martha was Jefferson's household manager and hostess, and a skilled pianist whom Thomas often accompanied on the violin or cello. Their reportedly very happy 10-year marriage ended when Martha, a diabetic, after bearing Thomas six children, died in 1782 at the age of 33—a few months after the birth of her eighth child, and 19 years before Thomas Jefferson became President. He never remarried.[301]

Only two of Martha Wales Skelton Jefferson's children, Martha and Mary, lived to adulthood. Their mother, before dying, copied the following lines from Laurence Stern's *Tristam Shandy*:

Time wastes too fast: every letter
I trace tells me with what rapidity
life follows my pen. The days and hours
of it are flying over our heads like
clouds of windy day never to return–
more. Every thing presses on–

To that, her husband added:

and every time I kiss thy hand to bid adieu, every absence which follows it,
are preludes to that eternal separation which we are shortly to make!

And he began her gravestone epitaph with Greek lines from Homer's *Iliad*. Translated:

Nay if even in the house of Hades the dead forget their dead,
yet will I even there be mindful of my dear comrade.

Thomas and Martha Jefferson's great-granddaughter Sarah N. Randolph stated:

Mrs. Jefferson is said to have been a singularly beautiful woman, and a person
of great intelligence and strength of character; and certainly, if the attractions
of a woman can be measured by the love borne her by her husband, hers
must have been great indeed, for never was a wife loved with more passionate
devotion than she was by Jefferson

There are many more eulogizations of Martha Wales Skelton Jefferson.[302]

Thomas Jefferson had an insatiable desire for fine things, kept redoing his home at Monticello for 40 years, spent the equivalent of over $1 million a year today on fine French, Spanish, and Italian wines, and spent prolifically on artwork, musical instruments, and books. His income never kept up with his expenditures and he died deep in debt. Thomas Jefferson Randolph, his oldest grandson and sole heir, sold everything he inherited from his grandfather and spent most of his life working to pay off that debt.[303]

Owning close to 200 Slaves at a time and about 600 overall made Thomas Jefferson the 2nd largest Slaveowner in Albemarle County, Virginia. He manumitted (formally freed) only two—males trained and qualified to hold employment. In his will, he freed five more: his Slave Sally Hemings' two youngest sons, her younger half-brother John Hemings, and her nephews Joseph Fosset and Burwell Colbert. (John and Joe each got an acre of land to build homes on and Burwell received $300 for supplies to be used in the *painter and glazier* trade.) When Jefferson died in 1826, his family then granted unofficial freedom (*their time*) to Sally Hemings and Wormley Hughes (Betty Hemings' grandson and Thomas Jefferson's head gardener). The rest of Thomas Jefferson's Slaves were sold at auction. So, in contrast with the post-revolutionary war increase in the number of free Blacks in Virginia from under 1% in 1782 to 7.2% in 1810, Thomas Jefferson formally freed only two of his Slaves (~0.3%) during his lifetime.[304]

A part of Jefferson's draft of the *Declaration of Independence* condemned King George for Slavery and was deleted by the Continental Congress. It stated:

> *he has waged cruel war against human nature itself, violating it's most sacred rights of life and liberty in the persons of a distant people who never offended him, captivating and carrying them into Slavery in another hemispere, or to incure miserable death in their transportation hither. this piratical warfare, the opprobium of infidel powers, is the warfare of the Christian king of Great Britain. [determined to keep open a market where MEN should be bought and sold,] he has prostituted his negative for suppressing every legislative attempt to prohibit or to restrain this execrable commerce; and that this assemblage of horrors might want no fact of distinguished die, he is now exciting those very people to rise in arms among us, and to purchase that liberty of which he had deprived them, by murdering the people upon whom he also obtruded them: thus paying off former crimes committed against the liberties of one people, with crimes which he urges them to commit against the lives of another.[305]*

Jefferson's autobiography further shows his moral opposition to Slavery by commenting on why the Anti-Slavery clause was deleted from the *Declaration of Independence*:

> *The clause...reprobating the enslaving the inhabitants of Africa, was struck out in compliance to South Carolina and Georgia, who had never attempted to restrain the importation of Slaves, and who on the contrary still wished to continue it. Our Northern brethren also I believe felt a little tender under these censures; for tho' their people have very few Slaves themselves, yet they had been pretty considerable carriers of them to others.[306]*

Jefferson's views on Slavery are apparent In his:[307]

- Earlier view that Blacks are naturally inferior to other races.
- Unsuccessfully advocating, as a young Virginia legislator, allowing citizens to free their Slaves, but later introducing a bill barring free Blacks from living in Virginia.
- Signing, as President, a bill outlawing the Transatlantic Slave trade.
- Writing, about Slavery, that: *Indeed I tremble for my country when I reflect that God is just; that his justice cannot sleep forever.* (Notes on the State of Virginia, 1782)
- Believing that most former Slaves could not survive independently.
- Fearing for his economic survival and the safety of Whites at the mercy of former Slaves who had experienced *unremitting despotism* and *degrading submissions.*

- Advocating, as an older man, freeing Slaves and returning them to Africa.
- Writing *There is nothing I would not sacrifice to a practicable plan of abolishing this moral and political depravity.* (Letter to Thomas Cooper, September 1814)
- Writing *Nobody wishes more than I do to see such proofs as you exhibit, that nature has given to our black brethren, talents equal to those of other colors of men, and that the appearance of a want of them is owing merely to the degraded condition of their existence.* (Letter to Banneker, August 30, 1791.)

In 1802, the year after Jefferson became President, James Callender, a (reputedly scandalmongering[308]) political journalist, reported that Jefferson fathered the children of the Slave Sally Hemings. There is no record of Jefferson's public denial of that, but he did not reply to political attacks, and several members of his family did deny it. For example, in the 1850s (decades after Thomas Jefferson's death), Thomas Jefferson Randolph said that Peter Carr, Jefferson's nephew (a son of his sister) had fathered Sally's children. And most major historians denied Thomas Jefferson's alleged paternity for the next 150 years.[309] {The oral tradition of the family of Thomas Woodson (1790-1879) is that he too is a son of Thomas Jefferson and Sally Hemings.}

British common law passed down a British father's Free or Slave status to his children. Free British Men were legally required to acknowledge their children born in or out of wedlock, support them with food, shelter, and financially, and arrange an apprenticeship that would enable them (male or female) to become self-supporting adults. But Africans and non-White foreigners were not British Subjects. And mixed-race children in the Colonies—who were generally not Christians—were considered foreigners without legal rights. Also, the subjecthood or citizenship of children of a British White man and an enslaved Black woman was beyond the authority of the Colonial Governments.

The Roman Civil Law doctrine of *Partus sequiter ventrum* (status follows the belly) makes a child's status that of the mother. It was used by the Dutch, Spanish, French, and Portuguese to enslave, as personal property (chattels personal), indigenous peoples of the Americas and Africa. As passed into law in 1662 in Virginia and adopted by the other North American Colonies, it enslaved every child of a Slave woman. That:

- Eliminated a White father's requirement to feed and shelter his Slave children.
- Made the enslaved their owner's chattels with no rights.
- Provided cheap manual labor to serve the increasing demand.
- Legitimized involuntary concubinage. (Slaves over age 11 legally had to accept a master's sexual advances.)
- Presaged permitting Slavery in the United States until 12/6/1865.

Partus sequiter ventrum also made the mixed-race children of White Women (including children of indentured servants) free people of color.

White Colonists had, by 1700, fathered many Half-White, Three-Quarter-White, and Seven-Eighth-White Slaves. The Virginia planter John Wayles (1715-1775) had over 100 Slaves including six Three-Quarter-White Slaves whom he sired with his Slave concubine Elizabeth (Betty) Hemings, a Half-White daughter of an English Sea Captain surnamed

Hemings and a Black Slave. Martha (Eppes) Wayles' daughter Martha (1748-1782) and her husband Thomas Jefferson inherited Wayles' Slaves when he died in 1773. The Half-White Slaves born to Betty Hemings and John Wales were Martha's half-siblings and the half-sisters-in-law and half-brothers-in-law (and distant cousins) of Thomas Jefferson. The youngest of those was Sally Hemings (1773-1835).

Sally, aside from being a companion to Martha Jefferson's daughters, apparently received typical House Slave treatment at Monticello. But her children with a White father were Seven-Eighths White, making them legally White (if their mother wasn't a Slave).

[There's no apparent record of Sally's cohabitation with Thomas Jefferson or any other potential father of her children. There also seems to be no alleged fathering of any other Slave's children by Thomas Jefferson.]

When Sally Hemings was "freed" after Thomas Jefferson died, she lived in Charlottesville with her sons Madison and Eston. The 1830 census listed them as free.[310]

The majority view appears to be that Thomas Jefferson "probably" sired Eston Hemings and "likely" sired Sally's other children. [311, 312, 313]

According to her son Madison, Sally's first child was born when she was 16, was fathered by Thomas Jefferson, and did not live long. {Thomas Jefferson was a widower for 13 years when Sally was 16.) Sally's children of record do not include that child and were:

- Harriet, b.1795 when Sally was 22, died in infancy.
- An unnamed daughter who died in infancy (1-2 years after the first Harriet)
- Beverly, b.1798 (1-2 years after the unnamed daughter) when Sally was 25. He was trained as a carpenter, schooled, allowed to leave Monticello as a White Man at age 22, moved to Washington, married a White woman, and raised a family.[314]
- Harriet (1801-1863). Reputedly beautiful, born (3 years after Beverly) when Sally was 28. Unofficially freed by Thomas Jefferson in 1822 at the age of 21 and given $50 for her journey to Washington (~120 road miles away), she was the only female Slave freed by Thomas Jefferson during his lifetime, and entered White "Society." [315]
- Madison (1805-1877). Born four years after Harriet and freed (at age 21) in 1826 by Thomas Jefferson's will, Madison went to Charlottesville (~4 road miles from Monticello) and married a free woman of color. Sally lived with them until she died in 1835. They then lived in Chillicothe, Ohio, where he worked as a farmer and skilled carpenter. Two of their 10 children were in the Union Army in the Civil War—one was in the *Colored Troops*, the other enlisted as a White Man.[316]
- Eston (1808-1856). Born three years after Madison, Eston was a cabinetmaker and musician. He was freed in 1827 (at age 19) by Thomas Jefferson's will and moved to Charlottesville, where he and his brother Madison purchased a lot, built a two-story wood and brick house, and lived with their mother. Eston married Julia Ann Isaacs, a free woman of color, in 1832. They sold their property and moved to Chillicothe, Ohio about 1838. Eston led a very successful dance band there and was considered a master of the violin and an accomplished "caller" of dances. About 1852, Eston and Julia and their three children took the surname Jefferson, moved to Madison, Wisconsin, and lived as Whites. Eston worked as a cabinetmaker there.[317] His and Julia's son John Wales Jefferson, a restauranteur and hotel manager, joined the Civil

War Union Army as a Major in the 8th Wisconsin infantry regiment, rose to Colonel in three years of fighting, and commanded the regiment for a time. He reportedly asked an Ohio acquaintance to not reveal his colored blood because no one in the regiment suspected it. After the war he settled in Memphis, Tennessee and became a prominent citizen, plantation owner, and wealthy cotton broker. He died in Memphis, where his obituary described him as a model man.[318] Eston's younger son, Frederick Beverly Jefferson, was a private in Company E of the 1st Wisconsin infantry regiment in 1861. Otherwise, he was a respected businessman, a Mason, a member of the Grand Army of the Republic (a Union veteran fraternal club) and a member of the Old Settlers Club (of Milwaukee County).[319]

A Thomas Jefferson Foundation analysis of the 1998 Y-DNA study of Jefferson DNA asserts that the study is reputable, meets current scientific standards, and compared 19 Chromosome markers of 5 male-line descendants of two sons of Thomas Jefferson's paternal uncle Field Jefferson, 3 male-line descendants of three sons of John Carr (Samuel and Peter Carr's grandfather), 5 male-line descendants of two sons of Thomas Woodson, and 1 male-line descendant of Eston Hemings.

[Males inherit their father's Y Chromosome genes intact (except for mutations). So, for example, cousins who are sons of brothers with the same father have the same male chromosome.] The male-line descendants of Field Jefferson and Eston Hemings Jefferson have identical Y Chromosomes—with less than 1% (one source says 0.1%) odds of that occurring by chance, making it ~100-1000 times more likely that Eston and Field are patrilineally related rather than by chance. So there's an ~99-99.9% chance that Eston Hemings' father was a Jefferson. [But because of the unlikely possibility that Thomas Jefferson's father and Field Jefferson had different fathers, Thomas Jefferson is not certainly the father of Eston.] Other known non-fathers of Eston include:

- Peter and Samuel Carr—because the Carr and Jefferson Y-DNA does not match.
- Thomas Woodson—because the Jefferson and Woodson Y-DNA does not match.

The study did not include John Wayles. (Daughters do not inherit Y-DNA.) Analysis of five local "old Virginia families" showed none that matched the Jefferson Y-DNA, which is considered quite rare. A few adult Jeffersons with that Y-DNA visited Monticello.[320]

[Among the considerations in whether Thomas Jefferson fathered Sally's children are:

- Prominent politicians get a lot of negative press, much valid, much not.
- Self-aggrandizing claims of having a prominent ancestor occur.
- Agenda-driven advocacy may invalidly ignore or contradict contrary information.
- There is no DNA evidence showing that that any other child of Sally Hemings was sired by a man with the same Y-DNA as Field Jefferson.
- That a widower in his mid-40s would begin a lasting affinity for and sexual relationship with the teenage half-sister of his beloved deceased wife is not far-fetched, especially when she is quite like his wife in appearance and voice (as has been claimed) and legally obliged to accept his sexual advances. (That's a *could be*, not a *did*.)

- There is no apparent evidence of Thomas Jefferson and Sally Hemings cohabitating.
- There was no Slavery in France when Sally Hemings was a companion to then U.S. Ambassador to France Thomas Jefferson's daughters in Paris. But Slaves who came to France had to apply for their freedom, and Sally did not. She did, however, live free and was (under)paid for her services there by Thomas Jefferson. Her return to Slavery in America (reputedly with the promise that her children would be freed at age 21) has been attributed to her attachment to her enslaved relatives in Virginia. But the lure of freedom is gigantic, and it seems unlikely that her feelings for her half-brother-in-law Thomas Jefferson played no significant role in her voluntary return to enslavement. Also, even free women were virtual chattels then, and being free in France may not have been as good a prospect as life at Monticello.
- Early assertions about Thomas Jefferson siring Sally Hemings' children were based on observed physical similarities.
- Elijah Fletcher (1789-1858) was an ~22-year-old bachelor when he met Jefferson at Monticello before going ~50 miles Southwest to Clifford to teach school.[321] In 1811, Elijah wrote: *the story of Black Sal is no farce – That [Jefferson] cohabits with her and has a number of children with her is a sacred truth.*[322] [Stating how he knew they shared the same bed could have made Elijah's allegation more convincing.]

An impartial jury might well conclude that Thomas Jefferson fathered Eston Hemmings but a reasonable doubt existed about Sally's other children. But Thomas Jefferson was and is venerated as the author of the *Declaration of Independence* and as one of the most prominent Founding Fathers—and also was and is a symbol of White enslavement of Blacks. So empaneling an unbiased jury to judge him was and is very unlikely, even in a civil trial where the standard is a preponderance of the evidence—not the absence of reasonable doubt. Nonetheless, the following circumstances might sway a reviewer into concluding that all of Sally Hemings' children were sired by Thomas Jefferson:

- The seven Slaves freed by Thomas Jefferson were all descended from Sally Hemings' mother Betty Hemings, included all four of Sally's surviving children, and represent only ~1.2% of the ~600 Slaves that Thomas Jefferson owned.
- After Thomas Jefferson's death, Martha's children freed Sally Hemings.
- Sally Hemings was a half-sister of Thomas Jefferson's beloved wife and chose returning from France to Virginia with him over freedom.

Whatever it was, Thomas Jefferson's relationship with Sally Hemings doesn't change the reality that ill-use and abuse of Slaves was (and is) common and there was (and is) strong Abolitionism among Slavers' peers. [U.S. Slavery's legality was based on political power—and myths of Black inferiority and any Black ancestry constituting Blackness. But many Blacks are genetically far more White than Black. And if **any** Black ancestry makes a person Black, the African origin of our species makes all of us Black.]

When Thomas Jefferson penned the *Declaration of Independence*, ~500,000 Black Slaves made up ~20% of the population of the North and ~40% of the population of the South. Jefferson owned ~100 Slaves then, but called Slavery a *hideous blot* on America.

He wasn't alone in such hypocrisy. George Washington said that Slavery was *repugnant* but his hundreds of (reputedly very well treated) Slaves weren't freed until he died. And James Mason, another Virginia Slave owner, condemned Slavery as "evil." But the South's tobacco, indigo, and rice crops—and then cotton—brought wealth and the determination to retain Slavery.[323]

4.5 Slavery and the Articles of Confederation

The Articles of Confederation, adopted in 1777 and ratified in 1783, established a weak Central United States Government. Each State had one vote, and most governmental power remained in the individual States. Slavery (as property and as persons) was protected in its Article IV as follows:

> *The better to secure and perpetuate mutual friendship and intercourse among the people of the different States in this Union, the free inhabitants of each of these States, paupers, vagabonds, and fugitives from justice excepted, shall be entitled to all privileges and immunities of free citizens in the several States; and the people of each State shall free ingress and regress to and from any other State, and shall enjoy therein all the privileges of trade and commerce, subject to the same duties, impositions, and restrictions as the inhabitants thereof respectively, provided that such restrictions shall not extend so far as to prevent the removal of property imported into any State, to any other State, of which the owner is an inhabitant; provided also that no imposition, duties or restriction shall be laid by any State, on the property of the United States, or either of them.*
>
> *If any person guilty of, or charged with, treason, felony, or other high misdemeanor in any State, shall flee from justice, and be found in any of the United States, he shall, upon demand of the Governor or executive power of the State from which he fled, be delivered up and removed to the State having jurisdiction of his offense.*
>
> *Full faith and credit shall be given in each of these States to the records, acts, and judicial proceedings of the courts and magistrates of every other State.*[324]

4.6 Slavery and the Constitution

In May 1787, during the writing of the U.S. Constitution, the more populous States wanted both the House and the Senate to be apportioned based on population. Smaller States wanted each State to have one vote in each House. The compromise gave each State two Senators and based each State's membership in the House on population—a major issue because population determined a State's number of House members, electoral votes, and the amount of tax it paid to the Federal Government. So the Slavery-enriched Southern States wanted to count Slaves and the Northern States didn't. The compromise was to count a Slave as three-fifths of a person in the census by inserting the following as U.S. Constitution Article I, Section 2, Clause 3:

> *Representatives and direct Taxes shall be apportioned among the several States which may be included within this Union, according to their respective Numbers, which shall be determined by adding to the whole Number of free Persons, including those bound to Service for a Term of Years, and excluding Indians not taxed, three fifths of all other Persons.*[325]

Until enough new territories became Free States, that gave the South much Congressional and Executive Power.[326] All 12 pre-Civil War Presidents except John Adams and John Quincy Adams owned Slaves.[327] And of the first 12 Presidents only John Adams (#2) and John Quincy Adams (#6) of Massachusetts, and Martin Van Buren (#8) of New York were from a Northern State.[328]

Importing Slaves was a Constitutional issue too. Ten States had banned that, but Georgia and both Carolinas threatened to walk out of the Constitutional Convention if that Slave Trade was banned. The compromise became Constitution Article I, Section 9, Clause I:

> *The Migration or Importation of such Persons as any of the States now existing shall think proper to admit, shall not be prohibited by the Congress prior to the Year one thousand eight hundred and eight, but a Tax or duty may be imposed on such Importation, not exceeding ten dollars for each Person.*[329]

In the five years before Congress overwhelmingly banned the International Slave Trade in 1808, South Carolina imported 40,000 Slaves.

The original U.S. Constitution also protected the International Slave Trade by specifying:

ARTICLE V. SECTION 1, CLAUSE 9:

> *The Congress, whenever two thirds of both houses shall deem it necessary, shall propose amendments to this Constitution, or, on the application of the legislatures of two thirds of the several states, shall call a convention for proposing amendments, which, in either case, shall be valid to all intents and purposes, as part of this Constitution, when ratified by the legislatures of three fourths of the several states, or by conventions in three fourths thereof, as the one or the other mode of ratification may be proposed by the Congress; provided that no amendment which may be made prior to the year one thousand eight hundred and eight shall in any manner affect the first and fourth clauses in the ninth section of the first article; and that no state, without its consent, shall be deprived of its equal suffrage in the Senate.*[330]

On 3/2/1807, Congress passed a bill that banned importing Slaves from any foreign place into any place under the jurisdiction of the United States. President Thomas Jefferson, who had promoted such legislation since the 1770s, signed that bill. It became effective on 1/1/1808, by which time all States except South Carolina had also abolished that Slave trade. But illegal importation of an estimated additional 50,000 Slaves into our Southern States occurred.[331] In 1859, *Clotilda* became the last *known* Slave ship to land on U.S. soil. The Africans she carried to Mobile, Alabama were sold as Slaves. (Matilda McCrear, *Clotilda's* last known survivor, died in 1940.)[332]

In regard to fugitive Slaves, the Constitution provided:

ARTICLE IV, SECTION 2, CLAUSE 3

No Person held to Service or Labour in one State, under the Laws thereof, escaping into another, shall, in Consequence of any Law or Regulation therein, be discharged from such Service or Labour, but shall be delivered up on Claim of the Party to whom such Service or Labour may be due.[333]

[Thus was Slavery permitted and protected by, and camouflaged In, the Constitution.]

4.7   The Northwest Ordinance

Abolitionists failed to get Slavery banned in the Colonies and in the original 13 States, but strove to ban its spread. Despite the South's knowledge that banning Slavery in new States would make the South progressively weaker politically, in 1789 the first U.S. Congress prohibited Slavery in the Northwest Territory by enacting the 1784 Northwest Ordinance of the Confederation Congress. That made the Ohio River the boundary between Free and Slave States from the Appalachians to the Mississippi River,[334] banning Slavery in U.S.-owned land West of Pennsylvania, East of the Mississippi River, and Northwest of the Ohio River. But for the quid pro quo of shipping and trade concessions for the New England States, the following fugitive Slave provision was put in as Article IV, Section 2, Clause 3 of the Constitution:

No Person held to Service or Labour in one State, under the Laws thereof, escaping into another, shall, in Consequence of any Law or Regulation therein, be discharged from such Service or Labour, but shall be delivered up on Claim of the Party to whom such Service or Labour may be due.[335]

Prohibiting Slavery in the Territories would have doomed the South's Electoral College advantage—and fostered ending Slavery. [But the Abolitionists' hope that Slavery would die out was doomed by its profitability.]

4.8 The Missouri Compromise

By 1820, there were 11 Free and 11 Slave States. Trying to balance the power between them led to the Missouri Compromise. It prohibited Slavery above 36° 30' N Latitude (allowing Missouri's admission as a Slave State and Maine's as a free one}.[336]

4.9 Nullification

Jefferson claimed that a State could nullify federal law that did not enact powers granted to the Federal Government by the Constitution. Resolutions to that effect were made in Virginia (Madison's wording) in 1788 and in Kentucky (Jefferson's wording) in 1789.

The 1828 Tariff of Abomination, as it was known in the South, protected Northern Industry by taxing imported goods by as much as 50%.[337] In 1829, John C. Calhoun of South Carolina, reputedly to protect the minority (a State) from majority (Federal) tyranny, further claimed that States only had to obey federal law when it was made an amendment to the Constitution and ratified by three-fourths of the States. When the Tariff of 1832 slightly modified the 1828 Tariff, South Carolina convened a Special Convention that, on 11/24/1832, declared the 1828 and 1832 Tariffs *null, void, and no law, nor binding upon this State, its officers or citizens.* Appealing such State action to Federal Court was forbidden. All State officeholders (except legislators) were required to take an oath of support for the ordinance. Secession was threatened if the federal government tried to collect tariff duties by force. No other State followed suit.

On 12/10/1832, President Jackson's *Proclamation to the People of South Carolina* asserted federal supremacy and warned that *disunion by armed force is treason.* On 3/1/1833 Congress passed the Force Bill authorizing the military to collect tariff duties and reducing the duties. Two weeks later, South Carolina rescinded its Nullification Ordinance but nullified the Force Bill three days later. The entire South then accepted the Tariff but was more acutely aware of Southern vulnerability to a Northern majority.[338]

4.10 Nat Turner's Rebellion (The Southampton Insurrection)

Nathanial (Nat) Turner (1800-1831), a Southampton County, Virginia Slave, had been sold three times as a child and was taught reading, writing, and religion. A fiery preacher and Slave leader, he believed in signs, in hearing divine voices, that he was chosen by God to lead the Slaves from bondage, and that a solar eclipse showed that the time had come. He and 10 other Slaves killed the Travis family on 8/21/1831, took their weapons and horses, enlisted ~75 more Slaves, and murdered ~55 more Whites. Nat hid for six weeks before being found, tried and convicted. He and 16 of his followers were hanged. Fifty-six other Blacks accused of participating in his Rebellion were executed. Over 200 more were beaten by White mobs and militias. The region's emancipation organization collapsed. Southern Anti-Abolitionism increased. New laws prohibited the education, movement, and assembly of Slaves.[339]

4.11 Reuben Crandall

Abolitionism in the United States proliferated from 1831 to 1835—when the two-year-old American Anti-Slavery Society mailed 175,000 pieces of Anti-Slavery literature across the country. On 7/25/1835, Amos Dresser was publicly whipped in Nashville, Tennessee for having such literature. On 7/30/1835, a mob broke into the Charleston, South Carolina Post Office and publicly burned Abolitionist literature. President Andrew Jackson and the Postmaster General supported Postmasters who refused to deliver it.

On 8/10/1835, Washington, D.C. Federal District Attorney Francis Scott Key (the *Star-Spangled Banner's* author and a Slave Owner) wrote the indictment for and had 29-year-old Reuben Crandall, M.D., arrested for seditious libel and inciting Slaves to revolt—the sedition being materials portraying Slavery as cruel and sinful. Crandall was jailed. The mayor had the militia surround the jail to avert the hanging of Crandall by a mob.

Crandall was tried eight months later. His defense was that he was not an Abolitionist, had opposed his educator sister's establishment of a school for Black girls, the Abolitionist literature had been taken from the attic of the family he lived with in Peekskill, New York and used by the lady of the family as packing materials for Crandall's belongings, and he had lent only one copy of the literature—to someone who had asked for it.

After a 10-day trial, the jury acquitted Crandall in three hours. That ended Francis Scott Key's political career. Crandall voluntarily remained in jail until he was smuggled out of Washington. After going to his parents' home in Connecticut, he went in late 1836 to Kingston, Jamaica—hoping to heal the tuberculosis that had infected him in jail. But it killed him in Kingston in January 1838, at the age of 32 years.[340]

4.12 The Snow Riot

On 7/25/1835, a Washington Navy Yard Mechanics' strike involving strong racial tension began. The strikers attacked Beverly Randolph Snow's *Epicurean Eating House* at the corner of 6th Street and Pennsylvania Avenue. Snow was an educated, mixed-race, manumitted Slave rumored to have insulted the mechanics' wives. Reputedly supported by sympathizers, the mob broke up and ransacked his restaurant, and drank all its whiskey and champagne. The Snows fled. White mobs continued to attack Black schools, churches, and businesses. The *United States Telegraph* stated: *The reason for all these attacks on the blacks is that they enter into competition for work at a lower rate.* President Jackson ordered a company of U.S. Marines to restore order. Mediation ended the strike on 8/15/1835 with little gain for the strikers. A new city ordinance banned Blacks from assembling after sundown. There was no compensation for damages.[341]

4.13 Elijah Parish Lovejoy

Elijah Lovejoy was the Valedictorian and a cum laude graduate of his Waterville College class. He was a school headmaster, a journalist, and a newspaper editor before studying at Princeton Theological Seminary in New Jersey and being ordained as a Presbyterian minister. He then returned to St. Louis, Missouri (a Slave State) and became the editor of the *St. Louis Observer*, a newspaper financed by his friends. In Spring 1834, his articles and editorials about the Catholic Church offended the city's large Catholic community. He also wrote critical articles on tobacco and liquor. Rumors of mob action against the *Observer* in October 1835 led prominent St. Louisans to ask him to stop discussing Slavery in the paper. He felt that martyrdom might result but refused.

In April 1836, Francis McIntosh, a mixed-race boatman, was arrested by two policemen. On the way to jail he grabbed a knife and stabbed them, killing one and seriously injuring the other. A mob caught him, tied him up, and burned him to death. Some mob members were brought before a Grand Jury presided over by Judge Lawless. He labeled the crime spontaneous with no one to prosecute, and insinuated that Lovejoy and the *Observer* were part of an Abolition group that had incited the stabbings. Lovejoy decided to move across the river to Alton, Illinois. (Illinois, a free State, had a strong Pro-Slavery contingent in Alton.) Before the move, the *Observer's* office was broken into and its press vandalized. Press remnants were put on the riverbank and thrown into the river overnight. (That was the third destruction of a Lovejoy press.) No police or city officials intervened.

In 1837, Lovejoy was the Upper Alton Presbyterian Church pastor. He became more strongly Anti-Slavery and started the Abolitionist *Alton Observer*. A March 1838 economic crisis prompted community speculation that his views contributed to hard times because harboring an Abolitionist could be having an adverse effect on business.

On 10/26/1837, Lovejoy held an Antislavery Conference at his church. On 11/7/1837, pro-Slavers approached the warehouse where Lovejoy's printing press was hidden. The *Observer* reported that the mob shot into the warehouse. Lovejoy and his men returned fire, hitting several and killing one. The attackers put up a ladder and sent a boy up it to torch the roof. Lovejoy and Royal Weller came out, pushed over the ladder, and retreated back into the warehouse. The ladder was put back. Lovejoy and Weller came out again. Weller was wounded. Lovejoy was killed by five shotgun slugs. The mob broke up his printing press and threw the pieces into the river.

John Quincy Adams stated that *the murder (gave) a shock as of an earthquake throughout the country.* John Brown said: *Here, before God, in the presence of these witnesses, from this time, I consecrate my life to the destruction of Slavery.* The *Boston Recorder* wrote that the event called forth from every part of the land *a burst of indignation which has not had its parallel in this country since the Battle of Lexington.*

The murder was prosecuted in Alton. The jury foreman was a mob member wounded in the attack. The presiding judge was a witness. The verdict was *Not Guilty.*[342]

4.14 Young Abraham Lincoln's Viewpoint

In 1/27/1838, 26-year-old, unmarried, Springfield, Illinois attorney Abraham Lincoln spoke the Young Men's Lyceum of Springfield. Part of that speech:

> *whenever the vicious portion of [our] population shall be permitted to gather in bands of hundreds and thousands, and burn churches, ravage and rob provision stores, throw printing-presses into rivers, shoot editors, and hang and burn obnoxious persons at pleasure and with impunity, depend upon it, this government cannot last. By such things the feelings of the best citizens will become more or less alienated from it, and thus it will be left without friends, or with too few, and those few too weak to make their friendship effectual.*

Lincoln continued by warning about tyranny:

> It is to deny what the history of the world tells us is true, to suppose that men of ambition and talents will not continue to spring up amongst us. And when they do, they will as naturally seek the gratification of their ruling passion as others have done before them. The question then is, Can that gratification be found in supporting and maintaining an edifice that has been erected by others? Most certainly it cannot. Many great and good men, sufficiently qualified for any task they should undertake, may ever be found whose ambition would aspire to nothing beyond a seat in Congress, a gubernatorial or a presidential chair; but such belong not to the family of the lion or the tribe of the eagle. What! think you these places would satisfy an Alexander, a Caesar, or a Napoleon? Never! Towering genius disdains a beaten path. It seeks regions hitherto unexplored. It sees no distinction in adding story to story upon the monuments of fame erected to the memory of others. It denies that it is glory enough to serve under any chief. It scorns to tread in the footsteps of any predecessor, however illustrious. It thirsts and burns for distinction; and if possible, it will have it, whether at the expense of emancipating Slaves or enslaving freemen. Is it unreasonable, then, to expect that some man possessed of the loftiest genius, coupled with ambition sufficient to push it to its utmost stretch, will at some time spring up among us? And when such an one does, it will require the people to be united with each other, attached to the government and laws, and generally intelligent, to successfully frustrate his designs. Distinction will be his paramount object, and although he would as willingly, perhaps more so, acquire it by doing good as harm, yet, that opportunity being past, and nothing left to be done in the way of building up, he would set boldly to the task of pulling down.

Lincoln also stated:

> Shall we expect some transatlantic military giant to step the ocean and crush
> us at a blow? Never! All the armies of Europe, Asia, and Africa combined, with
> all the treasure of the earth (our own excepted) in their military chest, with a
> Bonaparte for a commander, could not by force take a drink from the Ohio or
> make a track on the Blue Ridge in a trial of a thousand years. At what point
> then is the approach of danger to be expected? I answer. If it ever reach us
> it must spring up amongst us; it cannot come from abroad. If destruction be
> our lot we must ourselves be its author and finisher. As a nation of freemen
> we must live through all time or die by suicide.

Lincoln concluded by stating the need for *a political religion* with *reverence for the* laws
and reliance on *reason, cold, calculating, unimpassioned reason.*[343]

4.15 The Burning of Pennsylvania Hall

The religiously tolerant William Penn used the Greek words *phileo* (love) and *adelphosl*
(brother) to name Philadelphia. He also owned Slaves, exempted Blacks from many
Pennsylvania Charter protections, and excluded Catholics, Jews, and Muslims.[344]

Philadelphia became known as the *Cradle of Liberty* for hosting the Continental Congress
and the writing and signing of the *Declaration of Independence* and the U.S. Constitution.

In 1837-38, because they had a hard time finding meeting space, the Pennsylvania Anti-
Slavery Society built Pennsylvania Hall at Philadelphia's 109 N. 6th Street—near Independence
Hall, amidst a Quaker community that actively aided fugitive Slaves and strongly advocated
abolishing Slavery. Pennsylvania Hall's first floor held a 200–300-person lecture room; two
committee rooms; a reading room and bookstore; the office of the *Philadelphia Freeman,*
John Greenleaf Whittier's new Abolitionist paper; the Pennsylvania Anti-Slavery office; and
a store for selling products grown or produced by non-Slave labor. There was an auditorium
seating perhaps 3000 people on the second floor and three galleries on the third. The Hall's
appointments were luxurious, and Pennsylvania's motto, *Virtue, Liberty, and Independence*
was above the stage. The basement was to hold the as yet undelivered printing press for
the *Freeman.*

Meetings were held before the Hall's formal opening. Except for those held for women,
Blacks and Whites, male or female, were unseparated. That women and Blacks spoke to
audiences was viewed by some Philadelphians as a threat to social order.

One of the congratulatory letters read at the formal opening on May 14 was from former
President John Quincy Adams. It stated in part:

> *I learnt with great satisfaction...that the Pennsylvania Hall Association have
> erected a large building in your city, wherein liberty and equality of civil rights
> can be freely discussed, and the evils of Slavery fearlessly portrayed. ...I*

rejoice that, in the city of Philadelphia, the friends of free discussion have erected a Hall for its unrestrained exercise.

On Wednesday, May 16, some 50-60 people gathered outside the Hall and threatened the attendees, using increasingly abusive language. The crowd grew. Two watchmen were hired to keep the peace. That evening, with an audience of 3000 inside the Hall, the mob outside began smashing windows and breaking into the Hall. Whites and Blacks left the Hall arm in arm, through a hail of rocks and jeers.

On Thursday, May 17, the *Anti-Slavery Convention of American Women* refused Mayor John Swift's request to restrict attendance to White women and met in the Main Room. Three managers went to the Mayor to advise him of the problem and offer to name a mob ringleader. The Mayor said *There are always two sides to a question—it is public opinion that makes mobs—and 99 of a hundred of those with whom I converse are against you.* He also said that he would address the crowd but could do nothing further. In the early evening, the Hall was closed at the Mayor's request and the keys were delivered to him. He deferentially addressed the crowd, recommended that they go home to bed, wished them *a hearty good night,* and left amid cheers. About half an hour later, the mob forced the doors and set the Hall on fire. An eyewitness wrote that *No attempt of any kind was made to quell the riot.* Another wrote to the New Orleans *True American* stating:

> *A large number of splendid fire engines were immediately on the spot, many of which could throw water more than a hundred feet high: but the noble firemen, to a man, of all the numerous companies present, refused to throw one drop of water on the consuming building. All they did was to direct their engines to play upon the private buildings in the immediate vicinity of the blazing Hall, some of which were in great danger, as they were nearly joining the Hall. By the skil[l]ful exertion of these noble-hearted young men, however, no private property was suffered to receive the least damage — while the Hall was totally consumed with all its contents. Such conduct in the Philadelphia fire companies deserves the highest praise and gratitude of all the friends of the Union, and of all Southerners in particular.*

Another report said that the few firemen who tried to extinguish the fire were deterred by threats of violence and by the hoses of other firemen being turned on them. Also, the newspapers stated that most of the thousands who witnessed the conflagration were respectable and well-dressed and evidently watched approvingly—and that there was a universal shout of triumph when the roof of this noble temple of liberty fell in.

At night on Friday, May 18, strangers to the area set afire the Quaker *Shelter for Colored Children* at 13th Street above Callowhill. Total conflagration reportedly was averted *by the spirited conduct of the firemen and the police magistrate of the district.*

On Saturday evening, May 19, the Black, Bethel Church on South 6th Street, was attacked. Reportedly:

This would have shared the fate of Pennsylvania Hall, had not the Recorder of the city, with a spirit which does him great credit, interfered to do what the Mayor should have done on the first day, and forming a guard of well disposed citizens around the building, awed the rioters from their meditated violence.

Rewards were offered. They went unclaimed. Arrests were made. There were no trials. Philadelphia's official report blamed the fire and rioting on the Abolitionists, saying that they had encouraged *race mixing* and incited violence. Philadelphia County Sheriff John G. Watmough's report to the Governor stated:

I arrested with my own hands some ten or a dozen rioters; among them a sturdy blackguard engaged in forcing the doors with a log of wood, and a youth with a brand of fire in his hands. They were either forcibly rescued from me or were let loose again by those into whose hands I gave them. I appealed in vain for assistance—no one responded to me.

Abolitionist pilgrimages were made to the gutted shell lfor years. It took many years of litigation for the Anti-Slavery Society to recover part of its loss from the city. Their position became:

Ultimately the destruction of Pennsylvania Hall contributed to an awakening by the Northern public that was essential to the defeat of Slavery; and *In the destruction of this Hall consecrated to freedom, a fire has in fact been kindled that will never go out. The onward progress of our cause in the Key-stone State may now be regarded as certain.*

The *Philadelphia Public Ledger*, which was threatened with demolition by the rioters, asserted that its daily circulation increased by nearly 2000 after the disturbances despite its uncompromising opposition to mobs.[345]

4.16 The Amistad

In 1839, the Spanish schooner *Amistad, carrying 53 enslaved Africans,* sailed from Havana, Cuba. The Africans soon slipped their bonds, killed Captain Ferrer and the ship's cook, and ordered the crew to return them to Africa. Instead, the crew sailed up the East Coast. The U.S. Navy Brig *Washington* seized *Amistad* off Long Island in August. She was taken to Connecticut. The Africans were charged with murder and piracy. Those charges were dropped, and the Africans were imprisoned in New Haven. President Van Buren wanted the Africans extradited to Cuba.

In November 1839, the U.S. Court in Hartford ruled that these Africans were not Slaves, had been illegally captured, and should be returned to Africa. The District Court upheld that ruling. The U.S. Government appealed to the Supreme Court. There, former President John

Quincy Adams, the defense attorney, accused President Van Buren of abusing his power, defended the Africans' right to fight for their freedom, and asserted:

> *The moment you come to the Declaration of Independence, that every man has a right to life and liberty, an inalienable right, this case is decided. I ask nothing more in behalf of these unfortunate men, than this declaration.* [That was moral suasion, not law.]

On 3/19/1841, the Supreme Court, by a 7-1 vote, upheld the lower courts. It also awarded the Naval Officers of the Brig *Washington* the salvage rights to *Amistad*. Neither the Court nor the Government ordered that the Africans be returned to Africa. But the 34 surviving Africans departed for Africa in November 1841 on an Abolitionist-funded voyage.[346]

4.17 Prigg v. Pennsylvania

On 3/25/1826, Pennsylvania passed a law making it a felony to forcibly or violently remove or cause the removal from Pennsylvania of any negro or mulatto in order to sell or keep that person as a Slave or servant for any time whatsoever.

Margaret Morgan, a Black who had lived free in Maryland but had not been manumitted, moved to York County, Pennsylvania in 1832. Her owner's heirs decided to claim Margaret as a Slave and hired Slavecatcher Edward Prigg to recover her.

On 4/1/1837, Prigg and three others forcibly abducted Morgan and her children (one of whom was born free in Pennsylvania) and took them to Maryland to sell. On 5/22/1839, Prigg was convicted in York County of violating Pennsylvania law. He appealed to the U.S. Supreme Court, which reversed the conviction and held that Pennsylvania law violated Article IV of the U.S. Constitution and the Federal Fugitive Slave Law of 1793. The Court also ruled that State officials did not have to uphold Federal Law. Pennsylvania (and other Northern States) enacted laws that prohibited their doing so.[347]

Jerry Morgan, Margaret's husband, a free man, was captured with his family and later released. He returned to Pennsylvania, and went to Harrisburg to lobby the Governor. When he was returning home by boat, a White Man's jacket went missing. Jerry was blamed and threatened with violence. He jumped overboard and drowned. The fate of Margaret and her children is unknown.[348]

4.18 The Wilmot Proviso

The balance of power between Slave and Free States came into sharp contention when President Polk, on 8/8/1846, asked Congress for $2 Million to facilitate final settlement of the Mexican-American War. That request included the Wilmot Proviso. Modeled after the 1787 Northwest Ordinance, it specified:

Provided, That, as an express and fundamental condition to the acquisition of any territory from the Republic of Mexico by the United States, by virtue of any treaty which may be negotiated between them, and to the use by the Executive of the moneys herein appropriated, neither Slavery nor involuntary servitude shall ever exist in any part of said territory, except for crime, whereof the party shall first be duly convicted.

The proviso failed but resurfaced at the year's end in a $3 Million request. It was the sole matter considered and passed by the House from 2/8-15/1847—and stated that Slavery would be excluded from *any territory on the continent of America which shall hereafter be acquired.* The Senate omitted the Wilmot Proviso and prevailed.

When the Treaty of Guadalupe Hidalgo ending the war was submitted to the Senate in 1848, the mainstream Democrat concept of Popular Sovereignty had become:

Leave it to the people, who will be affected by this question to adjust it upon their own responsibility, and in their own manner, and we shall render another tribute to the original principles of our government, and furnish another for its permanence and prosperity.

Senator Stephen Douglas of Illinois joined the Southern effort to defeat the Wilmot Proviso again. He had earlier argued, when he was in the House, that Slavery should be addressed when a territory was organized by Congress.

Historian Alan Nevin described the Wilmot Proviso as involving two extremes: Northerners who demanded no new Slave Territories; and Southerners who demanded Slavery entry into all territories—with secession the penalty for denial.

The Proviso would have applied to California, which had Slavery during the 1848 Gold Rush. But no laws protected Slavery there, a lot of its Slaves escaped, and California entered the Union as a Free State in 1850. Nevada would have been covered too. It had no Slavery and became a Free State in 1864. Also covered were Utah and New Mexico, which had Slavery until it was banned in all Federal Territories in 1862. (The 1860 census recorded only 30 Slaves in Utah.)[349]

4.19 The Nashville Convention

From 6/3-11/1850, nine Southern States (Virginia, South Carolina, Georgia, Alabama, Mississippi, Texas, Arkansas, Florida, and Tennessee) held a convention in Nashville. They re-affirmed the Constitutionality of Slavery in 28 Resolutions and agreed to a concession extending the 1820 Missouri Compromise boundary to the Pacific Coast. The more extreme delegates urged secession if Slavery were restricted in any of the new territories. The presiding official, Judge William L Sharkey of Mississippi, said the Convention was not *called to prevent but to perpetuate the Union.* Secession was tabled. After the Compromise of 1850, the Convention reconvened, denounced the Compromise, and affirmed the right of a State to secede.[350]

4.20 The Compromise of 1850

In September 1850, multiple bills addressed Mexican-American War spoils by:

- Organizing part of the gained land into the New Mexico and Utah territories.
- Surrender of Texas' claims to New Mexico & Utah, & U.S. assumption of Texas' debt.
- Allowing each Territory to choose to be Slave or Free (Popular Sovereignty).
- Admitting California to the Union as a Free State.
- Banning the Slave Trade in Washington, DC.
- Enacting the Fugitive Slave Act of 1850.[351]

4.21 The Fugitive Slave Act of 1850

This Act provided for return of escaped Slaves to their owners. Arrest was required on a claimant's sworn testimony. Officials who didn't arrest a runaway Slave were liable to a $1000 fine (~$31,000 today). A provider of food or shelter to a runaway Slave was liable to six months' imprisonment and a $1000 fine. Officers capturing a fugitive Slave were entitled to a bonus or promotion. *Habeas corpus* wasn't allowed. An alleged fugitive Slave was brought before a Commissioner who received $10 for finding the individual a fugitive and $5 if he found the proof insufficient. There was no jury, and the alleged fugitive could not testify. Kidnapping and conscription of free Blacks into Slavery resulted.

In November 1850, Vermont enacted a *habeas corpus* law requiring State judicial and law enforcement officials to assist captured fugitive Slaves and establishing a State judicial review process paralleling the federal process. Virginia Governor John Floyd warned that such nullification could push the South toward Secession. President Fillmore threatened to use the Army to enforce the Act in Vermont. No test case came up there, but *Jury Nullification* occurred when Northern Juries acquitted accused violators of the Act. Secretary of State Daniel Webster, a key Act supporter, led the 1851 prosecution of the rescuers of Shadrach Minkins from Boston Officials who intended to return him to Slavery. They were acquitted. Webster's consequent unpopularity led the Whigs to pass him over as their 1852 presidential candidate.

The Act prompted shifting the *Underground Railroad's destination* from Northern cities to Canada. From 1850-60, the Black population of Canada increased from 40,000 to 60,000. And from 1850-55, the Black population of New York City dropped by almost 2000. In 1855, Wisconsin's Supreme Court ruled the Act unconstitutional. In 1859, the U.S. Supreme Court overruled that. Northerners who did business with the South and supported the Act contrasted with opponents like Reverend Luther Lee, pastor of the Wesleyan Methodist Church of Syracuse, New York, who wrote, in 1855:

> *I never would obey it. I had assisted thirty Slaves to escape to Canada during the last month. If the authorities wanted anything of me, my residence was at 39 Onondaga Street. I would admit that and they could take me and lock me up in the Penitentiary on the hill; but if they did such a foolish thing as that I*

*had friends enough on Onondaga County to level it to the ground before the
next morning.*

The Union Army returned some runaway Slaves to their owners until Congress barred
doing so in 1862. Military emancipation essentially superseded the Act, which was not
repealed until June 1864—whereupon the *New York Tribune* wrote: *The blood-red stain that
has blotted the statute-book of the Republic is wiped out forever.*[352]

4.22 Uncle Tom's Cabin (Life Among the Lowly)

In 1852, Abolitionist Harriet Beecher Stowe's 1851 Anti-Slavery newspaper serial was
expanded and printed as a book depicting Slavery and asserting that Christian love can
overcome Slavery's destructiveness. It was second only to the Bible in 19th Century book
sales. The stage plays and other works it triggered appear to have reached a far greater
audience than the book. *Uncle Tom's Cabin* has since been accompanied by the negative,
stereotypic connotations of its characters. For example:

- *Uncle Tom*, the noble Black who forgives his mistreatment, including being whipped
  to death, became an epithetic derogation of Blacks who kowtow to Whites.
- The *Happy Darky* image projected by the lazy, carefree character Sam arose.
- *Simon Legree*, the vicious Plantation Owner who used his female Slaves for sex, and
  who had Tom whipped to death, became an epithetic derogation of greed.
- *Mammy* became a descriptor of an affectionate [fat, older] Black woman.
- *Pickaninny* became an inferiority-connoting term for Black babies.[353]

4.23 The Slave Anthony Burns

In 1853, Anthony Burns (5/31/1834-7/17/1862), a Baptist and a *Slave Preacher* in
Falmouth, Virginia, escaped and survived near starvation to clandestinely make his way to
Boston. After a month of employment as a Free Man, he was captured under the Fugitive
Slave Act. Public outrage abounded in Boston. Federal troops kept Burns from being rescued.
Commissioner Loring, who heard the case, termed the Fugitive Slave Act a disgrace that he
had to uphold. On 5/56/1854, during Loring's deliberations, ≥25 armed men broke down the
courthouse door and fought with the guards. They killed one before the police foiled their
rescue attempt. President Pierce sent U.S. Marines to avert further violence. Three of the
courthouse attackers were prosecuted. One was acquitted. After several hung juries, the
federal government dropped the charges on the other two.

Loring ruled Burns a fugitive Slave. Boston's Mayor ordered in a militia brigade to support
the federal Marshal and his 125-man contingent of armed Bostonians. On 6/2/1854, with
the militia lining the streets and the marshal's men using bayonets to get through the crowd
at one point, Burns was escorted to and put on a vessel bound for Virginia. The estimated
government cost for the Burn's affair was >$40,000 (>$1 million in 2019).

Abolitionists purchased Burns' freedom for $1300. He studied at Oberlin College and a Cincinnati seminary, preached in Indianapolis, and moved to St. Catharine's, Ontario to serve the Zion Baptist Church. He died there from tuberculosis at the age of 28.

A new Massachusetts law prevented Slave claimants from being on State property, required jury trials for fugitive Slaves, and required two credible unbiased witnesses to prove their case. There were no more fugitive Slave hearings in Massachusetts.

Harvard University refused to re-hire Loring to their faculty. Massachusetts' Legislature voted to remove him as a Probate Judge. The Governor didn't do that but the next one did in 1857. President Pierce later appointed Loring to the Federal Court of Claims.[354]

4.24 The Ostend Manifesto

John Quincy Adams termed Cuba *of transcendent importance* and its annexation *indispensable to the continuance and integrity of the Union itself*. To mitigate against Cuba passing from Spanish to British or French control, President Jefferson instituted respect for Spain's sovereignty. In 1854, when Northern city growth and the admission of new Free States was raising Southern Democrats' concern., the South wanted to admit Cuba as a Slave State and to prevent it from becoming independent and/or abolishing Slavery. Purchase or intervention was their desired means of acquisition.

President Pierce (a New Hampshire Democrat) was committed to Cuban annexation and appointed like-minded officials. At the suggestion of his Secretary of State (William L. Marcy), the U.S. Ministers to Britain (James Buchanan), France (John Mason), and Spain (Pierre Soulé) met secretly in Europe and produced the Ostend Manifesto. It urged against inaction on Cuba and noted that, without U.S. intervention, there was a possibility of a Cuban Slave Revolt like the 1791-94 Haitian one. And it declared that:

- *Cuba is as necessary to the North American republic as any of its present members, and it belongs naturally to that great family of states of which the Union is the Providential Nursery.*
- *We should be recreant to our duty, unworthy of our gallant forefathers, and commit base treason against our posterity, should we permit Cuba to be Africanized and become a second St. Domingo (Haiti), with all its attendant horrors to the white race, and suffer the flames to extend to our own neighboring shores, seriously to endanger or actually to consume the fair fabric of our Union.*

Flamboyant statements by Soulé alerted the Congress and media to the Manifesto. Editorials chided the administration for its secrecy. The *New York Herald* published close to the truth aspects of it. President Pierce did not acknowledge the rumors. His opponents in the House called for the Manifesto's release. It was published. Northerners called it unconstitutional. Horace Greely of the *New York Tribune* labeled it *The Manifesto of the Brigands*. It became an anti-Slavery rallying cry during the fight for Kansas. The controversy irreparably damaged the Pierce administration and contributed to splintering the Democratic

Party. In 1856 the first Republican Party platform criticized the Ostend Manifesto as a *highwayman's* philosophy of *might makes right*.

Soulé was ordered to stop discussing Cuba. He resigned. President Pierce abandoned Expansionism. The Ostend Manifesto was described as one of a series of *gratuitous conflicts … that cost more than they were worth* to the Pro-Slavery forces.

James Buchanan, who was easily elected President in 1856, remained committed to annexing Cuba. But popular opposition prevailed. And Cuba didn't become nationally prominent again until 30 years after the Civil War.[355]

4.25 The Kansas-Nebraska Act

In 1854 the Kansas-Nebraska Act, proposed by Stephen Douglas of Illinois, rescinded the Missouri Compromise's use of latitude and allowed each new State to decide whether to permit Slavery (Douglas' Popular Sovereignty). Antagonism between Pro- and Anti-Slavery proponents increased and the violence called Bleeding Kansas ensued.[356]

4.26 Bleeding Kansas

From 1854-61, in the Kansas Territory and Western Missouri, Pro-Slavery *Border Ruffians* and Anti-Slavery *Free Staters* contested Slavery in Kansas. There was huge election fraud and ~200 killings. John Brown led the Abolitionists' violent response.

Pro-Slavers from Slave States, especially Missouri, emigrated to Kansas to foster the expansion of Slavery. Thousands of others entered to pose as residents and influence local politics. President Pierce appointed Pro-Slavery Kansas Territory Officials.

Abolitionists encouraged *Free Staters* to move to Kansas. *Beecher's Bibles* (Sharps rifles in crates labelled *Bibles*) were shipped to *Free Staters*, reputedly by Minister Henry Ward Beecher (Harriet Beecher Stowe's brother). The media fostered hysteria and the establishment of Abolitionist Republican strongholds (e.g., Lawrence, Topeka, and Manhattan, Kansas)

The November 1854 Kansas vote for a non-voting member of Congress "elected" Pro-Slavery Democrat John Whitfield. Subsequent Congressional Committee investigation reported 1,114 legal and 1,729 illegal votes with, in one location, only 20 of the 804 voters being Kansas residents and, in another, 35 resident and 228 non-resident voters.

In the 3/30/1855 election for the first Kansas Territorial Legislature, outsiders again streamed into Kansa and Pro-Slavers were elected to 37 of the 39 seats. *Free Staters* claimed fraud. Territorial Governor Andrew Reeder invalidated, as fraud-tainted, 11 of those seats. Eight of them went to *Free Staters in a* special election on 5/22. The (Lecompton) legislature's 29-10 Pro-Slavery majority invalidated the special election and seated the previously "elected" Pro-Slavery delegates. It also passed Pro-Slavery laws and adopted a Slave Code modeled largely on Missouri's. *Free Staters* called the Lecompton Legislature "bogus," elected their own, and located it in Topeka. It produced the Topeka Constitution and elected Charles Robinson Territorial Governor.

President Pierce fired Reeder (who left Kansas in disguise), made pro-South Wilson Shannon Territorial Governor, and refused to recognize the Topeka government. Congress refused to ratify the Topeka Constitution but sent a three-man Special Committee to investigate the voting fraud allegations. It reported that:

- If the 3/30/1855 election had been limited to *actual settlers*, a Free-State legislature would have been voted in.
- The Lecompton legislature was illegally constituted and could not pass valid laws.

When James Buchanan, a Northerner, became President in 1857, he endorsed the Pro-Slavery Lecompton Constitution for Kansas. It was submitted to Kansans for a vote, *Free Staters* refused to participate and it was approved by 6226 to 569. Congress ordered a revote because of irregularities. On 8/2/1858, Kansas rejected it by 11,812 to 1,929.

Meanwhile, the Leavenworth Constitution was produced. It extended suffrage to *every male citizen* regardless of race. *Free State* delegates passed it on 5/18/1858 in a low turnout vote. On 1/6/1859, it was sent to the U.S. Senate, where it died in committee.

The last *Free State* proposal, the Wyandotte Constitution, was approved in Kansas by a vote of 10,421 to 5,530 on 10/4/1859. Its confirmation was indefinitely postponed by the South-controlled U.S. Senate. But when the seceding States' Senators left Washington in January 1861, Kansas was admitted as a free state.[357]

4.27 The Brooks-Sumner Affair

Bleeding Kansas increased the polarization. Abolitionists accused Slaveholders of forced sex with Slave women (Hoffer, 2010). Pro-Slavers accused Abolitionists of promoting interracial marriage (Sinha, 2003). Fugitive Slave Act authors Senators Stephen A. Douglas of Illinois and Andrew Butler of South Carolina ridiculed and insulted, and Butler crudely race-baited, Republican Senator Charles Sumner of Massachusetts, a fervent Abolitionist. Sumner's 5/19-20/1856 *Crime Against Kansas* speech responded by arguing for immediate Kansas admission as a Free State, denouncing Slavery, and targeting the speech-impeded (by a recent stroke) Butler by saying:

> *Not in any common lust for power did this uncommon tragedy have its origin. It is the rape of a virgin Territory, compelling it to the hateful embrace of Slavery; and it may be clearly traced to a depraved desire for a new Slave State, hideous offspring of such a crime, in the hope of adding to the power of Slavery in the National Government....*
>
> *The senator from South Carolina has read many books of chivalry, and believes himself a chivalrous knight with sentiments of honor and courage. Of course, he has chosen a mistress to whom he has made his vows, and who, though ugly to others, is always lovely to him; though polluted in the sight of the world, is chaste in his sight—I mean the harlot, Slavery. For her*

his tongue is always profuse in words. Let her be impeached in character, or any proposition made to shut her out from the extension of her wantonness, and no extravagance of manner or hardihood of assertion is then too great for this senator....

[He] touches nothing which he does not disfigure with error, sometimes of principle, sometimes of fact. He cannot open his mouth, but out there flies a blunder.

During Sumner's speech, Senator Stephen Douglas reportedly said:

This damn fool is going to get himself killed by some other damn fool.

South Carolina Representative Preston Brooks, Butler's first cousin once removed, took umbrage at Sumner's speech. Two days later, along with South Carolina Representative Lawrence M. Kett and Virginia Representative Henry A. Edmundson, Brooks entered the floor of the Senate—late in the afternoon when no ladies were present. (Seven days earlier, about 36 hours into a House debate on the Kansas-Nebraska Act, Edmundson had tried to attack Ohio Representative Louis Campbell, and had opened his vest as if reaching for a weapon. He was restrained by other Representatives and order was restored by the Sergeant-at-Arms.[358]) Brooks went up to Sumner, who was writing at his desk in the nearly empty chamber, and calmly said: *Mr. Sumner, I have read your speech twice over carefully. It is a libel on South Carolina, and Mr. Butler, who is a relative of mine.* Sumner tried to rise. Brook struck him repeatedly with a thick, gutta-percha cane, knocking him under the desk. Sumner, though blinded by his own blood, managed to get up and tried to get away. Brook continued hitting him, breaking the cane several times and continuing the attack with the piece holding the cane's gold head. Sumner, losing consciousness, started to fall. Brooks held him up by the lapel with one hand and continued to strike *to the full extent of (my) power* with the cane.

Edmundson yelled at the other Senators and Representatives to leave Brooks and Sumner alone. Kett brandished his own cane and pistol and shouted *Let them be* and *let them alone, God damn you, let them alone.* Representatives Ambrose Murray and Edwin Morgan of New York finally restrained Brooks. After regaining consciousness and medical treatment (e.g., stitches), Sumner was helped to his lodgings. He convalesced for three years before returning to the Senate, and suffered from debilitating pain for the rest of his life—with symptoms akin to traumatic brain injury and PTSD.

The pieces of Brook's cane were retrieved from the bloody Senate floor. Boston's State House Museum put the piece with the gold head on display. Southern lawmakers made rings from the other pieces and wore them on neck chains. Brooks said that his cane's pieces *are begged for as sacred relics.*

Two weeks after the caning, Ralph Waldo Emerson said:

> I do not see how a barbarous community and a civilized community can
> constitute one state. I think we must get rid of Slavery, or we must get rid of
> freedom.

The *Cincinnati Gazette* wrote:

> The South cannot tolerate free speech anywhere, and would stifle it in
> Washington with the bludgeon and the bowie-knife, as they are now trying to
> stifle it in Kansas by massacre, rapine, and murder.

The *New York Evening Post's* William Cullen Bryant asked:

> Has it come to this, that we must speak with bated breath in the presence of
> our Southern masters?... Are we to be chastised as they chastise their Slaves?
> Are we too, Slaves, Slaves for life, a target for their brutal blows, when we do
> not comport ourselves to please them?

Over a million copies of Sumner's speech were distributed. Thousands attended Sumner-Support rallies in Northern cities.

A *Richmond Enquirer* editorial stated that Sumner should be caned *every morning*, praised the attack as *good in conception, better in execution, and best of all in consequences*, and denounced *these vulgar Abolitionists in the Senate* who *have been suffered to run too long without collars. They must be lashed into submission.*

Southerners sent Brooks hundreds of new canes, including one inscribed *Hit him again.*

Massachusetts Representative Anson Burlingame, a crack shot, goaded Brooks into challenging him to a duel and, as the challenged party, chose rifles and the Canadian side of Niagara Falls (where there were no anti-dueling laws). Brooks, citing the danger of violence while transiting the Northern States, withdrew the challenge. He also challenged U.S. Senator Henry Wilson of Massachusetts, who had termed the assault on Sumner *brutal, murderous, and cowardly.* Wilson said that the law and personal conviction prevented dueling. He continued his Senate duties, disregarding a rumor that Brooks might attack him in the Senate. There was no such attack.

Brooks was arrested and tried in the District of Columbia, and fined $300 (~ $8450 today). A motion to expel him from the House failed. He resigned to put the matter before his constituents and was re-elected. In the 1858 lame duck House session, he disappointed Southerners by calling for Kansas statehood *even with a constitution rejecting Slavery.* He was re-elected again, but died of the croup before taking up his 1858-60 duties.

4.28 The 1856 Presidential Election

Slavery was the major issue in the 1856 election. James Buchanan, the Democrats' candidate, endorsed Popular Sovereignty and claimed that a Republican victory would result in Civil War. James C. Frémont, the Republican candidate, ran on a platform opposed to expanding Slavery into the Territories. The Know Nothing candidate, ex-President Millard Fillmore, ran on an anti-immigration, anti-Catholic platform that ignored Slavery. Buchanan won with 43.6% of the vote and 174 electoral votes.[359] The new Republican Party's touting of *Bleeding Kansas* and of *Bleeding Sumner* did not keep the Democrats from winning the presidency and increasing their House majority. But State Legislatures chose U.S. Senators, and there was a dramatic Republican gain in State Legislature and U.S. Senate seats.[360]

4.29 The Dred Scott Decision

Two days after Buchanan's inauguration, in the case of the Slave Dred Scott, the U.S. Supreme Court ruled 7-2 that:

- Living in a Free State or Territory did not entitle a Slave to freedom elsewhere.
- Blacks were not and never could be U.S. citizens.
- The declaration that all territory West of Missouri and North of 36°30' North Latitude was Free Territory in the Missouri Compromise of 1820 was Unconstitutional. (Most of that Territory had been "free" since the Missouri Compromise.)[361]

Previously highly respected Chief Supreme Court Justice Roger Brooke Taney wrote the ruling. Taney was born in Calvert County, Maryland to a Slave-owning family but owned no slaves. And the Taney Court had unanimously ruled, in 1841, that the Slaves in the schooner *Amistad* were justified in attacking the crew and trying to gain their freedom. But Taney considered Slavery critical to *Southern life and values*.[362] His racial discrimination was couched as:[363]

> [Blacks] had for more than a century before been regarded as beings of an inferior order, and altogether unfit to associate with the white race, either in social or political relations; and so far inferior, that they had no rights which the white man was bound to respect; and that the negro might justly and lawfully be reduced to Slavery for his benefit. He was bought and sold, and treated as an ordinary article of merchandise and traffic, whenever a profit could be made by it.

Francis Scott Key, Taney's longstanding close personal and professional friend, brother-in-law, and lawyer, had represented runaway Slaves' owners and suppressed Abolition as District Attorney. He also had freed his seven Slaves in the 1830s, criticized Slavery's cruelty, and represented some freedom-seeking Slaves pro bono.[364, 365] That led Author F. Scott

Fitzgerald to remark: *The test of a first-rate intelligence is the ability to hold two opposed ideas in mind at the same time and still retain the ability to function.*[366]

Justice Benjamin R. Curtis (from Ohio) wrote one of the two strong dissents. It stated that Blacks are citizens because:

> *Of this there can be no doubt. At the time of the ratification of the Articles of Confederation, all free native-born inhabitants of the States of New Hampshire, Massachusetts, New York, New Jersey, and North Carolina, though descended from African Slaves, were not only citizens of those States, but such of them as had the other necessary qualifications possessed the franchise of electors, on equal terms with other citizens.*[367]

The Dred Scott decision further increased national polarization and strengthened the three-year-old Anti-Slavery Republican Party.

Law Professor Melvin I. Urofsky (b.1939) stated that:

- Taney ignored precedent, distorted history, imposed a rigid rather than a flexible construction on the Constitution, ignored specific grants of power in the Constitution, and tortured meanings out of other, more-obscure clauses.
- Taney admitted that Blacks could be citizens of a particular State and that they might even be able to vote, as they did in some States.
- Taney asserted that State Citizenship had nothing to do with National Citizenship and that Blacks could not sue in federal court because they could not be U.S. Citizens.
- If even one State considered a Black a Citizen, U. S. Constitution Article IV, Section 2 required that all States, and therefore the Federal Government, had to accord that person *all Privileges and Immunities of Citizens in the several States*, including the right to sue in Federal Court.
- U. S. Constitution Article III establishes the jurisdiction of the federal courts and does not mention National Citizenship but declares that *the judicial Power* shall extend, among other things, *to Controversies…between Citizens of different States.*[368]

But Constitution Article IV Sections 1 and 2 literally stated:

Section 1.

Full faith and credit shall be given in each state to the public acts, records, and judicial proceedings of every other state. And the Congress may by general laws prescribe the manner in which such acts, records, and proceedings shall be proved, and the effect thereof.

Section 2.

The citizens of each state shall be entitled to all privileges and immunities of citizens in the several states.

No person held to service or labor in one state, under the laws thereof, escaping into another, shall, in consequence of any law or regulation therein, be discharged from such service or labor, but shall be delivered up on claim of the party to whom such service or labor may be due.

A person charged in any state with treason, felony, or other crime, who shall flee from justice, and be found in another state, shall on demand of the executive authority of the state from which he fled, be delivered up, to be removed to the state having jurisdiction of the crime.[369]

The first sentence of Section 1 in effect asserts that, where Slavery was legal, if a State Legislature or Court declared all Slaves free there, Full Faith and Credit required all States to do the same. Its second sentence addresses the reality that *Full Faith and Credit* cannot be achieved where there are contradictory laws in different States—by specifying *Full Faith and Credit* in accordance with the general laws that the U.S. Congress enacts.

[The Constitution therefore enables States to deny *Full Faith and Credit* to other States' laws and court decisions. And conflicts between and within States' laws, Federal Laws, and Constitutional Provisions task the Courts with making case law in such cases.]

In practice, *Full Faith and Credit* means that the judgements of a State Court with authority over a case and its parties may determine the parties' rights in the other States. For example, a State's judgement on a gambling debt can be collected in another State where gambling is a crime. But States with conflicting laws about marriages by the young or close relatives can treat such marriages differently, while divorces legal in one State are legal in the rest. And State driver's licenses are valid in other States while fishing licenses are not. Congress has generally avoided this arena, but has enacted laws addressing child custody and child support for a family spread out over multiple States.[370] And the Constitutional right to bear arms has been affirmed 5-4 by the Supreme Court but restricted to in-home self-defense except as licensed by the individual State (District of Columbia, et al v. Heller, 2008).[371] [The Dred Scott decision may be the most egregious perversion of the *American Dream*. And the chicanery of altering the Constitution without amended it lessens the trustworthiness of the U.S. legal system.]

4.30 The Lincoln-Douglas Debates

In 1858, with Pro- and Anti-Slavery fervor rampaging, Republican Abraham Lincoln ran for the Illinois U.S. Senate seat held by Stephen Douglas, a Democrat seeking a third term. Their campaigns consisted primarily of seven debates held, at various Illinois locations, to convince the State Legislature whom to elect.

Stenographers' versions of the debates were nationally distributed. Newspapers corrected their candidate's stenographic and grammatical errors and left those of the other candidate alone. Lincoln had the debates published in a book that sold well and was a factor in his becoming the Republican candidate for President in 1860.

Douglas said that Lincoln's statement that the *Declaration of Independence* applied to

Blacks as well as Whites showed that Lincoln was an Abolitionist. [Lincoln also had said that "the electric cord… that links the hearts of patriotic and liberty-loving men (of different ethnic backgrounds) together" is a self-evident truth.]

Lincoln was a former Whig and one-term U.S. Congressman who had supported banning Slavery in lands into which the U.S. expanded (the Wilmot Proviso). He also opposed the Kansas-Nebraska Act and worked on developing the Republican Party. Before the debates, he said that Douglas had driven thousands away from the Republican Party by encouraging fear of amalgamation of the races.

At the Ottawa debate, Lincoln said that:

- Douglas was mistaken in seeing Popular Sovereignty and the Dred Scott decision as being in harmony with the Compromise of 1850.
- Popular Sovereignty would nationalize and perpetuate Slavery.
- Limiting Slavery (e.g., the Northwest Ordinance of 1787) was National Policy,
- The next Dred Scott decision could allow Slavery to spread into Free States.
- Douglas ignored the basic humanity of Blacks; Slaves had an equal right to liberty.
- He did not know how emancipation should happen.
- He believed in colonization in Africa by emancipated Slaves, but that was impractical.
- **It would be wrong for emancipated Slaves to be treated as *underlings*. But there was a large opposition to social and political equality and *a universal feeling, whether well or ill-founded, cannot be safely disregarded*.**
- Douglas' indifference would expand Slavery by molding public sentiment to accept it. *Public sentiment is everything.* **With public sentiment, nothing can fail; without it, nothing can succeed. Consequently, he who molds public sentiment goes deeper than he who enacts statutes or pronounces decisions. He makes statutes and decisions possible or impossible to be executed.**
- Douglas *cares not whether Slavery is voted down or voted up*, and would *blow out the moral lights around us and eradicate the love of liberty*.

Douglas said that:

- Popular sovereignty, as the Compromise of 1850 showed, was believed in by both Whigs and Democrats.
- *Black Republican Party* members, including Lincoln, were Abolitionists. The proof was Lincoln's statement that *I believe this government cannot endure permanently half Slave and half free.*
- Lincoln opposed the Dred Scott decision because *it deprives the negro of the rights and privileges of citizenship.*
- Lincoln wanted to overthrow State Laws excluding Blacks from States such as Illinois.

At Freeport, Lincoln asked Douglas to reconcile Popular Sovereignty and the Dred Scott decision. Douglas said that refusing to enact a Slave Code and other Slavery-Protecting-Legislation could keep Slavery out of a Territory (the Freeport Doctrine) despite the Supreme Court ruling. His support of Popular Sovereignty alienated Republicans and others opposed to Slavery, and also alienated Southerners and others disappointed by Kansas becoming a free State. His defeating of the Kansas Pro-Slavery Lecompton Constitution also alienated Southerners (and other pro-Slavers). [The 1858 Southern demands for Slave Codes split the Democrats into the Northern and Southern Democrats, who then had different presidential candidates in 1860.]

At Jonesboro, Lincoln said that expanding Slavery endangered the Union, citing the controversies in Missouri in 1820, in the territories conquered from Mexico, and in *Bleeding Kansas*. He also said that the crisis would be passed when Slavery was put *in the course of ultimate extinction*.

At Charleston, Lincoln said:

> *I will say then that I am not, nor ever have been in favor of bringing about in any way the social and political equality of the white and black races---that I am not nor ever have been in favor of making voters or jurors of negroes, nor of qualifying them to hold office, nor to intermarry with white people; and I will say in addition to this that there is a physical difference between the white and black races which I believe will for ever forbid the two races living together on terms of social and political equality. And inasmuch as they cannot so live, while they do remain together there must be the position of superior and inferior, and I as much as any other man am in favor of having the superior position assigned to the white race.*

Douglas declared that inconsistent with Lincoln's previous statements that *All men are created equal* applies to Blacks as well as Whites. He also said that Lincoln had an ally in Frederick Douglass in preaching *Abolition doctrines* and that Douglass told all the friends of negro equality and negro citizenship to rally around Abraham Lincoln.

In response to Douglas' questioning of his support of negro citizenship, if not full equality, Lincoln countered with: *I tell him very frankly that I am not in favor of negro citizenship*.

At Galesburg, quoting Lincoln's Chicago address, Douglas again claimed that Lincoln was an Abolitionist because of his insistence that *all men are equal*.

At Alton, Lincoln said that:

- The authors of the *Declaration of Independence intended to include all men, but they did not mean to declare all men equal in all respects*, but *meant to set up a standard maxim for the free society which should be familiar to all—constantly looked to, constantly labored for, and even, though never perfectly attained, constantly approximated, and thereby constantly spreading and deepening its influence, and augmenting the happiness and value of life to all people, of all colors, everywhere.*

- His support for the *Declaration of Independence* contrasted with statements by John C. Calhoun and Senator John Pettit of Indiana, who had called it *a self-evident lie.*

- Chief Justice Roger Taney and Stephen Douglas opposed Jefferson's self-evident truth by dehumanizing Blacks and preparing the public to think of them as property.
- *It is the eternal struggle between these two principles -- right and wrong -- throughout the world. ...It is the same spirit that says, You work and toil and earn bread, and I'll eat it. No matter in what shape it comes, whether from the mouth of a king who seeks to bestride the people of his own nation and live by the fruit of their labor or from one race of men as an apology for enslaving another race, it is the same tyrannical principle.*

At Quincy, Lincoln called Douglas' Freeport Doctrine *as thin as the homeopathic soup that was made by boiling the shadow of a pigeon that had starved to death.*

In the Illinois election, non-Republican former Whigs were the biggest block of swing voters. Douglas had the advantage of districts drawn in favor of his party and the endorsement of the influential former Whig and U.S. Senator from Kentucky John J. Crittenden. The Democrats won the State House 40-35 and the State Senate 14-11. Douglas was re-elected by a 54-46 vote. But Lincoln's 3402 votes gave him 50.6% of the popular vote and the debates made him a national figure[372]

[Douglas was correct in stating that Lincoln's statements about Blacks contrasted with his assertions that all men are equal. But those were campaign statements. It's far more significant how strongly Lincoln held to emancipation and to maintaining one-nation upon being elected—especially when Southern Battlefield Gallantry and Generalship were trouncing the Union—until the Battle of Gettysburg and Ulysses S. Grant's successes turned the tide of the Civil War. (Pragmatically, it's what a politician does after being elected that counts, not what was said to gain election.)]

4.31 The Oberlin-Wellington Rescue

On 9/13/1858, John Price, a runaway Slave from Kentucky, was arrested by a U.S. Marshall in Oberlin, Ohio, an Abolition hotbed. The Marshal promptly took Price to the nearby town of Wellington. A group of Oberliners followed and were joined by similar-minded Wellingtonians. They failed to negotiate Price's release, stormed the hotel where he was held, rescued him, and sent him to Canada on the Underground Railroad.

A federal grand jury indicted 37 of the rescuers. Ohio arrested the Federal Marshall and his Deputies and other helpers—freeing them when 35 indictments were dismissed. The other two Rescuers, Simon Bushnell, a White, and Charles Langston, a Black, were tried. At his trial, Langston gave a speech ending with:

> *But I stand up here to say, that if for doing what I did on that day at Wellington, I am to go to jail six months, and pay a fine of a thousand dollars, according to the Fugitive Slave Law, and such is the protection the laws of this country afford me, I must take upon my self the responsibility of self-protection; and when I come to be claimed by some perjured wretch as his Slave, I shall never be taken into Slavery. And as in that trying hour I would have others do to me, as I would call upon my friends to help me; as I would call upon you,*

your Honor, to help me; as I would call upon you [to the District-Attorney], to help me; and upon you [to Judge Bliss], and upon you [to his counsel], so help me GOD! I stand here to say that I will do all I can, for any man thus seized and help, though the inevitable penalty of six months imprisonment and one thousand dollars fine for each offense hangs over me! We have a common humanity. You would do so; your manhood would require it; and no matter what the laws might be, you would honor yourself for doing it; your friends would honor you for doing it; your children to all generations would honor you for doing it; and every good and honest man would say, you had done right!

The applause long resounded despite the Judge's and the Marshall's efforts to stop it.

Both men were convicted. Bushnell got 60 days in jail, Langston got 20. Their *habeas corpus* writ to Ohio's Supreme Court claimed that there was no right to arrest and try them because the 1850 Fugitive Slave Law was unconstitutional. That Court upheld the law by a 3-2 margin. Chief Justice Swan wrote that he was personally opposed to Slavery but an Act of the U.S. Congress was supreme and had to be upheld. Over 10,000 people participated in a Cleveland Rally to protest the decisions. Justice Swan failed to win re-election. His political career ended.

Two Rescuers and another Oberliner joined John Brown at Harper's Ferry. One was killed there, the other two were convicted of treason against Virginia and executed. And heightened national attention fostered adding repealing the Fugitive Slave Law of 1850 to the 1859 Ohio Republican Convention platform.

4.32 John Brown (1800-1859)

John Brown, the son of an Abolitionist who provided a Safe House on the Underground Railroad, was 20 years old when he married Dianthe Lusk in 1820. In 1825 they moved to New Richmond, Pennsylvania and built a tannery—with a secret room that was a major Underground Railroad stop for some 2500 fugitive Slaves during the next 10 years.

Dianthe died at age 31 in August 1832, three days after the birth of her seventh child. In June 1833, John married 16-year-old Mary Ann Day, who bore him 13 children. He often expressed pride in having seven sons to help him in the cause of abolishing Slavery. (Of Brown's 20 children, four sons and four daughters survived him.[373])

Brown moved to Ohio in 1836, dedicated himself to destroying Slavery in 1837, suffered great financial loss in the 1839 economic crisis, went bankrupt in 1842, and lost four children to dysentery in 1843. He became an expert in sheep and wool, partnered with Col. Simon Perkins of Akron, and he and his sons managed Perkins' farms and flocks.

In 1846 the partners moved to Springfield, Massachusetts, an Anti-Slavery community. Brown was deeply involved in making it a major Abolitionism Center and Underground Railroad stop. And, in one night's discussion, he made Abolitionist Frederick Douglass gloomy about achieving peaceful Abolition of Slavery.

Financial misfortune caused closure of the Perkins and Brown wool commission in late

1849. But no one was taken back into Slavery from Springfield after Brown responded to the 1850 Fugitive Slave Act by founding the militant League of Gileadites, saying:

> Nothing so charms the American people as personal bravery. [Blacks] would have ten times the number [of white friends than] they now have were they but half as much in earnest to secure their dearest rights as they are to ape the follies and extravagances of their white neighbors, and to indulge in idle show, in ease, and in luxury.

From Massachusetts, John Brown went to Timbuctoo in upstate New York's Adirondacks. He stayed there two years to support development of the 3000 40-acre lots given to Black New Yorkers by Land Baron Gerrit Smith. But only two of its families made the transition from being cooks, barbers, and domestic servants to farming, and Timbuctoo failed. (John Brown is interred in that beautiful area, at the farm he bought in North Elba.)

In 1855, Brown went to Kansas after hearing that his sons' families there were unprepared to face the militant Pro-Slavery forces—gaining funds, weapons, and militant support enroute.

On 5/21/1856, a Pro-Slavery sheriff-led posse destroyed two Abolitionist Newspapers and the Free State Hotel in Lawrence. On 5/24-25/1856, Brown and Abolitionist settlers took five "professional Slave hunters and militant Pro-Slavery settlers" from their residences and killed them (the Pottawatomie Massacre). That triggered three months of fighting and 29 deaths, the bloodiest part of *Bleeding Kansas*. (In the prior two years, there had been eight Slavery-related killings in Kansas.)

Before they sacked Lawrence, Missourians led by Captain Henry Clay Pate had captured John Brown's sons John, Jr. and Jason. On 6/2/1856, Brown, nine followers, and 20 local men defended Palmyra against Pate, captured him and 22 of his men, and forced Pate to trade the release of Brown's sons for Pate's and his men's freedom.

Over 300 Missourians led by General John W. Reid crossed into Kansas to destroy Osawatomie's *Free State* settlements and attack Topeka and Lawrence. On 8/30/1856, on Osawatomie's outskirts, they shot and killed John Brown's son Frederick and his neighbor David Garrison. Outnumbered 300-39, Brown and his men fired from cover beside the road, killing at least 20 of Reid's men and wounding 40 more. Reid had his men dismount and charge. Brown lost one man and had four captured while fleeing across the Marais des Cygnes River and hiding in the woods. The Missourians plundered and burned Osawatomie. Brown's role brought him national attention.

On 9/7/1856, Brown was among the defending *Free Staters* who skirmished with about 2700 invading Missourians near Lawrence—until Kansas' new Governor, John Geary, ordered both sides to disband and disarm, and offered them clemency. Brown then left Kansas with three of his sons, ostensibly to raise money. But he was intent on taking the U.S. Armory at Harpers Ferry, a large number of buildings that manufactured small arms and was thought to hold 100,000 muskets and rifles. As Frederick Douglass put it:

> His own statement, that he had been contemplating a bold strike for the freedom of the Slaves for ten years, proves that he had resolved upon his present course long before he, or his sons, ever set foot in Kansas. [374]

In 1859, using the alias Isaac Smith, Brown rented a farmhouse four miles North of Harpers Ferry, and credibly acted the part of a miner. He had 13 White and 5 Black companions, 198 breech-loading Sharps Carbines (Beecher's Bibles), and 950 pikes (recently obtained and never used). Expecting 200-500 Slaves to join him the first night of his assault, he planned to use his weapons and those he captured to arm rebellious Slaves and terrify Virginia Slaveholders.

Brown also ridiculed the militia and the potential U.S. Army opposition. He planned to send agents to nearby plantations to swell his ranks with White and Black recruits. Then he would rapidly follow the Appalachian Mountains into Tennessee and Alabama—foraging into the neighboring plains, freeing more Slaves and gaining food, horses, and hostages enroute. In an effort to get help in recruiting Blacks, he told Frederick Douglass his plan. Douglass declined and warned Brown that the plan was *an attack on the federal government* that *would array the whole country against us…. You will never get out alive.*

Brown's drillmaster, disgruntled over his pay, went to Washington, met with U.S. Senators William Seward and Henry Wilson, and revealed part of the plan. Wilson wrote a Brown backer advising the retrieval of weapons intended for use in Kansas. The backer [disingenuously?] replied that the weapons should not be used for other, rumored purposes. Brown returned to Kansas to bolster his support and discredit the drillmaster.

An estimated 80 people knew parts of Brown's plan. David Gue of Springdale, Iowa, knowing that Brown planned to attack the South and hoping to protect him from being killed, anonymously wrote Secretary of War John Floyd—stating that a secret association led by *Old John Brown*, late of Kansas, would enter Virginia at Harper's Ferry to liberate the South's Slaves by a general insurrection. There was a $250 reward for John Brown's capture (offered by President Buchanan). But Floyd did not connect the letter's *Old John Brown* to the Pottawatomie Massacre, regarded the letter as the work of a crackpot, and did nothing. He later [Naively? Disingenuously?] said *a scheme of such wickedness could not be entertained by any citizen of the United States.*

About 11 PM on Sunday, 8/16/1859, leaving his son Owen and three others as a rear guard, Brown led his force into Harpers Ferry, taking Col. Lewis Washington (George Washington's grandnephew) and several Brown's Ferry watchmen and townspeople hostage. The raiders cut the incoming and outgoing telegraph wires and shot Heyward Shepherd, a train station baggage handler and a free Black man, in the back when he refused to freeze and tried to return to the station. That attracted Dr. John Starry. When he said that Shepherd could not be saved, Brown let Starry leave. Starry raised the alarm. White townspeople began fighting back. But Brown's men took the Federal Armory.

Most Slaves were illiterate. But they knew about the Fugitive Slave Act and they didn't know John Brown. Some feared being taken and sold, and others ran away from him.

At Dawn on Monday, the Baltimore & Ohio train from Wheeling to Baltimore approached Harpers Ferry. A warning by the night watchman stopped it. Brown went aboard, talked to the passengers for about an hour, and released the train. Upon reaching a working telegraph ~7 AM., the Conductor sent a report to B&O Headquarters. A confirming report arrived ~10:30 AM. The B&O President notified President Buchanan, Secretary of War Floyd, Virginia Governor Wise, and General Stuart of the Maryland Volunteers.

Armory staff coming to work swelled the hostage count to over 60. Brown stayed at

Harpers Ferry—waiting for Slaves to flock to his cause. By Noon, he lost control of both bridges out of town—the only practicable escape routes. Sporadic but sometimes heavy fire exchanges with the Militia forced the Raiders to hole up in the (Fire) Engine House.

Eight Militiamen were wounded during the day. Four townspeople, including the Mayor, were killed. Brown sent his son Watson and Aaron Stevens out with a white flag. Watson was shot and mortally wounded. Aaron was shot and taken prisoner. William Leeman, one of the Raiders, tried to flee by swimming across the Potomac River but was shot and fatally wounded. Brown's son Oliver was fatally shot too, and died next to his father.

Late Monday afternoon, under President Buchanan's orders, Secretary of War Floyd asked the Navy for a Unit of U.S. Marines. Led by 1st Lt. Israel Greene, a Company of U.S. Marines (11 Sergeants, 13 Corporals, 81 Privates, 1 bugler) went from the Washington Navy Yard to Harpers Ferry. Lt. Col. Robert E. Lee, who was on leave just across the Potomac in Arlington, was sent to command them. He deployed in civilian clothes, and joined up with the Marines about 10 PM. They surrounded the Engine House where Brown and his Raiders and nine hostages were barricaded. Lee offered the storming of the Engine House to the Militia. They declined.

At 6:30 AM on Tuesday, Lee sent his aide-de-camp, Lt. J.E.B. Stuart, under a flag of truce, to negotiate Brown's surrender. Brown declined. [If he knew that the Marines outnumbered his raiders by over 5:1, he disregarded that.] Lee waved his cap, signaling Greene and 12 Marines to storm the Engine House. Two Marines tried to break through the door with sledgehammers but failed. Greene found a wooden ladder, ordered the other 10 Marines to use it as a battering ram, and was first to enter through the broken door. Hostage Lewis Washington identified John Brown to him. Greene struck the moving Brown with his saber, giving him a deep cut on the back of the neck. As Brown fell, Greene thrust his saber into his left breast, but the light sword's blade bent double and didn't penetrate. Greene thought, but wasn't sure, that Brown had just fired his Sharp's carbine and killed the first Marine to enter the Engine House after himself. In three minutes, four raiders were dead, the hostages were freed, and the rest of the Raiders were in custody. One Marine was dead, and another was wounded in the face. The next day, the Raiders were taken to Charlestown and turned over to Virginia civil authorities.[375]

Nine days later, Brown was declared fit to stand trial, and was tried in State Court for the murder of four Whites and one Black, for inciting Slaves to rebel, and for treason against the Commonwealth of Virginia. Brown's legal team included at least five attorneys. The defense argued that Brown could not be guilty of treason to a State where he didn't reside and to which he had no loyalty, that he had not killed anyone himself, and the raid's failure indicated that Brown had not conspired with Slaves. On November 2, after 45 minutes of deliberation, the jury convicted Brown on all three counts. The sentence was public hanging on December 2. Ralph Waldo Emerson said that John Brown *will make the gallows glorious like the Cross*. [Christ was glorious; the cross wasn't.]

The restriction against reporters talking to Brown was lifted after his conviction. Brown then talked freely. He also wrote "hundreds" of eloquent letters, many published in newspapers, gaining him more Northern support and more Southern hostility.

To protect against rescue attempts, Charles Town was filled with hundreds and sometimes thousands of troops and militia. The courthouse was protected by cannon. Brown's trips to and from the courthouse and to the gallows were heavily guarded. Governor Wise halted non-military transport on the Winchester and Potomac Railroad during the day of the execution and on the day before and the day after it.

Brown's Kansas friend Silas Soule infiltrated the jail to break him out to flee to New York and maybe Canada. But Brown refused—saying that, at 59, he was too old to live as a fugitive. And he wrote his wife and children that his blood will do vastly more towards advancing the cause I have earnestly endeavoured to promote, than all I have done in my life before and I am worth inconceivably more to hang than for any other purpose [thereby embracing martyrdom after Slaves and Abolitionists didn't flock to his cause].

French author Victor Hugo, who was in exile on the Channel Island of Guernsey and who had openly declared Napoleon III a traitor to France, tried unsuccessfully to gain a pardon for John Brown. And on the day of Brown's execution, Hugo wrote:

> *Politically speaking, the murder of John Brown would be an uncorrectable sin. It would create in the Union a latent fissure that would in the long run dislocate it. Brown's agony might perhaps consolidate Slavery in Virginia, but it would certainly shake the whole American democracy. You save your shame, but you kill your glory. Morally speaking, it seems a part of the human light would put itself out, that the very notion of justice and injustice would hide itself in darkness, on that day where one would see the assassination of Emancipation by Liberty itself. ... Let America know and ponder on this: there is something more frightening than Cain killing Abel, and that is Washington killing Spartacus.*

On the morning of December 2, Brown penned:

> *I, John Brown, am now quite certain that the crimes of this guilty land will never be purged away but with blood. I had, as I now think, vainly flattered myself that without very much bloodshed it might be done.*

He then read his bible and wrote a letter including his will to his wife. Having refused clergy because only Pro-Slavery ministers were available, and sitting in his coffin in a furniture wagon, he was taken through 2000 soldiers to the gallows at 11 AM, hanged at 11:15, and pronounced dead at 11:50. Stonewall Jackson and John Wilkes Booth were spectators. Walt Whitman's 1859-60 poem *Year of Meteors* contains the following lines:

> *I would bind in words retrospective, some of your deeds and signs;*
> *I would sing your contest for the 19th Presidentiad;*
> *I would sing how an old man, tall, with white hair, mounted the scaffold in Virginia;*
> *(I was at hand—silent I stood, with teeth shut close—I watch'd;*
> *I stood very near you, old man, when cool and indifferent, but trembling with age*
> *and your unhealed wounds, you mounted the scaffold.....*[376]

A bipartisan U.S. Senate Committee was appointed on December 14 to determine whether any citizens contributed arms, ammunition, or money to John Brown's men. Its Democrats tried to implicate Republicans in the raid; its Republicans tried to separate themselves from Brown and his acts. The report, written by Pro-Slavery Virginian James Mason, found no direct evidence of a conspiracy but implied that Republican doctrine caused the raid. The two-person minority report focused on denying Northern culpability. Republicans (e.g., Abraham Lincoln) disavowed the raid and called Brown *insane*. A Senator wrote his wife and stated: *The members on both sides are mostly armed with deadly weapons and it is said that the friends of each are armed in the galleries*. In the House of Representatives, after a heated exchange of insults, Pennsylvanian Thaddeus Stevens' friends prevented a Mississippian from attacking him with a Bowie Knife.

Ex-Slave Frederick Douglass, 20 years after the Civil War, said about John Brown:

His zeal in the cause of my race was far greater than mine—it was as the burning sun to my taper light—mine was bounded by time, his stretched away to the boundless shores of eternity. I could live for the Slave, but he could die for him.....

Did John Brown draw his sword against Slavery and thereby lose his life in vain? and to this I answer ten thousand times, No! ...If John Brown did not end the war that ended Slavery, he did at least begin the war that ended Slavery. If we look over the dates, places and men, for which this honor is claimed, we shall find that not Carolina, but Virginia — not Fort Sumpter, but Harper's Ferry and the arsenal — not Col. Anderson, but John Brown, began the war that ended American Slavery and made this a free Republic. Until this blow was struck, the prospect for freedom was dim, shadowy and uncertain. The irrepressible conflict was one of words, votes and compromises. When John Brown stretched forth his arm the sky was cleared. The time for compromises was gone — the armed hosts of freedom stood face to face over the chasm of a broken Union — and the clash of arms was at hand

The Harpers Ferry Raid intensified American polarization over Slavery.[377] [Brown's courage and dedication are indisputable. But his tunnel vision doomed hm and his raiders. And his embracing of martyrdom affirmed his realization that he had no other chance to further foster the end of Slavery.]

4.33 Lincoln at Cooper-Union

In February 1860, Abraham Lincoln spoke at Cooper-Union in Manhattan, New York. It was his first speech in the East and was widely circulated as campaign literature.

Willian Herndon, Lincoln's law partner, said that no former speech-making effort had cost Lincoln so much time and thought as this one. And an eyewitness said:

When Lincoln rose to speak, I was greatly disappointed. He was tall, tall, -- oh, how tall! and so angular and awkward that I had, for an instant, a feeling of pity for so ungainly a man. But when Lincoln warmed up: *his face lighted up as with an inward fire; the whole man was transfigured. I forgot his clothes, his personal appearance, and his individual peculiarities. Presently, forgetting myself, I was on my feet like the rest, yelling like a wild Indian, cheering this wonderful man.*

A New York writer said: *No man ever before made such an impression on his first appeal to a New York audience.*

The following partial description of Lincoln's speech, with some parts editorially italicized/ highlighted, was assembled with the intent of retaining enough of the original to depict the tenor of the times, the timbre of the speech, and the nature of the man.

Lincoln began by saying that the facts were old and familiar and only his presentation, inferences, and observations could be novel. He then made the following points.

The Constitution is the frame of our Government. Its 39 signers may fairly be called its Framers, and fairly represented the opinion and sentiment of the whole nation at the time.

Senator Douglas said that the Framers understood better than we do whether local and federal authority or anything in the Constitution forbids *Federal Government* control of Slavery in our *Federal Territories*—and the text of the original Constitution affirms that its Framers understood the Slavery question better than we do.

The evidence that the Framers understood that nothing prevented Federal Government control of Slavery in the Federal Territories is:

- In 1786, when the Confederation Congress considered prohibiting Slavery in the Territories, three of the four Framers in that Congress voted for prohibiting it.
- In 1787, the Confederation Congress considered the prohibition again. The two more Framers then in that Congress voted for it. And the Ordinance of '87 prohibited it.
- In 1789, the first U.S. Congress, which had 16 Framers as members, prohibited Slavery in the Northwest Territory (then the only Federal Territory). The bill passed both Branches of Congress without a word of opposition and without yeas or nays. President George Washington, another of the "39," signed it into Law. About a year later, Washington wrote Lafayette that he considered that prohibition a wise measure, and hoped that we should at some time have a confederacy of free States.
- North Carolina ceded Tennessee and Georgia ceded Mississippi and Alabama to the Federal Government on the condition that Slavery would not be prohibited in those Territories. But, in 1798 Congress, with 3 of the "39" being members, prohibited bringing Slaves into the Mississippi Territory from anywhere in the U.S.—by fines and by freeing any Slaves so brought. That Act also was passed without yeas or nays.
- Slavery was prevalent in New Orleans and other considerable towns and cities in the Louisiana Territory when the U.S. bought it in 1803. In 1804, Congress, which had 2 of the "39" as members, without yeas and nays, mandated no Slave importation into the Louisiana Territory from foreign parts or of Slaves imported into the U.S. after

5/1/1798; and no bringing in of Slaves except by the owner for his own use as a settler. The penalty for violation was a fine on the owner and freedom to the Slave.

- In 1818-19, both branches of Congress took many votes, with yeas and nays, on the Missouri question. Two of the "39" were members of that Congress. One, Rufus King, steadily voted to prohibit Slavery and against all compromises. The other, Charles Pinckney, steadily voted against prohibiting Slavery.
- Some Framers were members of Congress during more than one of the enumerated actions, with the actual number of different Framers involved being 23. Of these, 21 voted to prohibit or control Slavery in the Territories. And those 21 represent a clear majority of the "39." They did so while acting on their official responsibility and corporal oaths, and would have been guilty of gross political impropriety and willful perjury if their understanding was that Local or Federal Authority or anything in the Constitution prohibited Federal Control of Slavery in the Territories.

The remaining 16 of the "39" left no record (that Lincoln could find) of their position on Slavery, but there is much reason to believe that their understanding would have been the same as that of their 23 compeers.

We live under the original Constitution and the 12 Amendments framed by the first U.S. Congress. Those who insist that Federal Control of Slavery in Federal Territories violates the Constitution fix upon the Amendments, not the original Constitution. In the Dred Scott case, the Supreme Court plants itself on the 5th Amendment, which (contrarily) *provides that no person be deprived of life, liberty or property without due process of law.* Senator Douglas and his peculiar adherents plant themselves upon the 10th Amendment provision that *"the powers not delegated to the United States by the Constitution are reserved to the States respectively, or to the people.*

The 12 Amendments were introduced before and passed after the prohibition of Slavery in the Northwest Territory. Is it not a little presumptuous to affirm that the two things which that Congress deliberately framed, and carried to maturity at the same time, are absolutely inconsistent with each other? And does not such affirmation become impudently absurd when coupled with the other affirmation from the same mouth, that those who did the two things, alleged to be inconsistent, understood whether they really were inconsistent better than we - better than he who affirms that they are inconsistent?

It is surely safe to assume that the 39 Constitution Framers and the 76 members of the Congress that framed its Amendments certainly include those who may be fairly called *our fathers who framed the Government under which we live.* I defy any man to show that any one of them ever declared that, in his understanding, any proper division of local from federal authority, or any part of the Constitution, forbade the Federal Government to control Slavery in the Federal Territories—or that any man in the whole world ever did so prior to the present century. To those who now so declare, I give, not only *our fathers who framed the Government under which we live*, but with them all other men living in that century to search among, and they shall not be able to find the evidence of a single man agreeing with them.

I do not mean to say we are bound to follow implicitly in whatever our fathers did. That would disregard current experience - reject all progress - all improvement. But if we supplant the opinions and policy of our fathers in any case, we should do so upon evidence so conclusive, and argument so clear, that even their great authority, fairly considered and weighed, cannot stand; and most surely not in a case whereof we ourselves declare they understood the question better than we.

Any man who sincerely believes that a proper division of local from federal authority, or any part of the Constitution, forbids the Federal Government to control Slavery in the federal territories is right to say so, and to enforce his position by all truthful evidence and fair argument which he can. But he has no right to substitute falsehood and deception for truthful evidence and fair argument. And he should, at the same time, brave the responsibility of declaring that, in his opinion, he understands their principles better than they did themselves; and especially should he not shirk that responsibility by asserting that they *understood the question just as well, and even better, than we do now.*

But enough! Let all who believe that *our fathers, who framed the Government under which we live, understood this question just as well, and even better, than we do now,* speak as they spoke, and act as they acted upon it. This is all Republicans ask - all Republicans desire - in relation to Slavery. **As those fathers marked it, so let it be again marked, as an evil not to be extended, but to be tolerated and protected only because of and so far as its actual presence among us makes that toleration and protection a necessity. Let all the guarantees those fathers gave it, be, not grudgingly, but fully and fairly, maintained. For this Republicans contend, and with this, so far as I know or believe, they will be content.**

And now, if they would listen - as I suppose they will not - I would address a few words to the Southern people—I would say to them: - You consider yourselves a reasonable and a just people; and I consider that in the general qualities of reason and justice you are not inferior to any other people. Still, when you speak of us Republicans, you do so only to denounce us as reptiles, or, at the best, as no better than outlaws. You will grant a hearing to pirates or murderers, but nothing like it to "Black Republicans." In all your contentions with one another, each of you deems an unconditional condemnation of "Black Republicanism" as the first thing to be attended to. Indeed, such condemnation of us seems to be an indispensable prerequisite - license, so to speak - among you to be admitted or permitted to speak at all. Now, can you, or not, be prevailed upon to pause and to consider whether this is quite just to us, or even to yourselves? Bring forward your charges and specifications, and then be patient long enough to hear us deny or justify.

You charge that we stir up insurrections among your Slaves. We deny it; and what is your proof? Harper's Ferry! John Brown!! John Brown was no Republican; and you have failed to implicate a single Republican in his Harper's Ferry enterprise. If any member of our party is guilty in that matter, you know it or you do not know it. If you do know it, you are inexcusable for not designating the man and proving the fact. If you do not know it, you are inexcusable for asserting it, and especially for persisting in the assertion after you have tried and failed to make the proof. You need to be told that persisting in a charge which one does not know to be true, is simply malicious slander.

Some of you admit that no Republican designedly aided or encouraged the Harper's Ferry affair, but still insist that our doctrines and declarations necessarily lead to such results. You never dealt fairly by us in relation to this affair. When it occurred, some important State elections were near at hand, and you were in evident glee with the belief that, by charging the blame upon us, you could get an advantage of us in those elections. The elections came, and your expectations were not quite fulfilled. Every Republican man knew that, as to himself at least, your charge was a slander, and he was not much inclined by it to cast his vote in your favor.

Republican doctrines and declarations are accompanied with a continual protest against any interference whatever with your Slaves, or with you about your Slaves. Surely, this does not encourage them to revolt. True, **we do**, in common with *our fathers, who framed the Government under which we live*, **declare our belief that Slavery is wrong**; but the Slaves do not hear us declare even this. For anything we say or do, the Slaves would scarcely know there is a Republican party. I believe they would not, in fact, generally know it but for your misrepresentations of us, in their hearing.

Slave insurrections are no more common now than they were before the Republican party was organized. What induced the Southampton Insurrection (Nat Turner's Rebellion), twenty-eight years ago, in which, at least three times as many lives were lost as at Harper's Ferry? You can scarcely stretch your very elastic fancy to the conclusion that Southampton was "got up by Black Republicanism." In the present state of things in the United States, I do not think a general, or even a very extensive Slave insurrection is possible. The indispensable concert of action cannot be attained. The Slaves have no means of rapid communication; nor can incendiary freemen, black or white, supply it. The explosive materials are everywhere in parcels; but there neither are, nor can be supplied, the indispensable connecting trains.

Much is said by Southern people about the affection of Slaves for their masters and mistresses; and a part of it, at least, is true. A plot for an uprising could scarcely be devised and communicated to twenty individuals before some one of them, to save the life of a favorite master or mistress, would divulge it. Occasional poisonings from the kitchen, and open or stealthy assassinations in the field, and local revolts extending to a score or so, will continue to occur as the natural results of Slavery; but no general insurrection of Slaves, as I think, can happen in this country for a long time. Whoever much fears, or much hopes for such an event, will be alike disappointed.

John Brown's effort was not a Slave Insurrection. It was an attempt by White Men to get up a revolt among Slaves, in which the Slaves refused to participate. In fact, it was so absurd that the Slaves, with all their ignorance, saw plainly enough it could not succeed.

You will break up the Union rather than submit to a denial of your Constitutional rights. That has a somewhat reckless sound; but it would be palliated, if not fully justified, were we proposing, by the mere force of numbers, to deprive you of some right, plainly written down in the Constitution. But we are proposing no such thing. When you make such declarations, you have a specific and well-understood allusion to an assumed Constitutional right to take Slaves into the Federal Territories, and to hold them there as property. But the Constitution is literally silent about any such right. We, on the contrary, deny that such a right has any existence in the Constitution, even by implication.

Your purpose, then, plainly stated, is that you will destroy the Government, unless you be allowed to construe and enforce the Constitution as you please, on all points in dispute between you and us. You will rule or ruin in all events.

Perhaps you will say the Supreme Court has decided the disputed Constitutional question in your favor. Not quite so. The decision was made by a divided Court by a bare majority of the judges, not quite in agreement on the reasons for making it. And it was based mainly upon the untrue statement that *the right of property in a Slave is distinctly and expressly affirmed in the Constitution.* If the Judges had only pledged their judicial opinion that such right is affirmed in the instrument by implication, it would be open to others to show that neither the word "Slave" nor "Slavery" is to be found in the Constitution, nor the word *property*—and wherever in that instrument the Slave is alluded to, he is called a *person*—and wherever his master's legal right to him is alluded to, it is as *service or labor which may be due.* Also, it would be open to show that this mode of alluding to Slaves and Slavery was employed to exclude from the Constitution the idea that there could be property in man. To show all this is easy and certain.

When this obvious mistake of the Judges shall be brought to their notice, is it not reasonable to expect that they will withdraw the mistaken statement, and reconsider the conclusion based upon it? And it is to be remembered that our fathers long ago decided this Constitutional question in our favor—without division among themselves, and without basing it on any mistaken statement of fact. Do you really feel justified to break up this Government unless such a court decision shall be at once submitted to as a conclusive and final rule of political action?

You say you will not abide the election of a Republican president! In that supposed event, you say, you will destroy the Union; and then, you say, the great crime of having destroyed it will be upon us! That is cool. A highwayman holds a pistol to my ear, and mutters through his teeth, *Stand and deliver, or I shall kill you, and then you will be a murderer*!

To be sure, what the robber demanded— my money— was my own; and I had a clear right to keep it. But it was no more my own than my vote is my own; and the threat of death to me, to extort my money, and the threat of destruction to the Union, to extort my vote, can scarcely be distinguished in principle.

A few words now to Republicans. *It is exceedingly desirable that all parts of this great Confederacy shall be at peace, and in harmony, one with another. Let us Republicans do our part to have it so. Even though much provoked, let us do nothing through passion and ill temper. Even though the southern people will not so much as listen to us, let us calmly consider their demands, and yield to them if, in our deliberate view of our duty, we possibly can.* Judging by all they say and do, and by the subject and nature of their controversy with us, let us determine, if we can, what will satisfy them.

They will not be satisfied if the Territories be unconditionally surrendered to them. In all their present complaints against us, the Territories are scarcely mentioned. Invasions and insurrections are the rage now. Will it satisfy them, if, in the future, we have nothing to do with invasions and insurrections? We know it will not because we know we never had anything to do with invasions and insurrections. And yet this total abstaining does not exempt us from the charge and the denunciation.

What will satisfy them? Simply this: We must not only let them alone, but we must somehow convince them that we do let them alone. This, we know by experience, is no easy task. We have been so trying to convince them from the very beginning of our organization with no success. In all our platforms and speeches, we have constantly protested our purpose to let them alone; but this has had no tendency to convince them. Alike unavailing to convince them is the fact that they have never detected a man of us in any attempt to disturb them.

What will convince them? Only this: cease to call Slavery *wrong,* and join them in calling it *right.* And this must be done thoroughly—in *acts* as well as in *words.* Silence will not be tolerated—we must place ourselves avowedly with them. Senator Douglas' new sedition law must be enacted and enforced, suppressing all declarations that Slavery is wrong, whether made in politics, in presses, in pulpits, or in private. We must arrest and return their fugitive Slaves with greedy pleasure. We must pull down our Free-State Constitutions. The whole atmosphere must be disinfected from all taint of opposition to Slavery before they will cease to believe that all their troubles proceed from us.

They do not state their case precisely in this way. Most of them would probably say to us, "Let us alone, do nothing to us, and say what you please about Slavery." But we do let them alone—have never disturbed them. It is what we say that dissatisfies them—they will continue to accuse us until we cease saying.

Our Free-State Constitutions declare the wrong of Slavery with more solemn emphasis than all other sayings against it. And when all those other sayings have been silenced, the overthrow of these Constitutions will be demanded, and nothing be left to resist the demand. Holding that Slavery is morally right and socially elevating, they cannot cease to demand a full national recognition of it, as a legal right and a social blessing.

We cannot justifiably withhold this on any ground save our conviction that Slavery is wrong. If Slavery is right, all words, acts, laws, and constitutions against it, are themselves wrong, and should be silenced, and swept away. If Slavery is wrong, they cannot justly insist upon its extension—its enlargement.

All they ask, we could readily grant, if we thought Slavery right. All we ask, they could as readily grant, if they thought it wrong. The whole controversy depends upon their thinking it right and our thinking it wrong. Thinking it right, as they do, they are not to blame for desiring its full recognition as being right. But thinking it wrong, as we do, can we yield to them? Can we cast our votes with their view, and against our own? In view of our moral, social, and political responsibilities, can we do this?

Wrong as we think Slavery is, we can yet afford to let it alone where it is, because that much is due to the necessity arising from its actual presence in the nation. But can we, while our votes will prevent it, allow it to spread into the National Territories, and to overrun us here in these Free States? If our sense of duty forbids this, then let us stand by our duty, fearlessly and effectively. Let us be diverted by none of those sophistical contrivances wherewith we are so industriously plied and belabored—contrivances such as groping for some middle ground between the right and the wrong, vain as the search for a man who should be neither a living man nor a dead man—such as a policy of *don't care* on a question about which all true men do care—such as appeals beseeching true Union men to yield to Disunionists, reversing the divine rule, and calling, not the sinners, but the righteous to repentance—such as invocations to Washington, imploring men to unsay what Washington said, and undo what Washington did.

Neither let us be slandered from our duty by false accusations against us, nor frightened from it by menaces of destruction to the Government nor of dungeons to ourselves. LET US HAVE FAITH THAT RIGHT MAKES MIGHT, AND IN THAT FAITH, LET US, TO THE END, DARE TO DO OUR DUTY AS WE UNDERSTAND IT.[378]

4.34 The 1860 Presidential Election

In 1860, the deeply divided Country had multiple presidential competitors.

The Constitutional Union Party (former *Whigs* and *Know Nothings*) wanted to stave off secession by avoiding Slavery. Their slogan was: *The Union as it is, and the Constitution as it is.* Former U.S. Senator **John Bell** of Tennessee, a former *Whig*, who had opposed the Kansas-Nebraska Act and the Lecompton Constitution, was their candidate.

The Southern Democrats nominated Vice President **John C. Breckinridge**, a Kentuckian and a former member of both Houses of Congress. His party split from the Democratic Party when it decided not to not support extending Slavery where it wasn't wanted

The (Northern) Democrats nominated U.S. Senator **Stephen A. Douglas** of Illinois, who led on all their convention's votes but didn't gain the nomination until the 59th vote.

The four frontrunners of the eight candidates for the Republican candidacy were:

1. U.S. Senator **William H. Seward** of New York. He had been his State's Governor. His Anti-Slavery speeches predicted conflict, putting off moderates. He was wrongly seen as radical and his strong political ally, Horace Greely, had become his enemy.
2. Ohio Governor **Salmon Chase**, a former Democrat who opposed tariffs demanded by Pennsylvania and was short on charisma and political acumen.
3. Former U.S. Representative **Edwin Bates** of Missouri. His past association with the *Know Nothings* alienated German-Americans, but he had the support of Horace Greely.
4. Former U.S. Representative from Illinois **Abraham Lincoln**. His debating prestige, speech at Cooper-Union, adept "delegate wranglers," and Convention Delegate Horace Greely's strong opposition to Seward made him second to Seward on the first ballot. On the next ballot, there was a shift toward Seward and a bigger one toward Lincoln. On the third, Lincoln's moderate position on Slavery, economic position, Western origin, and oratorical reputation made him the Republican nominee by an overwhelming margin.

The remnants of the Liberty Party nominated the immensely wealthy former U.S. Representative **Gerrit Smith** of New York. He was an advocate of term limits, racial integration, women's suffrage and equality, a John Brown friend and financier, an opponent of land monopoly, and the founder of a non-sectarian Christian Church.[379]

Bell and Douglas claimed that electing Lincoln might not mean disunion. Army officers in Virginia, Kansas, and South Carolina advised of military preparations to the contrary. [Steven Douglas and Abraham Lincoln, and many others knew, well before 1860, that it was virtually inevitable that the South would go to war to save Slavery.]

In 1860, national election votes were cast for a State citizen pledged to vote for a candidate. In the 11 States that would secede, only Virginia had one pledged to vote for Abraham Lincoln, so the 1.15% of the vote that he got there was all he received from the Southern Confederacy to be.[380] But the Northern vote decided the issue as follows:

1860 PRESIDENTIAL ELECTION RESULTS[381]				
CANDIDATE	POPULAR VOTE %	POPULAR VOTES	ELECTORAL VOTES	ELECTORAL VOTE %
LINCOLN	39.82%	1,865,908	180	59.41%
BRECKINRIDGE	18.10%	848,019	72	23.76%
BELL	12.61%	590,901	39	12.87%
DOUGLAS	29.46%	1,380,202	12	3.96%
OTHER	00.01%	531	0	0.00%
TOTALS	100.00%	4,685.581	303	100.00%
ELECTORAL VOTES NEEDED TO WIN			152	

Four days after Lincoln's election, U.S. Senator James Chestnut of South Carolina resigned his Senate seat and went home to write an Ordinance of Secession.

On 12/3/1860, Vice President Breckinridge, as Chaplain, opened the 36th U.S. Senate's 2nd session with: *Hear our petitions, and send us an answer of peace. May all bitterness and wrath* be put away, and may Senators *deliberate…not as partisans, but as brethren and patriots, seeking the highest welfare… of the whole country…. Hear us… and heal our land.* The roll was then called. Ten (10) Southern Senators did not answer.[382]

On 12/20/1860, 169 South Carolina delegates convened in Charleston. Most were wealthy, middle aged planters and lawyers, and 153 were Slaveholders. They voted unanimously to secede. Their Secession Declaration stated that the non-slaveholding States had *denounced as sinful the institution of slavery* and had *encouraged and assisted thousands of our slaves to leave their homes; and those who remain, have been incited by emissaries, books and pictures to servile insurrection.*[383] And 44 days after Lincoln's election, South Carolina seceded. Alabama, Arkansas, Florida, Georgia, Louisiana, North Carolina, Mississippi, Tennessee, Texas, and Virginia followed suit.

4.35 The Civil War

On 4/12/1861, South Carolina's militia, commanded by Brigadier General P.G.T. Beauregard, started the War by bombarding Fort Sumter in Charleston's harbor.[384]

The Confederacy's population was 5.5 million free persons and 3.5 million Slaves. Their financial assets were $74 million. Jefferson Davis was elected President on 2/8/1861. The Union had 25 States: California, Connecticut, Delaware, Illinois, Indiana, Iowa, Kansas, Kentucky, Maine, Maryland, Massachusetts, Michigan, Minnesota, Missouri, Nevada, New Hampshire, New Jersey, New York, Ohio, Oregon, Pennsylvania, Rhode Island, Vermont, West Virginia (beginning in 1863) and Wisconsin. Of these, Delaware, Kentucky, Maryland, Missouri, and West Virginia were Border States (Slave States that did not secede), had 2.5

million free inhabitants, 500,000 Slaves, and $29 Million dollars in assets. The other Union States had 18.5 million people and $234 million in assets.

Agriculturally, the North had a large advantage outside of rice and tobacco. For example, the Union produced 550 million bushels of corn to the South's 250 million.[385]

Lincoln, concerned about premature emancipation causing loss of the Border States, particularly Kentucky, proposed gradual emancipation based on compensation and voluntary colonization. Congress passed that. Only the District of Columbia accepted it.

When a Horace Greeley editorial implied that Lincoln's administration lacked direction and resolve, Lincoln responded, on August 22, 1862, that:

- His personal wish is that all men everywhere could be freed.
- His duty is saving the Union, not saving or destroying Slavery. To do that, he would free all Slaves, or free none, or free some and not others. (Lincoln reputedly had a draft of the Emancipation Proclamation in his desk at the time.)[386]

On April 4, 1864, (*Honest Abe*) Lincoln averred in a letter to Kentuckian Albert Hodges, editor of the *Frankfort Commonwealth*,[387] that:

- *If Slavery is not wrong, nothing is wrong.*
- *I have never understood that the Presidency conferred upon me an unrestricted right to act officially upon this judgment and feeling. It was in the oath I took that I would, to the best of my ability, preserve, protect, and defend the Constitution of the United States. I could not take the office without taking the oath. Nor was it my view that I might take an oath to get power, and break the oath in using the power.*
- *I understood, too, that in ordinary civil administration this oath even forbade me to practically indulge my primary abstract judgment on the moral question of Slavery.*
- *I aver that, to this day, I have done no official act in mere deference to my abstract judgment and feeling on Slavery.*
- *My oath to preserve the Constitution to the best of my ability, imposed upon me the duty of preserving, by every indispensable means, that government -- that nation -- of which that Constitution was the organic law.*
- *Was it possible to lose the nation, and yet preserve the Constitution? By general law life and limb must be protected; yet often a limb must be amputated to save a life; but a life is never wisely given to save a limb.*
- *I felt that measures, otherwise unconstitutional, might become lawful, by becoming indispensable to the preservation of the Constitution, through the preservation of the nation. Right or wrong, I assumed this ground, and now avow it.*
- *I could not feel that, to the best of my ability, I had even tried to preserve the Constitution, if, to save Slavery, or any minor matter, I should permit the wreck of government, country, and Constitution all together.*
- *Early in the war, Gen. Fremont attempted military emancipation. I forbade it, because I did not then think it an indispensable necessity. When a little later, Gen. Cameron, then Secretary of War, suggested the arming of the blacks, I objected, because I did not yet think it an indispensable necessity. When, still later, Gen. Hunter attempted*

military emancipation, I again forbade it, because I did not yet think the indispensable necessity had come. When, in March, and May, and July 1862 I made earnest, and successive appeals to the border states to favor compensated emancipation, I believed the indispensable necessity for military emancipation, and arming the blacks would come, unless averted by that measure. They declined the proposition.

- *I was, in my best judgment, driven to the alternative of either surrendering the Union, and with it, the Constitution, or of laying strong hand upon the colored element. I chose the latter. In choosing it, I hoped for greater gain than loss; but of this, I was not entirely confident.*
- *More than a year of trial now shows no loss in our foreign relations, none in our home popular sentiment, none in our white military force. It shows a gain of quite a hundred and thirty thousand soldiers, seamen, and laborers. We have the men; and we could not have had them without the measure.*
- *I claim not to have controlled events, but confess plainly that events have controlled me. Now, at the end of three years struggle the nation's condition is not what either party, or any man devised, or expected. God alone can claim it.*
- *If God now wills the removal of a great wrong, and wills also that we of the North as well as you of the South, shall pay fairly for our complicity in that wrong, impartial history will find therein new cause to attest and revere the justice and goodness of God.*

On 9/171862, the Union's Army of the Potomac blunted Robert E. Lee's incursion into the Union at Antietam Creek in Maryland. That was the bloodiest one-day battle in American Military History and a military stalemate. Lee withdrew into Virginia. (But the battle reputedly ended France's and England's consideration of recognizing and aiding the Confederacy.) The Union declared victory. Lincoln repeatedly ordered General McClellan to pursue Lee. McClellan didn't, and Lincoln relieved him of command of the Army of the Potomac on November 5, 1862.[388]

On 4/9/1865, The Civil War's end began with Robert E. Lee surrendering the Army of Virginia to Ulysses S. Grant at Appomattox, Virginia. The last Confederate Army surrender was by Brigadier General Stand Watie on 8/23/1865 in what is now Oklahoma. But the Raider *CSS Shenandoah* terrorized Union commercial shipping in the Bering Sea until August 1865, when its Captain, LCDR James Waddell, learned of the war's end and covertly sailed to Liverpool, England, where he furled its Confederate flag.[389]

The Civil War death toll was put at 618,222, 360,222 Union and 258,000 Confederate. In 2010, demographic Historian J. David Hacker recalculated that based on digitized 19th Century Census data. He calculated a total of 750,000 Union and Confederate non-civilian deaths. If the relative proportions of the earlier figures are correct, the Union military lost 437,006 men and the Confederacy lost 312,994.[390] In any case, the Civil War killed more Americans than any other war.

Wars kill, regardless of how just the cause. And the ability to wage war is largely a function of the will of a nation's people—which erodes as the death rate climbs and war drags on. The Civil War affirmed that, especially during Christmas. Presents were fewer then, especially in the devastated South. In his Chronicle on Christmas during the Civil Was, Author Kevin Rawlings noted that some Southern children worried about the Union blockade and little Sallie Brock Putnam plotted the course Santa would take to avoid it. And excuses for a lack of Santa included his having been shot by Yankees. Also, in both the North and South, children reacted to their fathers who were on furlough as strangers. A representative depiction of the Northern viewpoint was the Christmas 1862 editorial cartoon by Thomas Nast. Published in the January 1863 issue of Harper's Weekly, it showed a husband and wife separated by the war in two adjacent circles. The left circle showed a wife praying at a window at the foot of the bed holding her two children— and the circle on the right showed her husband praying on the battlefield. The magazine's cover showed Santa holding a dancing puppet of Jefferson Davis hanging from a rope around his neck in one hand and passing out gifts like socks to Union Soldiers with the other hand. The Christmas 1863 Nast cartoon showed the couple back together. After the war, Nast made the North Pole Santa's home—so no one else could use him for propaganda the same way.[391]

William Gordon McCabe (1841-1920) was a Confederate soldier who enlisted as a private, served throughout the war, and rose to the rank of Captain. He also was a poet, and became an educator after the war. One of his poems depicts the soldier's humanity and the nature of war for him, mentioning the dead but not the killing. That poem follows.

CHRISTMAS NIGHT OF 1862

The wintry blast goes wailing by,
The snow is falling overhead;
I hear the lonely sentry's tread,
And distant watch-fires light the sky.

Dim forms go flitting through the gloom;
The soldiers cluster round the blaze
To talk of other Christmas days,
And softly speak of home and home.

My sabre swinging overhead Gleams
in the watch-fire's fitful glow,
While fiercely drives the blinding snow,
And memory leads me to the dead.

My thoughts go wandering to and fro,
Vibrating between the Now and Then;
I see the low-browed home again,
The old hall wreathed with mistletoe.

And sweetly from the far-off years
Comes borne the laughter faint and low,
The voices of the Long Ago!
My eyes are wet with tender tears.

I feel again the mother-kiss,
I see again the glad surprise
That lightened up the tranquil eyes
And brimmed them o'er with tears of bliss,

As, rushing from the old hall-door,
She fondly clasped her wayward boy
Her face all radiant with the joy
She felt to see him home once more.

My sabre swinging on the bough
Gleams in the watch-fire's fitful glow,
While fiercely drives the blinding snow
Aslant upon my saddened brow.

Those cherished faces all are gone!
Asleep within the quiet graves
Where lies the snow in drifting waves,
And I am sitting here alone.

There's not a comrade here to-night
But knows that loved ones far away
On bended knee this night will pray:
"God bring our darling from the fight."

But there are none to wish me back,
For me no yearning prayers arise.
The lips are mute and closed the eyes–
My home is in the bivouac. [392]

4.36 Emancipation

On 9/22/1862, 375 days into the War, Lincoln proclaimed: [393]

That on the first day of January in the year of our Lord, one thousand eight hundred and sixty-three, all persons held as slaves within any State, or designated part of a State, the people whereof shall then be in rebellion against the United States shall be then, thenceforward, and forever free; and the executive government of the United States, including the military and naval authority thereof, will recognize and maintain the freedom of such persons, and will do no act or acts to repress such persons, or any of them, in any efforts they may make for their actual freedom.

The Proclamation couldn't be enforced in Confederate-held territory. But it symbolized the Union's commitment to emancipation and greatly reduced the Confederacy's hope of getting foreign aid. Lincoln also played a leading role in getting the 13th Amendment passed, but all Union States except Delaware and Kentucky had abolished Slavery before its ratification on 12/6/1865. It states:

> Neither slavery nor involuntary servitude, except as a punishment for crime whereof the party shall have been duly convicted, shall exist within the United States, or any place subject to their jurisdiction.[394]

4.37 Post-Civil War Inequality

On 12/24/1865, the first Klu Klux Klan was founded in Pulaski, Tennessee. Similar Southern groups used threats, violence, and murder to intimidate Northern Leaders, their Southern Sympathizers, freedmen, and Politically Active Blacks. According to Historian Eric Foner, the 1870-71 Enforcement Acts restored order, reinvigorated Southern Republicans' morale, and enabled Blacks to exercise their citizenship rights. Historian George C. Rable argued that the first KKK was a political failure and was discarded, but similar paramilitary groups became the military arm of the Democratic Party, and were directed at suppressing Republican voting and turning Republicans out of office.[395]

Much has been since done to legislate Black equality. [But our over 10 million illegal aliens and illegal drug availability prove that poorly enforced laws aren't effective. And Prohibition and Colonial Smuggling showed that, when a great majority of a populace is against a law, it cannot be effectively enforced. Until Whites and Blacks work together, fairly and biracially, to eliminate unfair discrimination, equal treatment of Blacks by Whites or of Whites by Blacks will not be achieved. Moreover, the universal favoring of one's own children, families, and ethnicities means that inequalities will persist.]

4.38 The Ongoing Conflict

Acute emotional awareness of their history and mistreatment cannot be erased from the psyche of the descendants of Slaves. Other minorities, and women, carry an analogous burden. And individual and group efforts to improve don't stop with being equal but extend to excelling (being superior, winning) and take precedence over achieving equality.

The White Male is a stereotypical scapegoat for inequality. But we all belong to the same species—skin hue, sexual orientation, and ethnicity notwithstanding—and we all have the same basic emotional driving force and sensibility.

Treating people as individuals, not stereotypes, is essential. Yesteryear must not be forgotten, but it cannot be undone. And projecting yesteryear's sins onto those who did not commit them has a negative effect on "racial," sexual and other equality efforts. So does stereotypical castigation—of whomever.

Further, individual responsibility and accountability for one's own actions, not for those of others, is a fundament of the U.S. and of the Judeo-Christian ethic. An apt biblical statement of that is contained in Ezekiel 18:20:[396]

> The soul that sinneth, it shall die. The son shall not bear the inequity of the father, neither shall the father bear the inequity of the son: the righteousness of the righteous shall be upon him, and the wickedness of the wicked shall be upon him

5

Some Other Human Traits

5.1 Humor and Indomitable Spirit

Humor adds much to our quality of life and our ability to discount potential catastrophe. An example is evident in the Kingston Trio version of lyricist Sheldon Harnick's song *The Merry Minuet.* And people repeatedly surmount adversity, including personal tragedy, to enjoy life again. There's an example of that in the Louis Armstrong Dixieland Jazz version of the *New Orleans Funeral March.* [397]

5.2 Language Barriers

Language barriers (mini-Towers of Babel) endure and inhibit or prevent communication.

America's initial settlement was male-controlled. And many men label people and places indecorously. (Decorous language is fostered mostly by women. A likely false—but realistic—anecdote about that describes a friend of President Truman's wife Bess complaining about her inability to keep her husband from saying *horse manure!* Bess reputedly replied: *My dear, I've been trying for over 30 years to get Harry to say manure.*)

Typical Colonial American place names reflect "respectable" English culture. One that does not was evident during my childhood when our family made regular Summer Sunday afternoon trips to and from Bethany Beach, Delaware. Passing through Ocean View on the way took us over a little bridge over a creek identified by a State Highway Department sign as the *Assawoman Canal.* I took *Assawoman* to be an English language name. But *ass* was not a word to be used in front of my parents—nor dared I state that it sounded like a name for a place for having sex. But I was curious enough to ask about it. My father said that it's an "Indian" word that doesn't mean what it is spelled like. But he didn't know its meaning or how to pronounce it. And while I've often heard it spoken as *ass-a-woman* in male company, I've rarely heard it spoken in mixed company.

The *Assawoman Canal* was dug in the 1890s as part of the Intracoastal Waterway, runs South from *Indian River Bay* to *Little Assawoman Bay*, separates Fenwick Island (and Bethany Beach) from Mainland Delaware, and from 2006-2010 was dredged out to be 35' wide and 3' deep.[398] There's also a *Big Assawoman Bay* between North Ocean City, Maryland and Mainland Delmarva.[399] And ~50 miles further South there's an unincorporated community named *Assawoman* (formerly *Assawaman*) in Accomack County, Virginia. It reputedly was named for the matriarch of an Amerind Tribe.[400] [Many Amerind women were leaders. Among the Lenni-Lenape of the Central East Coast, for example, women farmed and hunted, were responsible for land management, and the older ones distributed the food.[401]] And the Amerind origin of *Assawoman* is consistent with nearby places like *Assateague, Chincoteague*, and *Chesapeake*.

An example of how *Assawoman* has been misconstrued is a 9/6/2012 online blog. It noted that Hamilton Kenny's *Place Names of Maryland* identifies *assa* as being from the Algonquin *acaw*, meaning *across*, or *asaw*, meaning *brown, yellow*. But, after acknowledging that the full meaning of *Assawoman* is unknown, the blog stated that it means *a woman with a fantastic ass*.[402] If that were true, it would follow that *Assateague Island*, where the *Chincoteague Ponies* live, is named for a Teague with a fantastic *ass* (or a place to have sex with a Teague?).

Teague is an anglicized Gaelic name that extends back to Ireland's County Galway in ancient times. Some Teagues arrived in Virginia and Maryland in the latter half of the 17th Century. Possible origins of the name include Cornish and Welsh words meaning handsome or fair.[403, 404] But the names *Assawoman* and *Assateague* appear to have existed long before Teagues arrived in North America.

The initial European male settlers of Delmarva might have named a locale as a *place to take (Amerind) women for sex*. But the only credible conclusion about *Assawoman* is that it is an Amerind name whose full meaning and proper pronunciation are generally, and perhaps totally, now unknown. Other connotations recur because of an indecorous aspect of *the nature of the human beast*, facilitated by the tendency to assign meaning to a word as if it originated in one's native tongue.

Another Delaware locale shows the mistranslation of Dutch names into English. In Southern Kent County, about 30 bayside miles North of Lewes, there's a stream named the *Murderkill River*. The *Murder* part, according to Dick Carter, Chair of the Delaware Heritage Commission, comes from the middle Dutch word *moeder,* meaning *mother*. And *kille* is the Dutch word for *river*, making *Mother River* a correct translation. Another possibility is *Muddy River*, if the original name were *Modderkille*—because the still used Dutch word *Modder* means Mud.[405] In either case, contrary to folklore and appearance, taking *Murderkill* as an English word is incorrect.

Yet another gory-sounding Delaware name is Slaughter Beach, in Sussex County about halfway between Lewes and the Murderkill River. It may have been named for its first postmaster, who lived there. Another conjecture is that it was named after the annual horseshoe crab exodus from the Delaware Bay to lay their eggs—with a host of crab deaths being caused by stranding of crabs by the tide. A third tale is that, to prevent massacre by Amerinds, a group of them were slaughtered by cannon fire.[406] {Some private citizens had cannons then. And when I was duck hunting on Chesapeake Bay about 50 years ago, I heard occasional unusually loud gunfire. My companions said it was from small, boat-mounted cannons used (illegally) as flock guns to down wildfowl.}

Another Delaware name mistranslation was *Whorekill*, an early English name for Lewes, Sussex County's first town. That's a reputed anglicization of *Hoerekill*, the name provided by the Dutch whose first settlers there, in 1631, were massacred by the Amerind Siconese (ancestors of the Lenni-Lenape and Nanticoke[407]). *Whorekill* could be from the Dutch words *Hoere*, meaning harlot, and *Kille meaning* river, making the Dutch name *Harlot River.* Speculation further attributes that name to the Siconese sharing their women with the settlers, with settler mistreatment of the women resulting in the "very peaceful" [??] Siconese killing every settler that the Dutch left behind to establish a Whaling Village in *HoereKill.* (Whorekill's unseemly connotation was set aside In 1682 when William Penn renamed the town Lewes after the town of that name in East Sussex, England.)[408]

The naming illustrations also show a penchant for pejoratively treating other cultures.

5.3 Competition and Cooperation

Our competitive nature[409] shows in Wars, Murders, Slavery, Theft, Inequalities, etc.—behavior as human as love, virtue, charity, and heroic selflessness.

The competitive exclusion principle states that two species cannot co-exist if they compete for exactly the same resources—because the more powerful reproduce more and their competition dies or is killed off.[410] Our Intraspecies counterpart of that includes genocides: the Cambodian (1975-79); the Holocaust (1941-45); the Ukrainian (1932-33), the Armenian (1915-22); the Irish (1845-1850), etc.[411]

A "scientific" term for wiping out competitive laggards is *Natural Selection.* Human competitiveness, as Author and Professor Loretta G. Breuning, PhD, put it,[412] has been naturally selected for by the development of brains that strive for social dominance and reward winning with a good feeling (a burst of serotonin). She also described our competitiveness as having been submerged in a warm fuzzy view of nature inconsistent with the reality that monkeys have been trying to one-up each other for 50 million years.

Business success, promotions, athletic matches and fan behavior, and band and chess contests, etc., all are competitive. And means of disposing of the competition and getting away with it better enable individuals, groups, and species to prosper.

Competition didn't take us out of our hand-to-mouth hunter-gatherer existence by itself. Concurrent cooperation[413] was required. Human physical frailty compared to other predators (e.g., bears, lions) and the dangers posed by human competitors necessitated team behavior for survival. Foraging and hunting success, development of better weapons and other tools, and establishment and protection of territory in which to hunt and gather benefitted from that. And competition, cooperation, big families, and a relatively high rate of offspring survival made H. sapiens Earth's dominant predator.

Cooperation often turns competitive. For example, America's early Colonists initially cooperated and traded with the Amerinds. But after learning necessary survival skills, the newcomers used superior weaponry and numbers to displace the Amerinds and make the Colonists' Europe-based culture dominant.

5.4 The World We Inherited

We strive for Goodness and Altruism, and even our pagan ancestors sought their own versions of doing Good. All of that has provided countless examples of virtue, selflessness, and heroic self-sacrifice.

After our Civil War, the U.S. continued to subdue Amerinds, took Spain's Pacific possessions (and freed Cuba and became dominant in the Caribbean) in the Spanish--American War, and occupied the Philippines in the Philippine-American War. But after WWI, allowing defeated Germany to remain sovereign changed the conquest paradigm. And, as is not atypical, the flaws in a new practice were devastating. The harsh and humiliating terms of the Armistice impoverished Germany, the Great Depression enabled its takeover by Hitler's National Socialist Party, Germany embraced anti-Semitism, and WWII began ~20 years after WWI.[414]

WWII's aftermath did not include a permanent takeover of the conquered either. The U.S. ended its post-war occupation of West Germany in 10 years—and included it in the Marshall Plan that provided about $100 billion (in today's dollars) to restore Western Europe.[415] Also, after Japan's unconditional (and first) surrender, we restored its sovereignty in seven years.[416]

Few of us are as dedicated to helping others as was Mother Teresa.[417] But when catastrophe strikes, we strive to restore a semblance of normal life to those affected—and many personally contribute to helping victims.

When loving parents tuck their children into bed at night and help them recite *Now I lay me down to sleep, I pray the Lord my soul to keep. If I should die before I wake, ...* they're providing security against the children's fears that exist despite their parents' dedication to their safety. We also lock our homes, turn on our security systems even when we're at home, and don't sleep when a teenage daughter stays out late. Moreover, we remain ensconced in our "civilized" world by knowing if and when we can safely go to some areas. And we're continually reminded by news telecasts about criminality, including murders. Moreover, the annual cost of U.S. identity theft and the $50 billion in annual losses to U.S. businesses due to employee theft[418] further attest to the dishonesty of a sizeable portion of our fellow man. And when someone tells us that *it's business, not personal* and/or *it's not the money, it's the principle*, it's a good bet that it's the money and very personal.

We nonetheless live well. The 2015 international poverty level, the minimum needed for food, shelter, and clothing, as determined by the World Bank, was $1.90/day.[419] That's less than one-thirtieth the $7.25/hour, $58 per eight-hour day U.S. federal minimum wage in 2015.[420] And the average U.S. welfare recipient's income of $25/day puts our government-subsidized poor in the top 20% of the world in income.[421]

Few Americans have seen real poverty. I saw a sharp depiction of it when I was stationed on a destroyer during a 1957-58 Mediterranean deployment. Our first African port was Addis Ababa, Ethiopia. From the desolate, salt-encrusted surrounding area came a poor native carrying a basket of peanuts over a slender, smooth-skinned arm that ended at the wrist. (The word quickly spread that he was a leper, and he made no sales.) Addis Ababa is now the relatively thriving capital city of Ethiopia, whose broad-based growth averaged 9.9% a year from 2007-08 to 2017-18, compared to a regional average of 5.4%. And as of 2018, Ethiopia was Africa's 2nd most populous nation, with about 109 million people, but its $709 per capita annual income also made it one of the poorest.[422]

The next African port we visited was Djibouti, French Somaliland. Its people were impoverished. Prostitution was rampant. The reputed venereal disease rate of over 90% attested to the lack of health care. (During my year 2000 trip to Kansas City, an African taxi driver relatively new to the U.S. told me, in an erudite British accent, that he didn't understand why people complained about health care here because he could just go to the hospital and get it—but there was no medical care at all where he came from.) Djibouti is now an Independent Republic, with a per capita income of about $2874/yr.[423]

Rich or poor, gentler people die rather than kill. (Some of them don't even realize that they are responsible for the killing of the meat they eat.) But it is police and military force, lethal when necessary, that assures our survival and freedom. That's clearly shown when government fails. For example, multiple references attest to federal, state, and local malfeasance when Hurricane Katrina hit the U.S. Gulf Coast in 2005. Reports of police and prison guard desertion and criminality abounded, as did tales of carjacking, looting, rapes, shootings, and murders. The Head of the Federal Emergency Management Agency was fired; the Governor of Louisiana didn't run for re-election; the New Orleans Police Superintendent resigned; the Mayor of New Orleans was convicted of 21 charges related to wire fraud, bribery, and money laundering before and after the hurricane; etc. And after the mandatory evacuation of New Orleans, the Coast Guard rescued about 33,500 of the 65,000 people still stranded there. Overall, about 2000 people died and over a million were displaced. And ~58,000 National Guardsmen from all 50 States were sent to combat the lawlessness and aid in the recovery. [e.g.,424]

Within the great cultural diversity in humans, there's a widespread belief that one's own slice of humanity is better than the rest. An ages-old example is Deuteronomy 14:2 (KJV), which states about Judaism that: *For thou art an holy people unto the LORD thy God, and the Lord hath chosen thee to be a peculiar people unto himself, above all the nations that are upon the earth.* Multitudes accept that literally, but Judaism also holds that God entered into a covenant with all humankind, and that non-Jews also have a relationship with God.[425] Another example is Nazi adoption of the Master Race ideology holding the Nordic (Aryan) race (predominant among Northern Europeans) to be superior.[426] Yet another is the belief in Whites superiority. (Such ideologies rationalize away the evils of unfair discrimination, subjugation, enslavement, maltreatment, murder, and genocide.)

We also too often misrepresent evil as good. The Old Testament's description of the Battle of Jericho as fulfillment of God's promise to reward the long-oppressed Hebrews with a homeland might be an example.[427] That was the first step in the Hebrew conquest of Canaan, and Jericho's entire populace, male and female, young and old, and all their animals (ox, sheep, and ass) were put to the sword. Such genocide is one of man's greatest deliberate tragedies. (Biblical literalism contributed to the lively spiritual *Joshua Fit the Battle of Jericho,* believed to have been *composed* by Slaves in the first half of the 19th Century. Its line *And the walls came tumblin' down* is considered to represent the dream of the end of Slavery.[428]) [In addition to biblical literalism, the lure of Freedom fostered acceptance of the belief that the blare of trumpets toppled walls.]

The *Art of War,* attributed to Sun-Tzu (544-496 BC),[429] is seen as representative of the cumulative knowledge of thousands of years of Chinese history—showing war to be a consequence of human nature.[430]

Without the ability to defend itself, militarily (competitively) and by alliance (cooperatively), a country faces eventual subjugation and/or enslavement (or killing off) of its people. And countries typically have been established by warfare—including peace-loving, neutral Switzerland (which still has conscripted military service and has armed 28% of its citizenry).[431] Even the attempt to peacefully separate India and Pakistan produced some 200,000-2,000,000 deaths from religious conflict.[432] And to continue to be able to prevent suffering the fate of the Amerinds whom we took our country from, the U.S. enacted a military budget of $693 billion for 2019.[433]

5.5 Unfair Colonial Discrimination

Colonial religion was basically divided between: the Anglicans (Church of England) in Maryland, New York, North Carolina, and Virginia; and the Puritans (Congregational Church) in Connecticut, Massachusetts, and New Hampshire. There was no official church in Delaware, Georgia, New Jersey, Pennsylvania, or Rhode Island. But most Colonies (e.g., Delaware) had religious restrictions on Government office holders.[434]

In Delaware, my generation was taught that Americans had immigrated to escape religious persecution. No emphasis was placed on how the Puritan fathers of the Massachusetts Bay Colony brooked no dissent, religious or political, and banned Catholics ("Papists") and other non-Puritans—or about the hanging of four Quakers between 1659 and 1661 for returning to Boston to stand up for their beliefs.[435] Nor did I learn that, in the 8 of the 13 Colonies that had their own established religion, people who sought to practice or preach a non-Christian or a different Christian religion typically were discriminated against and often persecuted.[436] The following more realistically depicts oppression practiced in the Colonies:[437, 438, 439, 440, 441, 442, 443]

During Virginia's first century, 100,000 of the 130,000 English immigrants were indentured servants. Most lived miserably. Nearly two-thirds died before their indenture ended.

Colonist enslavement of Amerinds failed because many escaped and hid among neighboring tribes, or were stricken by the White Man's diseases. Planters turned to Black Slavery. Black Slaves were brought to Jamestown in 1619, and their farming skills and labor were valued then The myth of inherent Black inferiority came later, facilitated by the effect of mistreatment and the denial of educational opportunity.

England, France, Holland, Spain, Portugal, and Denmark brought Black Slaves to the Americas. So did Massachusetts and Rhode Island. (Climate and landscape made New England's economy largely dependent on the sea.) After the earliest recorded New England Slave voyage sailed from Boston in 1644, the Massachusetts Slave trade developed. Rhode Island entered that trade about 1700. By the 1750s, the two-thirds of Rhode Island's fleet engaged in the Slave trade made up over 60% of the American mainland's Slave trade. Slave ships carried sugar and molasses from the Caribbean to New England. It was distilled into rum there, and taken to Africa and exchanged for Slaves—who were taken to the Caribbean and exchanged for sugar and molasses.

The vast majority of Slaves ended up on sugar plantations in the Caribbean and South

America. But ~500,000 Slaves ended up in North America and, by 1755, the cost and lack of Colonial labor resulted in there being over 13,000 Black Slaves in New England.

In the mid-17th Century, England's economy improved and indentured servant emigration decreased. That produced a Colonial labor shortage. And indenture's survivors were clamoring for land. When Colonists began settling in Virginia's Northern Neck frontier in the 1650s, some frontier freeholders demanded that the Amerinds, including friendly tribes living on treaty-protected lands, be driven out or killed. They also protested Virginia Governor Sir William Berkeley's government, which historian Stephen Saunders Webb called "incorrigibly corrupt, inhumanely oppressive, and inexcusably inefficient, especially in war." Berkeley reportedly kept the Colonists impoverished by unjust taxes and made a large "illegal" profit from the Amerind fur trade. The Legislature, or Governor's Council, made up of his friends, made the Colonists virtually powerless.

Amerinds (Doeg, Patawomeck and Rappahannock) moving into the region joined local tribes in disputing the settlers' claims. In July 1666, the colonists started warring on them. By 1670, they had driven most of the Doeg out of Virginia but continued to harass them. The Doeg retaliated by crossing the Potomac to steal hogs from Thomas Mathew, a reputed cheater and abuser of Amerinds, because he hadn't paid them for traded goods. Mathew and other colonists pursued the Doeg to Maryland and killed a group of them and some uninvolved Susquehannock. The Doeg retaliated by killing Mathew's son and two servants on his plantation.

Virginia Colonists seeking easier wealth and desirable land held by the Amerinds were led by Nathaniel Bacon. He was educated at the University of Cambridge, made a grand tour of Europe, studied law at Gray's Inn, and married Sir Edward Duke's daughter Elizabeth without permission. After he was accused of cheating another young man out of his inheritance, his father gave him a considerable sum (£1,800) and he emigrated to Virginia. There he bought two frontier plantations on the James River. His cousin, a militia colonel, was a friend of Governor Berkeley. Bacon settled in Jamestown. He was soon appointed to the Governor's Council, but ended up outside Berkeley's inner circle—disgruntled at being denied fur trading privileges and a military commission that would allow him to attack the Amerinds. (Early 20th Century History blamed the Amerinds for Bacon's attacks on them, and held Bacon to a be a hero whose insurrection against England's Sir William Berkeley's governorship was a precursor to the Revolutionary War.)

Bacon's forces attacked the Doeg and besieged the Susquehannock in Maryland. In 1676, they killed nearly fifty Pamunkey Amerinds in Virginia's Green Dragon Swamp on the Upper Pamunkey River. (The Pamunkey leader, "Queen" Cockacoeske, succeeded her husband when he was killed in 1656 while helping the English remove the Rickohockan Amerinds from the falls of the James River. She ordered her tribe to escape but keep their peace treaty and not harm anyone.)

Maryland Governor Calvert protested Bacon's incursion. But when the Susquehannocks retaliated, the Maryland militia and Virginia forces attacked a fortified Susquehannock village. Five chiefs accepted the Maryland force's invitation to parley. They were slaughtered. The Susquehannocks then killed 60 settlers in Maryland and 36 in Virginia. Other tribes joined in, killing settlers, burning houses and fields, and slaughtering livestock as far as the James and York rivers.

Governor Berkeley refused to help the Colonists, reputedly to protect his profitable fur trade. He advocated containment, proposed building defensive fortifications along the frontier, and urged frontier settlers to gather in a defensive posture. They dismissed that as expensive and inadequate, and also saw it as a possible excuse for raising taxes.

Bacon's force included thousands of Virginians of all classes, including indentured servants and Black Slaves. They chased Berkeley from Jamestown, looted his home, and burned the town. At the height of this "success," Bacon was stricken with dysentery and died. His rebellion collapsed. Berkeley returned, seized rebel properties, and hanged 23—many without trial. An investigative report to King Charles II criticized Berkeley and Bacon. Berkeley was relieved of his governorship, returned to England to protest, and died shortly thereafter Charles II later reputedly said *That old fool has put to death more people in that naked country than I did here for the murder of my father.*

Slavery's proponents responded to the alliance between indentured servants and Slaves by more strongly depicting Blacks as inferior. Poor Whites were given new opportunities (e.g., as overseers of Slaves) and began to identify with Wealthy Whites. As Abolitionism grew, Slavery's proponents stopped depicting it as a *necessary evil* and termed it a *positive good* instead. And the imputation of White superiority and Black inferiority intensified when Slavery was abolished.

White superiority has not only come into play in regard to Slavery. By the middle of the 19th Century, race was invoked not only to justify the enslavement of Africans, but also the taking of Mexican and Amerind lands, the exclusion of Asian immigrants, and then the acquisition of overseas territories such as the Philippine Islands, Guam and Puerto Rico. Racial superiority was seen not only as "natural" and inevitable but a moral responsibility for Whites. The notions of Manifest Destiny and the White Man's Burden were part of that ideology of "civilization" and racial difference.

Racial inferiority became institutionalized—explicitly and implicitly—in our laws, government, and public policies. And racial definitions were arbitrarily changed when politically expedient. Mexicans, for example, were classified as White until 1930, when nativists lobbied successfully for them to be classified separately (in order to target them for discrimination and emphasize their distinctness from Whites).

Blacks in the Jim Crow South were classified according to "blood" ancestry, but the amount (one quarter, one sixteenth, one drop) varied from State to State. As historian James Horton stated, "you could cross a state line and, literally, legally change race."

Historically, Whites, escaped Slaves, and other Amerinds were able to join Amerind tribes and be accepted as full members, regardless of "blood." But, in the 1930s, tribes wanting federal recognition were forced to follow government guidelines that specified tribal membership based upon "blood" degree. A 1991 Bureau of Indian Affairs inventory of 155 federally recognized tribes in 48 States showed that 4 out of 5 States conditioned membership on proof of blood, ranging in amount from 1/2 to 1/64th.

5.6 Limited Rights

A major lure of our United States was and is the powerful *American Dream* paraphrased as *all men are created equal and are endowed by their Creator with certain unalienable Right, and among these are Life, Liberty and the pursuit of Happiness.*

When the U.S. Constitution was ratified, its stated goal was:

> *We the People of the United States, in Order to form a more perfect Union, establish Justice, insure domestic Tranquility, provide for the common defense, promote the general Welfare, and secure the Blessings of Liberty to ourselves and our Posterity, do ordain and establish this Constitution for the United States of America.*

Depictions of the Founding Fathers who ratified the Constitution show them all to have been White Males. Any many have commented that only White Males were intended to be encompassed by the *American Dream*. For example, Author, Historian, and Professor Mary Beth Norton made the following points about the Constitution and women:[444]

- Women had no status in the Constitution of 1787. Wives and daughters were legally subordinate to husbands and fathers, and were seen solely as parts of households—which were then still the unit of society. Each household's male head controlled its property, activities, political activity, and militia service. But the 5th Commandment injunction to *Honor Thy Father and Mother* enabled Mothers to command the same obedience from even adult male children as their husbands could.
- Male status derived from England—where a woman took her father's' and husband's rank and was subject to men of her rank but had precedence over lower-status men.
- The theory that females were irrelevant outside the household was first formulated in ancient Greece. Aristotle articulated the sharp line drawn there. Men ruled the State. Females could not actively participate in family governance either, except women who ranked high in age, gender and wealth. (The young, beautiful, and rich advantage?)

Doctor Norton also noted that women's long-standing objections to male rule and men's insistence upon it was articulated by then future President John Adams and his wife Abigail. Letters[445] between those formidable souls show the erstwhile and lingering attitudes of both sexes about male dominance. Excerpts follow.

From Abigail Adams' March 31, 1776 letter to John Adams:

> *I have sometimes been ready to think that the passion for Liberty cannot be Eaquelly Strong in the Breasts of those who have been accustomed to deprive their fellow Creatures of theirs. Of this I am certain that it is not founded upon that generous and christian principal of doing to others as we would that others should do unto us. . . .*

I long to hear that you have declared an independancy—and by the way in the new Code of Laws which I suppose it will be necessary for you to make I desire you would Remember the Ladies, and be more generous and favourable to them than your ancestors. Do not put such unlimited power into the hands of the Husbands. Remember all Men would be tyrants if they could. If perticuliar care and attention is not paid to the Laidies we are determined to foment a Rebelion, and will not hold ourselves bound by any Laws in which we have no voice, or Representation.

That your Sex are Naturally Tyrannical is a Truth so thoroughly established as to admit of no dispute, but such of you as wish to be happy willingly give up the harsh title of Master for the more tender and endearing one of Friend. Why then, not put it out of the power of the vicious and the Lawless to use us with cruelty and indignity with impunity. Men of Sense in all Ages abhor those customs which treat us only as the vassals of your Sex. Regard us then as Beings placed by providence under your protection and in immitation of the Supreem Being make use of that power only for our happiness.

From John Adams' Aprill 14, 1776 letter to Abigail Adams:

As to your extraordinary Code of Laws, I cannot but laugh. We have been told that our Struggle has loosened the bands of Government every where. That Children and Apprentices were disobedient — that schools and Colledges were grown turbulent — that Indians slighted their Guardians and Negroes grew insolent to their Masters. But your Letter was the first Intimation that another Tribe more numerous and powerfull than all the rest were grown discontented. — This is rather too coarse a Compliment but you are so saucy, I wont blot it out.

Depend upon it, We know better than to repeal our Masculine systems. Altho they are in full Force, you know they are little more than Theory. We dare not exert our Power in its full Latitude. We are obliged to go fair, and softly, and in Practice you know We are the subjects. We have only the Name of Masters, and rather than give up this, which would compleatly subject Us to the Despotism of the Peticoat, I hope General Washington, and all our brave Heroes would fight. I am sure every good Politician would plot, as long as he would against Despotism, Empire, Monarchy, Aristocracy, Oligarchy, or Ochlocracy. — A fine Story indeed. I begin to think the Ministry as deep as they are wicked. After stirring up Tories, Landjobbers, Trimmers, Bigots, Canadians, Indians, Negroes, Hanoverians, Hessians, Russians, Irish Roman Catholicks, Scotch Renegadoes, at last they have stimulated the(m) to demand new Priviledges and threaten to rebell.

Abigail's entreaty seems faulty today only for ignoring tyranny's genderless nature. John's response has been dismissed by some because It's jocular. But it represented the innate human desire to control others. And it outlined some anti-independence problems that the Founding Fathers faced. John can be faulted for denigrating *rebells* when he was a leader of a rebellion—and for ignoring Abigail's undeniable assertion that vicious men used women cruelly with impunity—and for claiming (or having) no prior knowledge of women's discontent. But he was right not to embark upon an equality project that was doomed to fail and could have severely detracted from the support needed to achieve independence. Despite its faults, John's response showed recognition of and esteem for Abigail's (and therefore women's) intelligence and competence.]

5.7 Our Partisan Judiciary

The Dred Scott decision still stands out as a particularly egregious example of high "court" rulings based on a political agenda. Its 7-2 vote majority reputedly was achieved because President Buchanan had convinced one of the three Northern Justices to side with the South. That's directly contrary to the judiciary's inherent obligation to be independent, to be and to appear to be impartial, and to refrain from political activity. But even today the defining Code of Conduct for U.S. Judges is not applicable to the Supreme Court, which reputedly "consults" it.[446]

We've been taught that our judiciary is not political. But judges, especially Supreme Court "Justices," have been and are politically selected with the (sometimes erroneous) expectation that they will pursue the selector's agenda. A notable example of a judge being perceived as political was the celebrated, brilliant, Woman's Rights Activist Ruth Bader Ginsburg, who was appointed a Supreme Court Justice by Democrat Bill Clinton in 1993. University of Maine School of Law Associate Professor Dmitri Bam cited her public statement, during the 2016 presidential election campaign between Republican Donald Trump and Democrat and former First Lady Hillary Clinton: [447]

- *I can't imagine what this place would be - I can't imagine what the country would be - with Donald Trump as our president .... For the country, it could be four years. For the court, it could be - I don't even want to contemplate that.*
- In a later interview Ginsburg "lamented" that *she did not want to even consider the possibility of a Trump presidency.* She also said that she believed *her fears would not come to fruition because Hillary Clinton would likely be our next president.*
- In a third interview, Ginsburg "doubled down" by saying *He is a faker* and *He has no consistency about him. He says whatever comes into his head at the moment. He really has an ego .... How has he gotten away with not turning over his tax returns? The press seems to be very gentle with him on that.* [Reports that the Nixon administration had used tax return information to compile his infamous enemies list led to the Tax Reform Act of 1976, which prohibited disclosure of federal tax return information. Individual States have similar laws. But political candidates are encouraged to release

their tax returns, and some States reportedly are considering release of tax returns as a prerequisite for being put on the ballot.[448]]

Bam noted that Ginsburg's statements were excoriated by her biggest supporters and most ardent opponents, including the Political Left, the Political Right, the Media, Legal Academics, and Politicians. And Donald Trump, in his "signature" style, chimed in with:

- *Justice Ginsburg of the U.S. Supreme Court has embarrassed all by making very dumb political statements about me. Her mind is shot - resign!*
- Like Ginsburg, Trump "doubled down" by then tweeting: *Is Supreme Court Justice Ruth Bader Ginsburg going to apologize to me for her misconduct? Big mistake by an incompetent judge!*
- Trump also said: *I think it's highly inappropriate that a United States Supreme Court judge gets involved in a political campaign, frankly .... I think it's a disgrace to the court, and I think she should apologize to the court. I couldn't believe it when I saw it.*

Ginsburg responded:

On reflection, my recent remarks in response to press inquiries were ill-advised and I regret making them .... Judges should avoid commenting on a candidate for public office. In the future I will be more circumspect. She also reportedly told Nina Totenberg: I did something I should not have done.

The following (with bracketed comments added) condenses Bam's review of whether Ginsburg violated the obligations of a judge to both be and appear to be impartial.

- Judicial impartiality is one of the core tenets of a justice system, and entitlement to a neutral, impartial judge is a core principle of due process.
- The Code of Conduct for United States Judges and the Model Code of Judicial Conduct both require judges to recuse themselves if their impartiality could reasonably be challenged.
- The real question is whether Justice Ginsburg's expression of her thoughts raises an impartiality concern. But what matters most is her state of mind, not what litigants know about it. [That discounts the importance of appearing to be impartial.]
- Ginsburg did nothing more than express her sincere views on Donald Trump. [That's bald opinion.] Ginsburg's unusual remarks do not "suggest" her predetermination of any case involving Trump. [The furor far more than "suggests" otherwise.]
- The Supreme Court rejected the notion that mere expression of one's views—-even on legal issues that the judge is likely to decide—creates impartiality concerns. [A Woman's Advocate publicly derogating a male presidential candidate running against a woman candidate is very different from a Supreme Court Justice doing that.]
- A judge decides whether to be recused. A higher court can review that and take disciplinary measures, an option not available in the case of the Supreme Court.

- Recusal would almost certainly not be required in "all" future cases involving a Trump administration. [If failure to recuse is accompanied by the appearance of partiality, the credibility of the judge is in question. And Ginsberg's projected partiality tainted her and the Supreme Court's credibility, and set a precedent for judges in lesser courts. [Bam has also argued[449] that it is unconstitutional for a judge to decide her own recusal because it violates one of the most fundamental tenets of due process by allowing a judge to judge her own cause.]

- Ginsburg's views on Donald Trump, the person, would not lead a reasonable person to question her impartiality in a case nominally involving Donald Trump in his official capacity, or relating to his executive policy. [That opinion classifies as unreasonable everyone who concluded that Ginsburg's personal views constitute at least the appearance of prejudice against Trump—although Bam later stated that reasonable people could reach such a conclusion.]

- No reasonable person could believe that Justices Thomas and Scalia held no views on President Obama. Yet "nobody" called for recusal of those Justices in "every" case involving Obama. ["Nobody" is an absolute that Bam could not know. Also, using "every" instead of "any" is misleading because recusal should be based on the circumstances of each individual case.]

- Supreme Court Justices arrive with a lifetime of experience and well-established views, and are chosen largely because of their experience and expertise. [That discounts the political appointment process. An example of that process was then former Vice President Biden's March 2020 campaign promise discounting the selection of the best candidate available by promising that, if he is elected president, he will nominate a Black Woman to the Supreme Court.[450]]

- Ginsburg spent her career fighting against many of the things for which Donald Trump stands. Her partisan ideology was well-cemented by the time she made her comments. It seems unlikely that the mere expression of her thoughts (rather than the thoughts themselves) would influence her judicial decisions. [Discriminating between thoughts and their expression is toe-tapping around the issue of the judicial partiality indicated when a female Supreme Court Justice and Women's Advocate publicly inserts herself into a presidential election campaign to derogate the male candidate in a way that supports his female opponent.]

- There is no compelling or legitimate reason to create an appearance of impartiality solely to cover up actual bias by a judge. [There is if the judge wishes to appear to be impartial and/or for the judgement to be so viewed.] Ginsburg's statements only confirm what a reasonably informed person should know: that she is a reliable left-leaning voice on the Court, a trailblazer for women's rights, an icon in progressive circles, and likely supported Hillary Clinton over Donald Trump in the presidential election. [The question is whether she was impartial. And her public statements about Donald Trump are undeniably in favor of Hillary Clinton—consistent with Ginsberg being her advocate.]

- A reasonable person should recognize that judges have strongly-held political views that may influence judicial decisions. Term after term, the Court has decided a number of controversial cases by a 5-4 margin, with the two blocs-liberal and conservative-uniformly voting together. [That's true. It's also consistent with the "Justices" being partisan advocates, not objective jurists.]

- Justice Scalia's impartiality was challenged after his duck hunting trip with Dick Cheney, who was then a named party in a case pending at the Supreme Court. Scalia's rejection of recusal stated that no "reasonable observer who is informed of all the surrounding facts and circumstances" would conclude that he was biased towards his good friend and acquaintance. Doing so made an important distinction between Scalia's friendship with Cheney and his appearance in the lawsuit in his official capacity. A close friendship between a Justice and a President (or a presidential candidate) or a Justice's dislike of a President may not suffice to establish an appearance of bias. [That's true. But "may not" doesn't rule out "may," which constitutes an appearance of bias. Also, the bases stated in Justice Scalia's refusal to recuse himself included pointing out that the Court was being asked to decide the powers of the District Court under the Federal Advisory Committee Act and whether the Court of Appeals should have asserted mandamus or appellate jurisdiction over the Appellate Court—matters that did not affect Vice President Chaney. Scalia also rejected recusal based on press information because that would give the press unacceptable control over what Justices hear cases,[451] That's considerably different from the conditions leading to perceptions of Ginsburg's partiality.]
- When the Ohio Democratic Party later sought to enjoin the Trump campaign from improper voter intimidation, Ohio courts denied the injunction and the Supreme Court heard the Ohio Democratic Party's reinstatement application. Justice Ginsburg rejected that appeal and wrote separately to explain her vote in favor of Donald Trump—showing that judges do not simply decide cases according to their political preferences. [The phrase "improper voter intimidation" connotes impropriety that's not borne out by the Ohio or U.S. Supreme Courts' decisions. That, like much of Bam's presentation, seems consistent with his being an advocate of Ginsburg's anti-Trump stance—rather than being an objective reviewer. Nonetheless, that Ginsburg actually decided one case in favor of Trump is a point in her favor—though her statements about Trump would nonetheless have brought forth accusations of impropriety in any case in which she ruled against him.]
- Partisan judicial statements like Justice Ginsburg's raise impartiality concerns, especially if the statements solidify a Justice's views and make it more difficult for a judge to rule for (or against) a litigant. And regardless of the legal correctness of a ruling, the appearance of bias leads to a loss of confidence in the court. But these impartiality concerns are fairly minor. [The bipartisan furor over Ginsburg's statements about Trump show that many people did not consider the matter minor.]
- [A further demonstration of the political nature of the Supreme Court is the history of increasing the number of "justices" to 10 in 1863 to give Lincoln an extra appointment, the subsequent reduction to 7 to keep Andrew Johnson from making an appointment, and the subsequent expansion to 9 in 1869 to give Ulysses S. Grant extra appointments. It has remained at 9 despite FDR's attempt to allow him to replace federal judges over the age of 70. That would have enabled him to replace 5-6 Supreme Court "justices." His plan was abandoned when two "justices" started

supporting his New Deal legislation and thereby removed the incentive. But in an effort to counter Trump's appointments, there is reputedly serious Congressional consideration of again packing the Supreme Court, though President Biden reportedly is against doing that because of the likelihood that Republicans would respond in kind when they are able to do so.[452]

5.8 White Supremacy and the White Man's Burden[453]

The U.S. has been widely condemned for imperialism (extending its power, dominion, authority or influence by territorial acquisition or by control over the political or economic life of other areas[454]). The term carries a negative connotation even in Win-Win interaction. But most or all nations practice imperialism in their international relationships.

Rudyard Kipling, who lived in the U.S. from 1892-96, proffered a poem to and advocated U.S. annexation of the Philippines to New York Governor Theodore Roosevelt, saying:

Now, go in and put all the weight of your influence into hanging on, permanently, to the whole Philippines. America has gone and stuck a pick-axe into the foundations of a rotten house, and she is morally bound to build the house over, again, from the foundations, or have it fall about her ears. The poem follows.

The White Man's Burden

Take up the White Man's burden—
    Send forth the best ye breed—
Go bind your sons to exile
    To serve your captives' need;
To wait in heavy harness
    On fluttered folk and wild—
Your new-caught, sullen peoples,
    Half devil and half child.

Take up the White Man's burden—
    In patience to abide,
To veil the threat of terror
    And check the show of pride;
By open speech and simple,
    An hundred times made plain.
To seek another's profit,
    And work another's gain.

Take up the White Man's burden—
    The savage wars of peace—
Fill full the mouth of Famine
    And bid the sickness cease;
And when your goal is nearest
    The end for others sought,
Watch Sloth and heathen Folly
    Bring all your hopes to nought.

Take up the White Man's burden—
    No tawdry rule of kings,
But toil of serf and sweeper—
    The tale of common things.
The ports ye shall not enter,
    The roads ye shall not tread,
Go make them with your living,
    And mark them with your dead!

Take up the White Man's burden—
    And reap his old reward:
The blame of those ye better,
    The hate of those ye guard—
The cry of hosts ye humour
    (Ah, slowly!) toward the light:—
"Why brought ye us from bondage,
    Our loved Egyptian night?"

Take up the White Man's burden—
    Ye dare not stoop to less—
Nor call too loud on Freedom
    To cloak your weariness;
By all ye cry or whisper,
    By all ye leave or do,
The silent, sullen peoples
    Shall weigh your Gods and you.

Take up the White Man's burden—
    Have done with childish days—
The lightly proffered laurel,
    The easy, ungrudged praise.
Comes now, to search your manhood
    Through all the thankless years,
Cold-edged with dear-bought wisdom,
    The judgment of your peers!

Kipling saw the "White Race" as destined to civilize and bring God's empire to the brutish, non-Whites of the barbarous world. In 1901, Mark Twain reacted to that philosophy in a satirical protest titled *To the Person Sitting in Darkness*—describing Western military atrocities against the Chinese during the 1899-1901 anti-colonial Boxer Rebellion against European businessmen and Christian missionaries. Author and Humanities Professor Brook Thomas noted that Twain feared that policies claiming to civilize backward peoples would involve barbaric acts. That did happen in the fierce fighting on Samar Island during the US military campaign against the Filipinos. U.S. soldiers burned villages, killed wounded enemy soldiers, and tortured and killed civilians. There also were reports of rape and robbery. The war ended when US troops dressed as Filipino rebels infiltrated Filipino headquarters and captured the rebel leader, General Aguinaldo. The stated "justification" for the ruse was that, because Aguinaldo had not been a signatory of the Hague Convention (the first formal statement of the Laws of War), the U.S. had no obligation to follow it in the Philippine-American War. {The 1899 Hague Convention was largely based on the Lieber Code, which was signed by Abraham Lincoln during the Civil War and issued to the Union Forces on 4/24/1863.[455] Article 23(f) of the 1899 Hague Regulations provides: "It is especially prohibited ... to make improper use of ... the national flag or military ensigns and uniform of the enemy." [456]}

Mark Twain spoke out strongly in favor of American interests in the Hawaiian Islands and called the 1898 war with Spain the worthiest ever fought. He also stated that Lincoln's Emancipation Proclamation set Whites free as well as Blacks. And he sent at least one Black to law school, sent another to a University to study for the ministry, and convinced Connecticut's Legislature to vote a pension for Prudence Crandall for her efforts towards educating young Black ladies in Connecticut. He saw Amerinds as treacherous, ungrateful scum of the earth until concluding that, world-wide, "savages" have mercilessly been wronged by Whites by robbery, humiliation, and slow, slow murder through poverty and the White man's whiskey. He also argued that non-Whites did not get justice in the U.S., citing having seen Chinamen abused and maltreated in all the cowardly ways possible but never having a court right the wrongs done to one. Twain supported the Boxer Rebellion, saw War as incompatible with humanism and Christianity, felt that the French *Reign of Terror* paled in comparison to the terrors that preceded it, and averred that revolutions only occur to combat intolerable oppression. And he felt that the Filipinos' three centuries of suffering justified their having a miniature U.S. Constitution and being in a free republic—until he became a staunch anti-imperialist when he concluded that the U.S. was going to subjugate the Filipinos. Twain also campaigned for Women's Rights and Suffrage, derogated Capitalists and Kings, strongly supported Labor, and expressed enmity toward vivisection because it inflects pain upon unconsenting animals. At times he portrayed religious views, at others he stated sentiments like the conjecture that God created the world with all its tortures for some purpose of his own but was otherwise indifferent to humanity, which was too petty and insignificant to deserve his attention anyway. But he raised money to build a Presbyterian Church in Nevada, and he wrote a reverent portrayal of Joan of Arc. In the autobiography published 100 years after his death, he wrote: There is one notable thing about our Christianity: bad, bloody, merciless, money-grabbing, and predatory as it is – in our country particularly and in all other Christian countries in a somewhat modified degree – it is still a hundred times better than the Christianity of the Bible, with its prodigious crime – the invention of Hell. Measured by our Christianity of to-day, bad as it is, hypocritical as it is, empty and hollow as it is, neither the Deity nor his Son is a Christian, nor qualified for that moderately high place. Ours is a terrible religion. The fleets of the world could swim in spacious comfort in the innocent blood it has spilled.[457]

Twain's trenchant cynicism also is evident in the following quotes:[458]

- There is no distinctly native American criminal class save Congress. {Twain might have considered an example of that to be the about $4 trillion that Congress appropriated in COVID-19 stimulus packages over the past year—it averages out to over $27,000 for each of the 144.3 million U.S. taxpayers.]
- Reader, suppose you were an idiot. And suppose you were a member of Congress. But I repeat myself.
- If you pick up a starving dog and make him prosperous, he will not bite you. This is the principal difference between a man and a dog.

Twain's denouncement of the capture of Filipino leader Emilio Aguinaldo contrasts with that of Army Chief Historian Matthew J. Seelinger.[459] Seelinger's version contains no condemnation of the civilian government-ordered Philippine-American War [and could not]. And it claims that Twain's and other opposition was driven by a political agenda that misrepresented or glossed over the other side of the picture—and even disputed some significant Filipino and U.S. military heroism. An abbreviation follows.

When the U.S. defeated Spain, many Filipinos welcomed the Americans. They rebelled when annexation, not independence, loomed.

After repeated defeats in battle, the Filipinos discarded their ragged uniforms, blended into the general population, and became guerrillas. Their insurrection became a series of ambushes, reprisals, and patrol actions in the jungles. Captured American soldiers faced torture and murder. In retaliation, some suspect villages were destroyed. And by the time the rebellion was suppressed, over 6,000 American soldiers were killed or wounded, far more than in the Spanish-American War. Filipino casualties exceeded 16,000.

The war was won by one of the most daring exploits in U.S. Army history. That occurred when a small, disguised, American-led force ventured deep into enemy territory and captured Emilio Aguinaldo, the self-proclaimed President of the Philippine Republic. His capture was devised and led by Frederick C. Funston, whose experience with Cubans fighting Spain had taught him much about guerilla warfare. Funston's prior bravery at the Battle of Calumet on Luzon, and a glowing recommendation by Brigadier General Arthur MacArthur (5-Star General Douglas MacArthur's father), had earned him a Medal of Honor and promotion to Brigadier General of Volunteers. As Commander of the 4th District of Luzon, Funston destroyed rebel supplies, built an efficient intelligence system, conducted constant patrols, and gradually reduced guerrilla strength. But a small, elusive, hardcore group led by Aguinaldo assured that the insurrection would continue.

Funston learned that a small group of insurgents who had surrendered was commanded by a trusted, dispatch-carrying messenger of Aguinaldo. He had him brought to headquarters and questioned, and heard that Aguinaldo was in the village of Palanan in the mountains of northern Luzon—with no more than 50 guards. The dispatches were in Aguinaldo's handwriting and signed with code names that he used. A plan to land near Palanan and march to the rebel headquarters was ruled out because detection would enable Aguinaldo to flee. Funston then decided to disguise, as insurgents, a small group of loyal Macabebes, a Filipino tribe that despised Aguinaldo's Tagalogs but could speak Tagalog. They would march to Palanan with Funston and four other officers disguised as Prisoners of War and as privates. The Macabebes were to be equipped with captured rifles and dressed in peasant garb (few rebels wore uniforms). Funston would be in command, but the column would appear to be under the command of several Filipinos whom Funston recruited. At least two of them knew Aguinaldo personally.

General MacArthur approved the plan but realized the risks involved. And as Funston's party was preparing to depart, MacArthur grabbed Funston's hand and said, "Funston, this is a desperate undertaking. I fear that I shall never see you again."

Funston's night landing became riskier when the landing boats were swamped and the ferrying gunboat had to approach the beach. But the landing was undetected. The march to Casiguran began in the morning and took a day. They were welcomed, and rested and gathered supplies before continuing on. Funston sent two forged messages to Aguinaldo, one stating that the captured American "prisoners" were being brought in for questioning, the other that the 80 men that Aguinaldo had requested were being sent.

In Casiguran. Funston heard that Palanan had been reinforced by 400 men. He convinced his men that the element of surprise would compensate. But the villagers could only provide three days of rations and it was a seven-day trip to Palanan. Funston decided to continue on, hoping to forage enroute. On the first day out of Casiguran, his guide deserted. But a Casiguran bearer knew the way and the column pressed on, on two meals a day, through poor weather and rough terrain.

Aguinaldo received the forged messages and sent his Chief of Staff to meet the column. He did, telling the exhausted party that provisions would be arriving, that the prisoners were to be kept in the village of Dinundungan, and that the reinforcements hadn't arrived. That night, Funston produced a letter stating that the prisoners were to be brought to Palanan. It "arrived" about an hour after the column departed for Aguinaldo's headquarters. The "prisoners" and their 10 Macabebe guards then started for Palanan, narrowly avoiding the rebels sent to guard them in Dinundungan.

Two "rebel" officers crossed the rain-swollen Palanan River and made their way to Aguinaldo's headquarters. He took them to his residence and was given a time-consuming account of their victory over the Americans while the column crossed the river, formed ranks, and marched toward Aguinaldo's guards. When one of Aguinaldo's "guests" called out to them, they opened fire, killing two guards and scattering the rest.

Aguinaldo, thinking that the shots were a salute to the newcomers, moved towards the window to order the guards to conserve their ammunition. One of his "guests" wrestled him to the floor. The other rushed back in from the balcony where he had given the signal, saw that Aguinaldo's officers were drawing their weapons, and shot two of them dead. The others surrendered or escaped out the windows.

Funston's small group crossed the river as the gunfire erupted. He intervened to spare several of Aguinaldo's men from the Macabebes. Aguinaldo, who was inside and pinned to the floor, surrendered. Two of his chief officers also were taken prisoner.

Funston and his party rested and helped themselves to food left behind by villagers who fled when the shooting began. On the morning of 25 March, Funston rendezvoused with the gunboat *Vicksburg* in Palanan Bay and set out for Manila.

Aguinaldo told Funston that he had been completely fooled by the phony dispatches. He later confided that he could "hardly believe myself to be a prisoner" and that he was gripped by a "feeling of disgust and despair for I had failed my people and my motherland."

On 28 March 1901, *Vicksburg* arrived in Manila Bay with Funston's party and its three prisoners. Aguinaldo's capture was cause for great excitement there—and in the U.S. The American public was weary of this conflict with no end in sight until Funston's plan worked. But his exploits were condemned as treacherous and underhanded by opposers of American occupation of the Philippines. For example, Mark Twain wrote a sarcastic diatribe entitled "In Defense of General Funston," taking issue with Funston's "begging for food then capturing his benefactor."

On 19 April 1901, Aguinaldo issued a proclamation calling for the rebels to lay down their arms and accept American sovereignty. Not all did. The Muslim Moros in the Southern Philippines fought on for several years. But on 4 July 1902 President Theodore Roosevelt proclaimed the Philippine Insurrection over.

Funston was promoted to Brigadier General in the Regular Army, and to Major General on 17 November 1914. In early 1917, it seemed that he would become the Commander of any U.S. Expeditionary Force sent to Europe in WWI. But, on 19 February 1917, during dinner at a San Antonio hotel, he suddenly collapsed and died of heart failure.

Funston's capture of Aguinaldo showed a skilled use of intelligence, resourcefulness, and tremendous raw courage—matched by few actions in the history of the U.S. Army.

[There is merit in Twain's viewpoint and in Army Historian Seelinger's. But both were partisan—in Twain's case with vituperative denigration of the Army's method of carrying out the civilian government's orders. (He attacked the tool, not its wielder.) Imperialism was indubitably an element of the takeover of the Philippines, but Post-WWI-WWII U.S. actions show that the connotation of ruthless suppression and/or subordination and/or conquest by modern Democracies is outmoded. And while people and nations do and will hold dearly onto all the preferential treatment they can garner, the degree of good and evil involved in imperialism is a function of the composite before and after quality of life of the peoples involved. If they are better off as a result, and if that's worth the cost, then the imperialism is justified.]

There's no justification for the ongoing inequities in the *White Man's Culture* (or in the culture of Communist China). But the fact that immigration to the U.S. is a much bigger problem than emigration from the U.S. is strong evidence that, excluding the violent (e.g., KKK) kind of White Supremacy, the democratic *White Man's Culture* provides the highest standard of living that mankind has yet achieved.]

5.9 Criminality

Man's *You make it and I'll take it* criminality is evident, especially in Wars and Slavery. One of its current aspects is Identity theft. A DOJ study showed that it cost the U.S. $15.4 billion In 2014, with an average cost of $1343 per victim.[460] And according to a General Accounting Office survey, the estimated annual overall cost of U.S. crime ranges from $690 billion to $3.41 trillion.[461] For a populace of 335 million people, that's ~$2000 to ~$10,000 dollars per person—enough money to pay off the current national debt of $281 trillion (4/7/2021 estimate) in about 10-50 years (if we had a balanced budget).

6

A Planetary View

6.1 Impermanence

Over 5 billion species (>99% of all that ever existed on Earth) are extinct. And the million plant and animal species estimated to be at risk of extinction (e.g., due to habitat loss from human occupation)[462] are but one five-thousandth (0.02%) of that number.

Nonetheless, Man has not been a good planet steward. For example, in the 19th Century, Passenger Pigeons blocked out the sun for hours while they passed over a single spot. But the telegraph and railroad enabled commercial exploitation of this tasty bird—and in 1914 the last known specimen died.[463] Overall, we are estimated to have forced ~477 animal species into extinction in the last 500 years.[464]

Man also has been very unkind to his fellow man. WWI killed ~18 million people, or ~0.9% of the world's ~1.9 billion people. And WWII killed ~75 million people, ~3% of the world's ~2.5 billion. The human population boom has suffered but little from those prodigious death tolls. And disease hasn't done much to alter it either, despite the 14th Century bubonic plague killing off one-third of Europe and ~50 million people in Europe, Asia, and Africa. COVID-19 is another non-factor in the population boom. (Its toll of 3,530,151 deaths is 2% of the 169,880,421 known cases as of 5/28/2021[465] and less than 0.05% of the estimated human population of 7.8 billion.)

6.2 The Neanderthals

Homo sapiens' rise was accompanied by extinction of other species of the Genus Homo. A historically recent example is our cousin species, Homo neanderthalensis.[466] The Neanderthals left Africa some 350 KYA ago and lived in less numerous, more socially isolated groups than Homo sapiens (us). But 1-4% of the genome of most H. sapiens outside sub-Saharan Africa and even in some parts of sub-Saharan Africa is that of ancient Neanderthals. That has been attributed to interbreeding as long ago as 100 KYA, between

50-60 KYA, during out-of-Africa migration(s) of anatomically modern humans (AMHs), with ancestral Melanesian Neanderthals after they branched off, with Denisovans, and with East Asians. [The human sex drive is stronger than the separation effect of phenotypic and cultural dissimilarities between different human species.] And 3-5 KY after H. sapiens arrived in Neanderthal-land some 45-43 KYA, the Neanderthals started dying out—making H. sapiens the only living species in Genus Homo.

Hypothesized causes of the Neanderthal extinction include:

- Interspecies violence (akin to our own continual intraspecies warfare).
- Disease (consistent with the diseases that Europeans brought to Amerinds.)
- Competitive replacement/exclusion (consistent with human genocides and with occupying the habitats of other species). [Different non-human species competing for the same resources do coexist in some natural ecosystems.]
- Extinction by interbreeding (as Whites did with Amerinds?).
- Natural catastrophe. An example is the gigantic eruption of an 8.1-mile-wide caldera in the Phlegraean Fields (near Naples, Italy) about 39 KYA. It devastated about 3.7 million square kilometers.[467] (That's less than 7% of Eurasia.) The hypothesis also states that Neanderthal extinction was caused by H. sapiens competition and the inability of the Neanderthals to change their hunting practices when Europe became a sparsely vegetated steppe and semi-desert during the last Ice Age.
- Climate change. A 2018 Smithsonian Article[468] acknowledges factors like less Neanderthal reproduction than that of H. sapiens, slaughter of and introducing disease among the Neanderthals, and a catastrophic volcanic eruption. That article also attributes two cold snaps, one for 1000 years beginning about 44 KYA and the second a 600 year one beginning about 40.8 KYA, with below zero temperatures and year-round permafrost as an important Neanderthal extinction factor that the more adaptable H. sapiens survived. It also was noted that the cold snaps were not shown to have existed throughout the Neanderthal range, and that the Neanderthals had survived many previous periods of intense cold. The (questionable) conclusion that the (encroaching) newcomers didn't actively kill off the Neanderthals included the statement that *It seems we are off the hook on that one.*

The following seems more consistent with Human and Mother Nature:

- Catastrophic volcanic eruption affected H. neanderthalensis and H. sapiens equally.
- 300 KY of natural selection had adapted the Neanderthals to a cold climate and ice ages. {Since the mid-Pleistocene Transition of about 2 ± 0.25 MYA (million years ago), ice ages have occurred at about 100 KY intervals.[469]}
- H. sapiens cooperated and interbred with the burlier, bigger brained (~1400cc vs our ~1350cc[470]) Neanderthals as long as that was advantageous.
- Interbreeding-introduced Neanderthal genes better enabled H sapiens to survive cold.
- Out-populating the Neanderthals and superior weapons/tactics (e.g., throwing spears vs. the Neanderthals' thrusting spears) made H. Sapiens the more powerful predator.

- Competition, exacerbated by an ice age that drove the Neanderthals Southward, dominated. And, much like the American Colonists later treated the Amerinds, H. sapiens drove out and killed off most Neanderthals.
- There being even less mercy shown then to conquered competitors than during the Colonial and U.S. conquest of the Amerinds, the Neanderthals became extinct.

6.3 Hominin History

Our deep history is the history of Hominins (H. sapiens and directly ancestral and closely related species—but not other hominids such as bonobos, chimpanzees, gorillas, and orangutans). A peek at hominin history follows.

7.2 MYA Graecopithecus freybergi.[471] Possibly the oldest human ancestor before the human-chimpanzee lineage split (4-13 MYA). Known from a lower jaw found in Greece and an upper premolar tooth found in Bulgaria. (Those specimens may not have lived where their species originated.) Face probably ape-like with smaller teeth.

~7 MYA. Sahelanthropus tchadensis.[472] Known from a small cranium, 5 jaw pieces, and teeth found in the Djurab Desert of Chad. 320-380 cc brain.

6.1-5.7 MYA. Orrorin tugenensis.[473] More like Anatomically Modern Humans (AMHs) than A. afarensis was. Small toothed. Had bipedal and tree-climbing features.

5.8-1.98 MYA. Australopithecines.[474] 3.9-4.9' tall, 86-121 lb. upright walkers. Two types: gracile (Genus Australopithecus) and robust (Genus Paranthropus). A. kadabba was the first, A. sediba the last. Brains slightly larger than modern apes. Higher forearm to upper arm ratio than other hominins. More sexual dimorphism than H. sapiens and chimps (but less than gorillas and orangutans).

3.9-2.9 MYA. Australopithecus afarensis.[475] (e.g., Lucy) The most closely related australopithecine to the Homo Genus. A 380-430 cc brained primate and the first hominin that may have used stone tools (to cut meat from animal carcasses).[476] Adult males were ~4'11" tall and weighed ~100 lb; females were ~3'5" tall and weighed ~62 lb.[477]

2.8-1.9 MYA. Homo rudolfensis, aka Australopithecus rudolfensis.[478] Intermediate between australopithecines and modern humans. (Physical traits and tooth wear suggest that all early Homo in Africa were H. erectus.)

2.5 MYA-912 KYA?. (Dates based on features). Homo naledi. Specimens found in Rising Star Caves (~31 mi. from Johannesburg, S. Africa) date to 335-236 KYA. Possibly a relic species of early Homo. An anatomic mosaic. Brain size 450-610 cc. Adult males ~5' tall, 100 lb. Australopithecine-like torso/hip/pelvis/fingers; thumb/wrist/palm/teeth structure Homo-like (with better hand manipulation than Australopithecines). Upper body more primitive than Australopithecines. Modern brain temporal and occipital lobes. Teeth crowning and wear resisting enamel indicate an offshoot of modern human line rather than direct ancestry. Remains appear to have been deliberately placed in caves, but without artifacts like those accompanying ritualistic Homo burials.[479, 480]

2.4-1.4 MYA. Homo habilis. An ~70 lb., 3'4" to 4'5" human. The first known stone toolmaker. Coexistence with H. erectus suggests that an isolated subpopulation evolved into H. erectus while the rest existed as H. habilis until their extinction. H. habilis had legs more like AMHs than like Australopithecines and arms suitable for swinging and load bearing (more like chimps than like A. afarensis). Brain size was 550-687 cc (25% more than Paranthropus, 45% more than other archaic humans and Australopithecines), with relatively large parietal and frontal lobes (which govern humans' speech).[481, 482]

2 MYA? (Lifespan unknown) Homo georgicus, aka Homo erectus georgicus. Fossils dating to 800 KY before H. erectus were found in Europe in Dmansi, Georgia (near the Black Sea). About the size of H. habilis. Features intermediate between H. habilis and H. erectus. Their ~600 cc brains are the smallest, most primitive human ones found outside Africa. Males were significantly larger than females---much more sexually dimorphic than later Homo species. The care needed to sustain a toothless specimen's life indicates family/community care of the elderly.[483, 484, 485]

~2 MYA-250 KYA. Homo erectus (upright man). Lived in Africa and then Asia and Indonesia (and maybe Europe). Omnivorous. The longest lasting human. Evolved from a brain of ~550 to 1250 cc, a weight of from 90 to 143 lb, and a height of from 4'7" to 5'9".[486] More like AMHs than australopithecines in gait, body proportions, height, and brain size. Credited with speech, coordinated hunter-gathering, starting fires, caring for the ill and injured, and perhaps creating art. The proposed direct ancestor of H. heidelbergensis, H. antecessor, H. neanderthalensis, and H. sapiens. Encompasses many Homo species and subspecies.[487] (Evidence of sharpening tree branches for use as wooden spears 400 KYA in Germany—and observing Western Chimpanzees using their teeth to sharpen branches used for hunting indicates that spears were used not only by H. erectus but much earlier.[488])

1.9-0.6 MYA. Homo gautengensis.[489] Identified from South African fossils previously classified H. habilis, or H. ergaster, or Australopithecine. ~3' tall, 110 lb. Small-brained, big-toothed (probably primarily vegetarian) archaic human. No indication of speech. Might not be a direct H. sapiens ancestor.

~1.9-1.4 MYA. Homo ergaster, aka Homo erectus ergaster and African Homo erectus.[490] Mostly considered an early or African variety of H. erectus. Their stone tools were more diverse and sophisticated than those of H. habilis. They were ~20% less sexually dimorphic than australopithecines {but more so than AMHs}, more like modern humans in body, organization, and sociality than earlier species, and may have been the first humans to harness fire. (Predecessor species may have done that too)}

1.25 MYA-180 KYA. Homo heidelbergensis.[491] (Subspecies: H. heidelbergensis heidelbergensis, H. heidelbergensis daliensis, H. heidelbergensis steinheimensis.) Most recent common ancestor of modern humans and Neanderthals. Intermediate between H. erectus and H. neanderthalensis. Lived in Southern and East Africa and Europe. Brain size 1,250 cc. Dentition typically modern human. Phenotype otherwise more primitive than the Neanderthals. Males and females averaged 5'2" tall and 112 lb. (Reportedly, a 400-350 KYA grassland expansion led to large, hooved animals and a short period of H. heidelbergensis reaching over 7'.) Skeletons found in an Atapuerca, Spain pit suggest that this was the first Homo species to bury their dead.

~1.2 MYA-800 KYA. Homo antecessor.[492] Found in France, Spain, and England. Thought by some to be early Homo heidelbergensis or European Homo erectus. The ~5.5-6' tall, ~200 lb. adults had ~1,000-1150 cc brains. Tooth eruption patterns were like ours but probably occurred faster. Their auditory range reputedly was similar to ours and might have been accompanied by symbolic language. Cannibalism is indicated by numerous cuts where the specimens' flesh was flensed from the bones.

~850 KYA. (Origin/Lifespan unknown.) Homo ceprangensis.[493] (Also classified as H. heidelbergensis.) Known from one skull cap. Features intermediate between H. erectus and H. heidelbergensis. Possible direct ancestor of H. neanderthalensis.

800-120 KYA. Homo rhodesiensus.[494] Estimated brain size 1100 cc, with parietal and occipital regions H. sapiens-like. H. rhodesiensus dispersed throughout Africa and Eurasia. Now mostly considered to be H. heidelbergensis or an African subspecies thereof. A 400-260 KYA fossil gap is inconsistent with the proposal that H. rhodesiensus is the direct ancestor of H. sapiens. Used bows and arrows some 70-60 KYA in Africa, and likely to have invented that weapon.[495]

~200-≤50 KYA. Denisovans, aka Homo denisova, Homo altaiensis, and Homo sapiens denisova. Ranged from Siberia to Southeast Asia. Neanderthal and Denisovan nuclear DNA is ~17% alike. Denisovan mtDNA indicates an unidentified ancient human lineage (interbreeding). Anatomically Modern Humans (AMHs) also interbred with Denisovans (perhaps as recently as 15 KYA in New Guinea. That AMH ancestors and Denisovans interbred too is shown by Denisovan DNA comprising ~3-5% of the DNA of Melanesians and Aboriginal Australians and ~6% of Papuans' DNA. The Denisovan and Neanderthal ancestral lineage is estimated to have separated from that of AMHs ~744-600 KYA, after which Denisovan and Neanderthal DNA diverged significantly in only 300 generations.[496, 497]

≥65.7-≤50 KYA. Homo luzonensis.[498] Bones found on Luzon Island, Philippines. Bathymetric data shows Luzon to have always been an island. So H. luzonensis reached Luzon by sea. May be a locally adapted version of other archaic humans (e.g., H. erectus or Denisovans). Species height is unknown. Small molars indicate that, like H. floriensis, H. luzonensis may have experienced island dwarfing. Digit curvature is consistent with that of tree-climbers. The bones were found with those of deer, wild pig, and an extinct bovine. Potential cut marks on some of the quadrupeds' remains suggest that they were butchered. (Earlier stone tools and the almost complete fossil skeleton of a butchered rhinoceros dating back to ~700 KYA were found in nearby San Pedro, in Rizal, Kalinga.}

~90-50 KYA. Homo floriensis (the Hobbit). Hobbits lived on Flores island, Indonesia and went extinct about when H. sapiens arrived. Postulated to be an example of insular dwarfism like the ~1000 lb. Stegadons (elephants) they hunted. A typical Hobbit adult stood some 3'7" tall and weighed ~55 lb. (Even smaller skeletal hominin remains on Flores date to 700 KYA.) Hobbits reportedly are anatomically similar only to H. erectus, and H. erectus stone tools dating to 800 KYA (but no H. erectus fossils) have been found on Flores. H. floriensis brain size was ~380 cc (in the chimpanzee and australopithecine range) while H. erectus had an ~980 cc brain. But the Hobbits' Brodman's Area 10 (the brain's prefrontal cortex area associated with higher cognition) was about the same size as modern humans. Evidence of the use of fire for cooking and cut marks on the Stegadon bones indicate advanced behavior.

~14.5-11.5 KYA. (Species lifetime unknown.) Red Deer Cave People.[499] Recently identified archaic humans. Their fossils were found in Red Deer Cave and Longlin Cave in Southwest China. The fossils' mixed archaic and modern features are hypothesized to be those of a late surviving archaic human species, or of Denisovan and modern human hybrids, or of robust early modern humans probably related to Melanesians. They had flat faces, broad noses, jutting jaws without chins, large molars, prominent brows, thick skulls, moderately sized brains, and weighed ~110 lb.

Some mammal species live for the 10 MY typical for species, but a mammal species lifespan of 1 MY is more likely.[500] When H. erectus proliferated and spread, hominin speciation appears to have been replaced by rapid extinction and/or absorption into H. erectus. AMHs have followed a similar proliferation and extinction path. That indicates that conquest has been a primary human drive at least since the arrival of H. erectus.

6.4 Human Culture and the San

AMHs dominate other species and less powerful human groups and organizations. Sexual dimorphism generally enables men to physically dominate women, but domination of men by powerful women shows that the characteristic is genderless. The trait is obvious in war, athletics, business, the sandbox, denial of equal opportunity and pay to women and minorities, and the greater opportunities and better educations of children of the wealthy. Initiatives (e.g., scholarships, antitrust and equal opportunity laws) promote equality. But *Mother Nature's Order* is evident in the wealth and precedence of the more powerful, regardless of the form of government.

Egalitarianism (all people having equal rights and opportunities) is unlike *Mother Nature's Order*. Nonetheless, egalitarianism has been achieved to a considerable degree among the peaceful, semi-nomadic hunter-gatherer San people. Their male DNA is in subclades of the earliest human Y Chromosome Haplogroups. And the oldest mitochondrial (matrilineal) DNA of our species has its highest frequency among the Southern African San.[501] San ancestors produced AMHs' oldest art, the 70 KYA rock paintings in the San's sacred Tsodilo Hills in Ngamiland in Northwest Botswana. The San's ancestors are thought to be the first human inhabitants of Botswana and South Africa, probably due to originating in Northern Africa and being driven South by bigger and stronger Black Africans. (San adults are ~5' tall and have yellowish complexions.)[502]

The San speak ancient "click" languages and live in groups of up to 25. They do not trade for or buy goods or services but traditionally exchange gifts Instead. Most believe in a supreme God, recognize lesser Gods, and pay homage to the deceased. Believing in God-established order, they neither farm nor domesticate animals.

The San have no central authority and reach decisions by consensus. But they do have leaders in particular skills—long-time group members of a respectable age and good character. Women are highly regarded, included in family and group decision-making, may be family and group leaders, and own water holes and foraging areas.

San hunting is done by teams of men. The hunter whose arrow kills distributes the meat among the group and among visitors, and reciprocity is traditional. Women are the food gatherers and their harvest is consumed by their immediate families. But men sometimes help gather and women sometimes assist in hunting.

The San are now mostly concentrated in the Kalahari Desert and afflicted by poverty, alcoholism, violence, prostitution, disease, and despair. Their last hunter-gatherers were forcibly evicted from the Central Kalahari Game Reserve in April 2002 by the Botswana Government, ostensibly to bring the San into the modern world. But schools and medical services haven't materialized, and the government that claimed that San presence in the Game Reserve is "incompatible with wildlife conservation" allowed a $4.9 billion open pit diamond mine to open there in 2014.[503]

Botswana reputedly feels that the San need to become cattle-herders. But absorption and (mostly) extinction are dooming the San and their lifestyle to museums and history.[504] That's consistent with replacement of hunter-gathering by agriculture and its habitat-gobbling culture that, for hunter-gatherers, means *adapt or die.*

A study of two other hunter-gatherer groups (one in Africa, one in the Philippines) suggests that San-like egalitarianism existed until agriculture/pastoralism became dominant. Sex-based heritable resources then developed and led to wealth and to sexual inequality.[505] That's consistent with the hypothesis that, when there were few humans and food and shelter were plentiful, cooperation and sexual equality predominated. But as agriculture brought wealth and a population increase, competition, male domination and heritable ownership came to the fore.

The concept of an earlier egalitarian society has mythic overtones. There was competition for societal status and sexual advantage, and group competition for the best hunting grounds, etc. Drought and famine increased the competition. (Mother Nature ruthlessly removes more of the less competitively successful from the gene pool.) And ownership is an innate human drive—that's evident when a two-year-old claims *Mine* and only partially learns to share through extensive parental emphasis.

Hunter-gatherers like the San and the sea mammal-hunting Eskimos have drawn much interest from those striving for female equality. But Anthropology Professor Robert Kelly points out that other hunter-gatherer societies are different and considers the San an example of the *Noble Savage.* He and other anthropologists also point out that human aggression increases with population density.[506]

The San and their culture are dying out as the competitive modern world encroaches.

6.5 Rain Forest Pygmies

Genetically a little younger than the San, the ~500,000 African Rain Forest Pygmy hunter-gatherers are the smallest AMHs. (Men are up to ~4'11" tall.) In the Republic of the Congo, they are ~2% of the populace. Many are Bantu-owned Slaves and do much of the hunting, fishing, and manual labor in jungle villages. The ~360 million Bantu consider the Pygmies inferior and their Slavery a time-honored tradition. (Both the Pygmies and Bantu say the pygmies are paid in cigarettes, used clothing, or not at all—at the master's whim.) Under Belgian Colonial Authorities, Pygmy children were captured and exported to European zoos—and to the 1907 U.S. World's Fair.

The Rain Forest Pygmies are being forced from their homeland by deforestation for mining and farming. They often are marginalized, impoverished, and abused. Most African States do not recognize them as citizens and refuse them identity cards, deeds to land, health care, and proper schooling. They reportedly were hunted down and eaten as game animals during the Congo Civil War. And they were cannibalized by a death squad trying to clear and open up North Kivu Province for mineral exploitation. Much of the violence against Pygmies is attributed to the *Movement for the Liberation of the Congo* rebels, but they also have been targeted by many other armed groups.[507]

Extended on-scene study of the Congo-Brazzaville Mbendjele Yaka Pygmies by Jerome Lewis[508] and by Camille Oloa-Biloa[509] identified Pygmy egalitarian behavior and the contrasting behavior of their non-Pygmy fellow Africans. Mbendjele lore holds that the forest provides all they need. Most spend over half their time in it and some don't leave it for years. But many clear small areas and plant crops requiring little attention (e.g., bananas, plantain, chili) as a sideline, and aren't strictly hunter-gatherers.

The Mbendjele frequent their favored parts of the forest. No Mbendjele owns territory and they all consider it their inalienable birthright to go anywhere they wish in the forest and use whatever they want there. Forest-dwelling Pygmies spend three to five hours a day garnering food and are a communal, highly interactive people. They use intricate music/dance/speaking rituals (Massana) to communicate, air grievances, and maintain their egalitarianism. But within their societal constraints, each Mbendjele is free to do as he or she wishes, and need not submit to anyone else's authority.

That does not eliminate gender roles. The men hunt and the women gather. Mbendjele "clans" are determined by the male line, with primary male authority. For example, when a couple wants to marry, they approach their fathers, who decide the matter. And the groom often makes a bridewealth payment (~4-5 dollars U.S.) to the father of the bride. Mothers may or may not be informed of the impending marriage. But childbirth is hazardous, mothers fear for the health of their young daughters, and a groom's mother-in-law and his bride's younger siblings may instigate a huge row that lasts many hours when the groom sneaks into their hut to lie with his mate for the first time. (The groom lives with the bride's family and hunts as their agent for some time (another form of bridewealth payment) before his wife builds a hut for the two of them.)

The Pygmies' independence and egalitarianism coexist with the prestige and acceptance of advice of respected, experienced individuals. Hunting brings the largest dividend, and master hunters (tuma) are very highly regarded, especially forest elephant hunters. Tuma lead the hunts and their advice is readily followed during that dangerous process. (Elephants may have to be followed for half a day's time before they bleed out.) The tuma's authority lasts until the quarry is finally dispatched and the community begins the butchering and meat preservation (by smoking).

There is a continual Mbendjele battle against dominance. An example is the quasi-neutralization of elephant hunter prowess by a women-performed ritual that kills the elephant's spirit in preparation for, and necessary to, the men killing the elephant's body. Another leveling ritual is the moadjo, during which a woman, often a respected elder (kombeti), publicly mimics anti-egalitarian behavior (e.g., ordering others about, or dominating a wife or husband, or aggressiveness). With highly stylized theatrics, the kombeti ridicules the inappropriate behavior to publicly shame the culprit(s). That and the associated audience laughter serve to maintain egalitarianism. Ridicule also is used outside the moadjo, along with open criticism, by men, women, and children to counter individual or group attempts to control others' behavior.

A daily Mbendjele ritual is the Mosambo (every evening and often in the morning as well, and whenever somebody wishes to address the whole group). Any group member can hold forth, no one should interrupt the speaker, and everyone is expected to be silent during the speech. A morning Mosambo often features an individual's complaints about another individual or group, usually not identifying the person(s) directly but often identifying the behavior explicitly enough that there's no doubt about the alleged culprit(s). Women have their own area and address their comments to other women, but often come close to the men's area—so that the men are sure to hear criticism of them. Widows are permitted and expected to openly criticize those who have gravely transgressed. And the more comedic the criticism/mimicking, the more it's appreciated.

Shouting matches and even serious fights sometimes occur during Mosambo. Lewis described a wife's criticism of her husband so enraging him that he began to beat her. She fled. He followed. The other women grabbed sticks and beat him into submission.

[Mbendjele egalitarianism requires constant maintenance.]

6.6 Amerind Cultures

Another telling example of human nature is the Amerinds who spread throughout North and South America. They descended from Siberian immigrants who arrived 20-14 KYA. (Alaska's Inuit language speakers came later.) Those Amerinds' male descendants carry the Q-M3 Y-DNA Single Nucleotide Polymorphism (SNP), a mutation that arose about 15,000 years ago in the Americas, and there has been relatively little subsequent genetic diversity among them.[510] In Mesoamerica and South America, they developed the Maya, Andean (Inca), and Aztec civilizations.

The Maya[511] ritually sacrificed high-ranking enemy captives (and enslaved the lower ranks). During one such ritual, after ripping the heart out of the victim and skinning the corpse, the officiating priest donned the skin and performed a dance symbolic of rebirth.

Human sacrifice was more common among the Aztecs.[512] Their belief that all the Gods sacrificed themselves so that mankind could live entailed debt-repayment (nexttlahualli) by sacrificing captured enemies and chosen Aztecs. A typical ritual involved the victim being held fast by four priests on a stone slab while a fifth sliced through the abdomen and diaphragm with a ceremonial flint knife, ripped out the still beating heart, and placed it in a bowl held by the stone statue of a God. When cannibalism was involved, the stomach and chest were offered to the Gods and the meaty limbs went to the capturer(s).

The Inca[513] code was *do not lie, steal or be lazy.* But they practiced human sacrifice—including children. When their 11th Sovereign, Huayna Capac, died in 1527, up to 4000 servants, officials, favorites, and concubines were killed. (16th Century Spain's conquests sounded the death knell for the Amerind civilizations in Mexico and South America.)

The White Man also brought diseases that he had developed immunity to over many centuries of exposure. And Eurasian diseases (smallpox, typhus, measles, influenza, bubonic plague, cholera, malaria, tuberculosis, mumps, yellow fever, pertussis, etc.) were worse for the Amerinds because they all arrived with the White Man—and spread faster than the White Man did. Estimates of the Amerind population in 1492 ranged from 8-112 million (with a later estimate of 54 million), declining to less than six million by 1650.[514] Because the WWII death toll was some 75 million people, the disease-caused Amerind deaths weren't, as claimed,[515] the greatest catastrophe in human history. But the White Man's diseases caused a horrendous death toll among the Amerinds, and there were multiple reports of deliberate infection of the Amerinds by the Whites.[516]

The White Man's cruel treatment of the Amerind included wholesale slaughter of villages (like Joshua at Jericho?). But the Amerinds were ruthless too. In their wars among themselves, they either adopted (children and teenage girls) or sacrificially tortured and executed (men, women, and teenage boys) their captives. Torture victims were expected to maintain their composure, brag courageously, and be defiant. Entire villages took part in techniques like burning the captive (one hot coal at a time), cutting with knives, beating with sticks, jabbing with sharp sticks, ripping out fingernails, breaking fingers and having them twisted and yanked by children, scalping, forcing captives to eat their own flesh, and dissecting male genitals one slice at a time. By beginning on the legs with painful tortures that caused little bodily harm, progressing to the arms and then to the torso, torture was prolonged. Victims were revived, rested and fed so it could be further prolonged. And on the Northwest coast of the present U.S., Slaves were a significant part of the Amerind population and played a major economic role.[517]

6.7 Religious and Revolutionary Cultures

The Biblical tale of Jericho is consistent with the retribution of the newly empowered long oppressed. Another example was the French Revolution being preceded by long-standing clerical (1st Estate) and aristocratic (2nd Estate) mistreatment of commoners and peasants (the 3rd Estate). When the 3rd Estate gained control, they wreaked a *Reign of Terror* (e.g., massacres, executions summarily conducted without trial). The Revolution's Committee of Public Safety adopted the terror. Its leader Robespierre proclaimed:

> *If the basis of popular government in peacetime is virtue, the basis of popular government during a revolution is both virtue and terror; virtue, without which terror is baneful; terror, without which virtue is powerless. Terror is nothing more than speedy, severe and inflexible justice; it is thus an emanation of virtue; it is less a principle in itself, than a consequence of the general principle of democracy, applied to the most pressing needs of the patrie [homeland, fatherland].*[518]

"Enlightenment" (e.g., Democracy, Abolition of Slavery) accompanied the *Reign of Terror.* Robespierre outspokenly advocated: citizens having a voice; unrestricted admission to public office; the right to carry arms in self-defense; abolishing Slavery; and ending clerical celibacy. He also endorsed Deism, virtue, and nature's goodness. And he railed against clerical and aristocratic corruption by proclaiming:

> *Is it not He whose immortal hand, engraving on the heart of man the code of justice and equality, has written there the death sentence of tyrants? Is it*

not He who, from the beginning of time, decreed for all the ages and for all peoples liberty, good faith, and justice? He did not create kings to devour the human race. He did not create priests to harness us, like vile animals, to the chariots of kings and to give to the world examples of baseness, pride, perfidy, avarice, debauchery and falsehood. He created the universe to proclaim His power. He created men to help each other, to love each other mutually, and to attain to happiness by the way of virtue.[519]

Robespierre's "Godly" terror ended with his being guillotined one day after his arrest. . Expounding on the Russian Revolution would reinforce the tenor of the French one. And the tortures used by the church during the Spanish Inquisition were particularly revolting.

Religion is deeply involved in warfare, and not only in the assertion that *there ain't no atheists in foxholes.* Many Americans prayed, during WWII, that "our boys" would come home safely. But few Americans prayed for the enemy's "boys."

The Church's wartime role has sometimes been a primary one. For example:[520]

- Pope Alexander VI arranged the 1495 Holy League that forced the French out of Italy.
- Pope Julius II created the 1508-1516 anti-Venetian League of Cambria, and personally led the Papal Army in its successful 1510 Siege of Mirandola.[521]
- Pope Paul III arranged the 1538 Holy League, which lost to the numerically inferior Ottoman Empire's Admiral Barbarossa's fleet at the Battle of Preveza.[522]
- Saint Pius V, Pope from 1566-1572, arranged the 1571 Holy League that defeated the Ottoman forces in the sea Battle of Lepanto. At the battle's end, he reportedly went to a window, gazed out at the sky and cried out: *A truce to business; our great task at present is to thank God for the victory which He has just given the Christian army.* He also attributed the victory to the intercession of the *Blessed Virgin Mary* and instituted the *Feast of Our Lady of Victory.*[523]
- Pope Clement VIII established the 1594 Holy League of mostly Christian European countries allied against the Ottoman Empire during the 1591-1606 Long War.[524]
- Pope Innocent XI organized the 1684 Holy League that defeated the Ottomans in the 1683-1689 Great Turkish War.[525]
- The 1717 (last) Holy League organized the Papal States against the Ottoman Empire and ended Turkish supremacy in the Mediterranean at the Battle of Matapan,[526]

Germany's and Japan's WWII roles were infamous attempts to dominate by lethal force. So was Libya's 2nd Civil War (2014-2020). Some U.S. cities are notorious for murders, and we have had killing sprees elsewhere. But our murder rate, though unacceptable, is relatively minor. In 2016 our gunfire murders were 5.35 per 100,000 people—about one-fifteenth that of the worst in El Salvador (82.84 per 100,000 people),[527] (El Salvador has strong but laxly enforced gun control laws. It does not manufacture guns, many of which come from the U.S. by the same pathway that brings illegal drugs from El Salvador to the U.S. Other guns enter in shipments of old appliances and car parts to El Salvador, with the importers mostly being small-scale arms traffickers. Allegedly, corrupt military and police personnel add to the problem by selling captured weapons.[528])

7
The Gallowglass

The Gallowglass were mercenary warriors in Ireland. Initially, they were imported from Scotland's Hebrides by Irish Warlords.

7.1 Stage Setting by the Vikings

The Viking-related background for Ireland's employment of Gallowglass included:[529]

832—120 Viking ships attack Ireland's Northeast Coast.

836—Vikings begin to attack deeper inland in Ireland.

841—Vikings create Dublin (Dubhlinn).

846—Vikings create a settlement near Cork.

848—Vikings defeated in Sligo, Kildare, Cashel and Cork.

850—Vikings create Waterford (Vadrefjord).

851-895—Vikings raid Ireland.

851—Viking Battle at Dundalk Bay between Norwegian and Danish Vikings.

852—Vikings devastate the major monastery community of Armagh (which they also did subsequently—to take Slaves as well as plunder.[530])

860—Vikings attacking the King of Israige are slaughtered. Irish attacks on Vikings increase.

869—Connacht's King defeats the Norwegian Vikings near Drogheda.

902—The Irish drive Dublin's Vikings into Wales.

914—Large Viking Fleets that include Britain's Vikings land at Waterford. Viking settlements are built at Limerick and Wexford.

915—Vikings retake Dublin.

928—Massacre at Dunmore Cave in Kilkenny {According to the *Annals of the Four Masters,* Dublin Vikings marching to attack Waterford Vikings found a large number of women and children hiding in Dunmore Cave, hoped to sell them as Slaves, lit large

fires at the cave's mouth to force them out, and suffocated 1000 people when the fires consumed the cave's oxygen. In 1973 the bones of 44 people, mainly women, children and the elderly, were found in the cave.[531]}
980— Viking defeat at the Battle of Tara set the stage for the Irish to retake Dublin.[532]
1002—Brian Boru, King of Munster, and the Uí Néill slaughter Dublin's Vikings, and Brian becomes Ireland's High King.
1005—Máel Mórda mac Murchada, King of Leinster, his men, and Viking mercenaries from Dublin, the Orkneys, and The Isle of Mann—led by Sigtrygg Silkbeard, the Norse King of Dublin—rebel against Brian Boru.[533]
1014—At the Battle of Clontarf, Brian Boru is killed. Máel Mórda mac Murchada also dies, the Vikings are defeated, and Viking control in Ireland ends.

A melodramatic description (a second-hand account by German Abbot Walifrid Strabo) describes Vikings torturing, raping and killing Irish monks and nuns, whose dying screams echoed while their churches were being ransacked. It states that, in 825, the Vikings attacked Iona's monastery at first light and broke into the abbey where St. Blathmac and his followers were prostrate in prayer. All but Blathmac were slaughtered. Torture failed to force him to reveal where St. Columba's reliquary and other precious objects were hidden. Ropes attached to ponies' harnesses tore St. Blathmac limb from limb.

As a sacrifice to Odin, their war god, the Vikings also practiced blood-eagling. That involved carving a blood-eagle on their victim's back, hacking his ribs from his spine, pulling them outward like an eagle's wings, and wrenching his lungs out and draping them over his shoulders. King Edmund of East Anglia was a victim of that in 869 and Viking Earl Turf Einarr ordered the same ritual on Orkney in the 870s.[534]

7.2   Stage Setting by the Irish

Warfare between the Irish also set the stage for the Gallowglass. For example:

- The O'Reillys (Irish: Ó Raghallaigh) ruled a small area north of Loch Rahmor in East Breffny. Their cousins the O'Rourkes ruled the rest of Breffny. In 1161 Godfraid, a great-grandson of Raghallaigh, was killed by Melaghin O'Rourke in battle in Meath.
- The O'Reillys gained some independence from O'Rourke rule by siding with the Normans during their 1169 invasion of Ireland—and when Anglo-Norman invasion leader Hugh de Lacy killed clan king Tiernan O'Rourke in 1172.[535]
- O'Reilly support of the Normans ended when Walter De Lacy (Hugh's son) invaded central Breffny in 1220 and captured the O'Reilly crannog (a fortified artificial island) in Loch Uachtair. By 1224 the O'Reillys were besieging it. In 1226 they dismantled the Norman motte (a fortified, raised earthwork) at Kilmore. And when Walter De Lacy invaded O'Reilly East Breffny in 1233, they repulsed him with heavy casualties.[536]
- By 1240 the O'Reillys had usurped the O'Rourkes and Cathal O'Reilly ruled as King of Breffny from East Breffny. But when Cúchonnacht O'Reilly, the lead General of Connacht Province (Counties Leitrim, Mayo, Galway, Rosecommon, and Sligo) took

control of West Breffny and expelled the O'Rourke leaders,[537] the O'Rourkes re-allied with Connacht. Their combined forces pushed the O'Reillys out of West Breffny by 1250. By 1256 they had defeated the O'Reillys at Magh Slécht, killing Cathal and 14 other O'Reilly nobles. Cúchonnacht O'Reilly died there too, and the heavy losses among Connacht's forces made the O'Rourkes unable to retake East Breffny. So Breffny stayed divided into East Breffny (O'Reilly) and West Breffny (O'Rourke). [538]

7.3 Gallowglass Nature

In *The World of the Gallowglass*, Seán Duffy stated that Gallowglass is short-hand for *Warrior from Innse Gall* (Scotland's Hebrides Islands).[539] Norse-Hebridean ancestry has long been held to be the case for the Hebrides, for other formerly Scandinavian-held Scotch territory {e.g., the Orkneys and Shetlands), and for the lands along the Firth of Clyde (e.g., Caithness and Sutherland).[540]

In his book *Gallowglass (1250-1600)*, Fergus Cannan stated that Gallowglass means *Foreign Warrior* and has the implicit meaning of *Warrior from the Norsemen's Isles*. Among the first Gallowglass, Cannan identified the MacSweeneys, MacDowells, and many MacDonnells as exiles who had fallen afoul of the King of Scots. He also labeled the MacCabes as an "other" and more mysterious great Gallowglass tribe, one that probably found little chance of achieving their ambitions in Scotland, where they were an "alleged cadet branch of the great MacLeods of Harris." And he described other MacDonnells and the MacRorys as being enthusiastic about Robert and Edward Bruce's vision of an Ireland free of British rule—and as being attracted by the prospect of power and land in Ireland, and deeply attracted to participation in a heroic war against the English. Cannan also stated that there were relatively few Gallowglass and local Irishmen were recruited to fill out their ranks.[541]

The MacCabe Gallowglass presence in Ireland was first recorded in 1368, ~100 years after the first Gallowglass. The Gallowglass era ended about when Ulster was "Planted" by England—mostly with Scots (mostly Presbyterian) and with some Englishmen (mostly Anglican) beginning in 1606.[542] In 1921, over three centuries later, Ulster Counties Antrim, Down, Armagh, Londonderry, Fermanagh, and Tyrone became Northern Ireland.

When the Vikings established a combined Gaelic-Scandinavian culture in the 8th-10th Centuries, their warfare skills came to the British Isles.[543] Christianity was well established in Denmark and Norway by the mid-11th Century and took hold in Sweden in the 12th.[544] So, for at least the first 250 years of the 350-year Gallowglass era that began about 1250, the Gallowglass who had a religion were Roman Catholics. Some may have converted to Protestantism after Martin Luther began the Protestant Reformation in 1517.[545] And some may have become Presbyterian after Roman Catholic Priest John Knox brought that denomination to Scotland starting in 1560.[546] Others may never have allied themselves to a religious denomination.

The MacDonnells hired by England's (and Ireland's) Protestant Queen Elizabeth I (1533-1603)[547] during her attempt to plant Munster in the late 1590s were an exception to the Gallowglass role of fighting for the Irish.

The great poet Edmund Spenser (1552/53-1599), a favorite of Elizabeth I, was among the Anglo-Irish Rulers of Ireland. Like his friend Sir Walter Raleigh, he received substantial parts of the estates of the deposed Irish. Spenser argued for ruling Ireland firmly and ruthlessly, and for showing gentleness only for complete submissiveness.[548]

In 1598, during the *Nine Years War*, Spenser was driven from his Kilcolman Castle in Co. Cork by the forces of Aodh Ó Néill. The castle was burned. Spenser's infant son reportedly died in the blaze. He returned to England and died there in 1599 at the age of 46, and was buried in Westminster Abbey.[549] Spenser accused the Gallowglass and Kern (Irish light infantry) of *beastly behaviour inasmuch as they* oppress *all men, they spoil as well the subject, as the enemy, they steal, they are cruel and bloody, full of revenge and delighting in deadly execution, licentious, swearers, and blasphemers, common ravishers of women, and murderers of children.*[550] [A cynic might attribute Spenser's vitriol to his loss of filthy lucre upon being driven out of Ireland.]

Cannan, in *Gallowglass*, further stated:

- According to a 1537 statement by Robert Cowley, an Anglo-Irish government official: *amongst 200 of them* (the Gallowglass), a *scant eight* were *gentlemen*, with *all the residue* akin to *Slaves* from different parts of Ireland—and the Gallowglass *serveth for their wages, and not for love, nor affection.*
- The *gentlemen* were probably Scots of the same family name and the unit's officers.
- Most Gallowglass were probably Irish farm boys.
- Gallowglass personal honor counted more than gold or cattle, and material considerations rarely decided their loyalties. For example, the *Annals of the Four Masters* record Thomas Fitzmaurice of Kerry being under attack by the MacSheehy Gallowglass of his enemies, who knew that Fitzmaurice's MacSweeny Gallowglass' contract would soon expire. Constable Eamon MacSweeney *did not think it honourable* to desert Fitzmaurice and, with enmity and indignation, Eamon and his men enthusiastically *butchered* the MacSheehys.
- The *Annals of Connacht* state that *Fergal, son of Aed O'Rourke, son of the king of Breifne and a prince eligible for the kingship, was treacherously killed in his own house by Loughlin Calach MacCabe a fortnight before Easter.* And *the Annals of Ulster* state that in 1416 MacCabes were *retained Gallowglass* to the O'Rourkes. But those did not include Loughlin because the *Annals of the Four Masters* also state that he and others of the *Clann Cába*, and some O'Reillys, were killed by the English in 1413 in Meath because of committing *acts of conflagration and depredation.*[551]

Initially, Gallowglass were paid by a tax (*buannacht*) on their employer's feudal tenants. *Coyne and livery* (room and board provided by the employer's vassals) replaced that, with a Galowglass "quartered" in a household for three months (the reputed first use of *quarters* to describe lodging). These Gallowglass were noted for eating everything in sight, stealing, and stripping their hosts' homes bare before moving on.[552]

Author Ron Soodalter[553] stated that the Gallowglass practiced a generally accepted form of warfare. He also described their (Viking) two-handed battle-axes as having a razor sharp 8-12" blade on a 2-4 lb. iron socket mounted on a 5' wooden haft. And he quoted 16th Century alchemist and historian Richard Stonehurst's description of the Gallowglass he met as *grim of countenance, tall of stature, big of limb, burly of body, well and strongly timbered,* and as wearing iron battle helmets with peaks that added inches to their already prodigious stature. Soodalter further characterized Gallowglass assaults as Celtic giants screaming battle cries to the cacophonous squealing of bagpipes.

Other mercenaries came to Ireland in the mid-16th Century—*Redshanks* from the Highlands' Western Isles and the poorer parts of mainland Scotland—mostly from Clans MacLeod, MacQuarrie, MacLean, MacDonald, and Campbell. They wore kilts, waded bare-legged through icy rivers, and were armed with bows and two-handed claymore swords (~ 20" longer than a cavalryman's saber).[554]

7.4 Another Side of War

Invader devastation of one's homeland and being slaughtered or enslaved inspires defensive heroism. And personal honor and loyalty are typically more important to warriors than renumeration. An example is evident in the following 1854 poem by England's and Ireland's Poet Laureate *Alfred, Lord Tennyson*:[555]

The Charge of the Light Brigade

I
Half a league, half a league,
Half a league onward,
All in the valley of Death
Rode the six hundred.
"Forward, the Light Brigade!
Charge for the guns!" he said.
Into the valley of Death
Rode the six hundred.

II
"Forward, the Light Brigade!"
Was there a man dismayed?
Not though the soldier knew
Someone had blundered.
Theirs not to make reply,
Theirs not to reason why,
Theirs but to do and die.
Into the valley of Death
Rode the six hundred.

III
Cannon to right of them,
Cannon to left of them,
Cannon in front of them
Volleyed and thundered;
Stormed at with shot and shell,
Boldly they rode and well,
Into the jaws of Death,
Into the mouth of hell
Rode the six hundred.

IV
Flashed all their sabres bare,
Flashed as they turned in air
Sabring the gunners there,
Charging an army, while
All the world wondered.
Plunged in the battery-smoke
Right through the line they broke;
Cossack and Russian
Reeled from the sabre stroke
Shattered and sundered.
Then they rode back, but not
Not the six hundred.

V
Cannon to right of them,
Cannon to left of them,
Cannon behind them
Volleyed and thundered;
Stormed at with shot and shell,
While horse and hero fell.
They that had fought so well
Came through the jaws of Death,
Back from the mouth of hell,
All that was left of them,
Left of six hundred.

VI
When can their glory fade?
O the wild charge they made!
All the world wondered.
Honour the charge they made!
Honour the Light Brigade,
Noble six hundred!

War's cost in lives is horrendous. But Orson Welles, sardonically but not incorrectly, said in a reputedly unscripted statement in the movie *The Third Man: In Italy for 30 years under the Borgias, they had warfare, terror, murder, and bloodshed. They produced Michelangelo, Leonardo da Vinci, and the Renaissance. In Switzerland, they had brotherly love, five hundred years of democracy and peace. And what did that produce? The cuckoo clock.*[556]

Military inventions turned into civilian use[557] add some perspective:

- Sonar invented to detect submarines is used for undersea exploration.
- Radar invented for air defense is used for air traffic control.
- Walkie-Talkies became portable public safety communications devices.
- Night Vision technology is used for security surveillance and low light photography.
- Ballistic missile technology is used for space exploration and for placing satellites.
- Jet engines are used in airliners.
- Spy satellite digital photography was adapted to digital cameras.
- Computer networking led to the internet and world wide web.

Military-sponsored research also set the stage for today's computers and cell phones.

War's cruelty is not a characteristic of yesteryear but never-ending. For example, WWI Britain used poison gas—after Germany did. And WWI and WWII German and WWII American submarines practiced unrestricted submarine warfare by sinking merchant and naval ships without warning, and left the survivors to the merciless sea.

One of war's most shocking cruelties, the atomic bomb, killed ~250,000 Japanese (about half of them initially), and actually saved lives. That's because the U.S. estimated that 400,000 to 800,000 American and 5-10 million Japanese lives would be lost during the impending invasion of Japan.[558] But Vice Chief of the Imperial Japanese Navy General Staff Vice Admiral Takijirō Ōnishi predicted up to 20 million Japanese deaths.[559] And more recent assessments place the death toll even higher. One noted that the 73 million Japanese were prepared, and being trained and armed (children with spears), to defend their homeland to the last man, woman, and child, and estimated that 60-70 million Japanese might have died in the invasion.[560] (The 5-10 million estimate may be quite low and the 60-70 million estimate quite high, but nobody really knows.) In 2005, the Japanese government placed Japan's WWII death toll at 3.1 million, considerably fewer than the planned invasion would have added. Moreover, although WWI and WWII were only ~20 years apart, ~75 years have since passed without a WWIII. MAD, the mutually assured destruction of Nuclear, Biological, and Chemical (NBC) warfare combatants, is a major factor in that. Unfortunately, conventional warfare persists (e.g., the Bosnian Genocide, 1992-1995, and Libya's Civil War, 2014-2020). And the specter of NBC warfare remains.

8
Surname History

8.1 Language and Character Aspects

Language evolution brought about Breton, Cornish, Irish, Manx, Scotch and Welsh dialects of Gaelic. Irish Gaelic still has Connacht, Munster, and Ulster dialects. Scotch Gaelic, reputedly originated by Dalriada's settlers, also has a few remaining dialects.

Precise definition of ancient Gaelic is complicated by the dying out of many Gaelic dialects. Additional complexity is introduced by changes in word meanings

The choosing of perceived status-enhancing surnames is illustrated by the O'Neill surname being based on that Clan's origin being Ireland's legendary 5th Century King Niall of the Nine Hostages. And sports teams that illustrate complimentary naming include the Glasgow Celtics, the New York Yankees, the New England Patriots, the Philadelphia Eagles, the Toronto Maple Leafs, Los Indios (Indians) de Guantanamo, etc. The military psyche is typical in that regard (and Popes take a regnal name to associate themselves with their goals and/or a notable predecessor).

Some inherited surnames may be those of celibate clergy, perhaps as honorariums. Also, lay Clergy and individuals with clerical nicknames were not celibate. And the medieval clergy's behavior may have been like that of Pope Alexander IV, who sired at least four children in the 15th Century, including Lucrecia Borgia (b.1480).[561]

8.2 Basic Surname Development

Roman naming began in at least the 7th Century BC. It followed the forename (praenomen) with the family name (nomen) and a descriptive/epithetical name (cognomen).[562] For example, Caesar's full name was Gaius Julius Caesar. Caesar meant Hairy.[563] Surnames spread to Western Europe and the Mediterranean, died out in the early Middle Ages, and returned as bynames evolved into surnames.[564]

Our culture makes wives part of their husbands' families and a primary imparter of values to their children. But the family's name is the husband's surname. And that enables historically tracing patrilineal ancestry much farther than the matrilineal counterpart.

Early English language surnames discriminated between individuals with the same name, often by occupation or location. For example, a John could have become a *John Butcher,* another a *John Hill,* and a third a *John York.* (And each of their sons may have taken a different surname based on their different occupations/homes.)

Like the names of today's sports teams, many surnames undoubtedly were chosen to enhance the family's image. Also, surnames probably appeared first among prominent families and served as symbols of family status.

Today's surnames typically represent several male lineages (i.e., are polygenetic). Some non-mutually-exclusive potential causes are:

- Some Clan members unrelated to the family for which their Clan was named took the Clan name as their own.[565] [Early tribe/clan families also may have "recruited."]
- Early occupational (e.g., Carpenter), locational (e.g., Hill), and trait-based (e.g., Strong, Smiley) surnames included individuals who were not genetically related.
- Adoptions. Also, some men have married women pregnant with a child not their own, and some such have unwittingly given another man's child their own surname.
- Arbitrary surnaming (e.g., some cases of unmarried motherhood).
- Infidelity. An example among the mythical second settlers of Ireland was Partholon's wife Dealgnid. She slept with his servant while Partholon was hunting and fishing. Such infidelity sometimes accompanies the separation of spouses. It also has occurred with the reputed father's knowledge when an inherited status (e.g., a royal title or a priesthood) would be lost because the husband was sterile. [And there may have been some attempts to "improve" lineages with "better stock."]
- During the Middle Ages, it was not uncommon for the husband of a woman of a higher class/status family to take his father-in-law's surname when the family had no son to inherit the family name. [That also may have occurred if a son-in-law was chosen to lead the family.]

Estimates of misattributed paternity of between 10%-30% have been contradicted by ones in the 1%-3% range.[566] If there's a 95% chance (a guesstimate) that a boy's reputed father is his genetic father, the chance that his patrilineal ancestry conforms to his reputed father's surname drops below 20% over the about 33 generations that have passed since 10th Century. That would come to over 80% of males not having an unbroken patrilineal line of descent over that period of time.

8.3 Lower Sussex County Surnames

The surnames in my family, those of my high school classmates, and a sample of other Lower Sussex County, Delaware surnames are primarily English, Scotch, Irish, and Welsh names.[567] That affirms primary descent of the area residents from the people of the British Isles.

8.4 Irish Surnames

Ireland was the first country to adopt fixed surnames. The first one in the Irish Annals was Ó Cleirigh—recorded as the 916 AD death of Tigherneach Ua Cleirigh, Lord of Aidhne in Galway. Another mark of Irish surname use was Seán Ferghal Ó Ruairc, King of Connasht and Breifne (d. 964), the first O'Rourke surnamed after his grandfather, King Ruarc mac Tighearnán.[568]

The church's influence on pre-hereditary Irish surnames is evident still. An example is the anglicized version of the Celtic *Giolla* (Gil- or Kil-), meaning follower/devotee. Another is Mac, meaning son. Turlough mac Airt was Turlough, son of Art; and Turlough's son was Conor mac Turlough, Conor son of Turlough. And Mac Giolla Martin means *son of a follower of St Martin* while Mulrennan (Ó Maoilbhreanainn) means *descendant of a follower of St Brendan*. And their tonsure resulted in monks' names starting with the Mul- version of Maol (bald).[569]

Hereditary surnames took some time to spread. The 11th Century Brian Boru was Brian, High King of the Irish. His grandson Teigue called himself Teigue Ua Brian in memory of his grandfather, whereupon Ua Brian became a hereditary surname.

The earliest tribal names identified with a god, often one associated with a valued animal (e.g., the *Osraige*, or deer people). Next came names connoting divine ancestry (e.g., Boandrige, claiming descent from the goddess Boand, the divinized River Boyne). Then came names of a legendary ancestor (e.g., Eóganachta, for Eógan, the firstborn son of the semi-mythological 3rd-century King Ailill Aulom.). Later came surnames from a reputed or actual ancestor (e.g., O'Reilly). The initial beginning of hereditary Irish surnames with Ó or Mac or Ua, and the paucity of location-based Irish surnames, reflect the precedence of blood ties over where one is from.[570]

Author and genealogist John Grenham's *History of Irish Surnames*[571] points out that Irish surnames lasted just one generation until the 10th Century. So Ireland's High King *Niall Noígíallach*'s surname was his alone. And since he reportedly died somewhere between the middle and end of the 5th Century, descriptive non-hereditary surnames, at least in the case of the Irish kings, existed six centuries or more before Irish surnames became hereditary. The (embellished?) nature of such non-hereditary surnames is shown in the putative (but not continuous) tracing of the progenitor of the O'Neill Clan back via the all-Northern-Ui Neill line to *High King Niall Noígíallach*:

- ***Niall Noígíallach* (of nine hostages).** Most information about this Niall is legendary, but some presume him to have been real. His (re-analyzed) date of death is 452.[572]
- **Eógan mac Néill.** (d.465) Eponym of the Cenél nEógain (kindred of Eoghan) branch of the Northern Uí Néill. Allegedly baptized by and a close friend of St. Patrick.[573]
- **Muiredach mac Eógain.** (d. c.489) King of Ailech and head of the Cenél nEógain. Not mentioned in the Irish Annals.[574]
- **Muirchertach mac Muiredaig (macc Ercae).** (d. c.534), His "clearly legendary" mother Erc, daughter of "Lodarn, king of Alba," is the source of the alternative surname. Irish Annal entries about him may be of two different men.[575]
- **Domnall mac Muirchertaig.** (d. c.566. Aka **Domnall Ilchelgach** (Domnall of the Many Deceits) and **Domnall mac Maic Ercae**,[576]

- **Áed Uaridnach** (d.612) (aka **Áed mac Domnaill**, aka **Áed Allán**, a name used for his great-great-grandson of the same name)[577]
- **Máel Fithrich mac Áedo** (d. 630)
- **Máel Dúin mac Máele Fithrich** (d. 681) Defeated and slain at the Battle of Bla Sléibe. (in modern County Londonderry).[578]
- **Fergal mac Máele Dúin** (d. 722). One of his two sons was reputedly born from an illicit relationship with the daughter of High King Congal Cendmagair.[579]
- **Niall Frossach,** aka **Niall mac Fergaile. (d.** 778) *Frossach* (showery) is for the showers of silver, honey and wheat that fell on his home at his birth.[580]
- **Áed mac Néill.** (d. 819) Aka **Áed Oirdnide.**[581]
- **Niall mac Áeda** (d. 846), aka **Niall Caille** (Niall of the Callan) to distinguish him from his grandson Niall mac Áeda (d. 917),
- **Áed mac Néill** (d. 879), aka **Áed Findliath** ("fair-grey Áed"), Modern Irish: *Aodh Fionnadhliath*). Aka **Áed Olach** ("The anointing one").[582]
- **Niall Glúndub mac Áedo** (Modern Irish: ***Niall Glúndubh mac Aodha***) (d. 919), the O'Neill Clan eponym. His mother was Máel Muire, daughter of Kenneth MacAlpin, King of Scots. {Not all O'Neills are descended from the Ui Néill. And some of High King Niall's patrilineal descendants do not bear the O'Neill surname.}[583]

8.5 Scotch Surnames

Some hereditary surnames appeared in Scotland as early as the 10th Century. Factors such as ~30% of male Scots being named John, William, or Richard in the 13th Century prompted the use of bynames. For example, the Gaelic *cam* means *crooked*, *beul* means *mouth*, and *sron* means *nose*. Combined into *crooked mouth* and *crooked nose*, they're the sources of *Campbell* and *Cameron*. (The MacLeod surname was fixed in its chiefly lines by the mid-14th Century.[584]) But, for most Scots, consistent use of surnames didn't begin until the 16th Century and didn't spread to the Highlands and Northern Isles until the late 18th or early 19th Century.

Scottish surname development was complicated by influences like:

- *Daly* is from the Irish *O'Dalaigh*
- The forename *Andrew* came from the Greek
- Grant is derived from the French word *grand*
- Frasier is of Norman origin and from France's *Frasier* (strawberry plant)

Initially, patronyms in Scotland were given prefixes (mostly in the Highlands) or suffixes (mostly in the Lowlands). For example, a Lowland Scot named *Andrew* could have a son named *John* become *John Andrewson*. (*Andrewson* evolved into *Anderson*.) Similarly, a Highland Scot named *Craig* with a father named *Donald* could have become the first *Craig MacDonald*.[585] {Clan Donald/MacDonald is a Norse-Gaelic one whose descent has been traced to *Dòmhnall Mac Raghnuill* (d. c.1250). Anglicized as *Donald, Lord of the Isles*, he was the son of *Ranald, Lord of the Isles,* and the grandson of *Somerled, King of the Hebrides.*[586]}

The 13th Century MacSweeneys, MacDowells, and MacDonnells (who were among the first Gallowglass warriors in Ireland[587]) either were among the early adopters of Scottish surnames or their surnames were back-fits. But Gallowglass descendants probably inherited surnames at birth.

The common Gaelic background of Scotland and Ireland is reflected in similar surnames. For example, the Scotch name Gilchrist comes from *Gille Chriosd (servant of Christ)* and the name originated in Northeast Scotland, where the Pict ancestors of the Scotch Gilchrists lived.[588]

9
Ancient McCabes

9.1 Summary

In a nutshell, the McCabe history stated in the following is:

- The family eponym was Cába, a Gaelic nickname perhaps connoting a warrior's helmet, given to a warrior Scot or to an Irishman who became a Gallowglass warrior. (Cába became Mac Cába, then MacCabe and then McCabe.)
- The reputed ancestral McCabe link to Clan MacLeod is suspect and improbable.
- The MacCabes became a major Gallowglass tribe.
- The MacCabe Gallowglass were Scotch-Irish, not Ulster-Scots.
- The morality of the Gallowglass was that of the warriors of the time.

9.2 The Isles Celtic Background

Gaelic Celts settled in Ireland and expanded into Scotland and the Isle of Man. Brythonic Celts occupied Brittany (Northwest France) and "Brittain." Except for Wales and Cornwall, the Brythonic Celts were driven out of Brittain by Gaelic and Anglo-Saxon invasions.[589] {Some Brythonic Celts responded to the Roman invasion by going North of the Roman-built Hadrian's Wall to sally South and attack the Romans, who didn't pursue them into the rugged Scottish terrain. Like Wales and Cornwall, Hadrian's Wall provided a geographic and cultural barrier.}

9.3 Ancient Ireland

The following pictorial[590] shows how the provinces of Ulster, Connacht, Leinster, and Munster were previously approximated by Kingdoms.

When the Gallowglass era began in Ireland (~100 years before a McCabe Gallowglass surfaced), the country was subdivided into over-kingdoms made up of lesser kingdoms. Its High King received tribute from the other kings but did not rule them. The Norse-Irish port towns of Cork, Dublin, Limerick, Waterford, and Wexford had their own Rulers.[591]

Ulster then constituted parts of Breffny and the farther Northern parts of the island. Mide (middle) is Old Irish for Meath, a kingdom that lasted over 1000 years. It was the home of the Southern Uí Néilll, and was Ireland's 5th Province before becoming part of Leinster. Mide included all of County Meath, and parts of Cavan, Dublin, Kildare, Longford, Louth, and Offaly.[592] Argialla is Irish for Oriel. The Ulaid, who succeeded the Cruithne, were dominant in the North of Ireland until the Uí Néil took over. Osraige kingdom's name originated as a tribal name meaning deer-peole.[593] Bréifne comprised what is now County Leitrim, County Cavan and parts of neighboring counties.[594] After the loosely bounded Irish kingdoms became five provinces, most of Meath Province merged into Leinster Province—during the 1169-1571 Norman occupation.[595] According to historian John Gillingham, after that conquest, England's elite came to view their Celtic neighbors as inferior and barbarous.[596]

9.4 A Conventional McCabe Surname Perspective

The online Encyclopedia Wikipedia described the McCabe surname as follows:[597]

- McCabe and MacCabe are Scottish and Irish surnames anglicized from the Gaelic *Mac Cába*, meaning "Son of *Cába*."
- The nickname or personal name *Cába* is of uncertain origin.
- Patrick Woulfe[598] "considered" that *Cába* may have been derived from a nickname meaning *cap* or *hood*.
- Henry Harrison[599] "suggested" that the name was from the Gaelic *Mac Aba*, meaning *Son of the Abbot*. That would make the surname's etymology similar to *MacNab*, *McNab*, which are from the Gaelic *Mac an Aba*, *Mac an Abadh*.
- MacCabes are considered to have settled in Ireland from Scotland's Hebrides Islands about 1350, employed (as Gallowglass) by the O'Reillys and O'Rourkes of Breffny. (In the 12th Century, Breffny's western boundary was Drumcliffe in County Sligo, included Counties Leitrim and Cavan, and extended to Kells in County Meath[600])
- The pedigree written by Dubhaltach MacFhirbhisigh and cited by Patrick Woulfe shows the MacCabes to be descended from the MacLeods. (But it was considered an example of pedigree-faking as early as the 1860s.[601])
- The MacCabes became an Irish sept headed by the *Constable of the two Breffnys*.

[Notes. Constable = Chieftan. West Breffny = County Leitrim = the O'Rourke homeland. East Breffny = County Cavan = the O'Reilly homeland. Leitrim is in Northeast Connacht Province, adjoining Southwest Ulster Province. County Cavan, East of Leitrim, and County Monaghan, Northeast of Cavan, in the South of Ulster, were part of England's "Plantation" of Ulster, which began in 1606.[602] Ulster, the former center of Gaelic Ireland, Scotland, and the Isle of Mann, was changed by that planting.]

In 1921, when Northern Ireland was created from Ulster, three Ulster Counties (Cavan and Monaghan to the South and Donegal to the West) became part of the Irish Free State, which is now the Republic of Ireland.[603] About four-fifths of the Republic of Ireland professes to be Roman Catholic (i.e., 78.8% in 2016, down from 84% in 2011).[604] And in 2011 Roman Catholicism was the largest Northern Ireland religion, with its 46% nearly doubling Presbyterianism's 24% and more than tripling the Anglican Church's 14%.[605]]

According to MacLysaght's *Irish families*, a 12-year work of 365 text pages and 243 Coats of Arms,[606] the MacCabe lands were more associated with Cavan and Monaghan, and were lost after the Battle of Aughrim in 1691. [Catholic King James II of England and Ireland, VII of Scotland, lost that Jacobite war to his son-in-law, Dutch Protestant Prince William of Orange—beginning two centuries of Anglican Church of England rule of the mostly Catholic Ireland[607] that the Gallowglass had lived in and served since ~1250.]

MacCabe also is one of the over 8000 Scottish surnames and personal names identified over a 50 year stretch by *Dr. George Fraser Black* (1866-1948), who was a bibliographer and historical scholar for the New York Public Library from 1896 to 1931. The following was taken from his work, which was first published in 1946.[608]

MACCABE. G. *M'Caibe.*

- In the Book of the Dean of Lismore (p. 90) the name appears as M'Caybba, and the editor says 'the name is a rare one though still existing in the Highlands.'
- John McKape (McCabe or McRebb, as the name is also spelled) was sent prisoner to Edinburgh, 1689 (RPC., 3 ser. xiii, p 407, 430, 439).
- Angus filius M'Kabei, 1349 (REA., r. p. 80) is probably a miswriting of Maccabeus.
- The MacCabes are now widely spread through Ireland's midland counties, especially Leitrim, Cavan, Monaghan, and Meath, where they are remarkable for their xanthous complexions, vivacity, and vigor. They are evidently a branch of the MacLeods of Arran, and appear to have migrated to Ireland in the 14th Century. (*O'Donovan*).
- The First known record of the surname is documentation of the 1368 slaying of Hugh MacCabe in the Irish Annals. The MacCabas first appear in Irish history as leaders of *galloglach*s, mercenaries of Norse-Hebridean origin, under the Irish princes of Breffny and Oriel. Their chiefs were titled Constable of Oriel, Constable of Breffny, and Constable of the Two Breffnys, Fermanagh and Oriel. The tradition of their Norse origin is still known in East Breffny. Distinctive Hebridean forenames, such as Alan (Aleinn) and Somhai (Sumarlidi) were formerly frequent in their families.

Notes.

- The 16th Century poetic *Book of the Dean of Lismore* is a national treasure in Scotland.[609] It intermixes Irish and Scot Gaelic poetry.
- RPC = Register of the Privy Council of Scotland[610]
- REA = Registrum Episcopatus Aberdonensis[611]
- Xanthus is currently defined as yellowish, red, auburn, or brown hair.[612]
- O'Donovan's seven volumes of the *Annals of the Kingdom of Ireland by the Four Masters*[613] is one of *Black's* over 400 "principal" references.

- One MacCabe prisoner sent to Edinburgh in 1689 does not show a MacCabe clan/ Sept presence in Scotland. And the identification of a MacCabe presence in the Highlands doesn't mean that the MacCabe surname is native to Scotland.
- No record of MacCabes on Arran was identified by checking with the museum there.
- As discussed later, fine-Scale DNA testing found no Norse genes in the Hebrides, no doubt due to non-representative sampling in that respect. But Norse genes have been found in the MacDonalds, the MacNeils of Barra, and the MacLeods.[614]]
- Oriel (Arghíalla), ruled by the MacMahons, once consisted of Counties Monaghan, Armagh, and parts of Fermanagh, Louth, and Tyrone. The last MacMahon landownership in County Monaghan ended with the English putdown of the 1641 Irish uprising.[615] But County Fermanagh extends into central Ulster, and County Tyrone lies smack dab in Ulster's Center. And having MacCabe Constables (Chieftains) of Fermanagh and Oriel means that MacCabes expanded North of Ulster's Southern Counties—into what became Ulster-Scot territory.

The Clan MacLeod website[616] lists MacCabe as the 11th of 26 MacLeod septs and identifies it as, according to *Scots Kith & Kin*, a sept of MacLeod of Lewis.

The McCabes in Scotland today (e.g., in/near Glasgow) appear to be of Irish ancestry.

9.5 McCabe Castle [617]

A Castle is a large, typically medieval building fortified by thick walls, battlements, and towers. Tower is a synonym.[618] Fortified Tower Houses were built in Ireland by the Irish and Anglo-Irish for both defensive and residential purposes—and as status symbols, and as homes for the family's senior lineage. Tower Houses often were surrounded by a bawn (Irish: bábhún), a defensive wall. As cannon technology and tactics advanced, Tower Houses became increasingly obsolescent for defense. [619]

Until the early 21st Century, the site of McCabe Castle was pointed out as being near Moyne Hall (mansion) in County Cavan. Moyne Hall[620] is a few miles South of Cavan Town, just off the "old" Ballyjamesduff road. It and the ~196.5-acre Moynehall Townland are in an area that was known as Lisreagh before England's James I began "planting" Ulster. There's a Lisreagh Townland about three miles away—in the same Electoral Division of Moynehall, in the Civil Parish of Annegeliff, in the Barony of Loughtree Upper.[621] (The Townland is Ireland's smallest land division. By 2014, 61,098 Townlands were recognized.[622] Their average size is about 340 acres.)

In describing his land confiscation plan in a 1608 letter, Lord Deputy Chichester wrote that there were *many freeholders in the barony concerned (Loughtee)..., namely the McBradies, McCabes and others...* (A freeholder was a property owner, not a lessee.[623]) The area's confiscated land that was granted to Sir Thomas Lusher was sold by March 1616 to Sir George Mainwaring, and later became known as Moyneshall.

Tradition holds that:

- Lisreagh, (Grey Fort, from the Irish name *An Lios Riabahach*, with Lios = Ring-fort, Enclosure; Riabhach = Streaked, Grey[624]) is the site of McCabe Castle (Tower)
- The building was strong, well-fortified, and internally wainscoted with black oak from the bog of (nearby) Gortnakesh Townland.
- Many of the stones of the Castle became part of the Moyne Hall domain.
- A McCabe chief defied a whole garrison of English soldiers there and was killed at his post. (Garrisons vary widely in size.)

Captain Nicholas Pynnar's 1618-19 Survey[625] compliments the above and states: [626]

- A 2000-acre section called Lisreagh, whose original patentee was Reinald Horne, was held by Sir George Manneringe, knight.
- Upon this proportion was a 44' long, 20' high brick house and a 44' long, 12' high lime and stone bawne, and a small village of seven houses inhabited by English families.
- The said Sir George did, by deed of feoffment (grant of ownership of freehold property), grant the manor and great proportion of Lisreagh to Thomas, Bishop of Kilmore and Ardagh and his heirs and assigns forever. (Thomas Moigne was Bishop of the Anglican Church of Ireland's Kilmore and Ardagh diocese from January 13, 1613 until his death on January 1, 1629.[627])
- Roger Moyne was the reported tenant and possessor of the property in 1629, after the Bishop's death. {Inquisitions of Ulster, Cavan (23) Car. I.[628]}
- "Neither the said bishop, nor said other persons, did take the oathe of supremacy, and soe the said Sir George [Mainwaring] the proviso and condition did breake, whereby the premises unto the late King, his heirs and successors, did escheate (revert) and come."
- "There is erected upon the poll called Oughall al' Moynes-Hall, one fayer (fair, handsome) bawne of lyme and stone, and within the same a large fayer, and spatious castle, or capital mansion-house and building, of lyme-stone, vaulted with three storyes in height, and having within 26 fayer romes, with two flankers for the defence thereof; and alsoe a towne or village having 24 English-like howses and more, all inhabited with Englishe and Britishe families, in performance of the said plantation."
- To replace the old ruined parish church of Annakelly, a new edifice should be erected at the top of a hill at Gortneishe, where Roger Moyne, the landlord, was willing to grant an acre and a half for that purpose.
- "On the 13th of July, 1629, there was a grant to Abigail Moigne, widow of Roger Moigne, and John Greenham, of the great proportion of Lisreagh, to be called the manor of Moigne Hall, with all manorial rights, and subject to the terms for renewal of grants." (So the Oath of Supremacy of England could be bypassed?)

The lineage of the Fay family of Faybrook, near Cootehill (in Co. Cavan in Tullygarvy Barony) shows intermingling with the McCabes, in that James Fay (1800-1866), who owned the Moyne Hall Estate, married Susan, a daughter of James McCabe of Cavan.

The 2020 owners, Brendan and Terry (Higgins) Crowe have been accommodating to

McCabes in search of their roots. But a road by-pass planned by Cavan County, if constructed, will pass close to the house and threaten the integrity of the Estate.

There's also a Newtownmacabe Townland of 323 acres, 2 roods, 28 perches. (A rood is a quarter acre and is the size of 40 perches.[629]) It's in Straffan Electoral Division, in Taghadoe Civil Parish, North Salt Barony, Co. Kildare.[630] (Co. Kildare is West of the central eastern coastal counties of Dublin and Wicklow, which border on the Irish Sea.)

9.6 The Colla Legend

The Clan Knowles website[631] states that Cabe is Irish for cape, hood, or helmet, that McCabe means *Son of the Helmeted One*, and that (unidentified) ancient annalists trace the family to Colla da Croich, the founder of the Kingdom of Oriel (Irish: Airgíalla), which was at its largest in the 11th Century and later reduced to part of County Monaghan.[632]

Irish historians reputedly altered lineages to fabricate a Gaelic ancestry of settlement from Spain by the mythical sons of Mil (who took Ireland from the magical and immortal Tuatha de Danaan). The Collas might not be related to Ireland's High Kings. But they are credited with originating the *Tribe of the Arghíalla*.

Myths were (inaccurately?) updated when the Irish language changed drastically between the 4th and 7th Centuries. The following poem in the c.1634 *History of* Ireland, by the Reverend Father Geoffery Keating, is a reputed example:

> *Of the three Collas have you heard,*
> *Eocaidh's sons of highest fame,*
> *Colla Menn, Colla Da-crioch,*
> *And Colla Uais, the Ard-righ?*
>
> *Their names, all three, I know full well --*
> *Carrell and Muiredach and Aedh;*
> *By these was slain a mighty king,*
> *On yonder fair, well cultured plain.*
>
> *Carrell was Colla Uais, the king;*
> *Muiredach, Colla Da-crioch;*
> *And glorious Aedh was Colla Menn.*
> *Mighty were they beyond all braves!*

The Colla's Irish-Roman names were Carrell Colla Uais, Muiredach Colla Da-Crioch, and Aedh Colla Menn. {Da-Crioch may be from fo-Crioch—originally focrach (mercenary).}

The MacDonnell gallóglaigh descended from Colla Uais. Other Colla descendants included the McMahons, the McDonnells of Clan Kelly of County Fermanagh in Ulster, and the MacDonalds of Scotland's Southern Hebrides.

Irish Scholar Donald M. Schlegel postulated that the original three Collas were Romanized Britons (military commanders) from Southeast Britain's Trinovantes Tribe.[633] Late in Rome's rule, poor pay prompted Rome's Forces at Hadrian's Wall to rebel, enabling Picts to ravage Roman Britannia. And Saxons and Franks then assaulted Western and Southeastern Britain. Flavius Theodosius came to restore order in 367-368, and executed "mutineers" in the process. The Collas may have gone to Ireland then.

In Ireland the Collas hired out to Connach King Muiredach Tirech, whose people were generations-long enemies of the Ulaid (the Ulster name source). About 392 AD, Muiredach sent the Collas and six battalions from Olneemacht (Connacht) North to weaken the Ulaid and establish their own lands. In the first battle, at Carn Achadh Leth Derg, Ulaid King Fergus Foga killed Colla Menn and was killed by Colla Da Crioch. Seven battles were fought and won by the Collas (and condensed into one week of fighting by oral historians). That resulted in Counties Fermanagh, Tyrone, and Monaghan being ruled from Cloger in South Tyrone by Colla Da Crioch. The Collas remained subjects of King Muiredach's descendants, and took more Ulaid land by the sword for about 80 years.

About 425, Eoghan, Conal, and Enda, sons of Muiredach's grandson Néil Noíighíallach (High King Niall of the Nine Hostages), and Erc, the son of Colla Uais, and Erc's sons Carthend and Fiacha, took North-Central Ulster from the Ulaid. Niall's descendants settled in present County Donegal and became the Northern Ui Néill (among whom were the Ò Néills and Ò Donnells). The Arghíalla, led by descendants of Colla Uais, settled to their East. Carthend took land in the Faughan Valley, to the East of today's Derry. Descendants of other High King Niall sons became the Southern Ui Neill of Meath. They and other descendants of Colla Uais consolidated Mide and Brega,

The kingdom of Brega included the Hill of Tara, where the High King of Ireland was proclaimed. Brega extended from the Irish Sea to the Kingdom of Mide, and was bounded on the South by the River Liffey and on the North by the Sliabh Breagha, the line of hills in southern County Louth. When it was threatened by the rise of the Viking Kingdom of Dublin, Brega came under the control of the Kings of Mide.[634]

The tale that the Collas were the sons of Muiredach Tirech's uncle (Eochaid Dublin) was accepted from the 10th to the 20th Century. Reputedly, for the killing of Muiredach's father in battle, Muiredach exiled the Collas, who went to Alba—where their maternal grandfather King Ugari ruled. After three years they returned, were welcomed, and became military leaders. A skeptic who discredited this tale concluded that the three Collas were the sons of Néill who took the Northwest. Some later scholars followed suit.

A more conventional Colla legend[635] names them: Cairell Colla Uais: Muiredach Colla Fo Chrí (or Colla Dá Crich, or Fochrich); and Áed Colla Menn—4th Century sons of Eochaid Doimlén, the son of Cairbre Lifechair. Their mother, Allech, was Alba's (Scotland's) King Udhaire's daughter. The Collas killed their uncle, Ireland's High King Fíacha Sroiptine, at the Battle of Dubhchomar in Crioch Rois. Because of the prophesy that descendants of the killers of the Collas would never rule Ireland, Muiredach Tirech, Fíacha's son, exiled the Collas to Alba, where King Udhaire put them in command of three hundred warriors. The Collas returned to Ireland, hoping (?) that High King Muiredach Tirech would kill them and deprive his descendants of the throne. But Muiredach took them into his service and, several years later, sent them, with an army from Connacht, to conquer Ulster. They then seized the mid-Ulster territory that became Arghíalla.

Clan Colla's Families included: Agnew; Alexander; Boylan; Cassidy; Connolly; Corry;

Devin; Duffy; Hale; Hanratty; Keenan; Kearn; Kieran; Leahy; MacAllister; MacArdle; **MacCabe**; MacCann; MacClean; MacDonald; MacDonnell; MacDougald; MacDougall; MacDowell; MacElligott/Elliott; MacGilfinan; MacGilmichael; MacGilmore; MacKenna; MacMahon/ Matthews; MacManus; MacOscar/MacOsgar; MacTully; MacGrath; MacNeny; MacQuillan; MacRory; MacSheehy; Madden; Magee; Maguire; O'Carrol; O'Flanagan; O'Hanlon; O'Hart; O'Kelly; O'Neny; Rogers; Saunderson; Sheehy; etc. [636]

Male Clan Colla descendants carry the Z3000 SNP Y-DNA genetic marker. [637] I do not. So my patrilineal ancestors are not genetically of Clan Colla. But that does not rule out possible descent from a Colla Clan daughter with a MacCabe husband.

Another genealogy identifies the McCabes as descendants of Sitric Silkenbeard (c.970-1042), Dublin's Hiberno-Norse king who gathered a Viking army in 1014 to fight Ireland's Brian Boru at Clontarf. That may be false, but King Sitric's descendants flight to the Hebrides when the Anglo-Normans conquered Dublin in1170 lends it some plausibility.

By the mid-15th Century, the McCabes were being recorded in the Irish Annals as Irish. Their chief was known as *Constable of the two Breifnes, of Oriel,* and *of Fermanagh.*

The *Annals of the Four Masters* documents the McCabes' 1602 participation in the reputed last battle between opposing Gallowglass—when O'Donnell and McSweeney forces allied with England raided into Fermanagh and were attacked by a party of Donegal Gallowglass. Chieftain Donough McSweeney Banagh joined the forces of the Maguires and McCabes. Brian McCabe, the son of Dugal McCabe, was captured. Brian's ancestry was, according to Fermanagh genealogies compiled in the early 1700s: *Brian mc Dubhaill mc a Dubhaltaigh mac Duibh Dáira mc an Ghiolla dhuibh mc Alusdrainn mc Iomarleith mc Néill mhóir mc Somhairle na Madhmann mic Murchadh mhir mc Éogain féil mc Manchaigh mc Giolla Chríosd.* Giolla Chriosd (Servant of Christ) appears to have been an important Chieftain whose genealogy is taken back 20 generations past Sitric Silkenbeard to his original ancestor figure. [638]

9.7 The Knowles-MacLysaght Perspective

In the late 1940s, my Uncle, James McCabe, showed my parents a family history that he had commissioned, making two points that I remember:

- Our family's daughters could join the Daughters of the American Revolution (DAR).
- The McCabe name meant *Son of the Helmeted One.*

According to the Knowles Clan website, it is in Monaghan and Cavan that today we find the McCabe family numerically strongest—and the military profession was the field where they made their greatest mark. Historically they were Gallowglass (from gall = foreigner and oglach = soldier) mercenaries in the armies of the O'Reillys, the O'Rourkes and the MacMahons. That accounts for there being so many in Cavan as well as in their "original" home in Monaghan. After the 1691 Battle of Aughrim, the material fortunes of the McCabes followed those of the O'Reillys and other noble families to whom they were attached by alliance or kinship. They all lost everything in the confiscation that followed the defeat of the Stuarts and militant enforcement of the iniquitous penal laws in Ireland.[639] The Knowles website also cites MacLysaght's *Irish Families*, stating:[640]

> The MacCabes came from Scotland's Western Isles (Hebrides) about 1350 as Gallowglasses to the O'Reillys and the O'Rourkes, the principal septs of Breffny. They became a recognized Breffny sept, with a chieftain known as *Constable of the two Breffnys*. Modern statistics show that they are still most numerous in Breffny. As landed proprietors they were as much associated with County Monaghan as with County Cavan, but the principal MacCabe families lost their estates after Ireland's Royalist supporters of Charles I and Catholicism were defeated by England's Protestant Parliamentarians in the Battle of Aughrim in 1691.

9.8   The McNabs

Harrison speculated that the McNab and McCabe surnames may have the same origin.

Esteem for the clergy, and religion's involvement in war, could have made Mac an Aba (abbot) a warrior surname. But the McNab name variants similar to MacCába, M'Knabe and Maknabe, date to 1591,[641] long after the MacCábes surfaced in Ireland.

McNab is a quintessentially Scottish name that's traditionally attributed to the eponym *Abraruadh*, Abbot of Glen Dochart and Strathearn. Legend labels him a son of Scotland's Kenneth I (Kenneth MacAlpin), who is credited with uniting the Dalriadan and Pict kingdoms, and as a descendant of King Fergus of Dál Riata, and as a nephew of Saint Fillan, the 7th Century founder of the Glen Dochart Monastery.

The MacNab coat of arms shows a many-oared boat afloat beneath three crescent moons. (Crescents have been used in heraldry since at least the 13th Century.[642]) Also depicted is the reputed decapitated head of a Neish, a Clan exterminated by the MacNabs about 1612.[643] That coat of arms is very different from the MacCabe's.

Some McNabs emigrated to Ireland (mainly Ulster) in the 17th Century,[644] centuries after the MacCabe Gallowglass came to Ireland.

It seems highly unlikely that McNab and McCabe have the same name origin.

9.9   Clann Mc Cabe Society Family History.

A *History of the McCabes* was produced in 2020 by Ireland's Clann Mc Cabe Society.[645] A partially supplemented smattering of its content follows.

John Marsden, in *Galloglass*, asserts that the MacLeod genealogy is not impeccable historically. But he notes that the Mac Cabe's descent from the MacLeods (supported by old Fermanagh genealogies) represents the only evidence for the origin of this *most enigmatic of the galloglass kindreds, and for all the dubious detail of its earlier generations, can still be considered perfectly feasible.* [So can a well-faked "pedigree."] Leod reputedly had four sons, Tormod, Torquil, and two others. Later scholars considered Torquil a grandson.[646] The reputed MacLeod-McCabe link follows.

> *Brian, son of Dubhail,*
> *son of Dubhaltaigh mac Duibh Daira,*
> *son of Ghiolla Daira dhuibh,*
> *son of Alusdrainn,*
> *son of Iomarleith,*
> *son of Neill mhoir,*
> *son of Somhairle na Madhmann mic Muchadh mhir,*
> *son of Eogain feil,*
> *son of Manchaigh,*
> *son of Giolla Chriosd coirrshleigh mhicAlusdrainn Aran,*
> *son of Tarmoid, called* **mac an chaba**, *mhic Constantin Chaoimh Innsi Breatain,*
> *son of Lochluinn Leogusaigh,*
> *son of Loghairnn Loinngsigh.*

That would make *Giolla Chriosd* (follower of Christ) *coirrshleigh mhicAlusdrainn Aran* the son of *mac an chaba,* the son of Tormod, the son of *Lochluinn Leogusaigh, and the grandson of Loghairnn Loinngsigh* (Leod?).

Contemporary records of MacLeod chiefs start after Tormod. The main authority on earlier chiefs is the *Bannatyne Manuscript,* which identifies Tormod as Leod's grandson. {The MacLeods of Dunvegan label themselves Siol Thormoid (seed of Tormod)}.

Early 20th Century Historian R.C. MacLeod thought Tormod may have had a father also named *Tormod,* who married the daughter of an Irish chieftain named *M'Crotan.* Later historians consider that Tormod to be Leod's son. The *Bannatyne Manuscript* states that Tormod had three sons by his wife, namely: Malcolm, who succeeded Tormod; Leod, who was killed in Ireland without an heir; and Godfrey, a monk who died abroad. Late 20th Century Historian William Matheson considered the *Bannatyne manuscript* a dubious authority because it is the only identifier of Leod and Godfrey and omits Tormod's son Murdoch, the father of Torquil, founder of the MacLeods of Lewis (*Siol Torcaill*),

The 1299 Annals of Clonmacnoise identify the *Cabyes* as one of the families of the non-Cremthainne (a son of High King Niall) remnant of the Danes that *remaine in this Kingdome.* [The Annals of Clonmacnoise are not highly regarded for scholarliness.] Marsden also lists the Mac Cabas as a Galloglach family not of the original *Cremthainne,* but *with an appropriate pedigree from Sigtryg (Sitric) of the Silken Beard,* an 11th Century Hiberno-Norse king of Dublin. [Sitric's mother was a famed Irish beauty whose next marriage was to Brian Boru.]

Each Gallowglass had a servant to carry his mail coat and some of his weapons—and a boy to cook and carry his provisions. The trio was called a spar (as was the Gallowglass battle-axe). About 100 spars (or sparres) constituted a battalion. The spars in a Gallowglass battalion could drop as low as 80, but the battalion's pay didn't drop—and its constable acquired the pay and victuals of the non-existent (black) spars.

Fergus Gilbert-Cannan-Braniff, historian, author, Head of Religion & Philosophy at The

Skinners' School, Royal Tunbridge Wells, Kent, England, a descendant of the Scottish outlaw and folk hero Rob Roy MacGregor, described the Gallowglass as follows:

- Everything about the Gallowglass' tall and massive appearance spoke of strength and Gaelic male pride. He may have been bearded and/or heavily mustached, with long hair styled into a thick Irish fringe (glib) that the Tudors made illegal.
- William Camden described a 1562 trip to London to negotiate with Elizabeth I: *And now Shane O'Neill came from Ireland, to keep the promise he had made a year before, with an escort of gallowglass armed with battle-axes, bare-headed, with flowing curls, yellow shirts dyed with saffron, large sleeves, short tunics and rough cloaks, whom the English followed with as much wonderment as if they came from China or America.*
- The Gallowglass' saffron-dyed shirt (*léine crioch*) ranged from a simple wide-sleeved smock to a huge, flowing, richly dyed garment. At night, he wrapped up in a thick, rough, triangular cloak like a very heavy rug. Most seem to have worn hose, but many went barelegged, like most Scots and Irish. Their shoes were pieces of hide that usually rose no higher than the ankle and gripped so poorly that it could be better to fight barefoot.
- Battle dress consisted of a simple steel cap (clogad), a chain mail shirt (luireach), and an axe (tuagh). Spenser described the Gallowglass as *armed in a long shirt of mail down to the calf of the leg, with a long broad axe in his hand.* Most Gallowglass wore chain mail armor, but some wore coats of iron plate (jacks). When not in battle dress, the Gallowglass wore a thickly embroidered waist-length jacket over his saffron-dyed shirt. And after a Gallowglass became prosperous enough, he could vary his equipment based on personal preference.
- Every Gallowglass wore his armor over a quilted tunic (aketon), a leather or fabric coat stuffed with wool and stitched into vertical quilts—a splendid, warm garment waterproofed by waxing or pitching and able to stop a sword blow or an arrow.
- Early Gallowglass probably wore domed *spanglehelms* (conical helmets of three to six bronze or steel plates held together by metal strips). Those were replaced by tall, pointed helmets (basinets) that came into vogue from the 14th to 16th Century. And skullcaps became typical by the 17th Century. Morions (e.g., crested, flat-brimmed Spanish helmets), burgeonets (e.g., open-faced helmets with a peak or brim above the eye, cheek protectors, and a fore and aft crest on top) and cabosets (a 16th Century, Morion-like helmet) also were imported from Spain and Italy. And a series of iron plates riveted or threaded onto fabric or leather and made into segmented or quilted headpieces by Irish Smiths likely were in the mix.
- St Leger said that every Gallowglass had an axe resembling the axe of the tower (presumably the Tower of London Executioner's two-handed axe). Stanhurst wrote that *when they strike they inflict a dreadful wound,* and Dymock recounted that the axe was always *deadly where it lighteth.* The Annals of the Four Masters state that,

when Henry MacCabe died in 1460, he was carried to Cavan for burial, attended by 280 Gallowglass armed with axes.

- The spar is featured in MacSheehy, MacCabe and MacSweeny heraldry, but not all Gallowglass wielded one, though it was almost always his parade weapon. Common Gallowglass sidearms included a short hunting bow (boga), and a cruciform-hilted, single-handed broadsword (cloidem). His personal attendants carried javelins, glaives, (pole-mounted, knife-like, curved-blade weapons), bows, dirks, and spears.[647]

In 1521, the eminent German Artist Albrecht Dürer (1471-1528) drew a rare Gallowglass sketch that he identified as being of two soldiers and three peasants—from Ireland. One soldier wears a pointed helmet extending over the back of the neck (not resting on the body armor) with a brim shading the eyes (without limiting peripheral vision). His body armor is a chain mail neck and shoulder protector (pisane) over a belted and almost knee-length mail coat over a mid-calf-length robe. He's wearing open-toed sandals. His left hand holds a bow and his left arm holds four arrows tucked against his body. The cross guard (hand protector) of a huge two-handed broadsword (or claymore) rests on the back of his right shoulder, with its forward-extending hilt held near the pommel by his right hand. This gallowglass' physique is much like that of his companions'—unlike the typical description of prodigious Gallowglass stature.

The second soldier is in a protective gambeson and a "single-horned" skullcap. He has a light, sheathed sword, toed sandals, and a spear. That's Irish light infantry (kern) garb.

One peasant is shod, and carries a smaller broadsword than the Gallowglass does. The other two are barefoot. One grips the haft of a weapon resembling a kern glaive with his right hand and holds a curved machete-like weapon in his left. The other has his left hand on the haft of the glaive and a weapon resembling a Gallowglass spar on his right shoulder. None of these three are wearing protective clothing.[648]

{The two soldiers (but not the three peasants) in Dürer's drawing are also depicted on the cover of *The World of the Galloglass: Kings, Warlords and Warriors in Ireland and Scotland, 1200-1600*, by Sean Duffy.[649]} And the back cover of the Clan Mc Cabe Society's Mc Cabe History also shows that drawing—including the three peasants but with the blade of the sparre and with much of the blade of the glaive hidden.

[Dürer's drawing appears to depict a Galloglass, his servant carrying his back-up broadsword, and his boy carrying the battle-axe—accompanied by a kern and his boy, who is holding a machete and glaive.]

Dürer made the drawing in Antwerp. (His life is well-documented, but it is not apparent that he ever visited Ireland. He did, however, without ever having seen a rhinoceros, make a woodcut of one in 1515 from a written description and sketch by another artist. His devotion to accuracy in bodily proportions also suggests that his Gallowglass drawing wasn't based on his own observations.[650]) And his drawing has been labeled an *artist's impression* almost certainly based on the following pen-portrait by Vital:

> *These men deck themselves out in big hairy coats, over their heads in the same way as the women wear their cloaks in Brabant. This coat only goes a half-quarter beyond the belt, and over this is a long linen apron. Thus shorn,*

bearded, armed and barefoot—as I said—imagine how strange this costume is to look at. For sure, I have never seen anything like this before even in a painting.[651]

The following is primarily from the Clann Mc Cabe's listing of noteworthy McCabes:

- Thomas McCabe (1739-1820) owned a clock-making shop and a cotton mill. He was a leading Belfast liberal and radical who became a founding member of the 18th Century Revolutionary Society of the United Irishmen. A Presbyterian strongly opposed to Slavery, he wrote about Waddell Cunningham's and other Belfast merchants' plan to form a slave trading company: *May God eternally damn the soul of the man who contributes the first guinea.* And he prevented a slave-owning shipping company from setting up business in Belfast. Such behaviour led to his being called the *Irish slave*, a title he reputedly once displayed on a sign hanging outside his shop. The Ulster Historical Society erected a *Blue Plaque* (a historical marker) to Thomas and his son William Putnam McCabe (1775-1821), one of top organizers of the United Irishmen. It's on the wall of St. Malachy's College (a Catholic grammar school for boys), built on the site of the McCabe home.[652]
- William Gordon McCabe (1841-1920), who left the University of Virginia to enlist as a private in the Richmond Howitzers (of the Confederate Army of Northern Virginia), rose to Captain, and served throughout the U.S. Civil War. (His poem about a soldier's Christmas is included in the prior discussion of that war.)
- Edward Cardinal McCabe (1816-1885), a Roman Catholic Archbishop of Dublin (and Ireland's second Edward Cardinal McCabe[653]).
- American Methodist Bishop Charles Cardwell McCabe (1836-1906), of County Tyrone ancestry. He helped raise an infantry regiment for the Union, became Chaplain of the 122nd Ohio Infantry, and was captured by the Confederates and put in Libby Prison. There he taught his fellow prisoners *The Battle Hymn of the Republic* to maintain their spirit. (Libby prison in Richmond, Virginia, housed captured Union officers, and was second only to Andersonville in harshness.) About the Bishop's later visit to the U.S. Capitol, Julia Ward Howe's daughter Laura Elizabeth Howe Richards wrote: *Among other stirring tales, he told of the scene in Libby Prison; and once more, to a vast audience of loyal people, he sang the Battle Hymn of the Republic. The effect was magical. People sprang to their feet, wept and shouted and sang with all their might; and when the song was ended, above all the tumult was heard the voice of Abraham Lincoln, crying while the tears rolled down his cheeks, 'Sing it again!'* Poor health later forced the reverend to resign his chaplaincy.[654]
- William McCabe (1848-?), born in Belfast, was awarded, on 10/13/1875, the U.S. Congressional Medal of Honor, the country's highest award for bravery. The citation read: **The President of the United States of America, in the name of Congress, takes pleasure in presenting the Medal of Honor to Private William McCabe, United States Army, for gallantry in attack on a large party of Cheyennes on September 26 – 28, 1874, while serving with Company E, 4th U.S. Cavalry, in action at Red River, Texas**.[655]

- Edward P. McCabe (1850-1920). A Black, Republican, Kansas office-holder (and a fighter against racial persecution), he founded Langston, Oklahoma [where Langston University, the only Historically Black College in Oklahoma, opened in 1897.[656]]
- Alexander McCabe (1886-1972), a teacher who became heavily involved in the Irish War for Independence.
- Thomas B. McCabe (1892-1983), President and CEO of Scott Paper, and Chairman of the Federal Reserve from 1948 to 1951. He was born in Whaleysville, Maryland. In 1837, his great-great-great grandfather Arthur McCabe owned what was then all of Selbyville, Delaware. His father, William McCabe, founded and served as the first president of Selbyville Bank. Thomas graduated from Swarthmore College in 1915, and joined Scott Paper as a salesman in 1916. He enlisted as an army private in 1917 and rose to the rank of Captain. After WWI, he returned to Scott Paper, rapidly advanced, became its president and CEO at age 34, and took the company from a 500-person paper mill to a $2 billion international industry with 40,000 employees. He took leave of absence during WWII to serve as Deputy Administrator of the Lend-Lease Program and then as Deputy Director of the War Production Board. In 1946, he was awarded the Medal for Merit (the nation's highest civilian award from 1944-52) for meritorious service during WWII. He took another leave of absence from 1948-51 to serve as the eighth Chairman of the Board of Governors of the Federal Reserve. In 1952, he established Swarthmore's McCabe scholarships for ability, character, personality, leadership, and service to school and community. Two are awarded every year to students from the Delmarva Peninsula, or from Chester, Montgomery, or Delaware County, Pennsylvania.[657]
- Esther (Scanlon) McCabe (1889-1971) of Lilly, Pennsylvania. a teacher who became a full-time mother to her 12 children. She was widowed in 1933 and then raised her 12 children alone. Her 11 sons served overseas during WWII: eight in the Army, two in the Navy, and one in the Merchant Marine. The *War Mothers of the United States* named Esther *America's Number 1 Mother* and the *Pennsylvania Newspaper Publishers' Association* named her *Pennsylvania's Number 1 Mother*. All her sons survived the war, but two were haunted for life by wartime trauma. And it wasn't until Her son, Cpl. Leo (Rusty) McCabe, an anti-aircraft artillery technician, died that his six children learned that he had been awarded five bronze stars, the European-African-Middle Eastern Theater Service Medal, and the Distinguished Unit Badge.[658]
- Anna Mae Violet (McCabe) Hays (1920-2018), born in Buffalo, New York, was a U.S. Army Nurse in India in WWII and in Inchon during the Korean War. She became Head Nurse at Walter Reed Hospital, headed the Army Nurse Corps, and was the first woman promoted to Brigadier General.

McCabes in France's Military.

The 2005 Clogher record identifies the following McCabes among those who left Ireland after the 1690s, joined Louis XIV's army, served long terms, and were at Les Invalides (a home for aged and unwell soldiers set up in France by Louis XIV in 1670).

- Bernard Macabe, a Co. Fermanagh native, admitted 9/3/1730, died 4/11/1739.
- Felix Macabe, a Co. Fermanagh native, admitted 6/30/1726, died 4/11/1737.
- Hugh Macabe, a Co. Monaghan native, admitted 6/13/1726, died 10/31/1736

McCabes in England's Military.

McCabes participated in England's 1805 naval victory at Trafalgar, where England secured (until WWII) its position as the world's greatest naval power. The English fleet (27 ships, 17,000 men, 2148 guns) attacked and devastated the larger combined fleet of France and Spain (33 ships, 30,000 men, 2568 guns). Vice Admiral Horatio Nelson, England's greatest Naval Hero, who had earlier lost an eye and most of his right arm but none of his audacity, commanded the British. He told his Captains (his *Band of Brothers*) that *No Captain can do very wrong if he places his ship alongside that of the enemy.* Before joining combat, he signaled: *England expects that every man will do his duty.* In the battle, England lost less than 500 men and no ships. Their opponents suffered ~3000 dead and lost 22 ships. Nelson was fatally wounded by a sharpshooter and died before the battle ended.[659] Among his seamen and landsmen (apprentice seamen) were:

- James McCabe, from Dublin, an ordinary seaman.
- James McCabe, from Turvey Hill, a landsman.
- John McCabe, from Ballabay, a landsman.
- John McCabe, from Carrickmacross, a quarter gunner.
- John McCabe, from Dublin, a landsman.
- Michael McCabe, from Dublin, a landsman.
- Michael McCabe, from Longsfors, an ordinary seaman.
- Patrick McCabe, from Wicklow, a landsman.
- William McCabe, from Co. Dublin, a landsman.

When Napoleon was defeated at Waterloo in 1815, up to a third of the British Army was Irish. The McCabes among them included:

- James McCabe, from Co. Monaghan, a private in the 3rd Battalion, 1st Foot.
- Peter McCabe, from Co. Meath, a private in the 1st Battalion, 32nd Foot.

[In 1615, England began trying to reduce its criminal population by sending convicts to the Colonies. From 1700-1775, ~52,000 convicts sailed for the American Colonies, over 20,000 of them to Virginia. The unskilled became agricultural workers, the skilled were sold to tradesmen, shipbuilders, iron manufacturers, etc. (Convicts could be bought for less than indentured servants or Slaves, and were readily exploitable.) Virginia enacted laws prohibiting the practice. The Crown overturned them. By 1775, most convicts had completed their 7–14-year sentences and returned to England. Others went to distant parts of America and tried to blend in. The Revolutionary War ended the practice in the U.S.[660] But from 1788-1868, ~162,000 convicts were sent to Australian penal colonies from England and Ireland. Their crimes were typically minor because major crimes were punishable by death and few such convicts were transported. About one of seven transported convicts were women, and many of the well-known convicts were political prisoners. Most convicts in Australia stayed after serving their sentences. The stigma attached to being an Australian of convict descent later became a cause for celebration. {Almost 20% of Australians (and two million British) have convict ancestry.}[661]]

William (Tough Willie) McCabe, aka *the handsomest man on Broadway*, was an infamous New York West Side mobster. He supposedly was a bodyguard for Arnold Rothstein, the reputed fixer of the 1919 Baseball World Series. ([On the second day of that Series, the *Philadelphia Bulletin* newspaper printed the following poem reflecting high esteem for baseball's honesty and sportsmanship:

> Still, it really doesn't matter,
> After all, who wins the flag.
> Good clean sport is what we're after,
> And we aim to make our brag
> To each near or distant nation
> Whereon shines the sporting sun
> That of all our games gymnastic
> Base ball is the cleanest one![662])

The Chicago White Sox deliberately lost that series. That was termed *the Black Sox Scandal*. Eight players were permanently banned from organized baseball despite being tried and acquitted. One, Shoeless Joe Jackson (1888-1951), has baseball's third highest career batting average and set, in 1911, the highest rookie batting average record (.408). In 1999, *The Sporting News* named him #35 of the top 100 baseball players. (There were then ~210 players in the Hall of Fame.[663]} The ban precludes induction into the Hall, so Shoeless Joe hasn't been nominated. There are indications that he was party to the fix, but that's still a controversial issue. And *Say it isn't so, Joe* became famous as the reputed plea of a child fan who adored him.]

Tough Willie reputedly was cut in on $300,000 won from Rothstein by a mafia gangster in a poker game about five weeks before Rothstein was fatally shot (and refused to identify his shooter). Willie had supposedly tried to make Rothstein pay up by threatening him, and was a suspect in the murder. But he denied everything and the district attorney believed his "airtight" alibi about being in Savannah, Georgia to start a dog track.[664]

A ditty about Bessey Mc Cabe (?) from the historical pamphlets collection of the National Library of Ireland seemingly dates from the 1700s to the early 1800s follows. Its "timeless" moral could fit any surname.

Tie my Toes to the Bed

> When I first came to Dublin I viewed Barrack Street,
> I was a hearty young fellow and smart on my feet
> I met a girl called **Bessey Mc Cabe**,
> She brought me to a lodgin call'd Sweet Durty Lane

I had two hundred pounds and a good set of cloaths
And to tell you the truth I had a new pair of brogues
I'd a lovely felt hat and my waistcoat was red,
And young Bessey Mc Cabe tied my toes to the bed

When I wakened next morning young Bessey was gone
And five drunken girls to work they began
They had black eyes, broken noses, their blood ran in streams
Faith says I to myself but they will end my days

The mistress I asked her where was my cloaths
She told me my wife Brought them off I suppose
"Blugaronthers" says I "was I married last night"
And they told me I was "to a handsome young wife"

Call her in my good people 'till I see her face
I just came to Dublin to renew my lease
She has my two hundred pounds and my darling fine purse
And if she be my wife she served me bad enough

When I thought for to rise my two toes they are tied
And they told me it was tricks that was played by the bride
She covered me snug in the bed with the cloaths
But she never came back for to loosen my toes

They brought me to lodgement and lock{ed) me up tight
Without sheet or blanket the length of the night
The dickens a bed was there to lie down
But walking about like a bull in a pound

So all you young fellows to Dublin does go
Take care of young Bessey lest she serve you so
She took my two hundred pounds my big coat and my brogues
And she never came back for to loosen my toes

9.10 McCabe, MacLeod, and Viking Relatedness

As of this writing, neither DNA testing nor the historical record positively affirm either the national origin of the McCabe surname or a McCabe Sept of Clan MacLeod.

Information published in 2015 states that extensive DNA analysis shows that, while Anglo-Saxon DNA is evident across England, the Romans, Vikings, and Normans (Vikings who permanently settled in N.E. France) left surprisingly little genetic trace. An exception was finding that 25% of the DNA of the Orkney Islands is Viking DNA—with that being attributed to the Orkneys being part of Norway for 600 years.[665]

MacLeods came to Ireland to settle in the 17th Century during the Plantation of Ulster,[666] over two centuries after the first known presence of MacCabe Gallowglass in Ireland.

A 2011 analysis of the Y-Chromosomes of 45 MacLeods found that almost 47% carry the rare, classic Rib S68 Viking marker. S68 has been found in the MacLeod homelands of Lewis, Harris and Skye, in Scotland's Northern Isles of Orkney and Shetland, in Norway, and in a few cases in Sweden. The analysis concluded that S68's Norse descent is consistent with the MacLeod claim to descent from Leòd (Old Norse: Ljótr), a Norse aristocrat reputedly related to Olaf, King of Mann.[667] Leód, who reputedly died ~1280, may have been a younger son of Olaf the Bloody (1229-1237), King of Mann and of Lewis, or a third cousin (some removed) of Magnus (1252-1265), the last King of Mann.[668] (Subsequent Scottish rule of Mann was interrupted by Norse rule by Godfred Magnuson for part of 1275.[669] That may mean that Leód's descendants took the Clan surname by then—93 years before the first known McCabe presence in Ireland.)

In the other 53% of the MacLeods studied, nine other distinct lineages were found, with no Norse ancestry attributed to them. That, the 2015 finding of little Viking DNA in the Isles, and the non-identification of Scandinavian DNA in my genome indicate that, while Norse DNA has been found in (the chiefly lines of?) the Hebridean Clans and in the Northern Isles, much of the interaction of the people of the Isles with the Vikings did not involve intermarriage. (Also, the expulsion of the Vikings may have been followed by limiting Viking DNA propagation in the Isles, which may have been mostly to the families of Clan Heads who had intermarried with their Norse conquerors.)

Early MacLeod connections to Ireland included:

- Leòd (c.1200-1280), the Clan eponym, was related to the Crovan Dynasty, which is thought to be related to the earlier, 9th and 10th Century Ui Mair rulers of the Viking Kingdom of Dublin. [670]
- In 1594 Clan Chief Sir Roderick MacLeod (1573-1626) and his in-laws the MacDonalds each raised a 500-man force that supported (in 1594-1595) the rebellion of Hugh Roe O'Donnell (1572-1602), Earl of Tyrconnell, against the English in Ireland (during the 1593-1603 Nine-Year War). [671]

[Gallowglass (and other Scotch and Irish) adoption of Viking weapons and tactics is indisputable. So is Viking intermarriage with some Irish and some Scotch Clan leaders' families. How much more Viking admixture occurred is uncertain.]

9.11 McCabe Name Proliferation

McCabe is the world's 11,699th most common surname. It is most prevalent in the United States, and densest in Ireland. Scotland's 3398 McCabes are 6th, behind totals (which sum double listings) of: United States, 41602; England, 9826; Ireland, 6977, Australia, 5011; and Canada, 4226. (Northern Ireland's 2120 McCabes are listed separately.) [672]

The mid-2017 estimate of the population of Scotland was 5,424,800.[673] Its 3398 McCabes were ~0.06% of Scotland's people, 1/1596th of the populace. And the 41,602 U.S. McCabes were ~0.01% (1/7870th) of the 2018 U.S. population of 327,438,899.[674]

Informal checks with the museums on Arran and Lewis identified no knowledge of a McCabe family (as distinct from individual) history on those islands. And Ireland's Clann Mc Cabe did not identify any ancient McCabe family history in Scotland.

9.12 Translating Câba

Hat is one translation of Câba. Worn for protection against the weather, sun, or injury, as a status/occupation designator, as adornment and for ceremony, hats have been ubiquitous. Otzi, a bronze age man wearing a bearskin hat with a chin strap, was found frozen in the mountains between Austria and Italy (where he was killed about 3200 BC by an arrow wound and the associated blood loss).[675] The Tollund Man, who died about 400 BC, was found mummified in a Danish bog, wearing a pointed, sheepskin and wool cap. Warrior hats have included the Bearskin Caps worn by Buckingham Palace Guards, Berets, Bicorne Hats, and the Tam o' Shanter.[676] But middle age cold made hats so common that a generic name for *Hat* had no distinctiveness.

Woulfe's 1993 work "surmised" that McCabe is derived from the Gaelic name for cap or hood. "Cap" is translated to "caipin" and "hood" to "cochall" by an online English to Irish dictionary[677] while an English to Scotch-Gaelic one[678] translates "cap" as "caip," "hood" as "hood," and "hooded" as "sneachda."

Skullcap-like medieval protective headgear like the cervelière was much used by commoners and soldiers who could not afford better protection.[679] Hoods are not well suited to gallowglass-style hand-to-hand infantry combat because they may impede peripheral vision. And though protective skullcaps were worn by some middle age combatants, "cap" typically refers to headgear unsuited to protect its wearers in combat. So neither cap nor hood is a likely descriptor of infantry warrior protective headgear.

Câba also has been translated as cape.[680] Capes are historic, and prehistoric, fashion accessories, and symbols of the wearer's station. They also are part of some fictional Superhero (e.g., Superman, Batman) dress and of some military dress uniform ensembles. Queen Elizabeth I wore elaborate, foot-length capes. Capuchin Monks (Friars) wore hooded, waist-length capes. Some police uniforms include capes, ostensibly for warmth and as raingear.[681] But a functional cape could impede the range of motion needed for hand-to-hand combat. A warrior might wear one off the battlefield, but they seem to be an unlikely image choice for infantry warriors.

Helmet is another translation of Câba. Battle helmets have been worn since at least the 23rd Century BC. They were Initially made from leather and brass, then bronze, then iron. Forged steel ones debuted about 950 AD (while use of surnames was spreading).[682] So Câba could have referred to the distinctiveness of a warrior's battle helmet. And Mac Câba being translated as the *Son of the Helmeted One* is consistent with the 1940s genealogy commissioned by my Uncle and with the Clan Knowles website.

None of the identified translations of Câba can assuredly be either ruled out or considered correct. But *Son of the Helmeted One* is very consistent with being a surname based on a medieval warrior's (Viking-like?) distinctive battle headgear.

9.13 The Caob or Ceap Attribution.

The reference that identifies the Cabe in MacCabe as coming from the Gaelic Caob or of Ceap contains a caveat about the validity of its information. And Caob's and Ceap's meanings include bough, branch, clod, lump, a bit of anything, a hilltop, or a sign set up in time of battle. Those images lack favorable distinctiveness. Some (e.g., clod=clump of dirt) could have been taken by a warrior as insulting, relegating their use to his enemies and to warriors uninterested in amity and loyalty among their cohorts. It seems unlikely that such a surname was taken voluntarily by warriors. And Cába being more similar to Cabe than Caob or Ceap makes Cába a more likely source.

9.14 Cába Origin

Cába may well have originated as a vernacular, occupational byname. But defining its original meaning in an unknown Gaelic dialect ~700 years or more ago is speculation.

The first recorded identification of a Cába descendant being the death of Hugh MacCabe in Ireland in 1368 favors Ireland as being the country of the name's origin. But the name could have originated in Ireland or in Scotland in several ways. For example:

- A Scot (or several) who did not have a surname may have adopted the nickname of his (or their) father or grandfather as his (or their) Irish surname shortly before or upon becoming Gallowglass.
- Some Scots may have taken the MacCabe surname in Ireland to cut the tie to an unfavorable (ostracized?) status in Scotland.
- Some Irish recruits into the Gallowglass ranks may have taken the MacCabe surname to distance themselves from an unsavory personal or family reputation.
- Some Irish/Scot warriors may have had unacknowledged sons who took the MacCabe surname because they could not take their fathers' surnames.
- If the MacCabes were rare and disfavored Scots, after some became successful Gallowglass (aided by faking being part of a prestigious Scottish lineage?), they could have brought the rest of their surviving family to Ireland.

9.15 Coats of Arms, Weapons, and Armor

Coats of Arms may prestigiously overstate family values. The ~1689 MacCabe Coat of Arms attributed to Alexander MacCabe, a purported descendant of the last MacCabe chieftains, is described as: <u>*vert* *a fesse wavy between three salmons naint argent*</u>; crest a *demi-griffon segreant*; motto *aut vincere aut mori*.[683] That translates as:

- *Vert,* the green of the shield, connotes abundance, joy, hope, and loyalty in love.[684]
- *Fess* is a mid-shield military belt/girdle of honor. Its waviness "often" represents water.
- The *salmons* above and below the *fess* represent Christ, peace and sincerity.
- *Argent* is the salmons' lustrous silvery white (purity-connoting) color.
- A *griffon* is a mythical creature with an eagle's head (with upright, pointed ears) and a lion's body. Its four legs are eagle's feathered legs and claws. Female *griffons* have upwardly extended wings; male griffons are wingless and adorned with spikes on the body. A *griffon segreant* stands on its hind claws with its foreclaws extended.[685]
- The *demi-griffon MacCabe crest* shows the upper part of a griffon segreant (head, wings, extended foreclaws, and upper torso). [686]
- *Aut vincere aut mori* means *Either Conquer or Die.*[687]

Another version of the MacCabe coat of arms is a black and white drawing (by Katy Lumsden) of a MacCabe coat of arms from 18th Century graves at Balintemple, County Cavan. It shows the three salmons and fess on a shield flanked by battle-axes and topped with a crest consisting of a visored helmet with a *demi-griffon segreant* atop the helmet. The explanatory note states that the axes suggest an enduring Gallowglass identity among the MacCabes, who must have clung tightly to family tales and folk memories of the time when the MacCabes were mighty Galllóglaigh.[688]

There's also a McCabe Coat of Arms print with a crest displaying a helmet like a 15th Century armet.[689] (Some also have a demi-griffon segreant extending from the top of the helmet.) Such armet-like helmets appear on the crests of many families' Coats of Arms—and look much like those, visor down, on Hollywood versions of a mounted knight wearing plate armor (on which the heavy helmet's base rested) and armed with a lance. The weight and limited visibility and inhibition of communication of such helmets and the weight of plate armor are unsuited to hand-to-hand infantry combat. And the Gallowglass were heavy infantry who (gaining from better mobility and vision than a heavy, slit-visored helmet resting upon chain mail would have permitted?) typically wore open-faced helmets. Their other armor was neck and shoulder chain mail (pisanes) over chain-mail shirts (habergeons) over a heavy, loose-fitting multi-layered, quilted cloth coat (gambeson) that also provided armor-like protection. In addition to the fearsome two-handed battle-axe, Gallowglass arms included spears and two-handed swords, with dirks and one-handed broadswords as side-arms. And each Gallowglass' personal attendant(s) carried skirmishing weapons: dirks, spears, javelins, and glaives (pole-mounted, knife-like curved blades).[690]

The MacCabe Coat of Arms is unlike the O'Reilly or O'Rourke Coats of Arms, which both feature lions.[691] It's also unlike the MacLeods' coats of arms, one of which is a bull's head cabossed (cut off behind the ears) sable, horned Or (gold), between two flags Gules (red), staved at the first. The MacLeods' varied Armorial Bearings also show features such as a burning mountain (MacLeods of Lewis), three-turreted castles plus the three armored legs of the Isle of Man (MacLeods of MacLeod and MacLeods of Dunvegan), and a burning mountain plus the three armored legs of the Isle of Man plus a galley with sails furled and pennants flying plus a lion rampant (MacLeods of Rasay).[692] So, other than their warrior connotation, the MacLeod and McCabe Coats of Arms show no linkage between the families. That does not completely rule out a MacCabe-MacLeod heraldic link because the McCabe coats of arms were provided by McCabe Gallowglass descendants and their Gallowglass ancestors' armorial bearings (if they had them) could have been quite different.

9.16 *Cába* Armorial Implications

It has been common practice to depict a medieval family's warrior status by showing a battle helmet on the crest of their coat of arms. Typically, and in some versions of the McCabe coat of arms, the helmet displayed is like those of plate-armor-wearing mounted knights armed with lances. But such helmets' heavy weight and impediment to visibility and communication made them unsuitable for Gallowglass infantry combat. The following factors are relevant to the type of battle helmet that a MacCabe Gallowglass might have chosen from the many medieval helmet choices available (and to the choice of the helmet graphic on this book's cover being a Viking-style one with protective chain mail all around, with the chain mesh being open enough to enable communication).

- The Gallowglass' Viking-style warfare was learned before adoption of surnames.
- The MacCabes were a famed Gallowglass tribe.
- The putative *Cába* origin of the MacCabe name suggests surname selection based on having distinctive (Viking-style?) warrior headgear.

10
Genetic Inheritance

10.1 Background

Even if specific parentage is unknown, parents and children may recognize each other. That's evident in the ~400-year-old adage that *the apple doesn't fall far from the tree.*[693]

There's also an at least 2000-year-old perception that characteristics acquired during one's lifetime are inherited by one's offspring. Ancient Greece's most famous physician, Hippocrates (460-370 BC), believed that. And Charles Darwin's provisional pangenesis hypothesis of 1868[694] postulated that every part of the body produced tiny gemmules that migrated to the reproductive system, making acquired characteristics heritable.[695]

Before Darwin, a cohesive theory of biological evolution was proposed by the French taxonomist Jean-Baptiste Pierre Antoine de Monet, Chevalier de Lamarck (1744–1829). He postulated that the diversity of species and genera was created by two forces:

- A complexifying force drives animal body plans toward higher levels of complexity, creating a ladder of phyla. (That concept is scientifically credited.)
- A force that causes animals to adapt to their circumstances in accordance with two laws (condensed as follows):

1. Law of Use and Disuse: In developing animals, use of any organ gives it power, strength, and size proportional to that use; while the permanent disuse of any organ progressively diminishes its functional capacity, which finally disappears.
2. Law of Inheritance of Acquired Characteristics: Provided that the natural acquisitions or losses wrought are common to the offspring-producing individuals of both sexes, the characteristics acquired by any organ through predominant use or permanent disuse of any organ is inherited by the offspring.

Lamarck's acquired characteristics inheritance theory led to later repudiated postulations such as giraffes who stretch their necks to reach leaves higher in trees gradually lengthen them and have offspring with longer necks. Similar postulations like cutting off the tails of mice to produce tailless strains and blacksmith's sons inheriting the musculature that their fathers developed at work also have repeatedly been found to be untrue. (That blacksmith one also does not meet Lamarck's both sexes criterion.)

Beginning in 1928, Lamarck's acquired characteristics theory had disastrous consequences in the Soviet Union, where famine resulted from the Revolution's extermination of the originally affluent independent Russian Empire Kulaks (farmers) and expanded to killing farmers with a few more cows or acres than their neighbors. (Such farmers were labeled class enemies and were called "bloodsuckers, vampires, plunderers of the people and profiteers, who fatten on famine" by Lenin.[696])

Into that void stepped Trofim Lysenko, Director of the Lenin All-Union Academy of Agricultural Sciences, and an avid supporter of the Revolution. Lysenko rejected Mendelian Genetics and Darwin's Natural Selection, and claimed to have developed vernalization (a technique known since 1854) by exposing wheat seeds to high temperature and low humidity, thereby enabling the tripling or quadrupling of crop yields. Vernalization's proponents also claimed that rye could transform into wheat and wheat into barley, that weeds could spontaneously transmute into food grains, and that "natural cooperation" was observed in nature as opposed to "natural selection."

Lysenko's vernalization yielded only marginally greater food production. But Soviet propaganda lionized him. Many opposing scientists were executed and over 3000 mainstream biologists were fired or imprisoned. (Nikolai Vavilov, President of the Agricultural Academy and Lysenko's former mentor, died in prison.) Russia's genetic and much other biological research was adversely affected or banned until Stalin died in 1953—and Russia didn't discard Lysenkoism until 1964. Poland, Czechoslovakia, Germany, and China also unsuccessfully experimented with Lysenkoism.[697]

10.2 General Genetic Considerations

In non-sex-linked aspects, a daughter may be more like her father and a son more like his mother. Dominant and recessive genes are involved, as is the randomness of genetic recombination of the autosomes (non-sex-linked chromosomes) during reproductive cell formation (meiosis). That recombination can provide a virtually limitless combination of parts of the corresponding maternal and paternal autosomes.[698])

There also may be epigenetic traits. (quasi-Lamarckian inheritance of acquired traits?) Epigenetics involves heritable changes in gene activation and inactivation, with lifestyle being a factor.[699] Definitive scientific proof is lacking. But If epigenesis occurs, parental behavior prior to the conception of offspring and/or a mother's behavior and/or experiences during pregnancy may alter her children's inherited characteristics.

The general female superiority at some roles and the general male superiority at others are well known. And the premise that men and women are equally qualified for all non-reproductive activities will not be credible until the Ladies' Tees on the golf course are eliminated because women don't need them. {A few, like Mildred Ella (Babe) Didrikson Zaharias,[700] never did.} Still, many men and women now share or perform roles traditionally those of the opposite sex (e.g., male homemakers, female family income earners). But, except for matters like equal opportunity and equal pay for equal work, equality of the sexes is usually an apples and oranges comparison because of physical, behavioral, and thinking differences. Neither subordination nor lack of esteem is a necessary result. That was nicely stated by *Maurice Chevalier* in the movie *Gigi* as *Viva la difference!* There's a similar perspective in the song *There is Nothing Like a Dame* in the WWII musical *South Pacific*. Yesteryear's views have not, however, died out. My feisty great grandfather, who esteemed women highly throughout his 98-year life, was wont to proclaim, ashore or asea, that *I am the Captain of this ship, from stem to stern!* Such *King of the Mountain* claims/attitudes, often well camouflaged, persist in virtually every aspect of human interaction.

10.3 DNA

DNA (Deoxyribonucleic Acid) is a molecular chain in the nucleus of each of our (~37.2 trillion[701]) body cells. Human nuclear DNA contains 23 paired chromosomes {22 paired autosomes plus the Y (male) and X sex-determining chromosomes} that contain our ~10,000-20,000 genes. The chromosomes' telomeres (end caps) keep them intact and separate from each other. Those telomeres, except for the effect of their degradation as they age, do not affect chromosome function.

Less than 5 percent of the human genome codes for proteins. The vast bulk of human DNA lies between genes and in the introns that interrupt gene sequences. Some of the noncoding DNA plays a role in regulating gene activity; other parts may function in organizing the DNA into chromosomes and in chromosome replication (Alberts *et al.*, 1983; Lewin, 1987). But the functions of most noncoding DNA are unknown, and much of it may have no function.[702]

DNA has two "backbones," a repeating sequence of "vertebrae" made up of a Phosphate group {one Phosphorous atom bonded to four Oxygen atoms (PO_4) and to Deoxyribose, a five-Carbon sugar (Ribose with an Oxygen atom removed)}. Deoxyribose is the pentose monosaccharide $C_5H_{10}O_4$ {H–(C=O)–(CH$_2$)–(CHOH)$_3$–H}.[703]

Each Deoxyribose-Phosphate vertebra in each backbone is linked to one of four DNA Nitrogenous Bases: Adenine (A), Thymine (T), Guanine (G), or Cytosine (C). Adenine ($C_5H_5N_5$) and Guanine ($C_5H_5N_5O$) are double Carbon-Nitrogen ring compounds (Purines). Cytosine ($C_4H_5N_3O$) and Thymine ($C_5H_6N_2O_2$) are single Carbon-Nitrogen ring compounds (Pyrimidines).

The two backbones are analogous to the side rails of a ladder, with half of each ladder rung being a Nitrogenous Base attached to each Deoxyribose-Phosphate link in its side rail. Each half-rung is tied to its counterpart in the other side rail. The infinitesimal distance between the side rails is too small for two (double-ringed) purines to fit between them and too far apart for two (single-ringed) pyrimidines to connect them. So each ladder rung is a purine bonded to a pyrimidine. But A only bonds to T and C only bonds to G, so the ladder rungs are either *AT* or *CG* combinations. And a nucleotide sequence of, for example, ATCG along one side rail (backbone) is necessarily matched to the TAGC sequence on the other backbone—making the Nucleotide sequence of either backbone completely define the DNA

Nucleotide sequence. {Each rung in the DNA ladder therefore can be described by identifying it as a "T" or "C" base nucleotide (or allele).[704]} And the eight 100-millionths of an inch wide, three-inch long DNA ladder is twisted into a tightly coiled double helix in the nucleus of each of our ~37.2 trillion cells.

A change from TA to CG (or vice versa) in one "rung" in the DNA ladder is a SNP (pronounced snip), an acronym for Single Nucleotide Polymorphism. Everyone has 4-5 million SNPs, which correlates to a SNP about every 640-710 base-pairs (and to about 82,000-92,000 SNPs along the 59 million base pair Y Chromosome).

The terms haplogroup and haplotype are commonly encountered in genetic descriptions. Haplogroups are genetic groupings of individuals with a common patrilineal (Y Chromosome DNA) or Matrilineal (mitochondrial DNA) ancestor.[705] Haplotypes are groups of genes inherited together from one parent.[706]

Closely related SNPs are organized into alpha-numeric Haplogroups (e.g., R1b) which have a Key Marker SNP. Those Haplogroups are catalogued into "trees" that trace the ancestry of particular SNPs. And the known geographic incidence of specific SNPs and their Haplogroups enables tracing an individual's ancestry genetically and geographically.

Some short Nucleotide sequences are repeated. These STRs (Short Tandem Repeats), are statistically analyzed to genetically relate individuals to each other. An STR is usually shared by 5%-20% of humanity, but analysis of multiple STRs enables identification of the degree of relatedness of individuals (the more STRs analyzed, the better the discrimination.)[707] So, if 20% of us have the same STR at a specific DNA location and 20% have a different STR at another location, and if they are inherited independently, only 4% [(1/5) X (1/5)] of the unrelated population would have both STRs. For 8 independently inherited STRs, only 0.78% of the unrelated population have those 8.

DNA nucleotides close to each other on the DNA helix tend to be inherited together (linked) more than those farther apart, and that limits the degree of independent inheritance. Sophisticated statistical analysis of multiple STRs "projects" (predicts) the Haplogroup to which a tested individual belongs. Those analyses have a confidence level (accuracy) dependent on the quantity and consistency of the data, and the greater the number of STRs analyzed, the more accurate the projection. SNP haplogroup projections "confirm" Haplogroup membership. Analyses of a sufficiently large number of STRs (e.g., Family Tree DNA's 700 marker STR test) also confirms the testee's haplogroup.

The massive effect that a single nucleotide change can wreak is evident in mutation of the sixth amino acid in the 147 amino acid string of *Beta* Hemoglobin on Chromosome 11 from A to T. That changes glutamic acid (hydrophilic) to valine (hydrophobic). The result is Hemoglobin *S* (HbS), a recessive mutation. Its carriers (heterozygotes) inherit one copy of HbS from one parent and normal adult hemoglobin (HbA) from the other. Carriers who mate with carriers have children with a 25% chance of not inheriting HbS at all, a 50% chance of being carriers, and a 25% chance of inheriting two copies (being homozygotes). HbS homozygotes have Sickle Cell Disease (SCD).[708] A different single nucleotide mutation in the same amino acid changes glutamic acid to lysine. The result is Hemoglobin *C* (HbC), which causes less blood cell sickling than HbS. HbC heterozygotes have an increased (but incomplete) resistance to malaria infection. Individuals who inherit HbS from one parent and HbC from the other also have SCD. Individuals with one of their two Chromosome 11s carrying HbA and the other carrying HbS or HbC usually do not exhibit sickle cell disease.[709] But those sickle cell heterozygotes have Sickle Cell Trait (SCT), and some individuals with SCT experience complications of SCD (e.g., pain crises). SCT can be harmful in its extreme form and in rare cases (e.g., high or low air pressure (e.g., scuba diving, mountain climbing), or low air oxygen, or extreme physical stress, dehydration is experienced).[710]

The sickle cell mutation changes red blood cells from a round shape that flows smoothly to rod-like cells that clump together in sickle-like shapes. They die quickly, producing anemia. And they block blood vessels, causing pain, strokes, and damage to spleens, kidneys, livers, and lungs (e.g., acute chest syndrome). Victims, especially young ones, are highly susceptible to bacterial infections. CSD is not restricted to any human group(s). There are about a million carriers in the U.S., and about one in 12 Black Americans and about one in 100 Hispanics are among them. Modern medical care enables many SCD victims to live past the age of 50, whereas most prior victims didn't reach adulthood.

10.4 Patrilineal and Matrilineal Inheritance.

Mammalian females have paired X sex Chromosomes (XX), one from each parent. Males (XY) inherit an X sex Chromosome from their mother and a Y sex Chromosome from their father. When the autosomal (non-sex-determining) cells are produced during cell reproduction (meiosis), like chromosomes pair off, split, and recombine—exchanging genetic information. The Y-Chromosome's telomeres pair to some degree with the X-Chromosome's telomeres, but the Y-Chromosome is non-combining otherwise. Termed NRY (Non-Recombining Y), its about 59 million nucleotide base pairs and over 200 genes are the largest DNA segment inherited intact.[711] NRY, surnames, and histories all describe patrilineal ancestry.

The mitochondria, organelles in the cytoplasm external to the cell nuclei, supply energy (adenosine triphosphate) to the cells. Mammalian ova reject or destroy the mitochondria of the fertilizing sperm, giving both male and female offspring their mother's 37-gene mitochondria.[712] And mtDNA (mitochondrial DNA) describes their matrilineal ancestry.

Genome tracing has shown that we all have a common male and a common female ancestor who lived long after our species came into being. They are everyone's Most Recent Common Ancestors (MRCAs), aka Y-Chromosome Adam (the Y-MRCA) and Mitochondrial Eve (the mtMRCA). We're all descendants of both. The calculated time when the Y-MRCA and mtMRCA lived has varied, with a 2013 study placing the lifetime of the mtMRCA at between 99-148 KYA and the Y-MRCA at between 120-156 KYA.[713] (Analysis of 9.9 Mb of the Y-DNA of nine globally different populations has since calculated the Y-MRCA origin as 138±18 KYA[714] in Central-Northwest Africa.[715]) The odds against the Y-MRCA and mtMRCA being spouses are astronomical.

Inherited autosomal DNA has a 50-50 chance of being from the father, so the chance that an autosomal DNA gene that's inherited intact, even if the intact inheritance recurs every generation, will accompany inherited NRY for 1000 years (~30 generations) is less than one in 2^{30}, which is less than one in a billion (1×10^9). And the chance that such a gene has been inherited through the ~4000 generations that have followed the Y-MRCA is one in less than 1 in 10[444]). So living men have inherited virtually no autosomal DNA genes from the Y-MRCA. (But NRY traces them to him.)

Women have a similar chance of autosomal inheritance from Mitochondrial Eve. And while mtDNA provides the same identification of pre-surname and prehistory matrilineal inheritance that Y-DNA does patrilineal history, because women take their husbands' names and become more a part of their husbands' families than men join their wives' families, and most spouses are ethnically compatible, Y-DNA, surnames, and histories more readily trace patrilineal and ethnic ancestry.

10.5 Eurasian Patrilineal Ancestry

Y-DNA Haplogroup R1b (Key Marker SNP R-M343) is the most common Y-DNA haplogroup in International Society of Genetic Genealogy (ISOGG) databases. Its SNP R-M269 subclade is the dominant branch of R1b in Western Europe.[716] R-M269's alpha-numeric Haplogroup R1b1a1a2 was formerly identified as R1b1a2 (2003 to 2005), R1b1c (2005 to 2008), and R1b1b2 (2008 to 2011). Its East to West increase is shown by its estimated occurrence of 0.8% in China, 2.6% in Russia, 22.7% in Poland, 92.3% in Wales, and 85.4% in Ireland. It was estimated in 2010 to be carried by ~110 million Europeans. Once considered as young as 4 KYA, by 2010 it was concluded that it originated about 10 KYA in Europe or Western Asia.[717] (That's an outdated estimate if FTDNA's conclusion that R-M222, an R-M269 16-step descendant subclade, began 30 KYA in Central Europe is correct.) But R-M269 is still a link to European ancestry.

In 2004 researchers seeking STR markers for the great ancient families of Ireland connected an R1b cluster to medieval Irish Kings descended from the semi-legendary 5th Century Irish High King Niall of the Nine Hostages. They labeled it the IMH (Irish Modal Haplotype), which was definitively marked by Y-DNA SNP R-M222 in 2006. It's alpha-numeric Haplogroup was identified as R1b1c7 (2006, 2007), R1b1b2a1b6b (2008), R1b1b2a1a2f2 (2009, 2010), R1b1a2a1a1b4b (2011), R1b1a2a1a1b3a1a1 (2012), R1b1a2a1a2c1a1a1 (2013, 2014), & R1b1a2a1a2c1a1a1a1 (2015). R-M222 is not the most prevalent Haplogroup in any Irish County. But it is carried by ~12 million Irishmen and is most prolific in Northwest Ireland, where its incidence approaches 20% in some Counties (e.g., Donegal). It's also prolific in the rest of Ulster and in Lowland Scotland, and is found in Scotland's Western Isles and in Orkney, and near Scotland's border in England's North. There are a few R-M222 individuals in Iceland, Norway, and Germany. But R-M222's "heartland" can be envisioned as former Ulster Province plus the land in England and Scotland roughly bounded by lines running East-Northeast from Northernmost and Southernmost Ulster. RM-222 It is now called Northwest Irish.[718] Its carriers typically have Irish/Scot Gaelic ancestry.

FTDNA stated that R-M222 likely originated in Central Europe some 30 KYA, and identified it as being collectively defined by the following STRs:[719]

DYS390 = 25	DYS385b = 13	DYS392 = 14
DYS448 = 18	DYS449 = 30	DYS464 = 15-16-16-17
DYS456 = 17	DYS607 = 16	DYS413 = 21-23
DYS534 = 16	DYS481 = 25	DYS714 = 24

Having two of the DYS Markers 390, 385b, 392 and differing by one mismatching repeat means possible membership in R-M222. Confirmation requires SNP testing or the 700 STR Marker test (which checks some 14.5 million Y-DNA locations).[720]

FTDNA's Y-DNA tree leading to R-M222 and to McCabe Group T follows.[721]

Step	Key SNP	Step	Key SNP	Step	Key SNP
1	R-M207	10	R-P310	19	R-Z2976
2	R-M173	11	R-L151	20	R-DF23
3	R-M343	12	R-P312	21	R-Z2961
4	R-L754	13	R-Z290	22	R-Z2956
5	R-L389	14	R-L21	23	**R-M222**
6	R-P297	15	R-DF13	24	R-S568
7	**R-M269**	16	R-Z39589	25	R-566
8	R-L23	17	R-DF49	26	R-FGC440
9	R-L51	18	R-Z2980	27	R-FT125403

Each subclade carries all the SNPs of its parental clades. R-M22's 16-step subclade descent from R-M269 makes R-M222 far more ancestrally definitive, and the additional 4-step descent to R-FT125403 adds more definition.

10.6 McCabe Subgroup T

Decades of painstaking historical research by my 5th cousin Vernon McCabe[722] show our (and over 11,000 others') patrilineal descent from Revolutionary War Private John McCabe (1727-1800). Y-DNA tests that Vernon and I had done showed us to be in a distinctive Y-DNA subgroup of American McCabes. Four other distinctly separate Y-DNA haplotypes were in the FTDNA McCabe database at the time. Many more groups have since been identified, and Vernon McCabe, Russ McCabe, John David Mecabe, and I are in Group T, which is publicly identified as follows.[723]

Kit #	Paternal Ancestor	Origin	Haplogroup
493186	Unidentified	Unknown	R-M269
40344	Elisha Mecabe b.1799, Monmouth, NJ	Unknown	R-M269
9586	John McCabe b. 1790's to Sussex, DE	Scotland	R-M269
26901	John McCabe b. 1727? - d.1800 Sussex Co DE	Unknown	R-FT125403

Kit 40344 is that of John David Mecabe (deceased), accomplished at the behest of his mother, Brunhilde (Bruni) Wais Mecabe (deceased), who traced her family to Elisha Mecabe, born in 1799 in Monmouth, New Jersey.[724] That was a Y-DNA 67 marker STR test. (Bruni told me that Elisha's surname was McCabe in multiple records.)

Kit 9586 is that of Vernon McCabe and is a 37 marker Y-DNA STR test that confirmed Vernon's Historic tracing of his, my, and Russ McCabe's descent from Revolutionary War Private John McCabe (1727-1800).

Kit 26901 correlates to Russ McCabe. His DNA data was updated (as was mine) by taking the Y-DNA 700 STR Marker test. Before recent updates, FTDNA categorized Russ as being in the R-FGC440 Haplogroup. He correctly predicted that additional testing would show me to be R-FGC440 too. FTDNA has since expanded its Y-DNA tree and reclassified Russ and me as being in R-FT125403, a subclade of R-FGC440. {FTDNA also shows the R-FT12540 Haplogroup to be in the M1 subclade of Haplogroup M222+.[725] (Adding + to a SNP shows it to be "confirmed.")

According to Dr. Jim Freed, the FTDNA McCabe Project Coordinator when my initial, 67 Marker Y-DNA STR test was done, DNA testing showed that I, my 5th Cousin Vernon McCabe, and John David Mecabe should have a common Y-DNA Common Ancestor within the past 200-300 years. For Vernon and Russ and me, Vernon's work showed that was Revolutionary War Private John McCabe of Sandy Branch (Selbyville), Delaware. DNA testing done thus far doesn't identify the Most Recent Common Ancestor of Group T. {It may well be the father or grandfather of Revolutionary War Private John McCabe.}

Vernon, John David, and the Kit 493186 member of Subgroup T are projected to be in the R-M269 Haplogroup, but their DNA testing doesn't "confirm" their Haplogroup. The DNA correlation Dr. Freed made between Vernon's, John David's, and my relatedness nonetheless indicates that such testing would place Vernon and John David in the same R-M222 subclade as Russ and me (R-FT125403).

FTDNA STRs in R-M222 are tabulated below for FTDNA McCabe Subgroup T. (Blanks reflect non-identification of those STRs by the Y-37 and Y-67 STR tests.)

DYS	M422 STRs	Kit 491386 STRs	J. David Mecabe STRs	Vernon McCabe STRs	Russ McCabe STRs	Ebe McCabe STRs
390	25	25	25	25	25	25
385	13	11-13	11-13	11-13	11-13	11-13
392	14	14	14	14	14	14
448	18	18	18	18	18	18
449	30	32	32	32	32	32
464	15-16-16-17	15-16-16-17	15-16-16-17	15-16-16-17	15-16-16-17	15-16-16-17
456	17	16	16	16	17	16
607	16	16	17	16	16	16
413	21-23		21-23		21-23	21-23
534	16		16		16	16
481	25		26		25	25
714	24				24	24
R-M222 STR TABLE						

When my initial DNA testing was done, R-M222 was considered to represent patrilineal descent from Ireland's semi-legendary High King Niall. And my FTDNA page "badges" me as being in the "Niall" group. But even the earlier estimates of R-M222's European, non-British Isle origin significantly precede Niall's reputed lifetime.

It's hypothesized that the Irish historians who tried to make it appear that the Irish descended from the sons of Mil put Niall's death some 50 years earlier than it occurred. (Niall reputedly reigned from 379 AD until he was assassinated in 405 AD by Eochaida, a son of the King of Leinster, while Niall's forces were camped along the River Liane near Boulogne-sur-Mer in Northern France.[726])

R-M222 is most dense near the ancient Uí Néill stronghold (Dungannon Town in Co Tyrone[727]). So Niall may well have carried R-M222, and had many direct patrilineal descendants, but he isn't the progenitor of the two to three million R-M222 carriers in the world that he was once thought to be.

10.7 Matrilineal Ancestry

Over half of Europe and 25%-40% of the Near East are in mtDNA Haplogroup HV, the most frequent mtDNA lineage in that region. Its progenitor lived between 25-40 KYA. HV apparently spread from the Fertile Crescent (e.g., Mesopotamia) to Egypt, to the Horn of Africa, and to Central and Eastern Europe. Its Subclade HV-10 was passed on to all their children by my Kashubian Polish mother and by her mother, Joanna Szczypior.

HV-10 also is found in Europe around the Alps.[728] (The Alps range, in a 500-mile-long and 120-mile-wide arc, from France in the Southwest to Austria in the East, and from Monaco in the South to Germany in the North. Italy, Lichtenstein, Slovenia. and Switzerland also are Alpine countries.[729]) So the route from the mtMRCA to me and my matrilineal kin included an Alpine stopover.

My six generations of descent from my Great-Great-Great-Great (Great[4]) Grandfather John McCabe (1727-1800) means that my DNA is 1/64 (1.5625%) his. And my genome nominally comes just as much from his wife, Mary Hudson, making me and my siblings (using name origins from family information and Houseofnames.com):

50% my Kashubian Polish Mother Veronica (Coulis) McCabe
25% my nominally Anglo-Saxon English Grandmother Birdie May (Chandler) McCabe
12.5% my nominally Pict Scot Great Grandmother Julia Ann (Murray) McCabe
6.25%: my nominally Welsh Great[2] Grandmother Elizabeth (Williams) McCabe
3.125% my nominally English (Irish?) Great[3] Grandmother Elizabeth (Collins) McCabe
1.5625%: my nominally Anglo-Saxon Great[4] Grandmother Mary (Hudson) McCabe
0.78125% my Anglo-Saxon/Dutch/French Great[5] Grandmother Lydia (Winter) McCabe

10.8 Overall DNA Ancestry

Our 50-50 split between paternal and maternal genes can, over many generations, make one's overall genome far different nationality-wise from his or her birth surname's lineage. That's fostered by the genetic intermixing associated with immigration and/or conquest. In the U.S., that's been called the *Melting Pot* effect (based on the 1908 Stage Play with that name[730]).

My patrilineal ethnicity descends from (according to the work of University of Oxford Professor of Human Genetics Brian Sykes[731]): R1b {Clan Oisin), Iberia, 25 KYA, via Central Asia, N.W. Asia, Central Asia, S.W. Asia, the Middle East, and Ethiopia to N.E. Africa (60-80 KYA}. The mtDNA that I and my siblings share with our mother probably is very different than Vernon or Russ McCabe's and/or John David Mecabe's. (There are about 36 ancestral mtDNA Mother Clans v. 14 Y-DNA Father Clans.) And my mtDNA ancestry extends back via Clan Helena (S. France, 20 KYA) through W. Eurasia, the Near East, N. Africa, and Central Africa to Northeast Africa (140-200 KYA).

Analysis (by Ancestry.com) of all 23 pairs of a testee's chromosomes (706,393 SNPs, of which in men about 2% are Y-DNA SNPs) compares the results to a panel of reference samples whose relative incidence in specific regions is known.[732]

A possibility of my having inherited some Danish DNA existed because my maternal grandparents' were Kashubian Poles and there was a Danish Viking settlement in the Kashub homeland along the Baltic. But, as of 2/29/2020, ancestry.com's "updated" report showed no Scandinavian component in my genome and "estimated" my ancestry as:

- 39% (Range: 34-55%) Eastern Europe and Russia, highlighting Pomerania (an area split between Germany and Poland). Kashub is one of its languages.[733] (My Kashubian maternal grandparents emigrated to Canada from Prussia. The Kashubs were originally a Baltic Tribe, the Baltic is Prussia's Sea border, and the Kashubian homeland was West of Latvia in North-Central Poland.)
- 38% (Range 2-38%) England, Wales & Northwestern Europe, primarily Belgium, the Channel Islands, England, & Wales.
- 10% (Range 0-15%) Ireland & Scotland, including the Isle of Man and Northern Ireland. (Representing melting pot dilution of Gaelic genes?)
- 10% (Range 0-27%) Germanic Europe, primarily Germany. {The Angles and Saxons were Germanic, and the Celts were a combination of European tribes. Also, the map of this area includes a bit of Jutland (Southern Denmark)}.
  3% (Range 0-15%) Baltic, primarily Latvia & Lithuania.

My FTDNA page shows my overall ancestry as:

- 44% British Isles
- 35% East Europe (the associated map extends across the Baltic and Denmark's Bornholm Island to the S.E. tip of Sweden)
- 19% West and Central Europe
- 2% North African (Morocco/Algeria/Tunisia)

My having no Scandinavian DNA means that Revolutionary War Private John McCabe (1727-1800) and his wife Mary Hudson had no Scandinavian (Viking) ancestors either. (Scandinavian DNA inherited from their mothers may be in some of Revolutionary War Private John McCabe's grandsons and subsequent patrilineal descendants.

10.9 Ancient Occupants of the British Isles

Intermittent occupation of Britain by hominins began nearly 1 MYA.[734] Southeast England and Mainland Europe were then still connected by the Weald-Artois Anticline chalk ridge between Southeast England and Northern France. A megaflood broke through it ~425 KYA and created the English Channel. And rising sea levels separated Ireland and Britain ~11 KYA. The associated human occupation is shown by:

- ~900 KYO (thousands of years old), probably *Homo antecessor* stone tools and footprints at Happisburgh on the Norfolk coast (In Southern England, abutting on the North Sea, across from the Netherlands).
- ~500 KYO *Homo heidelbergensis* fossils were found in Boxgrove in Sussex (farther South than Norfolk). (*H. erectus*, the probable ancestor of *H. antecessor* and *H. heidelbergensis*, originated ~2 MYA.[735])
- ~400 KYO Early Neanderthal fossils were found at Swanscombe in Kent (in Southeast England), and ~225 KYO Classic Neanderthal Fossils were found in Pontnewydd in Wales (also in England's South). From 180-60 KYA, Britain was unoccupied by hominins—until the Neanderthals returned. They became extinct ~40 KYA, about when H. sapiens began intermittent occupation. After 11.7 KYA, permanent H sapiens occupation began.

Note: Hominins evolved during the Pleistocene Age (~2.6 MYA -11.7 KYA). The above suggests that ice then prevented hominin habitation of the Isles North of 53°N {~170 miles North of Southernmost Britain (Lizard Point) and 350 miles South of Northernmost Britain (Dunnet Head)}. And from ~425-11.7 KYA, mammals that couldn't survive Pleistocene cold and were unable to cross the English Channel may have been absent from even the slightly less than the Southernmost third of Britain that was then intermittently habitable.

10.10 A Study of the Isles' Ancestry

The genetic make-up of the Isles was the object of a study published in 2017 and updated in 2018 [736] It studied 2013 individuals (536 Irish, 101 Scots, 131 Welsh, 96 Orcadians, and 1239 English), with considerable extended ancestry from specific Irish regions. Fine-scale population clusters and admixture (interbreeding) in Ireland and high/low migration regions in Ireland and in Britain (England, Scotland, and Wales) were examined. The Study used the *Irish DNA Atlas* (194 Irish individuals with four ancestral generations linked to specific Irish regions) and the *Peoples of the British Isles* dataset (2039 individuals) to divide Ireland into

10 clusters: seven Gaelic ancestral Irish ones and three shared Irish and British ones. Data on 2225 Scandinavians was utilized to better assess the Norwegian component of British and Irish ancestry. The study also referenced findings showing that:

- The Irish Genome was established in the Irish Bronze Age (~3500 years ago).[737]
- Common Irish Y-DNA and mtDNA haplotypes show genetic continuity with other Western European populations and a general East-West decline of Y-DNA haplotype diversity in Ireland's North-West.[738]
- There is a predominant Y-DNA group in Gaelic Ireland.[739]
- There are distinctive North Munster and South Munster haplotypes.[740]
- Testing showed but little Norse Y-DNA presence in Ireland.[741]
- Irish haplotypes are less diverse than those of other European Populations.[742]
- Data insufficient to specify an Irish population structure indicated that Ireland's population diverges from those of neighboring Scotch and English ones.[743]
- There is fine-scale genetic structure within the British Isles.[744]

Scotland was divided into six genetic groups: Northeast, Southwest, Borders, the Hebrides, Orkney, and Shetland. Most Scottish samples were put in the Northeast or the Southwest group. That reflects a previously observed cline and the Scottish Mainland split apparently centered near the River Forth. {That river rises in a mountainous area of Central Scotland and meanders ~29 miles East-Southeast to the Firth of Forth, an estuary that extends ~49 miles East-Northeast to the North Sea.[745]) The split "echoes" the historical distribution of Gaels and Picts, with the Northeast clusters describing the Pictish Kingdoms' boundaries, and the Southwest grouping mapping the ancient Strathclyde Kingdoms (the *Sco-Ire* and Dál Riata clusters). Northeast Scotland has the *Tayside-Fife and Aberdeenshire* clusters. It also has the small *Buchanan-Moray* cluster, which exhibits isolation effects. The Isle of Man groups with Southwest Scotland, which also has some ancestry from the western coast area of Argyll (the *Argyll* Cluster). The *Borders* Cluster represents the boundary between Scotland and England.

Removing reputed admixture individuals from a sample of 6021 Europeans, configuring the remaining 5804 into 51 clusters, and applying regression analysis showed that:

- 80% of the seven 'Gaelic' Irish Clusters have French, Belgian, Danish, and Norwegian ancestry. The other 20% has Italian, Finnish, Swedish, Spanish, Polish, and German ancestry. European Cluster FRA1, four-fifths of which is from North-West France, provides 30% of the French ancestry of the 'Gaelic' Irish Clusters. That ancestry extends to the North Ireland, Scottish, Orcadian, Welsh, and Cornish Clusters.
- German ancestry is least evident in the 'Gaelic' Irish Clusters, next least in Orkney, and most evident in England.
- The low incidence of observed Belgian-like ancestry in Ireland, compared to Britain, shows the relative isolation of Ireland from Europe.
- The North Ireland Clusters' French-like ancestry increases as German-like ancestry decreases. North Ireland Clusters with the least Irish ancestry also had the lowest French-like ancestry.

- The best data fit for the Ireland-Britain link is to Scotland rather than England. Moreover, admixture in Ireland seems to have been gradual and perhaps confounded by the settling of Gallowglass mercenaries from the 13th-15th Centuries and/or the 16th Century hiring of large numbers of Scottish Redshank mercenaries.
- Norwegian-like ancestry was relatively low in Wales, higher in Orkney and Scotland, and unexpectedly high in Ireland.
- The upper limit of Norwegian ancestry in Ireland is estimated to be ~20%. (Causative uncertainties prevented estimation of a lower limit.) And the Norwegian ancestry in Ireland seems to be across Ireland, not just in Norse settlement areas (present day Annagassan, Arklow, Carlingford, Cork, Dublin, Limerick, Lough Foyle, Lough Ree, Strangford, Waterford, Wexford, and Youghal.[746])
- In Norway, mostly on the North and West Coasts, especially the West, significant Irish (6.82%), Scottish (2.29%), and Orcadian (2.13%) ancestry was found. (Slaves taken by the Vikings were an important commodity in trade.[747])
- The Fine-Scale Tree Building Algorithm put most Irish individuals in one 'Gaelic' Irish Branch and grouped it with the Orcadian Branch. That was likely due to Ireland and Orkney being similarly (but separately) distant genetically from the rest of the Isles. No large-scale gene flow was identified between Ireland and Orkney.
- It is unlikely that the Gallowglass descended from Celts who went or were taken to Scandinavia. That's shown by domination of a Nordic Y-DNA haplogroup and its subgroups in Sweden, Norway, Iceland, Finland, Denmark, and Germany, and in the migrating to the British Isles by Vikings. In contrast, the R1b Y-DNA (Celtic) haplogroup (SNP R-M343) links to Portugal, Spain, Andorra, France, Belgium, Luxemburg, Switzerland, the British Isles, Denmark, and the Netherlands.[748]

The primary differentiations in the Study findings are between England/Wales and Scotland/Ireland, the main sources of the Isles' genetic differences, and between Orkney/Shetland v. the rest. Scottish coverage was largely restricted to Northern Aberdeenshire and Southern Scotland. Limited sampling on one side of genetic barriers (e.g., the Scottish-English barrier and the Welsh-English barrier) limited the definition of migratory patterns. And the Study found or affirmed that:

- The Isles show Norse-Irish and Anglo-Irish admixtures dating, respectively, to the Vikings and to the Plantation of Ulster.
- The *Insular Atlantic Gene Pool* was established by the 4000-3000 BC influx of agriculturists and the Bronze Age metal shaping Beaker Culture starting ~2700 BC. Later alterations did not replace that gene pool.
- Hegemonies and migration altered South Britain and Ireland—effects less clear in Britain's North, Scotland, and the surrounding islands.
- The ~400-650 AD Anglo-Saxon invasions altered Southern England.
- Viking incursions altered Northern Britain.
- The "Plantation" of Ireland (Ulster) was with Scottish and English immigrants.
- There is high Northern Isles' Norwegian ancestry (23-28% in Shetland).
- There is High Germanic ancestry in the East and high "Celtic" ancestry in the West.

- There is broad (e.g., NE to SW division of Scotland's mainland) and fine (e.g., 3 km in the Northern Isles) geographic genetic structure. Much of that is consistent with the ancient kingdoms of the Gaels, the Picts, the Norse, and the Britons (P-Celtic Brythonic Language speaking ancestors of the Cornish, Welsh, and Bretons).
- Ireland has high levels of North-West French and West Norwegian-like ancestry.
- The seven "Gaelic" Irish clusters, with Viking and "Gaelic" Irish Cluster admixture from 788–1052, suggest homogenous levels of predominantly ancient Irish ancestry.
- The three Ulster (North Ireland) Clusters show Irish-British admixture consistent with the Plantation of Ulster, but Ulster "most likely" has a "Gaelic" ancestry genetically isolated from Britain.
- There are Gene Flow Barriers along the ancient boundaries between England, Wales, and Scotland, and between Scotland and Orkney. The strongest separates Wales from Ireland and from the rest of Britain. A Southwest England barrier appears to separate Devon/Cornwall from nearby England and Wales, and there's a North of England barrier in the Pennine Hills.
- The gene flow barrier in Ireland's West (including Connacht's coast), and the one in Leinster near its Munster Border may be due to the historical rivalry of those provinces, or to the genetic split of Munster from the rest of Ireland. If County Clare's shared Connacht and Munster history eliminated the barrier to Munster there, that would explain the low gene flow along Ireland's West Coast.
- A gene flow barrier separates West Ulster from East Ulster and Scotland. It represents the genetic divide between the "Gaelic" Irish Clusters and the North Ireland Clusters. And there's a major North to South barrier in Ulster.
- There's a relatively high gene flow corridor between Northeast Ulster and Southwest Scotland (indicative of shared ancestry and roughly representative of the North Ireland cluster's geographic distribution). There's another corridor between the two Scotland clusters, and another along the Welsh-English Border.
- There's a predominant related male group in the East to West decline in Y-DNA haplotype diversity in North-West Ireland, in a North of Munster haplotype, and in a South of Munster haplotype.
- Long and short runs of the same genetic variants (isolation effects) show high genetic fixation in the Hebrides, Highlands, Argyll, County Donegal, and the Isle of Man.
- The genetic axis in Ireland apparently ends in Donegal, the Republic of Ireland's Northwesternmost county.
- Southwest Scotland's majority lies in the *Sco-Ire* Cluster, whose people descend from either Northeast Ireland or Southwest Scotland. All *Sco-Ire* Irish appear to be from parts of North Ireland substantially "planted" by Brits/Scots. (That the 2011 census showed 84.2% of the Republic of Ireland and 40.8*% of Northern Ireland to be Catholic shows the "Plantation" effect. But 40.8% of Northern Ireland being Catholic[749] (its largest religious denomination) makes it considerably Irish as well as British.}
- English ancestry and a gene flow barrier separate *Borders* from the rest of Scotland. *Borders* coincides geographically with the Brythonic-language-speaking Kingdoms of Gododdin and Rheged. Gododdin was In Southeast Scotland and Northeast England. Rheged was considered to have been in Northwest England (Cumbria), but recent

archeologic findings[750] suggest that its stronghold was in Galloway in Southwest Scotland. That's an ~50-mile shift from East to North of the Isle of Man.)

- Northern Isles ancestry may be partly why *N. Scotland* is a genetic continuum between Scotland and the Northern Isles.

- The Hebrides appear genetically distinct from Mainland Scotland. Hebrideans cluster with *N. Scotland*, not other Western Scottish clusters, and have high proportions of ancestral components most frequent in Ireland. Isolation by distance may be the basis for the Hebrides' low gene flow rates and isolation effects.

- *Argyll* appears intermediate between *Sco-Ire* and the Hebrides.

- Orkney and Shetland are the most differentiated and the most genetically distinct from other British and Irish populations. The causes are isolation and Interbreeding with the later Norse Jarldom (Earldom) of Orkney. There's also a remarkable degree of differentiation between the individual Northern Isles.

- Most Scottish and Irish clusters have Celtic ancestry. *Aberdeenshire* and *Tayside-Fife* have more English-like ancestry, and the Isle *of* Man's 42% English ancestry is similarly high.

- Norwegian ancestry is highest in the Northern Isles (mean 18%), and substantially lower (4% avg.) in *N Scotland,* in the Southwest (*Argyll*), and on the Isle of Man—which differ but little from the rest of Mainland Scotland in that regard.

- The estimated average of 7% Scandinavian ancestry in Ireland is markedly lower than previous estimates.

- From high to low, Norwegian ancestry of the Isles is indicated to be: (1) Shetland; (2) Orkney (20-25%); (3) the Hebrides (7%); (4) the Isle of Man; and (5) Ireland.

- The largest source of Norwegian-like haplotypes in Britain and Ireland is in Clusters NOR9 and NOR10, which are predominantly from the Western Norwegian counties of Hordaland and Sogn & Fjordane—where most Viking voyages originated.

- Scandinavia is Iceland's major ancestral source. A Northwestern British or Irish source of the ancient Gaels who contributed to its early populating is suggested.

[Some additional studies are described online.[751] More studies undoubtedly will be done, with the entire genome being studied increasingly more. Selective sampling and incorporation of other findings made this study much more representative. But a study of ~10,000 individuals would encompass less than 0.02% of the Isles' population of 72 million—fewer than one of every 7000 inhabitants. That may be why the Study points out that it isn't comprehensive. And the Study's suggested/apparent findings, until more substantially corroborated, represent insights rather than proofs.]

Epilogue

This work tried to, in a small way, integrate history into Big Picture reality. Hopefully, that was accomplished consistent with the statement by Roman philosopher Marcus Tullius Cicero (106-43 BC) that: *For there is assuredly nothing dearer to a man than wisdom, and though age takes away all else, it undoubtedly brings us that.*[752]

(Cicero opposed Mark Antony and was executed. His severed head and hands were publicly displayed.[753] That the French who abandoned Fort Duquesne 1801 years later decapitated captured Scots and staked their heads on the Fort's walls illustrates the consistency of basic human nature. (Lasting major change can take a million years.[754])

Eulogization of the U.S. has been largely replaced by condemnation of its evils. This work has tried to present both Good and Evil aspects of our history—by refusing to throw out the baby with the bath water. Some of my related conclusions follow:

- Slavery and its (camouflaged) incorporation in the Constitution should be viewed in context with either keeping Slavery then or not having one nation, with subsequent progress, and with *the American Dream.*
- Lincoln made campaign statements about Black inferiority—ones inconsistent with his other statements. But performance after being elected is what counts, not campaign rhetoric. And Lincoln led the way to both ending Slavery and preserving the Union—in our deadliest war.
- The South fought for Slavery—initially skillfully trouncing the richer, more powerful, and more populous North. None of that should be swept under the rug.
- WWII Germany embraced anti-Semitism and the Master Race ideology, ignoring obvious Nazi atrocities. But the post-WWI reparations imposed had impoverished Germany and fostered Hitler's rise. And all mankind is susceptible to such evil.
- Symbols of our historic culture and civilization (e.g., the Ten Commandments and nativity scenes) should not be removed from public areas.
- Partisan polarization of all three government branches and the absence of media objectivity are fostering development of 4-year dictatorial Executive Branch administrations. Despite that and many other evils, we have much good to build upon. As Harlem-born U.S. Secretary of State Colin Powell said: *Look at the world. There is no pure competition to the United States of America.*[755]

Humanity's awareness of Good was shown in an ~1895 Rudyard Kipling poem, (He was awarded the 1907 Nobel prize for Literature for his power of observation, originality of imagination, virility of ideas, and talent for narration,[756] and also has had many critics.) But that poem[757] still applies to everyone. It follows.

If

If you can keep your head when all about you
Are losing theirs and blaming it on you,
If you can trust yourself when all men doubt you,
But make allowance for their doubting too;
If you can wait and not be tired by waiting,
Or being lied about, don't deal in lies,
Or being hated, don't give way to hating,
And yet don't look too good, nor talk too wise:

If you can dream—and not make dreams your master;
If you can think—and not make thoughts your aim;
If you can meet with Triumph and Disaster
And treat those two impostors just the same;
If you can bear to hear the truth you've spoken
Twisted by knaves to make a trap for fools,
Or watch the things you gave your life to, broken,
And stoop and build 'em up with worn-out tools:

If you can make one heap of all your winnings
And risk it on one turn of pitch-and-toss,
And lose, and start again at your beginnings
And never breathe a word about your loss;
If you can force your heart and nerve and sinew
To serve your turn long after they are gone,
And so hold on when there is nothing in you
Except the Will which says to them: 'Hold on!'

If you can talk with crowds and keep your virtue,
Or walk with Kings—nor lose the common touch,
If neither foes nor loving friends can hurt you,
If all men count with you, but none too much;
If you can fill the unforgiving minute
With sixty seconds' worth of distance run,
Yours is the Earth and everything that's in it,
And—which is more—you'll be a Man, my son!

All of mankind's progress and Goodness notwithstanding, the belief that Goodness will prevail is not supported by history. As Walt Kelly's cartoon character Pogo said: *We have met the enemy and he is us.*

Burgeoning populations and competition counter the hope that we will end our hundreds of millennia of Inequality and Warfare and Prejudice. But our quality of life is better than that of any preceding generation, we do get better tiny step by tiny step, and no other predator on Earth is less cruel. So, as the mortally wounded Captain James Lawrence of the *USS Chesapeake* said in battle on 6/1/1813, *Don't give up the ship.*

Glossary

Admixture. Interbreeding.

Alba. The Scotch Gaelic name for Scotland.

Allele. Different version(s) at the same place on a chromosome.[758] Mutated genes and mutated nucleotides are both alleles.

Amerind. The human inhabitants of the Americas (except the Inuit speaking tribes of Alaska) when European colonization began, and their descendants. (The term Native American is commonly used, but it's literally correct for all persons born in America, and our species is truly native only to Africa.)

AMH. Anatomically Modern Human. (aka EMH, for Early Modern Human). Early (Old Stone age, ~2.58 MYA) Homo sapiens phenotypes are consistent with the range of physical appearance among today's humans—as distinct from those of archaic humans. (Modern humans are sometimes referred to as Homo sapiens sapiens.)

Anglo-Irish. British rulers who lived in Ireland, and their descendants in Ireland

Anglo-Saxons (Angles, Saxons). Britain's Germanic/Danish invaders (Angles, Frisians, Jutes, and Saxons), who initially settled in Eastern Britain after the 410 AD departure of the Romans. The Frisians and Jutes were driven out or absorbed by the Angles and Saxons.[759] Merging with the indigenous inhabitants resulted in the adoption of Old (Saxon) English and establishment of England as a nation (with shires and hundreds). Charters and laws were established. Literature and language flourished. Britain became Christian during its Anglo-Saxon period, which dominated until the 1066 Norman Conquest. The term Anglo-Saxon was invented in the 8th Century to discriminate between the Saxons in Britain and the Saxons of Northern Germany. And the terms Angles, Saxons, and Anglo-Saxons came to represent the same source peoples.[760]

Argyll (Argyllshire). A Western Scotland County encompassing most of the part of the ancient *Dál Riata* kingdom on the Island of Britain. The name Argyll derives from Old Gaelic *Airer Goídel* (*Airer* meaning border/coast and *Goidel* meaning Gael).[761]

Armorica (Aremorica). The Northwestern extremity of Gaul (now Brittany) on the European mainland. It initially included what became Western Normandy.[762]

Bede. Saint Bede the Venerable (673-735). A church deacon at the age of 19 and a priest at the age of 30, Bede is widely regarded as the greatest Anglo-Saxon scholar. He wrote about 40 books, mostly on theology and history. His 731 AD *Ecclesiastical History of the English People* is a key to understanding early British History and the arrival of Christianity. It also was the first work of history to use the AD system of dating.[763]

Bretons. A Celtic ethnic group in the Brittany region of France. They trace their ancestry to Brittonic-speaking people who came, mainly during the Anglo-Saxon Invasion, from Southwestern Britain, especially Cornwall and Devon, during the 5th Century.[764]

Britain. The largest of the British Isles, located off the European Northwest Coast and comprised of England, Scotland, and Wales. (The English Channel, which is about 350 miles long and 20.7 to 150 miles wide, separates Southern England from Northern France and extends from the Southern North Sea to the Atlantic Ocean.)[765]

British. Citizens of England, Scotland, Wales, Northern Ireland, the British Overseas Territories, and the Crown Dependencies (Jersey, Guernsey, and Man).[766]

British Isles. A European Archipelago of over 6000 islands to the Northwest of Mainland Europe. Britain, Ireland, the Isle of Man, and the Isles of Scilly are prominent among them. The Channel Islands off the coast of France (Alderney, Guernsey, Jersey, Sark, and associated smaller islands are in a different archipelago but are British Crown dependencies, considered to be British Soil, and are sometimes considered part of the British Isles.[767] The British Isles also include the Hebrides, the Shetlands, and the Orkneys. (The Republic of Ireland's government does not officially recognize the common definition and uses *Britain and Ireland* instead.)[768]

British Overseas Territories. Territories with their own Constitutions and elected governments responsible for internal affairs. The Crown appoints their governors and is responsible for external affairs, security, defense, and air safety. The UK's 14 overseas territories include Bermuda, Gibraltar, the Falkland Islands, the Cayman Islands, the British Virgin Islands, the British Antarctic Territory, Pitcairn Island....)[769]

Brittany. A peninsula extending from Northwest France into the Atlantic Ocean, Brittany is the traditional homeland of the Bretons, and is recognized as one of the six Celtic Nations by the Celtic League. The name derives from the Latin Britannica, meaning Briton's Land. Its first known inhabitants were Neanderthals. Modern humans arrived there about 35,000 years ago. Before the Romans came in 51 BC, Brittany was occupied by five Celtic tribes. After the fall of the Roman Empire in 410, many Britons settled there and that peninsular part of Rome's Amorica became known as Britannia. It became the independent kingdom of Brittany in the 9th Century and then a Duchy before uniting with the French Kingdom in 1532—as a province governed as a separate nation. With the coming of the French Revolution in 1789, the Duchy was eliminated and Brittany became part of France.[770]

Britons (Celtic Britons, Ancient Britons). Celts who inhabited Britain from its Iron Age into the Middle Ages and spoke Common Brittonic, the ancestral Brittonic language. Their culture and language began diverging into modern Breton, Cornish, and Welsh in the 5th Century, when much of their territory was taken by the Anglo-Saxons and Scotch Gaels.[771]

Brittonic (Brythonic, British Celtic). An insular Celtic language that evolved into Breton, Cornish, Cumbric, and Welsh dialects. The Picts' language was a Brittonic or sister one. Brythonic initially referred to an indigenous Briton not an Anglo-Saxon or Gael.[772]

Celts. Indo-European people in Europe with cultural similarities that included the Celtic languages. The exact spread of the ancient Celts is disputed, but graves in Halstatt, Austria have led some to call that area the Celtic Homeland. Trans-cultural diffusion or migration expanded the Celtic Culture to the Insular Celts of the British Isles, to the Gauls of France, Belgium, the Netherlands, and Luxembourg, to Bohemia, to Iberia (Celtiberians, Celtici, Lusitanians, & Gallici), to Poland, to Northern Italy (the Golasecca culture and Cisalpine Gauls), and as far as Central Anatolia (Galatians) in modern-day Turkey. By the mid-1st millennium, Celtic culture and Insular Celtic languages were restricted to Ireland, Western and Northern Britain (Wales, Scotland, and Cornwall), the Isle of Man, and Brittany. Between the 5th and 8th centuries, Celtic-speakers in those regions had a common linguistic, religious and artistic heritage. Insular Celtic culture diversified into that of the Gaels (Irish, Scottish and Manx) and Britons (Welsh, Cornish, and Bretons). Celtic literary tradition begins with Old Irish texts around the 8th century. Irish, Scottish Gaelic, Welsh, and Breton are still spoken in parts of their historical territories, and Cornish and Manx reputedly are undergoing a revival.[773]

Celtic Nations. Six Western European Territories that share a Celtic language and/or Celtic cultural traits. They are: Brittany; Cornwall; Wales, where there are Brittonic (Brythonic) speakers; Ireland; Scotland; and the Isle of Man.[774]

Channel Islands. An archipelago in the English Channel, off France's Normandy Coast. They include two Crown dependencies: the Bailiwick of Jersey; and the Bailiwick of Guernsey (Guernsey, Alderney, Sark, and some smaller islands)—and are considered the remnants of the Duchy of Normandy.[775]

Clade. A set of haplotypes sharing a common ancestor.

Cornwall. The extreme Southwestern peninsula of the Island of Britain. Its people are recognized as a Celtic nation, and trace their roots to the ancient Britons.

Connacht. Connacht is the Midland-Western of Ireland's four Provinces. It contains Counties Leitrim, Sligo, Roscommon, Mayo, and Galway.[776]

Crown Dependencies. the Bailiwick of Guernsey, the Bailiwick of Jersey, and the Isle of Mann: self-governing island territories that are the responsibility of the English Crown but are not British Overseas Territories or part of the UK. They are not members of the Commonwealth of Nations or European Union (EU), but have relationships with them and are members of the British-Irish Council. All three are in the EU's customs area and Mann is in the EU's Value Added Tax area. Their legislative assemblies' laws govern, with the Crown's assent, local matters.[777]

Cumbric. An early Middle Age Brittonic dialect closely related to Old Welsh. It is thought to have died out in the 12th Century and was spoken in what is now Northern England and Southern Lowland Scotland.[778]

Dál Riata (Dalriada), The Gaelic kingdom that, from about the 5th Century until the early 9th Century, extended from Ulster's County Antrim in Northeast Ireland into part of Scotland's Inner Hebrides and Argyll. Extensive earlier immigration of the Irish (labelled Scoti by the Romans, and so known until the 12th Century) had (by displacing Picts) settled in Britain. About 500 AD, the ruling family of Irish Dalriada crossed into Scottish Dalriada and made Dunadd and Dunolly its chief strongholds. Irish Dalriada then declined, and lost its political identity after the early 9th Century Viking invasions. The Dalriadans in Britain were held in check by the indigenous Picts' onslaughts until the mid-9th Century, when Kenneth MacAlpin (reputedly King of the Picts and of the Dalriadans) united Pict-Land and Dalriada and became King Kenneth I of Scotland.[779] (The *Treachery of MacAlpin* legend holds that he did so by murdering the Pict Royal Families.)

England. The UK country located on the lower part of the Island of Britain. Scotland is to its North and Wales is to its West. 84% of the UK's population is in England.

Europe: Western Eurasia. Europe encompasses all of the British Isles, Scandinavia, and Iceland. The current discrimination between Europe and Asia locates some countries (e.g., Turkey, Russia, Kazakhstan, Georgia, and Azerbaijan) in both "continents." [780]

Gael. A Gaelic-speaking person or someone whose ancestors spoke Gaelic.[781] Also defined as a Gaelic-speaking inhabitant of Ireland, Scotland, or the Isle of Mann.[782] The terms *Irish* and *Scots* once generally described the Gaels, but a truer description is that the Gaels are Northwestern European natives ethnolinguistically linked to the Irish, Manx, and Scots and the Gaelic Language Branch of the Celtic languages. Gaelic remained the main language of Ireland's Gaeltacht and Scotland's Outer Hebrides.[783]

Gaeltacht. Ireland's Districts individually or collectively recognized as having the Irish language as the predominant in-home language. The 153 such districts in the 1920s have diminished to a population of about 120,000 with about 67,000 total Irish speakers (56%) in seven counties, each with the following percentage of the Irish-speaking populace: Donegal (25%), Galway (47%), Kerry (9%), Mayo (10%), Cork (4%), Waterford (2%), and Meath (3%).

A 2015 report considered it likely that Gaelic will not be used as a community language in the Gaeltacht within 10 years.[784]

Galloway. Southwestern Scotland's Counties of Wigtownshire and Kirkcudbrightshire, bounded on the West and South by the sea, on the East by the River Nith, and on the North by the rugged Galloway Hills. The name Galloway is derived from the Gaelic *i nGall Gaidhealaib* (amongst the *Gall Gaidheil*). *Gall Gaidheil* means *Stranger-Gaidheil* and originally referred to Middle Age Galloway's mixed Scandinavian and Gaelic population.

Brythonic-speaking Celts were the first known inhabitants of Galloway. Their kingdom was dominant until the 7th Century, when Galloway became a kingdom of the Anglo-Saxons, who were supplanted by Norse-Gaels (*Gall-Ghàidheal*) from the 9th to the 11th Centuries. That accompanied Norse domination of the Irish Sea and settlement in the Isle of Mann and in Cumbria just South of Galloway. Galwegian Gaelic's last recognized speaker was Margaret McMurray (d. 1760), of Carrick (outside modern Galloway).[785]

Gaul. An Iron Age Western European area inhabited by Celtic tribes. It encompassed present day France, Luxembourg, Belgium, most of Switzerland, Northern Italy, and the parts of the Netherlands and Germany on the west bank of the Rhine.[786]

Gray's Inn. One of London's Four Inns of Court. To become a barrister and practice law in England and Wales, it is necessary to be a member of one of those four inns.

Habeas Corpus. A writ requiring an arrested person to be brought before a judge or court to show either legitimate grounds for detention or secure release.

Haplogroup. A group sharing the same patrilineal (male, Y Chromosome) or matrilineal (male or female, mitochondrial) ancestry.[787] Also defined as the SNP/unique-event polymorphism (UEP) mutations that represent the clade to which a collection of particular human haplotypes belong. A haplogroup is a group of similar haplotypes that share a common ancestor with a specific SNP.

Haploid. Having one set of chromosomes. (e.g., the Y Chromosome is haploid, and the non-sex-determining (somatic) chromosomes (autosomes) are diploid (paired, with one set from each parent.)[788]

Haplotype (Haploid Genotype). A group of alleles inherited together from one parent; or a specific DNA sequence likely to be inherited intact for many generations; or a set of linked single-nucleotide polymorphism (SNP) alleles that tend to always occur together (i.e., are associated statistically); or an individual collection of specific mutations within a given genetic segment.

Hebrides. An archipelago off Scotland's West Coast. Its culture has been strongly affected by the occupying/conquering Celts, Norse, and English. Lewis and Harris, the largest Outer

Hebridean Island, has been politically divided into the land-linked Isles of Lewis and Harris. There are 15 inhabited Outer Hebridean Islands, 36 inhabited Inner Hebridean Islands (including Iona and Skye), and a host of uninhabited ones.[789]

Hominid. A bipedal primate mammal.

Hominim. The subset of Hominids that includes modern humans and their ancestral and closely related forms.

Indigenous. Historic (native-born) occupiers, as distinct from recent immigrants.

Innse Gall. Gaelic term for the Hebrides.[790] It connotes *islands of the foreigners*—the Vikings who imposed their culture and language on the Hebrides.

Ireland. The second largest of the British Isles, located West of and across the North Channel, Irish Sea, and St. George's Channel from Britain. Politically, Ireland is divided between the Republic of Ireland (officially named Ireland), which covers five-sixths of the island, and Northern Ireland, which is part of the United Kingdom.[791]

Ireland-Scotland Distance. Ireland and Scotland are geographically closest along the North Channel (where the currents are fast and unpredictable). One estimate of the shortest distance between Scotland (in Argyll) and Ireland (in Ulster's former County Antrim) is ~12.5 miles (~10.9 nautical miles).[792] Another is the (twice-accomplished solo) *Dál Riata Channel Swim* distance from Scotland's Mull of Kintyre (the Southwest end of the Kintyre Peninsula) to Ireland's Torr Head, Ballycastle, East Antrim of 10.5 miles (17 km).[793] Torr Head and the Mull of Kintyre are visible from each other on a clear day. {The migrations between Ireland and Scotland seem likely to have traveled between an Antrim seaport (Larne?) and a protected Scottish landing near but not in the North Channel—perhaps the former Cairnryan ferry landing or the present Stranyayer one.}

Iron Age. Ironworking began in Europe in the late 11th Century BC, and spread North and West for 500 years. In the British Isles, the Iron Age lasted from 800 BC to 100 AD.[794] (Ironworking continues, but the Iron Age ended when prehistory did.)

Jutes. A Germanic people who, with the Angles and Saxons, invaded Britain in the 5th Century. The Jutes have no recorded history on the European continent, but there is evidence of their being from Scandinavia (probably Jutland, the peninsular part of Denmark extending from the German part of that peninsula)—with the Jutes who stayed home having been absorbed by the Danes. According to St. Bede, the Jutes settled in Kent, the Isle of Wight, and parts of Hampshire. The social structure of Kent shows its settlers to have been a different "race" than their neighbors. Archaeological evidence confirms that the Isle of Wight and Kent were settled by the same people, and place-names confirm the Jutes' presence in Hampshire.[795]

KYA. Thousands of years ago.

KYO. Thousands of years old.

Leinster. The Eastern-Central of Ireland's four Provinces, Leinster contains 12 Counties: Carlow, Dublin, Kildare, Kilkenny, Laois, Longford, Louth, Meath, Offaly, Westmeath, Wexford and Wicklow.[796]

Manumission. The formal granting of freedom to a Slave.

Matrilineal. The line of descent from one's Mother and her's, etc.

Middle Ages (Medieval Period). The 5th to 15th Century, from the fall of the Western Roman Empire and merging into the Renaissance and Age of Discovery.[797]

Munster. The South-Southwestern of Ireland's four Provinces, Munster contains six Counties: Claire, Cork, Kerry, Limerick, Tipperary, and Waterford.[798]

MYA. Millions of years ago.

MYO. Millions of years old.

Native. A person is native to his or her birthplace. A species is native to its place of origin. (Mankind, to the best of current knowledge, is native to Africa.)

Normans. Descendants of the barbaric pagan Northmen who settled in Normandy, gave up sea roving, and became Christians. Known historically as almost foolhardy warriors of extreme courage, cunning, and brutality—and able to defeat much larger forces.

Patrilineal. The line of Descent from Fathers to Sons.

Pence. The plural of penny sterling or penny (symbol: p). The old penny sterling was 1/240 pound; there are 100p in the modern UK pound.[799]

Picts. Ancient indigenous Celtic-speaking tribes of Northeastern Scotland. By about the 11th Century, the Picts had lost their separate identity and become Scots.

Pleistocene Era. (the Ice age) The ~2.6 MYA to ~11.7 KYA glaciation era.

Republic of Ireland. The nation composed of 26 of the 32 counties in Ireland. When Northern Ireland was established as a nation of six of Ulster's nine counties, the other three Ulster counties (Cavan, Donegal, and Monaghan) became part of the Republic.

Scots. A synonym for Scottish.

Statutes of Iona. Laws passed in Scotland in 1609. They required child education in Lowland (Protestant) and Protestant ministers in Highland parishes; and prohibited extorting free quarters and provisions or protecting fugitives; outlawed beggars and bearers of traditional culture, etc.

UK. (United Kingdom.) England, Scotland, Wales and Northern Ireland.

Ulster. The Northernmost of Ireland's four Provinces. Pre-Northern Ireland Ulster contained nine Counties: Antrim, Armagh, Cavan, Donegal, Down, Fermanagh, Londonderry, Monaghan, and Tyrone.[800]

Younger Dryas. A 12.9-11.7 KYA return to glacial conditions that dropped England's annual temperature to 5°C (27°F), making most of the British Isles uninhabitable.

Endnotes

1.   McCabe, Ebe Chandler, Jr. (2011), *Celtic Warrior Descendants*, iUniverse, Bloomington, IN. {ISBN: 978-1-4502-9364-8 (pbk)}.

2.   McCabe, Vernon W., Jr. (2003), *Descendants of John McCabe (1727-1800) of Sussex County, Delaware, Edition III* (a self-published book available from the author at 9830 Keyser Point Road, Ocean City, MD 21842)

3.   https://www.brainyquote.com/authors/e-l-doctorow-quotes [accesed 6/22/2021]

4.   McCabe, Vernon, *Descendants of John McCabe*, pxv-xviii

5.   https://en.wikipedia.org/wiki/Province_of_Maryland#:~:text=Founding%20charter,-Henrietta%20Maria%2C%20the&text=Upon%20Baltimore's%20death%20in%201632,to%20the%202nd%20Baron%20Baltimore. [accessed 6/5/2020]

6.   https://en.wikipedia.org/wiki/Selbyville,_Delaware [accessed 6/30/2018]. Its references include: https://geonames.usgs.gov/apex/f?p=gnispq:3:::NO::P3_FID:214630; and Alotta, Robert I. *Signposts and Settlers: The History of Place Names in the Middle Atlantic States,* Bonus Books, Chicago, 12/31/1992.

7.   https://archives.delaware.gov/historical-markers-map/transpeninsular-line/ [accessed 6/24/2021]

8.   https://en.wikipedia.org/wiki/Penn%E2%80%93Calvert_boundary_dispute [accessed 10/5/2019]

9.   Worcester Co., MD Estate of John Aydelott Hudson, Inventory, 27 Feb 1752. John McCabe signed, as next of kin, that Inventory. {Vern Skinner: Abstracts of Inventories of Prerogative Court (MD): 1751-1756:15; & Account in the same Estate by Arthur Leatherberry, June 1763, stating that Mary McCabe was named in the distribution list to John Aydelott Hudson's siblings; John Aydelott Hudson had 3 sisters Mary, Ester, and Rachel} [Marjorie Adams 9/13/2019 7:05 PM email]

10.   https://en.wikipedia.org/wiki/Mason%E2%80%93Dixon_line [accessed 10/5/2019]

11.   https://en.wikipedia.org/wiki/Battle_of_Trenton [accessed 11/18/2019]

12.   McCabe, Ebe, *Celtic Warrior Descendants*, p32

13.   https://www.findagrave.com/cemetery/104408/memorial-search?firstName+&lastName=McCabe [accessed 1/7/2019]

14.   https://revolutionarywar.us/continental-army/delaware/ [accessed 10/5/2019]

15.   https://en.wikipedia.org/wiki/New_York_and_New_Jersey_campaign [accessed 10/5/2019]

16.   https://www.georgiaencyclopedia.org/articles/history-archaeology/nathanael-greene-1742-1786 [accessed 10/5/2019]

17.   Hancock, Harold B. (1976), *The History of Sussex County, Delaware* (self-published), p.25

18.   McCabe, Ebe, *Celtic Warrior Descendants*, p 1-2

19.   https://en.wikipedia.org/wiki/Baltimore_Hundred [accessed 7/2/2108]

20 https://en.wikipedia.org/wiki/Delaware#Counties [accessed 10/4/2019]

21 Ken Mamarella 1/13/2015 Article based on William H. William's *Delmarva's Chicken Industry, 75 Years of Progress,* available at https://www.delawareonline.com/story/life/2015/01/13/shipping-mistake-led-delmarva-chicken-industry/21718231/ [accessed 12/7/2018]

22 McCabe, Vernon, Paper presented at the August 2019 McCabe Family Reunion in Selbyville, Delaware.

23 https://en.wikipedia.org/wiki/Selbyville,_Delaware [accessed 6/30/2018]. Its references include: https://geonames.usgs.gov/apex/f?p=gnispq:3:::NO::P3_FID:214630; and Alotta, obert . *Signposts and Settlers: The History of Place Names in the Middle Atlantic Statesl,* Bonus Books, Chicago, 12/31/1992.

24 https://www.google.com/maps/place/Selbyville,+DE+19975/@38.4607475,-75.2195271,17z/data=!4m5!3m4!1s0x89b8c18456a91b8b:0x957b47bfd50f7ea6!8m2!3d38.4603917!4d-75.2207437 [accessed 10/4/209]

25 https://www.ducksters.com/history/american_revolution/life_as_a_revolutionary_war_soldier.php [accessed 10/6/2018]

26 https://militaryhistorynow.com/2014/07/04/americas-first-soldiers-12-amazing-facts-about-the-continental-army/ [accessed 10/6/2018]

27 McCabe, Vernon, *Descendants of John McCabe,* p xv-xvi, 7/9/2018 email from Vernon McCabe to Ebe McCabe

28 http://www.nationalarchives.gov.uk/currency-converter/#currency-result [accessed 10/7/2018]

29 https://homestead-honey.com/2014/12/22/afford-to-buy-a-cow/ [accessed 10/7/2018]

30 http://thewildgeese.irish/profiles/blogs/not-all-celts-are-gaels. Posted by Bit Devine 8/272013

31 https://www.genguide.co.uk/source/willstestaments-and-inheritance-scotland/70/ [accessed 6/28/2018]

32 https://en.wikipedia.org/wiki/Gavelkind_in_Ireland [accessed 6/28/2018]

33 https://en.wikipedia.org/wiki/Polyandry [accessed 6/28/2018]

34 https://www.celtic-weddingrings.com/celtic-mythology/5-waves-of-invasion-irish-mythology [accessed 6/23/2018]

35 https://en.wikipedia.org/wiki/Niall_of_the_Nine_Hostages [accessed 6/23/2018]

36 http://www.surnamedb.com/Surname/Hudson [accessed 7/29/2018]

37 https://en.wikipedia.org/wiki/Woodcroft_Castle [accessed 7/30/2018]

38 http://worcestermuseums.org/st-martins-episcopal-church.php [accessed 8/20/2018]

39 https://en.wikipedia.org/wiki/St._Peter%27s_Episcopal_Church_(Lewes,_Delaware) [accessed 1/8/2019]

40 https://en.wikipedia.org/wiki/Episcopal_Diocese_of_Delaware [accessed 1/8/2019]

41 https://en.wikipedia.org/wiki/Methodist_Episcopal_Church#Background_(1766%E2%80%931783) [accessed 11/20/2018]

42 https://en.wikipedia.org/wiki/Arthur [accessed 1/4/2019]

43 http://www.babynamewizard.com/baby-name/girl/alexa [accessed 1/4/2019]

44 https://www.wikitree.com/ [accessed 5/13/2019]

45 Year book of the Holland Society of New-York, Holland Society of New York., New York, 1887, p46

46 U.S., Dutch Reformed Church Records in Selected States, 1639-2000 [microfilm image on-line]. Ancestry.com Operations, Inc., 2014. Original data: Dutch Reformed Church Records from New York and New Jersey. Holland Society of New York, New York. Baptismal Records contained in

v1 of the Church Books of the German Lutheran Congregation at New York (aka Lutheran, Vol I, Book 85, pp.19 & 21.

47   Miller file, Putnam Co. (NY) Historian's Office.

48   Will of Edward McCabe written 12 Sept 1758, proved 16 Sept 1759, executor and "heir" was a John Waller, inn holder of New York. Abstracts of New Jersey Wills, 1730-1750. Middlesex County. (Inasmuch as the known family of Lydia (Winter) McCabe's husband Edward are not specified in this will, it could be a different Edward McCabe's will.)

49   The New York Genealogical and Biographical Record (quarterly-1906) - Extracts; New York, New York Genealogical and Biographical Society, p 285 at Ancestry.com [database on-line]. Ancestry. com Operations Inc, 2004.

50   https://www.wikitree.com/wiki/McCabe-1231 [accessed 5/18/2019]

51   https://www.wikitree.com/wiki/Winter-2307 [accessed 5/18/2019]

52   McCabe, Ebe, *Celtic Warrior Descendants*, p29

53   https://www.wikitree.com/wiki/McCabe-1638 [accessed 5/20/2019]

54   https://www.wikitree.com/wiki/McCabe-1639 [accessed 5/20/2019]

55   https://www.wikitree.com/wiki/McCaby-1 [accessed 5/20/2019]

56   https://www.wikitree.com/wiki/McCabe-1306 [accessed 5/20/2019]

57   McCabe, Vernon, *Descendants of John McCabe*

58   https://www.wikitree.com/wiki/Winter-243. [accessed 5/18/2019]

59   https://www.google.com/search?q=Port+Richmond%2C+Staten+Island&oq=Port+Richmond %2C+Staten+Island&aqs=chrome..69i57j0l5.8536j0j7&sourceid=chrome&ie=UTF-8 [accessed 5/23/2019]

60   https://www.wikitree.com/wiki/Winter-243 [accessed 5/24/2019]

61   https://www.wikitree.com/wiki/DePue-9 [accessed 5/24/2019]

62   https://www.houseofnames.com/Depue-family-crest [accessed 5/25/2019]

63   https://www.wikitree.com/wiki/Depuy-30 [accessed 5/24/2019]

64   https://www.wikitree.com/wiki/De_Vos-2 [accessed 5/21/2019]

65   https://www.wikitree.com/wiki/Du_Puy-1 [accessed 5/24/2019]

66   https://www.wikitree.com/wiki/UNKNOWN-128890 [accessed 5/25/2019]

67   https://www.wikitree.com/wiki/Du_Puy-2 [accessed 5/24/2019]

68   https://www.wikitree.com/wiki/Sanguin-2 [accessed 5/23/2019]

69   https://www.wikitree.com/wiki/De_Thou-1 [accessed 5/23/2019]

70   https://www.wikitree.com/wiki/Sanguin-2 [accessed 5/24/2019]

71   https://www.wikitree.com/wiki/De_Thou-1 [accessed 5/24/2019]

72   https://www.wikitree.com/wiki/Du_Puy-3 [accessed 5/24/2019]

73   https://www.wikitree.com/wiki/De_Jouven-1 [accessed 5/24/2019]

74   https://www.wikitree.com/wiki/Du_Puy-4 [accessed 5/24/2019]

75   https://www.wikitree.com/wiki/Pelissier-1 [accessed 5/24/2019]

76   https://www.wikitree.com/wiki/Dupuy-95 [accessed 5/24/2019]

77   https://www.wikitree.com/wiki/De_Claveyson-1 [accessed 5/24/2019

78   https://www.wikitree.com/wiki/De_Claveyson-2 [accessed 5/24/2019]

79   https://www.wikitree.com/wiki/Dupuy-96 [accessed 5/19/2019]

80   https://www.wikitree.com/wiki/De_Bellecombe-1 [accessed 5/23/2019]

81   https://www.wikitree.com/wiki/Astraud-1 [accessed 5/24/2019]

82   https://www.wikitree.com/wiki/Dupuy-97 [accessed 5/23/2019]

83   https://www.wikitree.com/wiki/De_Bellecombe-1 [accessed 5/24/2019]

84   https://www.wikitree.com/wiki/Puy-14 [accessed 5/23/2019]

85   https://www.wikitree.com/wiki/Hauteville-13 [accessed 5/24/2019]

86   https://www.wikitree.com/wiki/Hauteville-28 [accessed 5/24/2019]

87   https://www.wikitree.com/wiki/Puy-19 [accessed 5/23/2019]

88   https://www.wikitree.com/wiki/Bellecombe-1 [accessed 5/24/2019]

89   https://www.wikitree.com/wiki/Dupuy-100 [accessed 5/23/2019]

90   https://www.wikitree.com/wiki/Roland-533 [accessed 5/24/2019]

91   https://www.wikitree.com/wiki/De_Roland-2 [accessed 5/24/2019]

92   https://www.wikitree.com/wiki/Dupuy-101 [accessed 5/23/2019]

93   https://www.wikitree.com/wiki/Alleman-3 [accessed 5/24/2019]

94   https://www.wikitree.com/wiki/Alleman-2 [accessed 5/24/2019]

95   https://www.wikitree.com/wiki/Dupuy-102 [accessed 5/24/2019]

96   https://www.wikitree.com/wiki/Artaud-1 [accessed 5/24/2019]

97   https://www.wikitree.com/wiki/Dupuy-103 [accessed 5/23/2019]

98   https://www.wikitree.com/wiki/Unknown-7892 [accessed 5/24/2019]

99   https://www.wikitree.com/wiki/Dupuy-104 [accessed 5/23/2019]

100 https://www.wikitree.com/wiki/De_Moiran-1 [accessed 5/24/2019]

101 https://www.wikitree.com/wiki/De_Moiran-1 [accessed 5/24/2019]

102 https://www.wikitree.com/wiki/Dupuy-105 [accessed 5/23/2019]

103 https://www.wikitree.com/wiki/Ademar-1 [accessed 5/24/2019]

104 https://www.wikitree.com/wiki/Adhemar-1 [accessed 5/24/2019]

105 https://www.wikitree.com/wiki/De_Poisieu-1 [accessed 5/23/2019]

106 https://www.wikitree.com/wiki/Dupuy-106 [accessed 5/23/2019]

107 http://www.geneagraphie.com/getperson.php?personID=I161034&tree=1 [accessed 5/25/2019]

108 ibid

109 https://www.wikitree.com/wiki/De_Podio-1 [accessed 5/23/2019]

110 https://www.houseofnames.com/de+Podio-family-crest [accessed 5/25/2019]

111 http://www.emmigration.info/dutch-immigration-to-america.htm [accessed 10/15/2018]

112 https://en.wikipedia.org/wiki/New_Netherland [accessed 10/15/2018]

113 https://www.history.com/news/the-dutch-surrender-new-netherland-350-years-ago [accessed 3/29/2019]

114 https://www.mrnussbaum.com/history-2-2/delcolony/ [accessed 11/12/2018]

115 https://www.history.com/topics/immigration/u-s-immigration-before-1965 [accessed 10/15/2018]

116 http://mdroots.thinkport.org/library/georgecalvert.asp [accessed 6/30/2018]

117 https://en.wikipedia.org/wiki/Cecil_Calvert,_2nd_Baron_Baltimore [accessed 8/27/2018]

118 https://www.history.com/this-day-in-history/the-settlement-of-maryland [accessed 6/30/2018]

119 https://en.wikipedia.org/wiki/Richard_Ingle [accessed 8/26/2018]

120 https://www.catholic.com/index.php/magazine/print-edition/americas-catholic-colony [accessed 6/30/2018]

121 https://en.wikipedia.org/wiki/Province_of_Maryland#With_Pennsylvania [accessed 8/26/2018]

122 https://en.wikipedia.org/wiki/List_of_counties_in_Delaware#References [accessed 2/6/2019]

123 Gerken, Sandie, (2018), *Storied Sussex*, Layman Enterprises, Ocean View, DE, p.35-36

124 https://en.wikipedia.org/wiki/Penn–Calvert_boundary_dispute#The_1732_Agreement [accessed 11/04/2018]

125 https://sussexcountyde.gov/history [accessed 6/19/2018]

126 https://classroom.synonym.com/catholic-vs-protestant-religions-colonial-times-7288.html [accessed 6/30/2018]

127 http://www.stedmond.org/parish-history [accessed 6/28/2018]

128 https://en.wikipedia.org/wiki/Sussex_County,_Delaware#2010_census [accessed 6/28/2018]

129 https://en.wikipedia.org/wiki/Sussex_County,_Delaware#Cities [accessed 7/1/2018]

130 https://en.wikipedia.org/wiki/Baltimore_Hundred [accessed 7/2/2108]

131 http://www.thecatholicdirectory.com/directory.cfm?fuseaction=search_directory&country=US&state=DE&county=SUSSEX [accessed 6/28/2018]

132 https://en.wikipedia.org/wiki/Penn%E2%80%93Calvert_boundary_dispute [accessed 11/06/2018]

133 https://observer.com/2017/07/soldiers-militia-american-revolution/ [accessed 10/15/2018]

134 https://books.google.com/books?id=aVeAAQAAQBAJ&pg=PA364&lpg=PA364&dq=Colonial+Sussex+County,+Delaware%27s+Country+and+Court+parties&source=bl&ots=aV0X1kX8Re&sig=ACfU3U0IZB4CECEQaXjFtc8SAgJjeR6UhA&hl=en&sa=X&ved=2ahUKEwii2JHH9-vpAhUvmXIEHZN8BekQ6AEwAHoECAcQAQ#v=onepage&q=Colonial%20Sussex%20County%2C%20Delaware's%20Country%20and%20Court%20parties&f=false [accessed 6/5/2020]

135 Purcell, Richard J, *Irish Settlers in Early Delaware,* https://journals.psu.edu/phj/article/viewFile/21669/21438 [accessed 9/25/2018]

136 https://en.wikipedia.org/wiki/Loyalist_(American_Revolution) [accessed 11/04/2018]

137 https://en.wikipedia.org/wiki/Origins_of_the_War_of_1812 [accessed 11/04/2018]

138 https://en.wikipedia.org/wiki/Kiliaen_van_Rensselaer_(merchant) [accessed 2/10/2019]

139 https://vocwreckssulawesi.wordpress.com/walvis/ [accessed 2/10/2019]

140 https://www.google.com/maps/place/Hoornkill+Ave,+Lewes,+DE+19958/@38.78019,-75.1594289,17z/data=!3m1!4b1!4m5!3m4!1s0x89b8b9ff98fc47af:0x91e8be1722380f67!8m2!3d38.7801859!4d-75.1572402 [accessed 9/26/2019]

141 John Clark Ridpath, *The New Complete History of the United States of America*, (12 Volumes), Vol II, Ch XIV, p566. Eliot Madison Co: The Jones Brothers Publishing Company, Chicago, Cincinnati, 2012 https://books.google.com/books?id=2gREAQAAMAAJ&pg=PA566&lpg=PA566&dq=Pieter+Heyes&source=bl&ots=BzYfLks9jV&sig=ACfU3U19SbpMyk0Sq6bk2xlkr9H4Q4XhMA&hl=en&sa=X&ved=2ahUKEwim38XEg6rgAhVNqIkKHY50DLMQ6AEwBHoECAQQAQ#v=onepage&q&f=false [accessed 2/7/2019]

142 https://books.google.com/books?id=9wd5AAAAMAAJ&pg=PA32&lpg=PA32&dq=Captain+Peter+Heyes...sailed+from+Texel,+Holland...&source=bl&ots=qSMIHKzXdK&sig=ACfU3U1beq0uG62vpy9j8JvmRgZLR1g_zg&hl=en&sa=X&ved=2ahUKEwjKxs7Ly6rgAhXhuFkKHTBIDs8Q6AEwA3oECAcQAQ#v=onepage&q=Captain%20Peter%20Heyes...sailed%20from%20Texel%2C%20Holland...&f=false {accessed 2/7/2019}

143 Richard Solomon, *Sexual Practice and Fantasy in Colonial* America, Indiana University Journal of Undergraduate Research, Vol III, 2017, p 27-28. 23364-Article%20Text-55389-2-10-20180218%20(1).pdf [accessed 9/27/2019]

144 https://capacitybuilders.info/prevention/sex-marriage-views.php [accessed 2/11/2019]

145 Hancock, Harold, *The History of Sussex County, Delaware*, p 25-26, 37 *istory of Sussex County, Delaware*

146 McCabe, Ebe Chandler, Jr. (2011), *Celtic Warrior Descendants, Appendix 1*

147 Cannan, Fergus, *Gallowglass, 1250-1600*, Osprey Publishing (2010), Great Britain & New York, NY, p4

148 http://ebooks.grsu.by/british_society/2-the-highlands-and-the-lowlands-cultural-differences.htm

149 http://ebooks.grsu.by/british_society/2-the-highlands-and-the-lowlands-cultural-differences.htm [accessed 11/11/2018]

150 https://www.quora.com/What-do-Lowlands-Scots-and-Highlands-Scots-think-of-each-other, [A 12/07/2017 statement by Peter Mirtitish, and another by Graham Niven on o7/16/2017, both accessed 11/11/2018]

151 151 http://www.ulsterscotssociety.com/about.html [accessed 11/04/2018]

152 http://www.askaboutireland.ie/learning-zone/secondary-students/history/tudor-ireland/the-plantation-of-munster/ [accessed 9/26/2021]

153 https://en.wikipedia.org/wiki/John_Knox [accessed 11/18/2018]

154 https://www.britannica.com/biography/Anne-queen-of-Great-Britain-and-Ireland [accessed 11/18/2018]

155 https://en.wikipedia.org/wiki/Penal_Laws_(Ireland) [accessed 12/5/2018]

156 Paterson, Raymond Campbell, *The Scots-Irish: The thirteenth Tribe* https://electricscotland.com/books/paterson/scots_irish.htm [accessed 12/2/2018]

157 https://www.newenglandhistoricalsociety.com/shattuck-and-the-devil-try-to-stop-quaker-persecution-in-new-england/ [accessed 10/12/2020]

158 https://www.newenglandhistoricalsociety.com/1662-robert-pike-halts-quaker-persecution-massachusetts/#:~:text=In%201661%2C%20the%20King%20of,stop%20executing%20and%20imprisoning%20Quakers.&text=Active%20persecution%20of%20the%20Quakers,had%20fled%20to%20New%20Hampshire.[accessed 10/12/2020]

159 https://www.dover.nh.gov/government/city-operations/library/history/the-whipping-of-the-quaker-women.html [accessed 10/12/2020]

160 https://en.wikipedia.org/wiki/Salem_witch_trials#Reversals_of_attainder_and_compensation_to_the_survivors_and_their_families [accessed 1/27/2021]

161 https://www.irishcentral.com/roots/history/irish-native-last-witch-hanged-boston [accessed 1/27/2021]

162 https://en.wikipedia.org/wiki/Cotton_Mather [accessed 1/27/2021]

163 https://en.wikipedia.org/wiki/Salem_witch_trials [accessed 1/27/2021]

164 https://salemwitchmuseum.com/2013/02/15/spectral-evidence/ [accessed 1/29/2021]

165 https://www.thoughtco.com/salem-witch-trials-timeline-3530778 [accessed 1/29/2021]

166 https://en.wikipedia.org/wiki/Abigail_Faulkner#Aftermath_and_exoneration [accessed 1/29/2021]

167 Lewis, Jone Johnson. "Salem Witch Trials Timeline." ThoughtCo, Jan. 7, 2021: thoughtco.com/salem-witch-trials-timeline-3530778. [accessed 1/30/2021]

168 https://www.history.com/topics/american-revolution/boston-massacre [accessed 7/9/2020]

169 https://www.historyplace.com/unitedstates/revolution/rev-prel.htm [accessed 7/21/2020]

170 https://www.history.com/news/george-washington-french-indian-war-jumonville [accessed 7/26/2020]

171   https://en.wikipedia.org/wiki/Battle_of_Fort_Necessity [accessed 7/26/2020]

172   https://www.history.com/news/george-washington-french-indian-war-jumonville   [accessed 7/26/2020]

173   https://en.wikipedia.org/wiki/Joshua_Fry [accessed 8/1/2020]

174   https://www.phrases.org.uk/meanings/keep-your-powder-dry.html [accessed 8/11/2020]

175   https://en.wikipedia.org/wiki/Battle_of_Fort_Necessity [accessed 7/30/2020]

176   https://en.wikipedia.org/wiki/Braddock_Expedition [accessed 7/30/2020]

177   https://en.wikipedia.org/wiki/Action_of_8_June_1755 [accessed 8/1/2020]

178   https://en.wikipedia.org/wiki/Braddock_Expedition [accessed 7/30/2020]

179   https://www.ancient.eu/Boudicca/ [accessed 8/3/2020]

180   https://en.wikipedia.org/wiki/Forbes_Expedition [accessed 8/1/2020]

181   https://en.wikipedia.org/wiki/Battle_of_Fort_Duquesne [accessed 8/3/2020]

182   https://en.wikipedia.org/wiki/Battle_of_Fort_Ligonier [accessed 8/3/2020]

183   https://en.wikipedia.org/wiki/Treaty_of_Easton [accessed 8/1/2020]

184   https://en.wikipedia.org/wiki/Battle_of_Fort_Duquesne [accessed 8/3/2020]

185   https://en.wikipedia.org/wiki/Forbes_Expedition [accessed 8/1/2020]

186   https://www.uswars.net/pontiacs-rebellion/#:rebellion/#:~:text=Pontiac's%20Rebellion%20was%20a%20Native,than%20that%20of%20the%20English [accessed 7/22/2020]

187   https://en.wikipedia.org/wiki/Battle_of_Bloody_Run#:~:text=The%20Battle%20of%20Bloody%20Run,surprise%20attack%20on%20Pontiac's%20encampment. [accessed 7/21/2020]

188   https://en.wikipedia.org/wiki/Pontiac%27s_War#Amherst's_policies [accessed 2/7/2021]

189   https://en.wikipedia.org/wiki/Eastern_Continental_Divide [accessed 9/1/2020]

190   https://www.history.com/topics/native-american-history/1763-proclamation-of   [accessed 7/21/2020]

191   https://www.history.com/topics/american-revolution/stamp-act [accessed 11/5/2020]

192   https://www.ushistory.org/declaration/related/sons.html#:~:text=In%20Boston%20in%20early%20summer,as%20the%20Sons%20of%20Liberty. [accessed 11/5/2020]

193   https://www.history.com/topics/american-revolution/samuel-adams#section_6   [accessed 7/7/2020]

194   https://www.history.com/news/the-stamp-act-riots-250-years-ago [accessed 11/5/2020]

195   https://en.wikipedia.org/wiki/Declaratory_Act [accessed 11/5/2020]

196   https://www.history.com/topics/american-revolution/townshend-acts [accessed 11/5/2020]

197   https://www.ushistory.org/declaration/signers/hancock.html [accessed 7/12/2020]

198   https://alphahistory.com/americanrevolution/seizure-of-liberty/ [accessed 7/12/2020]

199   https://en.wikipedia.org/wiki/John_Hancock [accessed 7/12/2020]

200   https://en.wikipedia.org/wiki/HMS_Liberty_(1768) [accessed 7/11/2020]

201   https://en.wikipedia.org/wiki/Christopher_Seider#:~:text=Seider%20was%20born%20in%201758,shop%20of%20Loyalist%20Theophilus%20Lillie. [accessed 7/7/2020]

202   http://www.bostonmassacre.net/players/Samuel-Maverick.htm [accessed 7/6/2020]

203   https://en.wikipedia.org/wiki/Kilroy_was_here#In_popular_culture [accessed 7/7/2020]

204   http://www.bostonmassacre.net/players/Patrick-Carr.htm [accessed 7/7/2020]

205   https://www.history.com/topics/american-revolution/american-revolution-history   [accessed 7/7/2020]

206 https://www.history.com/topics/american-revolution/boston-massacre [accessed 7/9/2020]

207 https://www.brainyquote.com/quotes/robert_kennedy_745981?src=t_mob [accessed 7/19/2020]

208 https://en.wikipedia.org/wiki/Demagogue#The_enduring_character_of_demagogues [accessed 7/19/2020]

209 https://www.history.com/topics/american-revolution/townshend-acts#:~:text=All%20of%20 the%20Townshend%20Acts,of%20tea%20in%20Boston%20Harbor.[accessed 10/30/2020]

210 https://en.wikipedia.org/wiki/Gaspee_Affair [accessed 7/14/2020]

211 http://www.gaspee.org/WilliamDudingston.htm [accessed 7/14/2020]

212 https://www.britannica.com/event/Boston-Tea-Party [accessed 7/15/2020]

213 http://www.john-hancock-heritage.com/boston-massacre-boston-tea-party/ [accessed 7/15/2020]

214 https://en.wikipedia.org/wiki/Boston_Tea_Party#Standoff_in_Boston [accessed 7/15/2020]

215 https://www.bostonteapartyship.com/john-adams-boston-tea-party [accessed 7/15/2020]

216 https://www.mentalfloss.com/article/625061/boston-tea-party-facts [accessed 7/15/2020]

217 https://www.varsitytutors.com/earlyamerica/early-america-review/volume-17/english-lcolonial-policy#.:~:text=Being%20enacted%20on%20May%2020,were%20appointed%20by%20the%20 King. [accessed 7/19/2020]

218 ibid

219 ibid

220 https://www.britannica.com/event/Intolerable-Acts [accessed 7/19/2020]

221 http://www.ouramericanrevolution.org/index.cfm/page/view/m0072 [accessed 7/19/2020]

222 https://en.wikipedia.org/wiki/First_Continental_Congress#Declaration_and_Resolves [accessed 7/22/2020]

223 https://poets.org/poem/paul-reveres-ride [accessed 7/23/2020]

224 https://en.wikipedia.org/wiki/Concord_Hymn [accessed 7/22/2020]

225 https://www.history.com/topics/american-revolution/battles-of-lexington-and-concord [accessed 7/22/2020]

226 https://www.americanrevolutioninstitute.org/exhibition/a-revolution-in-arms/ [accessed 9/23/2020]

227 https://en.wikipedia.org/wiki/Siege_of_Boston#:~:text=The%20Siege%20of%20Boston%20 (April,city%20of%20Boston%2C%20Massachusetts%20Bay. [accessed 8/12/2020]

228 https://en.wikipedia.org/wiki/Israel_Putnam [accessed 7/24/2020]

229 https://en.wikipedia.org/wiki/Second_Continental_Congress [accessed 11/20/2020]

230 https://www.encyclopedia.com/history/encyclopedias-almanacs-transcripts-and-maps/ continental-army-social-history [accessed 2/7/2021]

231 http://www.loc.gov/teachers/classroommaterials/presentationsandactivities/presentations/ timeline/amrev/contarmy/accepts.html#:~:text=On%20June%2015%2C%201775%2C%20 the,the%20defence%20of%20American%20liberty.[accessed 8/12/2020]

232 https://ivn.us/2016/11/28/modern-lessons-george-washingtons-expense-accounts [accessed 5/14/2021]

233 ccountingin.com/accounting-historians-journal/volume-17-number-1/george-washingtons-expense-account/ [accessed 5/12/2021

234 https://ivn.us/2016/11/28/modern-lessons-george-washingtons-expense-accounts [accessed 5/12/2021]

235 https://www.history.com/topics/american-revolution/battle-of-bunker-hill [accessed 9/26/2021]

236 https://en.wikiquote.org/wiki/William_Prescott [accessed 7/24/2020]

237 https://en.wikipedia.org/wiki/Battle_of_Bunker_Hill#:~:text=The%20Battle%20of%20Bunker%20 Hill%20was%20fought%20on%20June%2017,peripherally%20involved%20in%20the%20battle. [accessed 2/13/2021]

238 http://www.revolutionaryday.com/usroute4/whitehall/default.htm [accessed 2/15/2021]

239 https://www.history.com/topics/american-revolution/capture-of-fort-ticonderoga [accessed 9/3/2020]; https://en.wikipedia.org/wiki/Capture_of_Fort_Ticonderoga [accessed 2/14/2021] https://en.wikipedia.org/wiki/Capture_of_Fort_Ticonderoga#Crown_Point_and_the_raid_on_ Fort_Saint-Jean [accessed 2/15/2021]

240 https://en.wikipedia.org/wiki/Ethan_Allen#Raids_on_St._John [accessed 9/26/2021]

241 https://www.battlefields.org/learn/biographies/philip-schuyler#:~:text=On%20June%20 19%2C%201775%2C%20he,deferred%20to%20General%20Richard%20Montgomery.[accessed 2/14/2021]

242 https://en.wikipedia.org/wiki/Battle_of_Longue-Pointe [accessed 2/15/2021]

243 https://en.wikipedia.org/wiki/Invasion_of_Quebec_(1775) [accessed 2/15/2021]

244 https://en.wikipedia.org/wiki/Benedict_Arnold#Quebec_Expedition [accessed 10/26/2020]

245 https://en.wikipedia.org/wiki/Invasion_of_Quebec_(1775) [accessed 2/15/2021]

246 https://www.history.com/news/9-things-you-may-not-know-about-benedict-arnold#:~:text=6.,the%20surrender%20of%20West%20Point. [accessed 9/3/2020]

247 https://en.wikipedia.org/wiki/Burning_of_Norfolk#Continental_Army_occupation_of_Norfolk [accessed 9/10/2020]

248 https://en.wikipedia.org/wiki/Burning_of_Norfolk#Continental_Army_occupation_of_Norfolk [accessed 9/10/2020]

249 https://en.wikipedia.org/wiki/Burning_of_Norfolk#Continental_Army_occupation_of_Norfolk [accessed 9/13/2020]

250 https://en.wikipedia.org/wiki/Burning_of_Norfolk#Continental_Army_occupation_of_Norfolk [accessed 9/13/2020]

251 https://en.wikipedia.org/wiki/Burning_of_Norfolk#Continental_Army_occupation_of_Norfolk [accessed 9/13/2020]

252 https://en.wikipedia.org/wiki/Burning_of_Norfolk#Continental_Army_occupation_of_Norfolk [accessed 9/13/2020]

253 https://en.wikipedia.org/wiki/Burning_of_Norfolk#Continental_Army_occupation_of_Norfolk [accessed 9/13/2020]

254 https://en.wikipedia.org/wiki/Burning_of_Norfolk#Continental_Army_occupation_of_Norfolk [accessed 9/13/2020]

255 https://www.history.com/topics/american-revolution/declaration-of-independence [accessed 9/24/2020]

256 https://en.wikipedia.org/wiki/Burning_of_Norfolk#Continental_Army_occupation_of_Norfolk [accessed 9/13/2020]

257 https://en.wikipedia.org/wiki/Esek_Hopkins [accessed 10/27/2020]

258 https://en.wikipedia.org/wiki/Esek_Hopkins [accessed 10/27/2020]

259 https: https://en.wikipedia.org/wiki/Burning_of_Norfolk#Continental_Army_occupation_of_ Norfolk [accessed 9/13/2020]

260 https://en.wikipedia.org/wiki/Esek_Hopkins [accessed 10/27/2020]

261 https://en.wikipedia.org/wiki/Esek_Hopkins [accessed 10/27/2020]

262 https://www.history.com/topics/american-revolution/declaration-of-independence [accessed 9/24/2020]

263 https://nmaahc.si.edu/blog-post/vermont-1777-early-steps-against-Slavery [accessed 10/25/2020]

264 https://www.brainyquote.com/authors/otto-von-bismarck-quotes [accessed 5/13/2021]

265 https://en.wikipedia.org/wiki/Esek_Hopkins [accessed 10/27/2020]

266 https://www.history.com/topics/american-revolution/battles-of-trenton-and-princeton [accessed 10/26/2020]

267 https://en.wikipedia.org/wiki/Benedict_Arnold#Quebec_Expedition [accessed 10/26/2020]

268 https://en.wikipedia.org/wiki/Battle_of_Ridgefield#Ridgefield [accessed 10/26/202]

269 https://www.historycentral.com/Revolt/Bticonderoga.html#:~:text=British%20recapture%20Ticonderoga%201777,a%20peak%20overlooking%20the%20fort.&text=The%20British%20plan%20for%201777,Canada%2C%20to%20divide%20the%20colonies.[accessed 10/24/2020]

270 https://www.history.com/this-day-in-history/the-battle-of-brandywine-begins [accessed 10/24/2020]

271 https://www.history.com/topics/american-revolution/battle-of-germantown [accessed 10/24/2020]

272 https://en.wikipedia.org/wiki/Battles_of_Saratoga [accessed 8/24/2020]

273 https://en.wikipedia.org/wiki/Esek_Hopkins [accessed 10/27/2020]

274 https://en.wikipedia.org/wiki/Franco-American_alliance#Treaty_of_Alliance [accessed 8/24/2020]

275 https://en.wikipedia.org/wiki/HMS_Drake_(1777) [accessed 10/26/2020]

276 Bonhomme Richard v. Serapis, https://www.youtube.com/watch?v=9Yb5w_UlCyY; https://en.wikipedia.org/wiki/USS_Bonhomme_Richard_(1765); https://www.history.com/this-day-in-history/john-paul-jones-wins-in-english-waters [accessed 10/26/2020]

277 https://en.wikipedia.org/wiki/Siege_of_Charleston [accessed 1/22/2021]

278 https://en.wikipedia.org/wiki/Battle_of_Camden#Casualties [accessed 1/22/2021]

279 https://www.fold3.com/page/642791252-john-andre-arrested-benedict-arnold-exposed#:~:text=Andr%C3%A9%20finally%20left%20the%20house,Van%20Wart%20and%20David%20Williams. [accessed 9/3/2020]

280 https://en.wikipedia.org/wiki/Benedict_Arnold#Saratoga_Campaign [accessed 10/25/2020]

281 https://en.wikipedia.org/wiki/Battle_of_Kings_Mountain#Battle [accessed 1/22/2021]

282 https://en.wikipedia.org/wiki/Battle_of_Cowpens [accessed 1/24/2021]

283 https://en.wikipedia.org/wiki/Battle_of_Guilford_Court_House [accessed 1/24/2021]

284 https://www.nps.gov/york/learn/historyculture/lafayette-and-the-virginia-campaign-1781.htm#:~:text=On%20March%2014%2C%201781%2C%2023,their%20defeat%20six%20months%20later. [accessed 1/25/2021]

285 https://en.wikipedia.org/wiki/Siege_of_Yorktown_(1781) [accessed 1/25/2021]

286 https://www.nps.gov/york/learn/historyculture/lafayette-and-the-virginia-campaign-1781.htm#:~:text=On%20March%2014%2C%201781%2C%2023,their%20defeat%20six%20months%20later. [accessed 1/25/2021]

287 https://en.wikipedia.org/wiki/Battle_of_the_Chesapeake [accessed 1/26/2021]

288 https://en.wikipedia.org/wiki/Siege_of_Yorktown_(1781) [accessed 1/27/2021]

289 https://www.allpeoplefree.com/faq/when-was-Slavery-abolished?gclid=EAIaIQobChMI5fLZ1MWb7QIVwfezCh2qYQDOEAAYASAAEgluMfD_BwE [accessed 11/24/2020]

290 https://www.khanacademy.org/humanities/world-history/world-history-beginnings/origin-humans-early-societies/a/what-were-paleolithic-societies-like [accessed 11/22/2020]

291 https://hbr.org/1998/07/how-hardwired-is-human-behavior [accessed 5/15/2021]

292 https://www.freetheSlaves.net/about-Slavery/Slavery-in-history/?gclid=EAIaIQobChMIjv_VtlyX7QIVFmKGCh2VIQ42EAAYASAAEgl_1vD_BwE [accessed 11/22/2020]

293 https://en.wikipedia.org/wiki/Slavery_among_Native_Americans_in_the_United_States [acessed 11/22/2020]

294 https://www.brown.edu/news/2017-02-15/enslavement#:~:text=Native%20American%20Slavery%20%E2%80%9Cis%20a,to%2012.5%20million%20African%20Slaves.%E2%80%9D [accessed 11/22/2020]

295 https://www.history.com/news/american-Slavery-before-jamestown-1619#:~:text=The%20arrival%20of%20the%20first,as%20early%20as%20the%201500s. [accessed 11/20/2020]

296 http://www.medfordhistorical.org/medford-history/africa-to-medford/slaves-in-new-england/ [accessed 2/28/2021]

297 https://en.wikipedia.org/wiki/Esek_Hopkins [accessed 10/27/2020]

298 https://nmaahc.si.edu/blog-post/vermont-1777-early-steps-against-Slavery [accessed 10/25/2020]

299 https://en.wikipedia.org/wiki/Abolitionism_in_the_United_States#:~:text=In%20the%2018th%20century%2C%20Benjamin,Abolitionists%20in%20the%20United%20States. [accessed 5/16/2021]

300 https://www.independent.co.uk/voices/top-10-misattributed-quotations-a7910361.html [accessed 11/29/2020]

301 https://en.wikipedia.org/wiki/Thomas_Jefferson#Monticello,_marriage,_and_family [accessed 11/7/2020]

302 https://www.monticello.org/site/research-and-collections/martha-wayles-skelton-jefferson [accessed 5/16/2021]

303 https://www.varsitytutors.com/earlyamerica/why-thomas-jefferson-died-broke [accessed 11/7/2020]

304 https://en.wikipedia.org/wiki/Thomas_Jefferson_and_Slavery [accessed 11/29/2020]

305 http://www.let.rug.nl/usa/documents/1776-1785/jeffersons-draft-of-the-declaration-of-independence.php [accessed 9/24/20w20]

306 https://www.history.com/news/declaration-of-independence-deleted-Anti-Slavery-clause-jefferson [accessed 12/6/2020]

307 https://www.poplarforest.org/learn/thomas-jeffersons-life-and-times/the-enslaved-people-of-poplar-forest/jeffersons-views-on-Slavery/ [accessed 11/24/2020]

308 https://en.wikipedia.org/wiki/James_T._Callender [accessed 11/15/2020]

309 https://en.wikipedia.org/wiki/Sally_Hemings [accessed 11/8/2020

310 https://www.monticello.org/sallyhemings/ [accessed 11/15/2020]

311 https://en.wikipedia.org/wiki/Sally_Hemings [accessed 11/8/2020]

312 https://www.monticello.org/thomas-jefferson/jefferson-Slavery/thomas-jefferson-and-sally-hemings-a-brief-account/research-report-on-jefferson-and-hemings/appendix-h-sally-hemings-and-her-children/ [accessed 11/8/2020]

313 https://www.monticello.org/thomas-jefferson/jefferson-Slavery/thomas-jefferson-and-sally-hemings-a-brief-account/ [accessed 11/8/2020]

314 https://www.monticello.org/site/research-and-collections/beverly-hemings [accessed 11/17/2020]

315 https://en.wikipedia.org/wiki/Harriet_Hemings [accessed 11/17/2020]

316 https://en.wikipedia.org/wiki/Madison_Hemings [accessed 11/17/2020]

317 https://www.monticello.org/getting-word/people/eston-hemings-jefferson [accessed 11/17/2020]

318 https://www.monticello.org/getting-word/people/eston-hemings-jefferson [accessed 11/17/2020]

319 https://www.wisconsinhistory.org/Records/Image/IM35742 [accessed 11/17/2020]

320 https://www.monticello.org/thomas-jefferson/jefferson-Slavery/thomas-jefferson-and-sally-hemings-a-brief-account/research-report-on-jefferson-and-hemings/ii-assessment-of-dna-study/ [accessed 11/8/2020]

321 https://en.wikipedia.org/wiki/Elijah_Fletcher [accessed 5/16/2021]

322 https://en.wikipedia.org/wiki/Harriet_Hemings#Life_after_Monticello [accessed 5/16/2021]

323 https://www.crf-usa.org/black-history-month/the-constitution-and-Slavery [accessed 6/18/2020]

324 https://billofrightsinstitute.org/founding-documents/primary-source-documents/articles-of-confederation/?gclid=EAIaIQobChMI5Paqmc267QIViMDICh0rPAtkEAAYASAAEgLrwvD_BwE [accessed 12/6/2020]

325 https://www.archives.gov/founding-docs/constitution-transcript [accessed 6/4/2020]

326 https://www.heritage.org/constitution/#!/articles/1/essays/6/three-fifths-clause   [accessed 12/6/2020]

327 https://en.wikipedia.org/wiki/List_of_presidents_of_the_United_States_who_owned_Slaves [accessed 12/6/2020]

328 https://en.wikipedia.org/wiki/List_of_presidents_of_the_United_States_by_home_state [accessed 6/14/2020]

329 https://www.archives.gov/founding-docs/constitution-transcript [accessed 6/4/2020]

330 https://en.wikipedia.org/wiki/Article_Five_of_the_United_States_Constitution#Text [accessed 12/6/2020]

331 https://www.politico.com/story/2018/03/02/congress-votes-to-ban-Slave-importation-march-2-1807-430820#:~:text=On%20this%20day%20in%201807,1%2C%201808. [accessed 12/12/2020]

332 https://en.wikipedia.org/wiki/Atlantic_Slave_trade#Triangular_trade [accessed 12/12/2020]

333 https://constitution.congress.gov/browse/article-4/section-2/clause-3/#:~:text=No%20Person%20held%20to%20Service,or%20Labour%20may%20be%20due. [accessed 12/10/2020]

334 https://en.wikipedia.org/wiki/Northwest_Ordinance [accessed 12/11/2020]

335 Ibid

336 https://www.google.com/search?q=missouri+compromise+of+1820&oq=Missouri+Compromise&aqs=chrome.1.0i131i433i457j0j0i131i433l2j0i433j0i131i433l2j0.13893j0j7&sourceid=chrome&ie=UTF-8 [accessed 12/11/2020]

337 https://en.wikipedia.org/wiki/Tariff_of_Abominations [accessed 12/121/2020]

338 https://www.britannica.com/topic/nullification-crisis [accessed 12/12/2020]

339 https://www.history.com/topics/black-history/nat-turner [accessed 12/13/2020]

340 https://en.wikipedia.org/wiki/Trial_of_Reuben_Crandall [accessed 12/11/2020]

341 https://en.wikipedia.org/wiki/Snow_Riot [accessed 12/13/2020]

342 https://en.wikipedia.org/wiki/Elijah_Parish_Lovejoy [accessed 12/14/2020]

343 https://en.wikipedia.org/wiki/Abraham_Lincoln%27s_Lyceum_address [accessed 12/14/2020]

344 https://philadelphiaencyclopedia.org/archive/city-of-brotherly-love/ [accessed 12/14/2020]

345 https://en.wikipedia.org/wiki/Pennsylvania_Hall_(Philadelphia) [accessed 12/15/2020]

346 https://www.history.com/topics/Abolitionist-movement/amistad-case [accessed 12/17/2020]

347 https://en.wikipedia.org/iki/Prigg_v._Pennsylvania [accessed 12/17/2020]

348 Margaret Morgan, MSA SC 5496-8784 (maryland.gov) [accessed 12/19/2020]

349 https://en.wikipedia.org/wiki/Wilmot_Proviso [accessed 12/19/2020]

350 https://en.wikipedia.org/wiki/Nashville_Convention [accessed 12/20/2020]

351 https://en.wikipedia.org/wiki/Compromise_of_1850 [accessed 12/20/2020]

352 https://en.wikipedia.org/wiki/Fugitive_Slave_Act_of_1850 [accessed 12/21/2020]

353 https://en.wikipedia.org/wiki/Uncle_Tom%27s_Cabin [accessed 12/21/2020]

354 https://en.wikipedia.org/wiki/Anthony_Burns#Trial [accessed 12/22/2020]

355 https://en.wikipedia.org/wiki/Ostend_Manifesto#:~:text=The%20Ostend%20Manifesto%2C%20also%20known,declare%20war%20if%20Spain%20refused. [accessed 12/22/2020]

356 https://www.history.com/topics/19th-century/kansas-nebraska-act [accessed 12/22/2020]

367 https://en.wikipedia.org/wiki/Bleeding_Kansas#:~:text=Bleeding%20Kansas%2C%20Bloody%20Kansas%2C%20or,the%20proposed%20state%20of%20Kansas. [accessed 12/26/2020]

358 https://en.wikipedia.org/wiki/Henry_A._Edmundson [accessed 12/24/2020]

359 https://en.wikipedia.org/wiki/1856_United_States_presidential_election#:~:text=The%201856%20United%20States%20presidential,American%20Party%20nominee%20Millard%20Fillmore. [accessed 6/8/2020]

360 https://en.wikipedia.org/wiki/Caning_of_Charles_Sumner [accessed 12/24/2020]

361 https://en.wikipedia.org/wiki/Dred_Scott_v._Sandford [accessed 6/4/2020]

362 https://www.google.comsearch?q=Chief+Justice+Haney&oq=Chief+Justice+Haney&aqs=chrome..69i57.15720j0j7&sourceid=chrome&ie=UTF-8 [accessed 6/7/2020]

363 https://www.acslaw.org/expertforum/no-rights-which-the-white-man-was-bound-to-respect/ [accessed 6/8/2020]

364 https://en.wikipedia.org/wiki/Francis_Scott_Key [accessed 6/8/2020]

365 https://en.wikipedia.org/wiki/Francis_Scott_Key [accessed 6/12/2020]

366 https://www.brainyquote.com/quotes/f_scott_fitzgerald_100572 [accessed 6/12/2020]

367 https://en.wikipedia.org/wiki/Dred_Scott_v._Sandford [accessed 6/8/2020]

368 https://www.britannica.com/event/Dred-Scott-decision [accessed 1/7/2021]

369 https://www.archives.gov/founding-docs/constitution-transcript [accessed 1/7/2021]

370 https://constitutioncenter.org/interactive-constitution/interpretation/article-iv/clauses/44 [accessed 1/6/2011]

371 https://www.supremecourt.gov/opinions/07pdf/07-290.pdf [accessed 6/12/2021]

372 https://en.wikipedia.org/wiki/Lincoln%E2%80%93Douglas_debates [accessed 12/28/2020]

373 https://www.nps.gov/articles/wives-and-children-of-john-brown.htm#:~:text=She%20married%20James%20Fablinger%20in,the%20Bible%20in%20the%20other.[accessed 5/1/2021]

374 https://en.wikipedia.org/wiki/John_Brown_(Abolitionist) [accessed 1/11/2021]

375 https://en.wikipedia.org/wiki/John_Brown's_raid_on_Harpers_Ferry, & https://en.wikipedia.org/wiki/Israel_Greene; [accessed 1/12/2021]

376 https://www.bartleby.com/142/100.html [accessed 1/13/2021]

377 https://en.wikipedia.org/wiki/John_Brown_(Abolitionist) [accessed 1/13/2021]

378   http://www.abrahamlincolnonline.org/lincoln/speeches/cooper.htm,\ referencing the *Collected Works of Abraham Lincoln,* edited by Roy Basier, et al [accessed 1/14/2021].

379   https://en.wikipedia.org/wiki/1860_United_States_presidential_election [accessed 1/13/2021]

380   https://en.wikipedia.org/wiki/1860_United_States_presidential_election [accessed 1/17/2021]

381   ibid

382   https://www.senate.gov/artandhistory/history/minute/Civil_War_Begins.htm [accessed 1/17/2021]

383   https://www.nps.gov/articles/000/south-carolina-secession.htm#:~:text=%2D%20Charleston%20Mercury%20on%20November%203,Union%20on%20December%2020%2C%201860. [accessed 1/17/2021]

384   https://en.wikipedia.org/wiki/Battle_of_Fort_Sumter [accessed 1/17/2021]

385   https://www.nps.gov/civilwar/facts.htm#:~:text=Civil%20War%20Facts%3A%201861%2D1865&text=The%20Confederacy%20included%20the%20states,Missouri%20were%20called%20Border%20States. [accessed 1/17/2021]

386   http://www.abrahamlincolnonline.org/lincoln/speeches/greeley.htm#:~:text=Written%20during%20the%20heart%20of,Abraham%20Lincoln's%20most%20famous%20letters.&text=He%20stated%20that%20Lincoln%20did,Washington [accessed 6/14/2020]

387   http://www.abrahamlincolnonline.org/lincoln/speeches/hodges.htm [accessed 6/14/2020]

388   https://www.history.com/topics/american-civil-war/battle-of-antietam [accessed 6/14/2020]

389   https://www.history.com/news/why-the-civil-war-actually-ended-16-months-after-lee-surrendered [accessed 1/17/2021]

390   4/12/2012 Guy Gugliotta New York Times Article, https://www.nytimes.com/2012/04/03/science/civil-war-toll-up-by-20-percent-in-new-estimate.html#:~:text=New%20Estimate%20Raises%20Civil%20War%20Death%20Toll,-A%20lithograph%20of&text=For%20110%20years%2C%20the%20numbers,numbers%20were%20far%20too%20low. [accessed 1/17/2021]

391   https://en.wikipedia.org/wiki/Christmas_in_the_American_Civil_War [accessed 3/26/2021]

392   http://suvcw.org/mollus/journal/2010-67-4-Winter.pdf]accessed 3/26/2021]

393   https://en.wikipedia.org/wiki/Emancipation_Proclamation [accessed 1/19/2021]

394   https://www.archives.gov/historical-docs/13th-amendment [accessed 1/19/2021]

395   https://en.wikipedia.org/wiki/Ku_Klux_Klan#First_KKK [accessed 11/25/2020]

396   https://www.biblegateway.com/passage/?search=Ezekiel+18%3A20&version=KJV [accessed 8/6/2021]

397   The Merry Minuet was popularized in the 1959 LP music album *The Kingston Trio from the Hungry I.* As of 6/5/2021, It and the individual song could be accessed on YouTube, and the song is also accessible via Alexa. YouTube also has Louis Armstrong's *New Orleans Funeral March,* showing the practice of mourning death on the way to the cemetery and celebrating life on the return.

398   https://en.wikipedia.org/wiki/Assawoman_Canal [accessed 2/6/2019]

399   https://en.wikipedia.org/wiki/Assawoman_Bay [accessed 22/5/2019]
      https://babel.hathitrust.org/cgi/pt?id=wu.89058322223;view=1up;seq=13 [accessed 2/5/2019]
      https://en.wikipedia.org/wiki/Gender_roles_among_the_indigenous_peoples_of_North_America [accessed 2/5/2019]
      http://opheliaexplainsitall.blogspot.com/2012/09/unusual-town-name-extravaganza.html?m=1 [accessed 2/5/2019]

400   https://babel.hathitrust.org/cgi/pt?id=wu.89058322223;view=1up;seq=13 [accessed 2/5/2019]

401 https://en.wikipedia.org/wiki/Gender_roles_among_the_indigenous_peoples_of_North_America [accessed 2/5/2019]

402 http://opheliaexplainsitall.blogspot.com/2012/09/unusual-town-name-extravaganza.html?m=1 [accessed 2/5/2019]

403 https://www.houseofnames.com/Teague-family-crest [accessed 2/19/2019]

404 https://www.ancestry.com/name-origin?surname=teague [accessed 2/19/2019]

405 https://en.wikipedia.org/wiki/Murderkill_River [accessed 2/5/2019]

406 https://en.wikipedia.org/wiki/Slaughter_Beach,_Delaware [accessed 2/5/2019]

407 http://nanticokelenapemuseum.org/museum/628/the-keepers-of-the-land/ [accessed 11/03/2018]

408 Delaware Legends & Lore, the History Press, 2010 information posted by David Healy on 2/16/2016: https://davidhealeyauthor.com/2016/02/14/how-legend-says-delawares-whorekill-murderkill-and-slaughter-beach-got-their-names/ [accessed 11/03/2018]

409 https://en.wikipedia.org/wiki/Competition_(biology) [accessed 11/30/2019]

410 https://en.wikipedia.org/wiki/Competitive_exclusion_principle [accessed 12/1/2019]

411 https://en.wikipedia.org/wiki/List_of_genocides_by_death_toll [accessed 2/26/2019]

412 Loretta Graziano Breuning, PhD, Professor Emerita of Management, California State University, East Bay, Author of *Habits of a Happy Brain*. Textual information taken from: https://www.psychologytoday.com/us/blog/your-neurochemical-self/201608/why-winning-feels-good [accessed 11/30/2019]

413 https://en.wikipedia.org/wiki/Co-operation_(evolution) [accessed 11/30/2019]

414 https://www.britannica.com/place/Germany/Germany-from-1918-to-1945 [accessed 6/27/2020]

415 https://en.wikipedia.org/wiki/Marshall_Plan [accessed 11/4/2019]

416 https://en.wikipedia.org/wiki/Occupation_of_Japan [accessed 11/4/2019]

417 https://en.wikipedia.org/wiki/Mother_Teresa [accessed 1/15/2020]

418 https://www.cnbc.com/2017/09/12/workplace-crime-costs-us-businesses-50-billion-a-year.html [accessed 11/13/2019]

419 https://en.wikipedia.org/wiki/Poverty_threshold#Basic_needs [accessed 9/30/2019]

420 https://www.peoplekeep.com/blog/minimum-wage-rates-for-2015-by-state [accessed 10/3/2019]

421 https://www.forbes.com/sites/timworstall/2015/05/04/the-average-us-welfare-payment-puts-you-in-the-top-20-of-all-income-earners/#595548e7316f [accessed 9/30/2019]

422 https://www.worldbank.org/en/country/ethiopia/overview [accessed 11/5/2019]

423 https://en.wikipedia.org/wiki/Djibouti#Economy [accessed 11/5/2019]

424 https://en.wikipedia.org/wiki/Hurricane_Katrina;
https://www.google.com/search?q=Katrina+police&oq=katrina&aqs=chrome.0.69i59j69i5 7j0j69i61j69i60l2.2430j0j7&sourceid=chrome&ie=UTF-8:;https://www.history.com/topics/ natural-disasters-and-environment/hurricane-katrina;
https://www.npr.org/sections/thetwo-way/2016/12/20/506282657/new-orleans-to-pay-13-3-million-over-police-killings-after-hurricane-katrina;
https://www.wave3.com/story/3904630/police-chief-249-new-orleans-officers-left-posts-without-permission-during-katrina/;
https://www.pbs.org/newshour/show/crime-increases-in-new-orleans-as-the-city-recovers-from-hurricane-katrina; https://en.wikipedia.org/wiki/Ray_Nagin [accessed 11/11/2019]

425 https://en.wikipedia.org/wiki/Jews_as_the_chosen_people [accessed 11/4/2019]

426 https://en.wikipedia.org/wiki/Master_race [accessed 11/4/2019]

427   https://en.wikipedia.org/wiki/Battle_of_Jericho [accessed 2/26/2019]

428   https://en.wikipedia.org/wiki/Joshua_Fit_the_Battle_of_Jericho [accessed 6/19/2020]

429   https://en.wikipedia.org/wiki/Sun_Tzu [accessed 2/26/2019]

430   https://en.wikipedia.org/wiki/Sun_Tzu [accessed 2/26/2019]

431   https://en.wikipedia.org/wiki/Switzerland [accessed 11/4/2019]

432   https://en.wikipedia.org/wiki/History_of_the_Islamic_Republic_of_Pakistan [accessed 11/4/2019]

433   https://en.wikipedia.org/wiki/Military_budget_of_the_United_States#Total_overview [accessed 9/26/2019]

434   https://sites.google.com/site/americachristiannation/home/religion-in-the-13-colinies [accessed 6/29/2020]

435   https://www.smithsonianmag.com/history/americas-true-history-of-religious-tolerance-61312684/ [accessed 6/29/2020

436   https://www.facinghistory.org/nobigotry/religion-colonial-america-trends-regulations-and-beliefs [accessed 6/29/2020]

437   http://Slaveryandremembrance.org/articles/article/?id=A0145 [accessed 6/19/2020]

438   https://www.pbs.org/race/000_About/002_03-godeeper.htm [accessed 6/21/2020]

439   http://Slaveryandremembrance.org/articles/article/?id=A0145 [accessed 6/21/2020]

440   https://en.wikipedia.org/wiki/Nathaniel_Bacon_(Virginia) [accessed 6/21/2020]

441   https://en.wikipedia.org/wiki/Cockacoeske [accessed 6/21/2020]

442   https://www.legendsofamerica.com/ah-nathanielbacon [accessed 6/22/2020]

443   https://www.choices.edu/wp-content/uploads/2017/08/choices-Slavery-reading.pdf [accessed 6/23/2020]

444   Mary B. Norton, The Constitutional Status of Women in 1787, 6 Law & Ineq. 7 (1988). https://scholarship.law.umn.edu/cgi/viewcontent.cgi?article=1558&context=lawineq [accessed 6/1/2020] (Norton is the *Mary Donlon Alger Professor of History at Cornell*.)

445   https://www.americanyawp.com/reader/the-american-revolution/abigail-and-john-adams-converse-on-womens-rights-1776/ [accessed 6/1/2020]

446   https://fas.org/sgp/crs/misc/LSB10255.pdf [accessed 6/10/2020]

447   Dmitry Bam, *Seen and Heard; a Defense of Judicial Speech.* https://digitalcommons.mainelaw.maine.edu/cgi/viewcontent.cgi?article=1098&context=faculty-publications [accessed 6/10/2020]

448   https://www.findlaw.com/tax/federal-taxes/tax-return-confidentiality-and-disclosure-laws.html [accessed 4/15/2021]

449   https://papers.ssrn.com/sol3/papers.cfm?abstract_id=2830129 [accessed 6/10/2020]

450   https://rewire.news/article/2020/03/16/joe-biden-says-hell-nominate-a-black-woman-to-the-supreme-court-here-are-6-options/ [accessed 6/10/2020]

451   https://www.supremecourt.gov/opinions/03pdf/03-475scalia.pdf [accessed 6/11/2020]

452   https://www.washingtonpost.com/politics/2020/09/22/packing-supreme-court/ [accessed 5/2/2021]

453   https://en.wikipedia.org/wiki/The_White_Man%27s_Burden [accessed 6/29/2020]

454   https://www.merriam-webster.com/dictionary/imperialism [accessed 6/28/2020]

455   https://en.wikipedia.org/wiki/Hague_Conventions_of_1899_and_1907 [accessed 6/29/2020]

456   https://ihl-databases.icrc.org/customary-ihl/eng/docs/v2_rul_rule62 [accessed 6/29/2020]

457   https://en.wikipedia.org/wiki/Mark_Twain#Anti-imperialist [accessed 6/30/2020]

458 goodreads.com/author/quotes/1244.Mark_Twain [accessed 6/30/2020]

459 https://armyhistory.org/a-desperate-undertaking-funston-captures-aguinaldo/   [accessed 6/30/2020]

460 https://www.csid.com/2016/09/real-cost-identity-theft/ [accessed 1/22/2021]

461 https://www.gao.gov/products/GAO-17-732#:~:text=Researchers%20have%20estimated%20 varying%20annual,committed%20in%20the%20United%20States.[accessed 1/22/2021]

462 https://en.wikipedia.org/wiki/Extinction [accessed 1/16/2019]

463 https://www.audubon.org/magazine/may-june-2014/why-passenger-pigeon-went-extinct [accessed 2/26/2019], Article by Barry Yeoman.

464 https://www.techtimes.com/articles/64542/20150630/humans-cause-of-extinction-of-nearly-500-species-since-1900.htm [accessed 9/26/2021]

465 https://www.worldometers.info/coronavirus/ [accessed 5/28/2021]

466 https://en.wikipedia.org/wiki/Neanderthal_extinction [accessed 10/10/2019]

467 https://en.wikipedia.org/wiki/Campanian_Ignimbrite_eruption [accessed 10/1/2019]

468 Daley, Jason, *Climate Change Likely Iced Neanderthals Out of Existence*, August 18, 2018, https://www.smithsonianmag.com/smart-news/modern-humans-didnt-kill-neanderthals-weather-did-180970167/ [accessed 10/1/2019]

469 https://en.m.wikipedia.org/wiki/Mid-Pleistocene_Transition [accessed 11/17/2019]

470 https://www.discovermagazine.com/planet-earth/neanderthal-brains-bigger-not-necessarily-better [accessed 1/15/2020]

471 https://en.wikipedia.org/wiki/Graecopithecus [accessed 5/29/2021]

472 https://www.nature.com/scitable/knowledge/library/overview-of-hominin-evolution-89010983/ [accessed 1/14/2020]

473 https://en.wikipedia.org/wiki/Orrorin [accessed 5/29/2021]

474 http://www.macroevolution.net/australopithecines.html [accessed 12/20/2019]

475 https://en.wikipedia.org/wiki/Australopithecus_afarensis [accessed 1/13/2020]

476 Sharon P. McPherson, et al, Nature, Vol. 466, Issue 7308, pp 857-860, August 2010, as cited in https://ui.adsabs.harvard.edu/abs/2010Natur.466..857M/abstract [accessed 1/3/2020]

477 https://www.pbs.org/wgbh/evolution/humans/humankind/d.html [accessed 1/13/2020]

478 https://en.wikipedia.org/wiki/Homo_rudolfensis [accessed 12/20/2019]

479 https://en.wikipedia.org/wiki/Homo_naledi [accessed 1/17/2020]

480 https://www.nationalgeographic.com/news/2017/05/homo-naledi-human-evolution-science/ [accessed 1/17/2020]

481 http://humanorigins.si.edu/evidence/human-fossils/species/homo-habilis [accessed 12/7/2019]

482 https://www.britannica.com/topic/Homo-habilis [accessed 12/19/2019]

483 https://simple.wikipedia.org/wiki/Homo_georgicus [accessed 12/22/2019]

484 http://www.macroevolution.net/homo-georgicus.html [accessed 1/13/2020]

485 https://milnepublishing.geneseo.edu/the-history-of-our-tribe-hominini/chapter/homo-georgicus/ [accessed 1/20/2020]

486 https://www.nhm.ac.uk/discover/homo-erectus-our-ancient-ancestor.html [accessed 12/22/2019]

487 https://en.wikipedia.org/wiki/Homo_erectus#Anatomy [accessed 12/22/2019]

488 https://en.wikipedia.org/wiki/Spear [accessed 1/17/2020]

489 https://en.wikipedia.org/wiki/Homo_gautengensis [accessed 1/15/2020]

490 https://en.wikipedia.org/wiki/Homo_ergaster [accessed 12/22/2019]

491 https://en.wikipedia.org/wiki/Homo_heidelbergensis [accessed 5/29/2021]

492 https://en.wikipedia.org/wiki/Homo_antecessor [accessed 12/18/2019]

493 https://en.wikipedia.org/wiki/Ceprano_Man [accessed 1/152020]

494 https://en.wikipedia.org/wiki/Homo_rhodesiensis [accessed 1/15/2020]

495 https://en.wikipedia.org/wiki/Bow_and_arrow [accessed 1/17/2020]

496 https://en.wikipedia.org/wiki/Denisovan#Taxonomic_placement [accessed 12/17/2019]

497 https://www.sciencealert.com/we-finally-have-some-idea-of-when-the-mysterious-denisovans-walked-the-earth [accessed 12/22/2019]

498 https://en.wikipedia.org/wiki/Homo_luzonensis [accessed 1/14/2020]

499 https://en.wikipedia.org/wiki/Red_Deer_Cave_people [accessed 12/22/2019]

500 https://www.pbs.org/wgbh/evolution/library/03/2/l_032_04.html [accessed 1/14/2020]

501 https://en.wikipedia.org/wiki/San_people [accessed 12/3/2019]

502 https://www.southafricatoursandtravel.com/sanpeople.html# THE%20SAN%20PEOPLE%20 (BUSHMEN) [accessed 12/2/2019]

503 https://www.survivalinternational.org/news/10410 [accessed 12/4/2019]

504 http://www.krugerpark.co.za/africa_bushmen.html [accessed 12/2/2019]

505 https://science.sciencemag.org/content/348/6236/796 [accessed 11/28/2019]

506 https://www.youtube.com/watch?v=iNJnfKBLWlE [accessed 12/4/2019]

507 https://en.wikipedia.org/wiki/African_Pygmies [accessed 1/25/2020]

508 Lewis, Jerome. The Mbendjele Yaka Pygmies of Congo-Brazzaville, a PhD Thesis, https://discovery.ucl.ac.uk/id/eprint/18991/1/18991.pdf [accessed 1/25/2020]

509 https://discovery.ucl.ac.uk/id/eprint/1522643/1/Oloa-Biloa%20PhD%20thesis%20final%202017.pdf [accessed 2/16/2020]

510 https://en.wikipedia.org/wiki/Genetic_history_of_indigenous_peoples_of_the_Americas [accessed 3/12/2019]

511 https://en.wikipedia.org/wiki/Maya_civilization#Correlation_of_the_Long_Count_calendar [accessed 3/12/2019]

512 https://en.wikipedia.org/wiki/Human_sacrifice_in_Aztec_culture [accessed 3/12/2019]

513 https://en.wikipedia.org/wiki/Inca_Empire#Religion [accessed 3/12/2019]

514 *The Native Population of the Americas in 1492*, 2nd Revised Edition, 1992, edited by William M. Denevan, Carl O' Sauer Professor of Geography and Environmental Studies at the niversity of Wisconson-Madison. https://uwpress.wisc.edu/books/0289.htm [accessed 2/26/2019]

515 https://en.wikipedia.org/wiki/Population_history_of_indigenous_peoples_of_the_Americas [accessed 3/12/2019]

516 https://en.wikipedia.org/wiki/Population_history_of_indigenous_peoples_of_the_Americas#Formal_apology_from_the_United_States_government [accessed 2/26/2019]

517 https://en.wikipedia.org/wiki/Captives_in_American_Indian_Wars [accessed 9/26/2019]

518 https://en.wikipedia.org/wiki/Reign_of_Terror [accessed 9/30/2019]

519 https://en.wikipedia.org/wiki/Maximilien_Robespierre#Arrest [accessed 9/30/2019]

520 https://en.wikipedia.org/wiki/Holy_League [accessed 9/29/2019]

521 https://en.wikipedia.org/wiki/Siege_of_Mirandola_(1510) [accessed 9/29/2019]

522 https://en.wikipedia.org/wiki/Holy_League_(1538) [accessed 11/5/2019]

523 https://en.wikipedia.org/wiki/Pope_Pius_V [accessed 9/29/2019]

524 https://en.wikipedia.org/wiki/Holy_League_(1594) [accessed 11/5/2019]

525 https://en.wikipedia.org/wiki/Holy_League_(1684) [accessed 11/5/2019]

526 https://en.wikipedia.org/wiki/Holy_League_(1717) [accessed 11/5/2019]

527 https://en.wikipedia.org/wiki/List_of_countries_by_intentional_homicide_rate   [accessed 2/27/2019]

https://www.techtimes.com/articles/64542/20150630/humans-cause-of-extinction-of-nearly-500-species-since-1900.htm [accessed 10/3/2019]

528 https://www.lawg.org/arming-the-conflict-el-salvadors-gun-market/#:~:text=On%20paper%2C%20El%20Salvador%20has,automatic%20rifles%2C%20among%20other%20measures. [accessed 3/21/2121]

529 https://www.yourirish.com/history/medieval/vikings-invade-ireland [accessed 10/1/2018]

530 https://celt.ucc.ie/General%20Vikings%20in%20Ireland.pdf [accesses 10/26/2019]

531 https://www.ancient-origins.net/ancient-places-europe/dark-reputation-dunmore-cave-ireland-002828 [accessed 10/2/2018]

532 http://www.battleofclontarf.net/the-battle-of-clontarf-23rd-april-1014/the-battle-of-tara/3475 [accessed 10/1/2018]

533 https://wildeyedsoutherncelt.com/tag/mael-morda-mac-murchada/ [accessed 9/1/2018]

534 https://www.scotsman.com/lifestyle/scotland-s-dna-who-do-you-think-you-are-part-4-1-1503458 [accessed 10/17/2018]

https://en.wikipedia.org/wiki/Blood_eagle. [both accessed 10/17/2018]

535 https://www.clanoreilly.com/history/ [accessed 6/12/2018]

536 https://www.clanoreilly.com/history [accessed 6/9/2018]

537 https://en.wikipedia.org/wiki/West_Breifne [accessed 6/12/2018], &

https://en.wikipedia.org/wiki/East_Breifne [accessed 6/13/2018]

538 https://en.wikipedia.org/wiki/Battle_of_Magh_Slecht [accessed 6/9/2018]

539 Duffy, Seán, (2007, 2016) Editior, *The World of the Gallowglass, Kings, warlords and warriors in Ireland and Scotland, 1200-1600*, Four Courts Press, LTD, p.1

540 https://en.wikipedia.org/wiki/Scandinavian_Scotland [accessed 6/22/2018]

541 Cannan,*Gallowglass*, p.3-4, 6,8

542 https://en.wikipedia.org/wiki/Plantation_of_Ulster [accessed 9/5/2018]

543 https://en.wikipedia.org/wiki/Hat#Styles [accessed 1/11/2019]

544 http://www.bbc.co.uk/history/ancient/vikings/religion_01.shtml [accessed 11/20/2018]

545 https://en.wikipedia.org/wiki/Reformation [accessed 11/20/2018]

546 https://en.wikipedia.org/wiki/Church_of_Scotland [accessed 11/20/2018]

547 Cannan, Fergus (2010), *Gallowglass 1250-1600.* (artwork by Seán Ó'Brógáin) Osprey Publishing Ltd, Oxford, UK, p 32

548 https://www.britannica.com/biography/Edmund-Spenser [accessed 10/3/2018]

549 https://en.wikipedia.org/wiki/Edmund_Spenser#Life [accessed 9/20/2019]

550 Cannan, *Gallowglass*, p 44

551 Cannan, *Gallowglass,* p 10, 25

552 Cannan, *Gallowglass*, p 28-30

553 Soodalter, Ron, *Scourge of the Gallowglass*, Military History Magazine, 1/1/2016:

https://www.historynet.com/scourge-of-the-Gallowglass.htm [accessed 4/1/2019]

554 https://www.monreaghulsterscotscentre.com/the-redshanks-donegal/ [accessed 12/01/2018]

555 Copied from https://www.poetryfoundation.org/poems/45319/the-charge-of-the-light-brigade on 10/3/2018

556 https://en.wikiquote.org/wiki/Orson_Welles [accessed 4/21/2019]

557 https://en.wikipedia.org/wiki/List_of_military_inventions [accessed 4/25/2019]

558 https://en.wikipedia.org/wiki/William_Shockley [accessed 4/22/2019]

559 https://en.wikipedia.org/wiki/Atomic_bombings_of_Hiroshima_and_Nagasaki#Preparations_to_invade_Japan [accessed 4/21/2019]

560 https://www.fosters.com/news/20170807/bombs-dropped-on-japan-saved-millions-of-lives [accessed 4/21/2019]

561 https://en.wikipedia.org/wiki/Pope_Alexander_VI#Slavery [accessed 1/10/2019]

562 https://en.wikipedia.org/wiki/Roman_naming_conventions [accessed 1/15/2019]

563 https://www.ebabynames.com/#!meaning-of-Caesar [accessed 1/17/2019]

564 httgps://en.wikipedia.org/wiki/Surname [accessed 1/17/2019]

565 https://www.scottish-at-heart.com/scottish-surnames.html [accessed 10/6/2018]

566 http://theconversation.com/what-are-the-chances-that-your-dad-isnt-your-father-24802 [accessed 2/4/2019]

567 McCabe, Ebe, *Celtic Warrior Descendants*, p 88-93

568 https://en.wikipedia.org/wiki/O%27Rourke [accessed 10/6/2018]

569 https://www.johngrenham.com/browse/retrieve_text.php?text_contentid=478 [accessed 3/20/2021]

570 https://www.johngrenham.com/browse/retrieve_text.php?text_contentid=478 [accessed 3/21/2021]

571 https://www.johngrenham.com/browse/retrieve_text.php?text_contentid=478 [accessed 6/24/2018]

572 https://en.wikipedia.org/wiki/Niall_of_the_Nine_Hostages#Historicity_and_dates [accessed 3/20/2021]

573 https://en.wikipedia.org/wiki/Special:BookSources/9780521363952 [accessed 3/20/2021]

574 https://en.wikipedia.org/wiki/Muiredach_mac_E%C3%B3gain [accessed 3/20/2021]

575 https://en.wikipedia.org/wiki/Muirchertach_mac_Muiredaig_(Mac_Ercae) [accessed 3/20/2021]

576 https://en.wikipedia.org/wiki/Domnall_Ilchelgach [accessed 3/20/2021]

577 https://en.wikipedia.org/wiki/%C3%81ed_Uaridnach [accessed 3/20/2021]

578 https://en.wikipedia.org/wiki/M%C3%A1el_D%C3%BAin_mac_M%C3%A1ele_Fithrich [accessed 3/20/2021]

579 https://en.wikipedia.org/wiki/Fergal_mac_M%C3%A1ele_D%C3%BAin [accessed 3/20/2021]

580 https://en.wikipedia.org/wiki/Niall_Frossach [accessed 3/20/2021]

581 https://en.wikipedia.org/wiki/%C3%81ed_Oirdnide#:~:text=%C3%81ed%20mac%20N%C3%A9ill%20(died%20819,reckoned%20High%20King%20of%20Ireland. [accessed 3/20/2021]]

582 https://en.wikipedia.org/wiki/Muirchertach_mac_Muiredaig_(Mac_Ercae) [accessed 3/20/2021]

583 https://en.wikipedia.org/wiki/Niall_Gl%C3%BAndub [accessed 3/20/2021]

584 03/05/2020 email from Andrew MacLeod to Ebe McCabe

585 https://www.scottish-at-heart.com/scottish-surnames.html [accessed 10/6/2018]

586 https://en.wikipedia.org/wiki/Clan_Donald [accessed 11/11/2018]

587 Cannan, Fergus, *Gallowglass, 1250-1600*, Osprey Publishing Ltd, UK, 2010,p6

588 https://www.houseofnames.com/GilChrist-family-crest [accessed 5/29/2021]

589 http://thewildgeese.irish/profiles/blogs/not-all-celts-are-gaels. Posted by Bit Devine 8/272013.

590 https://ireland-calling.com/viking-cities-in-ireland/ [accessed 9/26.2021]

591 https://en.wikipedia.org/wiki/Kingdom_of_Meath [accessed 6/3/2021]

592 https://en.wikipedia.org/wiki/Osraige#Origins_and_prehistory [accessed 5/20/2021]

593 https://en.wikipedia.org/wiki/Kingdom_of_Breifne [accessed 5/20/2021]

594 https://www.irishcentral.com/roots/four-irish-provinces [accessed 6/1/2021]

595 https://en.wikipedia.org/wiki/Norman_invasion_of_Ireland [accessed 6/7/2018]

596 https://en.wikipedia.org/wiki/List_of_Irish_kingdoms [accessed 8/6/2021]

597 https://en.wikipedia.org/wiki/McCabe_(surname) [accessed 5/31/2018]

598 Wolfe, Patrick (1993), *Irish Names and Surnames*. Genealogical Publishing Company, p.324. ISBN 978-0-8063-0381-9 (cited by the Wikipedia Article on the McCabe Surname)

599 Harrison, Henry (1996), *Surnames of the United Kingdom; A Concise Etymological Dictionary* (Reprinted.). Genealogical Publishing Company. P.M2 ISBN 978-0-8063-0171-6 (cited by the Wikipedia Article on the McCabe Surname)

600 https://en.wikipedia.org/wiki/Kingdom_of_Breifne [accessed 6/1/2018]

601 03/05/2020 Macleod Clan Genealogy Coordinator Andrew MacLeod email to Ebe McCabe

602 https://en.wikipedia.org/wiki/Plantation_of_Ulster [accessed 9/9/2018]

603 https://en.wikipedia.org/wiki/Ulster [accessed 9/20/2018]

604 https://en.wikipedia.org/wiki/Religion_in_the_Republic_of_Ireland [accessed 9/20/2018]

605 https://en.wikipedia.org/wiki/Religion_in_Northern_Ireland [accessed 11/20/2018]

606 MacLysaght, Edward, D.Litt., M.R.I.A (1957), Chairman of the Irish Manuscripts Commission, Former Chief Herald of Ireland, *Irish Families, Their Names, Arms and Origins. Dublin*: First Published by Hodges, Figgis & Co. 1957; Third Edition, Revised, first published in the USA by Crown Publishers, Inc., New York, 1972. pp. 69–70.

607 https://en.wikipedia.org/wiki/Williamite_War_in_Ireland#Athlone,_Aughrim_and_the_Second_Siege_of_Limerick [accessed 6/1/2018]

608 Black, George Fraser, Ph.D (1946), *The Surnames of Scotland, Their Origin, Meaning, and History*, Churchill & Dunn Ltd. ISBN: 978-1-6265-4059-0. © 2015 George F. Black, p. 461

609 Per https://www.nls.uk/collections/manuscripts/archives [accessed 6/16/2018], The Book of the Dean of Lismore is a restricted access, 16th Century manuscript, handwritten by James MacGregor (c.1480-1551), of mostly Celtic poetry with items in Scots, Latin, and English.

610 Register of the Privy Council of Scotland.1.series. v. 1-14 (1545-1625); 2. series. V. 1-8 (1625-1660; 3. series. V. 1-14 (1661-1689). Edinburgh, 1841

611 C. Innes, Editor, (1845) *Registrum Episcopatus Aberdonensis*, (Two Volumes, Spalding & Maitland Clubs, Edinburgh)

612 https://www.merriam-webster.com/dictionary/xanthous [accessed 6/13/2018]

613 O'Donovan, John, Editor (1856), Annals *of the Kingdom of Ireland by the Four Masters*, 7 Volumes, Dublin, Hodges, Smith and Company

614 03/05/2020 email from Andrew MacLeod to Ebe McCabe

615 http://www.mcmahonsofmonaghan.org/the_fall_of_the_macmahons.html [accessed 9/8/2018]

616 http://www.clanmacleod.org/about-macleods/macleod-septs.html [accessed 6/13/2018]

617 Taken from the 9th Issue of the *Gallowglass*, Ireland's McCabe Clan newsletter

618 https://www.google.com/search?q=castle+definition&oq=castle+definition&aqs=chrome.
0.69i59j0l5.8687j1j7&sourceid=chrome&ie=UTF-8]accessed 9/16/2019]

619 https://en.wikipedia.org/wiki/Tower_houses_in_Britain_and_Ireland [accessed 9/19/2019]

620 https://www.townlands.ie/cavan/loughtee-upper/annagelliff/moynehall/moynehall/ [accessed 9/14/2019]

621 https://www.townlands.ie/cavan/loughtee-upper/annagelliff/moynehall/lisreagh/ [accessed 9/17/2019]

622 https://en.wikipedia.org/wiki/Townland [accessed 9/16/2019]

623 https://en.wikipedia.org/wiki/Freehold_(law) [accessed 9/16/2019]

624 https://www.logainm.ie/en/61062 [accessed 5/12/2020]

625 Captain Nicholas Pynnar's survey, commissioned as one of four British Surveys of the Plantation of Ulster, is printed in full in George Hill, *An Historical Account of the Plantation of Ulster at the Commencement of the Seventeenth Century* (Belfast, 1877). A copy is also available in the Manuscripts Room in Trinity College, Dublin. Pynnar was commissioned to do his survey on 11/18/1618 and spent 119 days at it. He visited most Plantation Estates and described the buildings, agricultural practices, and the numbers of tenants—discriminating between freeholders, leaseholders, and cottagers. https://www.ancestryireland.com/plantation-ulster/?page_id=21 [accessed 3/20/2021]

626 From *The Conquest of Ireland, Pinnar's Survey, Special Census of Northern Ireland, by Rev. George Hill,* published by the Irish Genealogical Foundation in 2004. See:
https://books.google.com/books?id=tW6edf80pIC&pg=PA467&lpg=PA467&dq=English +Bishop+Roger+Moyne&source=bl&ots=zzUcl502fu&sig=ACfU3U27ZTb4_QABqpJ05zpqzkM Te0kg_A&hl=en&sa=X&ved=2ahUKEwiY3ajI7tvkAhWiSt8KHZ9HCXcQ6AEwDnoECAYQAQ#v= onepage&q=English%20Bishop%20Roger%20Moyne&f=false [accessed 918/2019]

627 https://en.wikipedia.org/wiki/Bishop_of_Kilmore_and_Ardagh [accessed 9/16/2019]

628 See: the Inquisitions of Ulster reference at: thttps://books.google.com/books?id= C_Y0kleJMJcC&pg=PA282&lpg=PA282&dq=Inquisitions+of+Ulster,+Cavan+(23)+Car.+I&source=bl&ots= zr3AKncDxI&sig=ACfU3U2HRGKeW9y4G8vIsOJ_zDzfqodm=en&sa=X&ved=2ahUKEwiZ5ffz_ NjkAhVQU98KHaz1BDkQ6AEwAHoECAcQAQ#v=onepage&q&f=false [accessed 9/16/2019]

629 https://en.wikipedia.org/wiki/Rood_(unit) [accessed 9/16/2019]

630 https://www.townlands.ie/kildare/north-salt/taghadoe/straffan/newtownmacabe/ [accessed 9/16/2019]

631 http://www.knowlesclan.org/mccabe.htm [accessed 5/12/2020]

632 https://en.wikipedia.org/wiki/Airg%C3%ADalla [accessed 6/16/2018]

633 http://www.mcmahonsofmonaghan.org/collas_alternate_explanation.html [accessed 1/15/2019]

634 https://en.wikipedia.org/wiki/Kings_of_Brega [accessed 8/26.2019]

635 https://en.wikipedia.org/wiki/The_Three_Collas [accessed 1/18/2019]

636 https://www.libraryireland.com/Pedigrees2/clan-colla.php [accessed 1/18/2019]

637 http://www.peterspioneers.com/colla.htm [accessed 1/18/2019]; Colla Clan Administrator Patrick McMahon 1/21/2019 email to Ebe McCabe

638 McGettigan, Darren, *The McCabe Gallowglass Family, 3/25/2011:* http://www.familyhistoryireland. com/genealogy-blog/item/12-galloglass-families-of-ireland [accessed 11/17/2018]

639 http://www.knowlesclan.org/mccabe.htm [accessed 9/12/2018]

640 MacLysaght, Edward, *Irish Families, Their Names, Arms and Origins*

641 Black, *The Surnames of Scotland*, p 547

642 https://en.wikipedia.org/wiki/Star_and_crescent [accessed 9/27/2018]

643 https://en.wikipedia.org/wiki/Clan_Macnab [accessed 9/19/2018]

644 https://www.johngrenham.com/findasurname.php?surname=MacNab [accessed 9/19/2018]

645 *Clann Caba: A History of the McCabes, 2020,* researched/compiled by Brian Mc Cabe, Secretary of the Mc Cabe Clan Society [accessed 3/22/2021] (The Clann's newsletter was a primary information source.) Copies may be purchased from Brian McCabe, Ivy Cottage, Johnstown, Naas, Co. Kildare (brianfrancismccabe@gmail.com) or Aidan McCabe, Kisaderg, Cootehill, Co. Cavan (aidnmccabe04@gmail.com).

646 https://en.wikipedia.org/wiki/Leod [accessed 3/24/2021]

647 Cannan, Fergus, *Gallowglass 1250-1600, Gaelic Mercenary Warrior,* Osprey Publishing Ltd, UK, 2010, p12-24

648 http://www.albrechtdurerblog.com/albrecht-durers-only-irsh-drawing-happy-st-pattys-day/ [accessed 3/21/2021]

649 https://www.amazon.com/World-Galloglass-Warlords-Warriors-1200-1600/dp/1846826241/ref=pd_lpo_14_img_0/142-8406336-1512433?_encoding=UTF8&pd_rd_i=1846826241&pd_rd_r=95c3e6d1-785b-4676-bc51-4aad47eb8ab2&pd_rd_w=uTp69&pd_rd_wg=Cfv82&pf_rd_p=337be819-13af-4fb9-8b3e-a5291c097ebb&pf_rd_r=E0XS5X0RGE6KK6X10V42&psc=1&refRID=E0XS5X0RGE6KK6X10V42&asin=1846826241&revisionId=&format=4&depth=1 [accessed 3/21/2021]

650 https://en.wikipedia.org/wiki/Albrecht_D%C3%BCrer [accessed 3/21/2021]

651 https://www.historyireland.com/early-modern-history-1500-1700/basis-for-durers-drawing/ [accessed 3/28/2021]

652 https://en.wikipedia.org/wiki/Thomas_McCabe_(United_Irishmen) [accessed 3/26/2021]

653 McCabe, Brian, *The Second Cardinal Edward McCabe,* https://www.jstor.org/stable/30101352?seq=1#page_scan_tab_contents [accessed 9/12/2018]

654 https://en.wikipedia.org/wiki/Charles_Cardwell_McCabe [accessed 9/12/2018]

655 https://valor.militarytimes.com/hero/3162 [accessed 3/25/2021]

656 https://en.wikipedia.org/wiki/Langston_University [accessed 3/21/2021]

657 https://en.wikipedia.org/wiki/Thomas_B._McCabe [accessed 4/3/2021]

658 http://www.americainwwii.com/articles/war-mother/ [accessed 3/25/2021]

659 https://en.wikipedia.org/wiki/Battle_of_Trafalgar [accessed 3/24/2021]

660 https://encyclopediavirginia.org/entries/convict-labor-during-the-colonial-period/#:~:text=In%201615%2C%20English%20courts%20began,alleviating%20England's%20large%20criminal%20population.&text=Between%201700%20and%201775%2C%20approximately,20%2C000%20of%20them%20to%20Virginia. [accessed 3/29/2021]

661 https://en.wikipedia.org/wiki/Convicts_in_Australia#:~:text=Between%201788%20and%201868%2C%20about,in%20the%20early%2018th%20century. [accessed 3/29/2021]

662 https://en.wikipedia.org/wiki/Black_Sox_Scandal [accessed 3/29/2021]

663 https://baseballhall.org/explorer?page=13 [accessed 4/3/2021]

664 https://erenow.net/biographies/rothstein-the-life-times-and-murder-of-the-criminal-genius/21.php [accesed 3/30/2021]

665 Cannan, *Gallowglass,* p8

666 O'Laughlin, Michael C. (1992), *The Book Of Irish Families, Great and Small,* 1st Ed., Irish Genealogical Foundation, p iv

667 https://en.wikipedia.org/wiki/Leod#DNA_and_the_founder_of_Clan_MacLeod [accessed 3/2/2020]

668 https://www.scotweb.co.uk/info/macleod/ [accessed 9/17/2018]

669 http://www.qualtrough.org/history/Kings-of-Man.pdf [accessed 9/17/2018]

670 https://texasmacleods.com/2015/03/15/macleods-in-ireland/ [posted 3/15/2015, accessed 10/17/2018]

671 https://en.wikipedia.org/wiki/Roderick_Macleod_of_Macleod [accessed 9/26/2021]

672 https://forebears.io/surnames/mccabe [accessed 4/21/2019]

673 https://www.bbc.com/news/uk-scotland-scotland-politics-43822306 [accessed 10/16/2018]

674 http://www.worldometers.info/world-population/us-population/ [accessed 10/17/2018]

675 https://en.wikipedia.org/wiki/Haplogroup_A_(Y-DNA) [accessed 4/26/2019]

676 https://en.wikipedia.org/wiki/%C3%96tzi#Health [accessed 1/11/2019]

677 http://imtranslator.net/translation/english/to-irish/translation/ [accessed 1/10/2019]

678 https://translate.google.com/#view=home&op=translate&sl=en&tl=gd&text=cap [accessed 1/10/2019]

679 https://en.wikipedia.org/wiki/Cervelliere [accessed 5/14/2020]

680 https://www.teanglann.ie/en/eid/Cába [accessed 1/11/2019]

681 https://capes.com/the-origin-of-the-cape/ [accessed 1/11/2019]

682 https://en.wikipedia.org/wiki/Combat_helmet [accessed 1/11/2019]

683 D'Alton, John (1861). *Illustrations, Historical and Genealogical, of King James's Irish Army List. 2 (2nd enlarged ed.).* London: John Russell Smith. pp. 753–755. (cited in the Wikipedia article on the McCabe surname)

684 ww.thetreemaker.com/design-coat-of-arms-symbol/meaning-of-colors.html [accessed 6/8/2018]

685 https://en.wikisource.org/wiki/A_Complete_Guide_to_Heraldry/Chapter_13 [accessed 6/1/2018]

686 MacLysaght, Edward, *Irish Families,* Plate III, MacCabe Crest

687 http://www.irishsurnames.com/cgi-bin/gallery.pl?name=mccabe&capname=Mccabe&letter=c [accessed 5/31/2018]

688 Cannan, *Gallowglass*, p.47

689 https://en.wikipedia.org/wiki/Components_of_medieval_armour [accessed 6/3/2018]

690 e.g., Cannan, Fergus, *Gallowglass*, p.19, 24. Also, the book's covers and ~20 internal images show many different helmets, with the sole visored one being on the p.47 drawing by Katy Lumden.

691 MacLysaght, Edward, *Irish Families,* Plate XXV, O'Reilly and O'Rourke Crests.

692 http://www.scotclans.com/scottish-clans/clan-macleod/macleod-coat-of-arms [accessed 6/8/2018]

693 https://knowyourphrase.com/apple-does-not-fall-far-from-tree [accessed 6/3/2019]

694 https://en.wikipedia.org/wiki/Lamarckism [accessed 9/16/2019]

695 https://en.wikipedia.org/wiki/Pangenesis [accessed 9/22/2019]

696 https://en.wikipedia.org/wiki/Kulak [accessed 9/22/2019]

697 https://en.wikipedia.org/wiki/Lysenkoism [accessed 9/22/2019]

[698] http://hihg.med.miami.edu/code/http/modules/education/Design/Print.asp?CourseNum=1&LessonNum=5 [accessed 11/19/2019]

[699] https://www.whatisepigenetics.com/what-is-epigenetics/ [accessed 6/3/2019]

[700] https://www.biography.com/athlete/babe-didrikson-zaharias [accessed 6/5/2019]

[701] https://www.wonderopolis.org/wonder/how-many-cells-are-in-the-human-body [accessed 5/29/2020]

[702] https://www.ncbi.nlm.nih.gov/books/NBK218247/ [accessed 9/18/2021]

[703] https://en.wikipedia.org/wiki/Deoxyribose [accessed 1/24/2019]

[704] https://www.ebi.ac.uk/training/online/course/human-genetic-variation-i-introduction-2019/what-genetic-variation/what-are-variants-alleles [accessed 11/19/2019]

[705] https://isogg.org/wiki/Haplogroup [accessed 5/29/2020]

[706] https://www.nature.com/scitable/definition/haplotype-haplotypes-142/ [accessed 3/19/2021]

[707] https://en.wikipedia.org/wiki/STR_analysis [accessed 11/24/2019]

[708] https://labtestsonline.org/tests/sickle-cell-tests#:~:text=Sickle%20cell%20tests%20determine%20the,people%20with%20sickle%20cell%20trait. [accessed 6/1/2021]

[709] https://en.wikipedia.org/wiki/Hemoglobin_C#:~:text=Hemoglobin%20c%20(abbreviated%20as%20HbC,mild%20sickling%20of%20the%20RBCs. [accessed 6/1/2021]

[710] https://www.cdc.gov/ncbddd/sicklecell/documents/scd%20factsheet_sickle%20cell%20trait.pdf [accessed 6/3/2021]

[711] https://en.wikipedia.org/wiki/Y_chromosome [accessed 1/28/2019]

[712] https://en.wikipedia.org/wiki/Mitochondrial_DNA#In_mammals [accessed 5/11/2019]

[713] https://en.wikipedia.org/wiki/Mitochondrial_Eve#Early_research [accessed 2/28/2020]

[714] http://science.sciencemag.org/content/341/6145/562, *Sequencing Y Chromosomes Resolves Discrepancy in Time to Common Ancestor of Males Versus Females*, by G. David Poznik[1,2], Brenna M. Henn[3,4], Muh-Ching Yee[3], Elzbieta Sliwerska[5], Ghia M. Euskirchen[3], Alice A. Lin[6], Michael Snyder[3], Lluis Quintana-Murci[7,8], Jeffrey M. Kidd[3,5], Peter A. Underhill[3], Carlos D. Bustamante[3],* [1]Program in Biomedical Informatics, Stanford University School of Medicine, Stanford, CA, USA; [2]Department of Statistics, Stanford University, Stanford, CA, USA;

[3]Department of Genetics, Stanford University School of Medicine, Stanford, CA, USA;

[4]Department of Ecology and Evolution, Stony Brook University, Stony Brook, NY, USA; [5]Department of Human Genetics and Department of Computational Medicine and Bioinformatics, University of Michigan, Ann Arbor, MI, USA; [6]Department of Psychiatry, Stanford University, Stanford, CA, USA; [7]Institut Pasteur, Unit of Human Evolutionary Genetics, 75015 Paris, France. [accessed 1/25/2019], [8]Centre National de la Recherche Scientifique, URA3012, 75015 Paris, France. *Science* 02 Aug 2013, Vol. 341, Issue 6145, pp. 562-565

[715] https://en.wikipedia.org/wiki/Y-chromosomal_Adam#Likely_geographic_origin [accessed 1/25/2019]

[716] https://isogg.org/wiki/Haplogroup_R1b_(Y-DNA) [accessed 2/19/2020]

[717] https://en.wikipedia.org/wiki/Haplogroup_R-M269 [accessed 2/19/2020]

[718] https://isogg.org/wiki/NW_Irish [accessed 2/19/2020]

[719] https://www.familytreedna.com/groups/r-1b-1c-7/about/background [accessed 2/25/2020]

[720] https://www.familytreedna.com/groups/r-1b-1c-7/about/background [accessed 2/19/2020]

[721] https://www.familytreedna.com/my/y-dna-haplotree [accessed 2/20/2020]

[722] McCabe, Vernon, Descendants of John McCabe, Edition III

723 https://www.familytreedna.com/public/McCabe?iframe=yresults [accessed 2/19/2020]

724 McCabe, Ebe, *Celtic Warrior Descendants,* p29

725 https://www.familytreedna.com/public/R-DF49?iframe=yresults [accessed 2/19/2020]

726 https://floridairishheritagecenter.wordpress.com/2011/08/19/are-you-a-descendant-of-irish-king-niall-of-the-nine-hostages/ [accessed 2/23/2020]

727 https://www.irishcentral.com/travel/oneill-locations-ireland [accessed 2/24/2020]

728 https://www.eupedia.com/europe/Haplogroup_HV_mtDNA.shtml [accessed 5/31/2019)

729 https://en.wikipedia.org/wiki/Alps#Geography [accessed 5/31/2019]

730 https://en.wikipedia.org/wiki/The_Melting_Pot_(play) [accessed 6/10/2019]

731 Sykes, Bryan (2006), *Saxons, Vikings, and Celts, the Genetic Roots of Britain and Ireland,* W.W. Norton & Company, New York-London (published in the UK as *Blood of the Isles*)

732 https://www.ancestry.com/dna/resource/whitePaper/AncestryDNA-Ethnicity-White-Paper.pdf [accessed 5/11/2019]

733 https://en.wikipedia.org/wiki/Pomerania [accessed 2/20/2020]

734 https://en.wikipedia.org/wiki/Prehistoric_Britain [accessed 5/23/2020]

735 https://en.wikipedia.org/wiki/Homo_erectus [accessed 5/23/2020]

736 https://www.nature.com/articles/s41598-017-17124-4 [accessed 7/1/2018]: *The Irish DNA Atlas: Revealing Fine-Scale Population Structure and History Within, Ireland.* Authors: Gilbert, Edmund; Reilly, Seamus; Merrigan, Michael; McGettigan, Darren; Molloy, Anne M.; Brody, Lawrence C.; Bodmer, Walter; Hutnik, Katarzyna; Ennis, Sean; Lawson, Daniel J.; Wilson, James F; Cavalleri, Gianpiero L., 12/8/2017, Scientific Reports, Volume 7, Article Number: 17199 (2017). An Author Correction to this article was published on May 3, 2018.

737 Cassidy, L.M., et al. Neolithic and Bronze Age Migration to Ireland and Establishment of the Insular Atlantic Genome. *Proc Natl Acad Sci* USA 113(2), 368-73 (2016)

738 Hill, E.W., Jobling, M.A. & Bradley, D.G., Y-Chromosome Variation and Irish Origins, *Nature* 404(6776), 351-2 (2000); and McEvoy, B., et al, The Longue Durée of Genetic Ancestry-Multiple Genetic Marker Systems and Celtic Origins on the Atlantic Facade of Europe *Am J Hum Genet* 75(4), 693-702 (20004).

739 Moore, L.T. et al. A Y-Chromosome Signature of Hegemony in Gaelic Ireland. *Am J Hum Gen* 78(2), 334-8 (2006)

740 McEvoy, B., Simms, K. & Bradley. D.G., Genetic Investigation of the Patrilineal Kinship Structure of Early Medieval Ireland. *Am J Phys Anthropol 136(4), 415-22 (2008).*

741 McEvoy, et al. The Scale and Nature of Viking Settlement in Ireland from Y-Chromosome Admixture Analysis, Eur J Hum Genet 14(12), 1288-94 (2006)

742 O'Dushlaine, C.T. et al, Population Structure and Genome-Wide Patterns of Variation in Ireland and Britain, Eur J Hum Gen 14(12), 1288-94 (2006); and Lao, O. et al, Correlation Between Genetic and Geographic Structure in Europe, Curr Biol 18(16), 1241-8 (2008)

743 O'Dushlaine, C.T. et al, Population Structure and Genome-Wide Patterns of Variation in Ireland and Britain; and Cronin, S. et al, A Genome-Wide Association Study of Sporadic ALS in a Homogenous Irish Population. Hum Mol Genet 17(5), 768-74 (2008)

744 Leslie, S. et al, The Fine-Scale Population Structure of the British Population, Nature 519, 309-14 (3015)

745 This geographic information was culled from multiple google maps and Wikipedia articles.

746 http://thedockyards.com/norse-settlements-in-ireland/ [accessed 121/01/2018]

747 https://en.natmus.dk/historical-knowledge/denmark/prehistoric-period-until-1050-ad/the-viking-age/power-and-aristocracy/Slaves-and-thralls/ [accessed 10/26/2018]

748 https://www.quora.com/What-is-the-difference-between-Nordic-and-Celtic-countries [accessed 6/26/2018]

749 https://en.wikipedia.org/wiki/Religion_in_Northern_Ireland#Comparison_with_the_Republic_of_ Ireland [Re-accessed 5/28/2020]

750 https://en.wikipedia.org/wiki/Rheged [accessed 5/20/2020]

751 https://en.wikipedia.org/wiki/Genetic_history_of_the_British_Isles#Vikings [accessed 5/5/2021]

752 https://www.rightathome.net/blog/proverbs-sayings-old-age-wisdom [accessed 6/17/2021]

753 https://en.wikipedia.org/wiki/Cicero [accessed 6/18/2021]

754 https://today.oregonstate.edu/archives/2011/aug/lasting-evolutionary-change-takes-about-one-million- [accessed 6/20/2021]years#:~:text=Across%20a%20broad%20range%20of,a%20 %22remarkably%20consistent%20pattern.%22

755 https://www.brainyquote.com/authors/colin-powell-quotes_2 [accessed 6/16/2021]

756 https://www.nobelprize.org/prizes/literature/1907/summary/ [accessed 4/18/2021]

757 https://www.poetryfoundation.org/poems/46473/if---[accessed 4/18/2021]

758 https://isogg.org/wiki/Haplogroup [accessed 5/30/2020]

759 https://www.timeref.com/episodes/saxons1.htm [accessed 10/27/2018]

760 https://en.wikipedia.org/wiki/Anglo-Saxons [accessed 10/27/2018]

761 https://en.wikipedia.org/wiki/Argyll [accessed 10/29/2018]

762 https://www.britannica.com/place/Armorica [accessed 10/28/2018]

763 http://www.bbc.co.uk/history/historic_figures/bede_st.shtml [accessed 10/31/2018]

764 https://en.wikipedia.org/wiki/Bretons [accessed 10/28/2018]

765 https://en.wikipedia.org/wiki/English_Channel [accessed 10/28/2018]

766 https://en.wikipedia.org/wiki/British_people [accessed 10/27/2018]

767 https://www.historic-uk.com/HistoryUK/HistoryofBritain/The-UK-Great-Britain-Whats-the-Difference/ [accessed 10/27/2018]

768 https://en.wikipedia.org/wiki/British_Isles [accessed 10/27/2018]

769 https://en.wikipedia.org/wiki/British_Overseas_Territories [accessed 10/28/2018]

770 https://en.wikipedia.org/wiki/Brittany#Middle_Ages [accessed 10/28/2018]

771 https://en.wikipedia.org/wiki/Celtic_Britons [accessed 10/28/2018]

772 https://en.wikipedia.org/wiki/Brittonic_languages [accessed 10/27/2018]

773 https://en.wikipedia.org/wiki/Celts [accessed 5/29/2020]

774 https://en.wikipedia.org/wiki/Celtic_nations:/ [accessed 10/28/2018] 0/28/2018]

775 https://en.wikipedia.org/wiki/Channel_Islands [accessed 10/28/2018]

776 https://en.wikipedia.org/wiki/Connacht#Geography_and_political_divisions   [accessed 10/28/2018]

777 https://en.wikipedia.org/wiki/Crown_dependencies [accessed 10/28/2018]

778 https://en.wikipedia.org/wiki/Cumbric [accessed 10/28/2018]

779 https://www.britannica.com/place/Dalriada [accessed 10/29/2018]

780 https://www.worldatlas.com/articles/what-physical-and-political-features-delineate-the-border-between-europe-and-asia.html [accessed 10/27/2018]

781 https://en.oxforddictionaries.com/definition/gael [accessed 11/01/2018]

782 https://www.merriam-webster.com/dictionary/Gael [accessed 11/01/2018]

783 https://en.wikipedia.org/wiki/Gaels [accessed 11/01/2018]

784 https://en.wikipedia.org/wiki/Gaeltacht [accessed 11/1/2018]

785 https://en.wikipedia.org/wiki/Galloway [accessed 11/02/2018]

786 https://en.wikipedia.org/wiki/Gaul [accessed 10/31/2018]

787 https://isogg.org/wiki/Haplogroup [accessed 5/30/2020]

788 https://en.wikipedia.org/wiki/Haplotype [accessed 5/30/2020]

789 https://en.wikipedia.org/wiki/Hebrides#Inner_Hebrides [accessed 10/28/2018]

790 https://en.wikipedia.org/wiki/Hebrides [accessed 10/31/2018]

791 https://en.wikipedia.org/wiki/Ireland [accessed 11/1/2018]

792 https://www.latitudesinformation.com/scotland-ireland-mi.html [accessed 10/29/2018]

793 http://infinitychannelswimming.com/dal-riata-channel-swim/ [accessed 10/30/2018]

794 https://en.wikipedia.org/wiki/Iron_Age_Europe#Western_Europe [accessed 10/31/2018]

795 https://www.britannica.com/topic/Jute-people [accessed 10/31/2018]

796 https://en.wikipedia.org/wiki/Leinster [accessed 11/01/2018]

797 https://en.wikipedia.org/wiki/Middle_Ages#Late_Middle_Ages [accessed 11/1/2018]

798 https://en.wikipedia.org/wiki/Munster [accessed 11/02/2018]

799 https://en.wikipedia.org/wiki/Penny_sterling [accessed 5/12/2021]

800 https://en.wikipedia.org/wiki/Ulster [accessed 11/02/2018]

Printed in the United States
by Baker & Taylor Publisher Services